Comparative Policy Agendas

Comparative Policy Agendas

Theory, Tools, Data

Edited by
Frank R. Baumgartner, Christian Breunig,
and Emiliano Grossman

OXFORD
UNIVERSITY PRESS

OXFORD
UNIVERSITY PRESS

Great Clarendon Street, Oxford, OX2 6DP,
United Kingdom

Oxford University Press is a department of the University of Oxford.
It furthers the University's objective of excellence in research, scholarship,
and education by publishing worldwide. Oxford is a registered trade mark of
Oxford University Press in the UK and in certain other countries

© Oxford University Press 2019

The moral rights of the authors have been asserted

First Edition published in 2019
Impression: 1

Published in the United States of America by Oxford University Press
198 Madison Avenue, New York, NY 10016, United States of America

British Library Cataloguing in Publication Data
Data available

Library of Congress Control Number: 2018954690

ISBN 978–0–19–883533–2

Printed and bound by
CPI Group (UK) Ltd, Croydon, CR0 4YY

Contents

Contents

Part III. Comparative Perspectives

List of Figures

List of Figures

List of Tables

List of Contributors

Petya Alexandrova, analyst in the Research Sector of the Information and Analysis Unit, European Asylum Support Office and coordinator of the EU Policy Agendas Project.

Frank R. Baumgartner, professor of political science, University of North Carolina Chapel Hill.

Ana Maria Belchior, associate professor of political science and public policy, ISCTE University Institute of Lisbon/Centre for Research and Studies in Sociology.

Shaun Bevan, senior lecturer in quantitative political science, University of Edinburgh.

Zsolt Boda, director of the Institute for Political Science/Centre for Social Sciences, Hungarian Academy of Sciences.

Enrico Borghetto, postdoctoral researcher in political sciences, New University of Lisbon, Interdisciplinary Centre of Social Studies.

Amber E. Boydstun, associate professor of political science, University of California at Davis.

Gerard Breeman, assistant professor of policymaking and research design, Leiden University and scientific director of the Institute of Public Administration.

Christian Breunig, professor of comparative politics, Department of Politics and Public Administration, University of Konstanz.

Sylvain Brouard, senior research fellow, Sciences Po and CEVIPOF.

Alper Tolga Bulut, research scholar, Karadeniz Technical University, Turkey.

Marcello Carammia, lecturer in European politics, Institute for European Studies, University of Malta and senior researcher, European Asylum Support Office.

Amnon Cavari, lecturer at Lauder School of Government, Diplomacy and Strategy Interdisciplinary Center, Herzliya, Israel.

Laura Chaqués-Bonafont, professor of political science at the University of Barcelona and IBEI.

Teresa Cornacchione, political science PhD candidate, Florida State University.

Keith Dowding, professor of political science, Australian National University/Centre for European Studies/Australian Centre for Federalism.

Rebecca Eissler, government PhD candidate, University of Texas at Austin.

Rhonda L. Evans, senior lecturer and director, University of Texas at Austin/Edward A. Clark Center for Australia and New Zealand Studies.

Kevin Fahey, research fellow at the Centre for Political and Legal Analytics at Cardiff University's School of Law and Politics.

Guy Freedman, project manager and public opinion researcher, Lauder School of Government Diplomacy and Strategy and managing director, IDC Center for Statistical Consulting.

Jean-Philippe Gauvin, assistant professor of political sciences, Université de Montréal/ Centre de recherche sur les politiques et le développement social.

Roy Gava, lecturer, Department of Political Science and International Relations, University of Geneva.

Christoffer Green-Pedersen, associate professor of political science and government, Aarhus University.

Emiliano Grossman, associate professor of political science, Centre d'études européennes, Sciences Po.

Jay Jennings, postdoctoral fellow, Annette Strauss Institute for Civic Life University of Texas at Austin.

Will Jennings, professor of political science and public policy, University of Southampton.

Jeroen Joly, lecturer, Universiteit Gent/Ghent Institute for International Studies.

Bryan D. Jones, professor, J. J. "Jake" Pickle Regents Chair in Congressional Studies, University of Texas Austin and director of the US Policy Agendas Project.

Stefanie Kasparek, assistant program director for the Pennsylvania Policy Database Project, Temple University Institute for Public Affairs.

Nir Kosti, research assistant at Hebrew University of Jerusalem.

David Levi-Faur, professor of political science and public policy, Hebrew University of Jerusalem.

Luz Muñoz Marquez, assistant professor of political science, University of Barcelona.

Aaron Martin, lecturer at the Department of Political Science, University of Melbourne, Australia.

Joseph McLaughlin, professor of American politics, Department of Political Science, College of Liberal Arts and director of the Institute for Public Affairs.

Patrick Merle, assistant professor, Communication and Public Relations, College of Communication and Information, Florida State University.

Éric Montpetit, vice-dean and professor of political science, Faculty of Arts and Sciences, Université de Montréal.

Peter B. Mortensen, associate professor of political science, Aarhus University.

Julien Navarro, associate professor of political science, Department of the European School of Political and Social Sciences, Lille Catholic University.

Dario Nikić Čakar, postdoctoral researcher in political science, University of Zagreb.

Anna M. Palau, associate professor of political science, University of Barcelona.

Federico Russo, assistant professor (Ricercatore Senior), University of Salento.

Tinette Schnatterer, CNRS researcher, Centre Emile Durkheim, Sciences Po, Bordeaux.

Pascal Sciarini, professor of politics, University of Geneva.

Miklós Sebők, senior research fellow at Hungarian Academy of Sciences.

Julie Sevenans, FWO postdoctoral research at University of Antwerp.

Ilana Shpaizman, assistant professor, Department of Political Studies, Bar Ilan University and co-director of the Israeli Agendas Project.

Daniela Širinić, postdoctoral researcher in political science, University of Zagreb.

Arco Timmermans, professor of public affairs, Institute of Public Administration, Leiden University.

Anke Tresch, associate professor, University of Lausanne and project director Swiss Election Studies.

Frédéric Varone, professor, Department of Political Science and International Relations, University of Louvain and Geneva.

Rens Vliegenthart, professor of communication science, University of Amsterdam.

Stefaan Walgrave, professor of political science, University of Antwerpen.

Carol Weissert, professor of political science, Florida State University and director of the LeRoy Collins Institute.

Tevfik Murat Yildirim, Department of Political Science, University of Missouri

Part I
Roots, Foundations, and Evolution

1

The Comparative Agendas Project

Intellectual Roots and Current Developments

Frank R. Baumgartner, Christian Breunig, and Emiliano Grossman

1.1 Roots and Goals of the Comparative Agendas Project

In compiling research for their 1993 book *Agendas and Instability in American Politics*, Frank Baumgartner and Bryan Jones developed a very simple methodology for tracking the attention of media and government institutions to particular issues: code a minimum of information for every activity on a particular topic. They looked at a total of over 22,000 media stories and over 6,500 congressional hearings in tracing attention to nuclear power, pesticides, and other topics (see Baumgartner and Jones, 1993, Appendix A). The key methodological innovation was to use public indices (at the time, published annual volumes such as the *New York Times Index* or the Congressional Information Service annual abstracts of congressional hearings) and to record the date as well as a minimum of additional information about each issue. Rather than closely analyze the entire article or document, they simply looked at the title or abstract. If the key issue is how much attention is being directed at an issue, and if the attention reflects enthusiasm or criticism, then traditional "deep reading" of the text was not needed. Plus, if the goal is to look at long-term trends over several decades, these broad patterns should emerge, complementing the deeper chronological histories other scholars may have completed. They found that student coders could quickly be trained to record such basic information quickly and accurately. Immediately on finishing the book, the two put forward an audacious proposal to the US National Science Foundation: create a database of all US congressional hearings from 1947 through the present, comprehensively documenting the congressional agenda and making it possible to track the rise and fall of every issue on the congressional agenda over more than forty years. The proposal was rejected on the grounds of being impossible.

Thirty years later we are glad to note that not only is that original idea now a reality, but that the simple idea of creating an infrastructure for research on the history and dynamics of public attention to all activities of government has become widely accepted. The US Policy Agendas Project (PAP) now makes available records of over one million government activities from all branches of the US federal government, and we recognize the support of the National Science Foundation for making much of this possible. The project is now an important part of the comparative study of public policy, as the Comparative Agendas Project (CAP) makes available similar data for over a dozen countries.

Christoffer Green-Pedersen of the University of Aarhus was the first to create an agendas project outside of the United States, doing so for his native Denmark after an extensive stay at the University of Washington in the early 2000s. Baumgartner was a visiting professor in 2004–5 in Italy and France, spending significant time visiting colleagues in various European countries just as *The Politics of Attention* (Jones and Baumgartner, 2005) was about to be released. Stefaan Walgrave, well integrated into a separate international community interested in the study of social movements and protest, had already begun a large data collection project for Belgium that he was able to adapt to the CAP standards, recognizing the value of comparable data. By the mid-2000s, a number of CAP-focused projects were underway, and major funding was made available through the European Science Foundation to support several of them (see Green-Pedersen and Walgrave, 2014). As we write, there are agendas projects in over a dozen countries ranging from Hong Kong to Central and Western Europe, Canada, Australia, for some US states, with the US project being the most established in time, but the center of gravity now clearly in Western Europe where the bulk of the scholars focusing on comparative agendas studies now reside.

In 2016 the CAP went online with a single integrated website allowing users to download datasets and information from many of the associated projects and to analyze the data online in an easy interactive user-interface. Previously, only the US Policy Agendas Project had such a high functioning website. The new comparative site will be continuously updated with new databases, greater time coverage, and more countries as the project continues to expand.

As Green-Pedersen and Walgrave wrote in the introduction to their 2014 edited volume, the CAP is united by data, not by theory. The vision that brings us together is that political science, and comparative studies of public policy in particular, will be moved forward by the common use of large infrastructure projects that make possible the types of comparative research that many would like to do, but previously could not undertake because the questions demanded data of a scope and reach that was not available. Political science, we believe, has too long worked following a "lone scholar" model. While the solitary scholar working alone can have many insights, the discipline can also benefit from teams of scholars that share their research efforts to create a research infrastructure larger than any single scholar, or small group of collaborators, could envision. Contributing to a shared infrastructure need not preclude continued independent work on one's own, of course. So we have sought to create a large network of scholars contributing to something perhaps bigger than any of us need for our individual research, but by working with just a few common elements, we coordinate our efforts and seamlessly generate something collective, even while each individual scholar or small national group can continue on their particular research tracks. Other scholarly disciplines have certainly benefitted from collective projects, often discipline-wide ones, such as mapping the human genome, the construction of mega-infrastructure projects such as massive particle accelerators, space- or mountain-based telescopes, or other data collection or observational projects of use to hundreds or thousands of scholars within a given field. Closer to our own discipline, the American National Election Studies, the General Social Survey, and the Eurobarometer constitute such shared infrastructure. The Correlates of War project serves as such a thing within the field of international relations.

A key element in the CAP is to generate a shared data resource without imposing constraints on its use. Such constraints could be methodological or theoretical. We strive to reduce any such constraints: there are no restrictions on the use of our databases, as they are distributed over open websites. Similarly, whereas Baumgartner and Jones focused substantially on a theoretical perspective drawn from punctuated equilibrium, there is no reason why a study using the underlying data from the larger project would necessarily draw from this (or any other) theory. Indeed, in Green-Pederson and Walgrave's (2014) edited volume drawing from the CAP, "punctuated equilibrium" appears in the index only once: to refer to the part of the introduction where the editors explain that none of the contributions to the volume draw from it (2014: 3–4).

Perhaps the only shared methodological point that scholars using CAP data would need to have in common is a desire to base their analysis on a systematic review of what governments do. Beyond that, the data can used by themselves to study such things as the interplay between media coverage and parliamentary debate, or they can be used as a starting point, for example as a means of identifying all activities or documents on a given topic (say, endangered species protection), permitting the scholar to do a more in-depth analysis of that topic by reading those primary sources and developing further qualitative or quantitative indicators going beyond what is made available on the CAP website. Our goal is to promote, facilitate, and subsidize new research, including research that goes well beyond the data we make available. By making it available, we hope to raise the floor for all scholars, allowing them to start from a base much higher than if we had not created the CAP, and allowing them to envision projects that are much more systematic and larger in scope. This ambition includes encouraging international comparisons where previously many projects would have been done within a single country.

A defining characteristic of the CAP is that our policy topic categories are focused on issues, not left–right positions. We concentrate on issues for two reasons. First, we care about the allocation of attention. Governments can't identify and tackle all problems at the same time. Hence, we are interested in when certain issues are addressed and which ones are ignored. Second and most importantly, we cannot determine, except by forcing some outside value structure on a given issue, which position is "left" and which is "right" on many policy topics. Consider a bill to set a minimum wage of some amount; this would seem a bill motivated from the political left. But what if the bill actually replaces a higher amount with a lower one? What if the bill increases the minimum wage but adds flexibility for employers to dismiss workers? Our point is that without deep knowledge of the political context, even a bill as central to the traditional left–right dimension as one relating to worker wage regulation could be difficult to classify. When we consider that our goal is to classify every activity of government, including professional regulation, but also water infrastructure, health research, and other topics that do not correspond to the traditional left–right cleavage structure at all, it is clear that we cannot expect to classify every activity by political position. However, we do know who is the speaker or the sponsor of the activity (for example, any parliamentary question is associated with the Member of Parliament or a political party sponsoring the question), so we can often infer the position by the speaker. But we never impose in our coding system any assumption that a statement or an activity by an actor of the left is necessarily a leftist action; that is an empirical question. Another reason why we do not categorize activities within the CAP by "directionality" is that the left and the right positions on various issues can change over time. In any case, the need for deep historical and contextual knowledge about individual issues during particular time periods suggested to us at the very beginning of the CAP (and even before, in the US-based Policy Agendas Project), that we should code systematically by policy topic, not by partisan or ideological directionality, and we have remained true to this philosophy throughout the creation of all the databases that constitute the CAP. Its focus on policy however, does not preclude researchers to combine measures of attention based on CAP data with directional measures as Adams (2016) suggests. Similar to measures of policy mood (Stimson et al., 1995), researcher might also employ CAP data for recovering the dimensions and positions of a particular political space (see Breunig et al. (2016) for legislation).

Similar to our decision not to incorporate ideological positions into our coding, we have also not coded frames or issue-definitions. When Baumgartner and Jones (1993) studied pesticides or nuclear power, they coded activities by whether they promoted or criticized the industry in question, a crude indicator of framing. But when they expanded their study to all congressional hearings as the PAP was beginning, they discovered, as discussed in the previous paragraph with regards to ideology, that they could not impose a consistent definition of framing without making unwarranted assumptions. So framing, like ideological position, is a topic dear to the hearts and concerns of many of the scholars who participate in (indeed, who designed) the CAP (e.g., Baumgartner et al., 2008), but one that is not systematically incorporated into the publicly available databases. As it requires close contextual knowledge, it needs to be added on, typically by a scholar or team with an interest in a particular question. For example, several scholars have looked at abortion, stem-cell research, and other morality issues by starting with CAP databases on those topics in several countries, then developing issue-specific definitions of the various positions or frames on the issue (see Engeli et al., 2012).

While the CAP does not code by frame or by directionality, we encourage scholars to do so. Indeed, a main motivation of the project is to subsidize or make possible research projects on diverse topics, allowing scholars to start with our data and add anything else to them. For certain topics, it would indeed be feasible to add directionality codes to the items we identify, to code them by policy frame, or to add other codes of theoretical interest. We could not feasibly do so for the entire universe, so we have left it to others to share in that work. This is not because many of us involved in the CAP are not interested in those topics; it is purely a matter of feasibility and scope. In smaller-scope projects not covering the entire range of public policies, these constraints might not apply. We look forward to seeing the studies that might result.

1.2 Using Agendas to Study Public Policy across and within Nations

The CAP today covers an increasing number of countries and agendas. As the number of country projects increased the original goals and ambitions also changed. The first central change is clearly the move towards comparative research. Comparative research on public policy is strongly dependent on the availability and comparability of data. Most of this data is compiled by international organizations, such as the OECD, on topics as diverse as pensions, healthcare, education, unemployment etc. While there have been attempts, of course, to combine research into different areas, this endeavor has usually proven difficult. The comparison of welfare states is probably the area where most large-scale comparative research has taken place across a set of neighboring policies. Beyond welfare states, large-scale comparisons have suffered from the focus on government *spending*. Alternatively, the OECD collects certain performance indicators for health or education that are used extensively in comparative research on policymaking. The development of indicators such as those of the "PISA" survey on education certainly represent an important improvement.

CAP is making a contribution at several levels. Initially most of the national CAP projects drew their inspirations from the US policy agendas project. Several projects examined their newly collected data in an analysis over time for an individual data series or single question within the country of interest (for example, Mortensen, 2010; Walgrave and Vliegenthart, 2010; Brouard et al., 2014; John and Jennings, 2010). Due to the common interest in agenda-setting, those projects insisted early, at least since 2007, on a certain degree of coordination regarding the topic codes, agendas to code and coding techniques and protocols. As Shaun Bevan explains in Chapter 2 of this volume, this coordination has increased over time. The launching of the common website has, moreover, set the pace for recoding existing agendas where necessary to comply with the common CAP Master Codebook. The original goal of these coordination efforts clearly has been to facilitate comparative research, but effective comparative research has become possible only recently. The first comparative contributions of CAP have for instance provided a more in-depth assessment of the evolution of spending priorities over time and across countries (Breunig, 2011). Since then, contributions have covered very different topics regarding the contents of executive speeches (Jennings et al., 2011), the media (Vliegenthart et al., 2016), or parliamentary questions (Green-Pedersen and Mortensen, 2010). An extension of indicators of government activity made it possible to examine a more diverse set of policy fields and also contribute to various fields of research in comparative politics.

Beyond new agendas, the CAP should allow for cross-country comparison in new policy fields. CAP data will, moreover, allow study of those areas that lack both budgetary or performance indicators. Virtually any policy can be compared with regard to timing, relative attention, and, possibly subject to some recoding or additional coding, the type of reforms or attention that was adopted, as illustrated by comparative work on "morality" issues and policies (see Engeli et al., 2012).

CAP data also allows for the study of policy dynamics. The long-term evolution of aggregate agendas can be compared across political systems. Doing so enables researchers to explore reactions to common problems or shocks (Gourevitch, 1986). Long time series data on public policies opens up a host of new research questions that have been studied in case-study research in public policy, but that may now be studied in large-n comparisons. This type of inquiry includes the role of elections and electoral calendars, for instance. We may study the consequences of elections on agenda-setting and policy change. Studies on individual countries, such as France (Baumgartner et al., 2009) or the United Kingdom (Bevan and Jennings, 2014) have tended to show the rather limited impact of elections, which contrast to some findings in comparative politics (e.g., List and Sturm, 2006; Rogoff and Sibert, 1988) but comparative research should shed more light on this question. Similarly, the proximity of election is likely to favor attention to certain issues more than others.

Another element regarding agenda dynamics concerns the size and diversity of the agenda itself. The substantive content of the agenda, as well as its macro-characteristics can be analyzed in a way not previously possible. Baumgartner and Jones' 2005 *Politics of Attention* analyzed the way in which attention evolved over time and how it spread from just a few core issues to many other policy domains. CAP data will help to compare country-specific agenda dynamics and also understand whether there are common dynamics across countries regard the size or the diversity of agenda-setting. For example, Green-Pedersen and Wilkerson (2006) show that the evolution of health policy is strikingly similar across two very different institutional contexts, namely the United States and Denmark. In an early study of policy processes, across three countries, Baumgartner et al., (2009: 619) conclude that "in the democracies we studied, the effects of the policy process dominate the country effects." Instead of focusing on institutional differences across countries and their consequences, these studies suggest that a fruitful avenue for future work would be to examine if various policy domains are organized differently across countries and if these organizational differences can still produce similar outcomes. Studying multiple policy domains across polities at the same time requires demanding research designs. The CAP database can ease this burden considerably by offering a unified inventory of all policy areas within a large set of countries.

A different type of question concerns the possible correlations and inter-actions across national agendas. For instance, scholars have observed that certain types of "moral issues", e.g., related to genetically modified food, cloning, and other similar concerns have emerged on national policy agendas more or less at the same time. While this partly responds to scientific discoveries, there other forces at work. The diffusion of policy ideas across borders may explain some of these developments, while political traditions and the structure of the party system may account for continuing differences in the political treatment of such kind of questions (see Engeli et al., 2012). The possibilities for further research in this area are certainly very important. Hypotheses on policy learning, diffusion, the power of ideas and related questions should be put to the test, thanks to the consolidation of CAP data. This data may also help us identify first movers or pace-setters more easily, as solutions developed in some countries progressively spread to other countries. We may also consider at greater length the importance of EU legislation and the degree of "Europeanization" of national legislation in EU member states (for example, Brouard et al., 2012).

When considering all its components within and across countries, the CAP database is unique in its design. To our knowledge, it is the first dataset that makes it easy to study policymaking along four dimensions: along the policy cycle, across policy domains, among at least a dozen countries, and over long periods of time. This richness and flexibility can serve policy specialists as a sophisticated index for initiating a topic-specific research project more easily. For example, one can easily identify various legislative activities ranging from hearings to lawmaking on healthcare in the United States in the 1990s (Hacker, 1999). It also can serve for offering a broad overview of long-term patterns of policy change. These can indeed be assessed within the confines of the project and not just using it as a starting point. Vliegenthart et al. (2016) employ CAP data from six Western European countries in order to explore how heightened media coverage of protests on a particular policy issue leads to parliamentary questioning on that issue. The authors make clear that certain political opportunity structures, such as majoritarian democracy, enhance protestors' ability to place a particular issue on the political agenda. Both examples, a qualitative study of a particular reform proposal in the United States and a quantitative study of all protests in six European democracies, showcase the wealth of data and the versatility of its usage.

1.3 Comparative Policy Agendas as a Field of Study

The trends and perspectives apparent in the study of agendas are becoming increasingly diverse. While most of the original research focused on intra- or inter-agenda dynamics, a lot of work was interested in understanding the consequences of agenda-setting for policy outputs. As we have seen, this diversification of research goals, strategies, and objects is a central feature of the CAP. As the project expanded to new countries, it also expanded to new research communities and questions. While our goal is not to define the emerging field of study, we can identify a certain number of directions that have emerged in recent CAP-based work.

The study of agenda dynamics remains a goal in itself. Even though research has moved away from the study of punctuated equilibrium and the distribution of attention more generally, intra- and inter-agenda dynamics remain a central feature of CAP. The existence of multiple parallel CAP-coded agendas allows for fine-tuned studies of the interdependence of different agendas and their evolution. This is the case for, instance for studies on media effects on the parliamentary agenda (Vliegenthart et al., 2016) or on the influence of social movements on either the media or the government (Hutter and Vliegenthart, 2016). The study by Froio et al. (2016) studies the interaction of party agendas with present and future problem flows. These examples illustrate how the CAP may eventually contribute to a much better understanding of processes in other fields of study, thanks to its research infrastructure.

A second trend is thus also that CAP has moved away from study of bills or adopted laws as its main objects of study: social movements, party platforms or media are now regularly studied by CAP researchers. And while these objects, of course, are part of large separate and autonomous strands of literature, the fact that they have been integrated into the CAP frameworks opens up new opportunities to study them within new research designs. For the study of parties, for instance, CAP research has allowed for new perspectives concerning the study of issue ownership and related party strategies (e.g., Tresch et al., 2015).

One of the most important recent directions adds to existing work on responsiveness and the quality of democracy. As for the studies of parties, media, or social movements, this field possesses a lively research tradition of its own that has produced an increasing amount of original research and results. Again, the combination of multiple agendas may open up new perspectives, ask new questions and generate original results. The concentration on policy areas may show a diversity of relationships between, say media, public opinion, and political institutions. So far most work has tended to assume a stable relationship across all policy areas. This assumption, common in institution-based studies, stands in stark contrast to the traditions in policy studies, where entire literatures often focus on given policy domains, such as pensions, health-care, defense, foreign policy, or trade. Even a cursory look at recent conference papers within the CAP community or among the wider group of researchers using CAP data illustrates the importance of this new direction, seeking to show systematically the importance not only of institutional structures, but also the peculiarities of individual policy domains.

1.4 The Current State of the CAP Infrastructure

The developments explained above have become possible thanks to a greatly expanded wealth of data that is now mostly stocked on the new CAP website. Table 1.1 summarizes all available data from three levels of political system: the European Union, eighteen countries, and two US states. The table lists nine common series ranging from policy inputs such as public opinion to policy outputs including laws and budgets. It becomes immediately apparent

Table 1.1. Current datasets of the Comparative Policy Agendas Project

Political system	Public opinion	Media	Courts	Government speeches	Party platforms	Parliamentary questions	Bills	Laws	Budgets
European Union	2003–16			1945–2013		1994–2001[a]	1994–2001[b]	1975–2014[c]	
Australia	1992–2013	1996–2013	1903–2016	1992–2008		1980–2013	1966–2015	1966–2015	
Belgium[d]		1999–2008		1960–2009	1978–2008	1988–2010	1988–2010	1988–2010	
Canada[e]	1987–2009					1982–2004	1960–2010		
Croatia[f]		1990–2015			1990–2015	1992–2015	1990–2015	1990–2015	
Denmark[g]		1984–2003		1953–2013	1953–2011	1953–2013	1953–2013	1953–2013	1953–2013
France[h]		1981–2013	1951–2009		1981–2012	1996–2010	1974–2013	1978–2013	
Germany	1986–2005			1976–2005	1976–2005	1976–2005	1976–2005	1976–2005	
Hungary		2010–14			1990–2010	1990–2014			1991–2013
Israel[i]								1948–2014	
Italy				1979–2014	1983–2008	1997–2014		1983–2013	1990–2012
Netherlands[j]		1990–2008		1945–2015	1981–2012	1984–2009	1981–2009	1981–2009	
New Zealand			2004–15			2008–11			
Portugal		1995–2015		2002–11	1995–2011	2003–15			
Spain	1993–2015	1996–2012		1982–2015	1982–2000	1978–2015	1977–2015	1980–2015	
Switzerland[k]		1995–2003				1995–2003	1978–2008	1978–2008	
Turkey	2003–13	1980–2005		1983–2007	2002–11	1991–2011		2002–13	1841–2016
United Kingdom[l]	1944–2016	1960–2008		1911–2016	1983–2008	1998–2008		1911–2016	1911–2007
United States[m]	1947–2012	1946–2013	1945–2009	1946–2016	1948–2008	1947–2013[n]		1948–2014	1947–2015
State of Florida		1989–2015					1989–2015	1989–2015	
State of Pennsylvania[o]	1994–2017	1979–2016	1979–2012	1979–2017		1979–2010[p]	1979–2014	1979–2014	1979–2014

Notes: [a] Council Conclusions (laws), 1995–2014 1995–2014, Council Working group meetings, European Commission Documents [b] Council Working group meetings 1995–2014. [c] European Commission Documents 1995–2014. [d] Additionally: Coalition agreements 1978–2008. [e] Also: 1960–2009 intergovernmental meetings. [f] Government Weekly sessions 1990–2015. [g] Plus three series on local political agenda. [h] Also Government communications and decrees 1974–2013. [i] Regulations 1948–2014 and Cabinet Decisions 2003–16. [j] Coalition agreements 1963–2012; some agency publications 1990–2006; local coalition agreements 1986–2014; policy agendas of think tanks related to political parties 2000–11; introductory section to the budget of the minister of the interior 1985–2008; EU COM proposals EU-directives and changes to directives 1974–2007. [k] Direct Democracy 1848–2014. [l] Public opinion, Scotland ("most important issue"), Bills/Acts of Scottish Parliament, Hearings of Committees of Scottish Parliament 1998–2007, Reports of Select Committees of UK Parliament 1997–2014, Statutory Instruments of UK Parliament 1987–2008, Prorogation Speech 1975–2016. [m] Roll Calls 1947–2013; Executive Orders 1945–2015; Interest Groups 1966–2001. [n] Congressional hearings. [o] Executive Orders 1979–2008; Legislative Service Agency Reports 1979–2009; General Fund Balance 1979–2014. [p] Hearings.

Source: Comparative Agendas Project

that the loose network structure is consequential for data collection and availability. For most systems, laws and some form of legislative inquiry (i.e., hearings or parliamentary questions) have been coded. For more than half of the entities, information on media (albeit in different formats), government speeches, party platforms, and bills are accessible. Public opinion, budgets, and Supreme Court decisions are among the more fragmented data series. The time frame of each data series also fluctuates among projects. While most of the British data goes back to the early twentieth century, the most frequent coverage starts in the early 1990s. This is obviously true for the Eastern European cases, but also holds for most EU-related series. Variability in data coverage for each political system has multiple reasons, including researchers' own interests and resources as well as simple data availability. For example, data on most important problems surveys only became publicly available in the last three decades and in a limited number of countries with an established survey industry.

The codebook is highly adaptable to a diverse set of political activities that can be classified by policy content. The summary table also highlights how many different activities have been coded in addition to the nine core series. These include, for example, working group meetings of the European Union Council. Several European countries added coalition agreements, referenda as a direct democratic tool in Switzerland, executive orders and regulatory action by bureaucracies, as well as policy agendas or mission statements from think tanks and interest groups. The plethora of applications indicates the wide utility and versatility of the underlying coding scheme.

1.5 Structure of the Book

This book is divided into three parts. The two remaining chapters of Part 1 provide overviews of the entire CAP project. Chapters in Part 2 give information related to individual country-based projects—the databases and time periods covered, data sources, institutional context, and so on. Each short chapter in this section also provides an illustration of a country-specific question that can be addressed with the project's data. Part 3 includes comparative and analytical chapters including cross-national studies using CAP data. These are by no means exhaustive, but the selection of chapters provides a series of illustrations of relevant questions that can be addressed.

In Chapter 2, Shaun Bevan introduces the specifics of data retrieval and coding within the CAP. The chapter explains that the CAP emerged out of a loose network structure among scholars with related but diverse interests. The common ground is a desire to classify political agendas according to the policies they address. Based on voluntary coordination, a group of roughly a dozen country project teams settled on a common coding scheme that made it possible to include national particularities and still ensure cross-national comparison. A concerted effort by Bevan and individual project team leaders enabled the creation of a Master Codebook. Another challenge of the collective endeavor is to figure out what types of government activities are employed and what records are publicly available. On that basis, most countries in the CAP were able to collect data throughout all stages of the policy process, ranging from public opinion and media, to parliamentary process, such as speeches and interpellation, to bills and laws. Depending on researchers' interests, these core series are supplemented with additional data, e.g., on courts or interest groups. Indeed, it is possible to apply the basic coding scheme to a variety of political settings ranging from authoritarian regimes to international organizations. Bevan concludes his chapter by showing the descriptive power of the existing online database and stating some limitations of the CAP data.

Chapter 3 by Stefaan Walgrave and Amber Boydstun narrates how the research topics and design of the CAP community have evolved over time. The two authors assemble all the abstracts of papers presented at CAP conferences in the last ten years in order to canvass the collective work. Over ten conferences more than 250 papers have been presented by over 200 authors. The authors show how diverse the group is. The papers used thirteen different agenda series covering many political processes. In fact, the most often studied agenda involved mass media (23 percent) but several other series follow closely. At least half the papers related two or more series with each other. This design suggests that many CAP papers are interested in how political processes interact with each other. The most apparent connection are studies of responsiveness and representation. Because of the steady evolution of the network, the predominant research design entails a one-country study of changes in a political agenda over time. But even these studies are typically comparative because they consider agenda-setting across all policy fields. All in all, the chapter indicates that the CAP data has been applied to a wide range of political science research and that comparative research using it has been flourishing, a trend that should accelerate now that the CAP data are mostly available online.

Part 2 of the book provides descriptive elements for all CAP projects. Each chapter sketches out the main features of the political system and how agendas are generated in those systems. The chapters outline agendas data at three levels of governance: supra-national (European Union), national (Australia, Belgium, Canada, Croatia, Denmark, France, Germany, Hungary, Israel, Italy, Netherlands, New Zealand, Portugal, Spain, Switzerland, Turkey, United Kingdom, and United States), and sub-national (Florida and Pennsylvania). The diversity of institutional and political setting is quite broad and range from democratic to semi-democratic, presidential to parliamentary, and from unitary to federal systems. Within these different institutional settings a large array of political activities occurs. Moreover, the institutional rules for employing these activities sometimes change over time. Electoral reforms in Italy or New Zealand are well known, but parliamentary rules, such as agenda-setting procedures or structures of debate, also change quite frequently (Sieberer et al., 2016). Providing detailed descriptions of the institutional setting for each agenda series therefore enables scholars to assess the possibility of cross-case comparison of political activities and policies.

Part 3 highlights the analytical advantages of using CAP data. The chapters demonstrate a variety of approaches and usages of the data, while all feature cross-country and longitudinal analyses. Papers illustrate various possible uses for areas as diverse as media, social movements, parties, lawmaking, speeches etc. The chapters also exemplify different types of methodological approaches, ranging from qualitative research to very sophisticated multivariate regression designs and time-series analysis. Those chapters summarize or illustrate existing research, while suggesting new research directions and possibilities. Our concluding chapter then assesses some of the future possibilities of the CAP, in particular how it relates with other large research projects prominent on the international scene.

References

Baumgartner, F. R., Breunig, C., Green-Pedersen, C. et al. (2009). Punctuated Equilibrium in Comparative Perspective. *American Journal of Political Science*, 53(3): 602–19.

Baumgartner, F. R., De Boef, S. L., and Boydstun, A. E. (2008). *The Decline of the Death Penalty and the Discovery of Innocence*. New York: Cambridge University Press.

Baumgartner, F. R., Foucault, M., and François, A. (2009). Public Budgeting in the French Fifth Republic: The End of *La République des Partis? West European Politics*, 32(2): 401–19.

Baumgartner, F. R., and Jones, B. D. (1993). *Agendas and Instability in American Politics*. Chicago: University of Chicago Press.

Bevan, S., and Jennings, W. (2014). Representation, Agendas and Institutions. *European Journal of Political Research*, 53(1): 37–56.

Breunig, C. (2011). Reduction, Stasis, and Expansion of Budgets in Advanced Democracies. *Comparative Political Studies*, 44(8): 1060–88.

Breunig, C., Elff, M., and Workman, S. (2016). Dynamics of Policy Change. Paper presented at the *European Political Science Association Meeting*.

Brouard, S., Costa, O., and Koning, T. (eds) (2012). *The Europeanization of Domestic Legislatures*. New York: Springer.

Brouard, S., Grossman, E., and Guinaudeau, I. (2014). The Evolution of the French Political Space Revisited: Issue Priorities and Party Competition. In *Agenda Setting, Policies, and Political Systems: A Comparative Approach*, ed. C. Green-Pedersen and S. Walgrave. Chicago: University of Chicago Press.

Engeli, I., Green-Pedersen, C., and Larsen, L. T., eds. (2012). *Morality Politics in Western Europe: Parties, Agendas and Policy Choices*. Basingstroke: Palgrave Macmillan.

Froio, C., Bevan, S., and Jennings, W. (2016). Party Mandates and the Politics of Attention: Party Platforms, Public Priorities and the Policy Agenda in Britain. *Party Politics*, 23(6): 692–703.

Gourevitch, P. (1986). *Politics in Hard Times: Comparative Responses to International Economic Crises*. Ithaca: Cornell University Press.

Green-Pedersen, C., and Mortensen, P. B. (2010). Who Sets the Agenda and Who Responds to it in the Danish Parliament? A New Model of Issue Competition and Agenda-Setting. *European Journal of Political Research*, 49(2): 257–81.

Green-Pedersen, C., and Walgrave, S. eds (2014). *Agenda Setting, Policies, and Political Systems: A Comparative Approach*. Chicago: University of Chicago Press.

Green-Pedersen, C., and Wilkerson, J. (2006). How Agenda-Setting Attributes Shape Politics: Basic Dilemmas, Problem Attention and Health Politics Developments in Denmark and the US. *Journal of European Public Policy*, 13(7): 1039–52.

Hacker, J. S. (1999). *The Road to Nowhere: The Genesis of President Clinton's Plan for Health Security*. Princeton: Princeton University Press.

Hutter, S., and Vliegenthart, R. (2016). Who Responds to Protest? Protest Politics and Party Responsiveness in Western Europe. *Party Politics*, 24(4): 358–69.

Jennings, W., Bevan, S., and John, P. (2011). The Agenda of British Government: The Speech from the Throne, 1911–2008. *Political Studies*, 59(1): 74–98.

John, P., and Jennings, W. (2010). Punctuations and Turning Points in British Politics? The Policy Agenda of the Queen's Speech, 1940–2005. *British Journal of Political Science*, 40(3): 561–86.

Jones, B. D., and Baumgartner, F. R. (2005). *The Politics of Attention: How Government Prioritizes Problems*. Chicago: University of Chicago Press.

List, J. A., and Sturm, D. M. (2006). How Elections Matter: Theory and Evidence from Environmental Policy. *The Quarterly Journal of Economics*, 121(4): 1249–81.

Mortensen, P. B. (2010). Political Attention and Public Policy. A Study of How Agenda Setting Matters. *Scandinavian Political Studies*, 33(4): 356–80.

Rogoff, K., and Sibert, A. (1988). Elections and Macroeconomic Policy Cycles. *The Review of Economic Studies*, 55(1): 1–16.

Sieberer, U., Meißner, P., Keh, J. F., and Müller, W. C. (2016). Mapping and Explaining Parliamentary Rule Changes in Europe: A Research Program. *Legislative Studies Quarterly*, 41(1): 61–88.

Stimson, J. A., Mackuen, M. B., and Erikson, R. S. (1995). Dynamic Representation. *American Political Science Review*, 89(3): 543–65.

Tresch, A., Lefevere, J., and Walgrave, S. (2015). 'Steal Me If You Can!' The Impact of Campaign Messages on Associative Issue Ownership. *Party Politics*, 21(2): 198–208.

Vliegenthart, R., Walgrave, S., Wouters, R. et al. (2016). The Media as a Dual Mediator of the Political Agenda–Setting Effect of Protest: A Longitudinal Study in Six Western European Countries. *Social Forces*, 95(2): 837–59.

Walgrave, S., and Vliegenthart, R. (2010). Why Are Policy Agendas Punctuated? Friction and Cascading in Parliament and Mass Media in Belgium. *Journal of European Public Policy*, 17(8): 1147–70.

2

Gone Fishing

The Creation of the Comparative Agendas Project Master Codebook

Shaun Bevan

For the past decade, I have spent more time discussing fishing than I would have ever expected when I started my career in political science. Amazingly this is not because of an advisor's obsession with fishing,[1] the need to escape my work with a nice day along a river, or due to the unending series of *Deadliest Catch* marathons on the Discovery Channel since I started my graduate training. Instead my time contemplating and deliberating on fishing has been about policy, namely the difficulties in conducting comparative analyses of public policy across nations. To allow the pun, this research note fishes through the creation of the Comparative Agendas Project (CAP) the finalization of the CAP Master Codebook and my time as a student, researcher, manager, faculty member, and ultimately director of the Master Codebook for the CAP. It is an effort to better understand CAP coding and data as well as the difficulties and limitations of a comparative approach to coding policy agendas.

Policy issues such as healthcare, national defense, and social welfare are often grouped in a logical manner based on one's own interpretation and understanding of the world. This inherent grouping extends to both human and computer coding techniques, including methods of scaling that group items based on the usage of keywords. However, as considerable work has shown scaling techniques are only applicable in a single language as different languages or even contexts can lead to considerable differences in the categories (e.g., Klüver, 2009). As datasets, languages, countries, and time periods change so does our interpretation and understanding of the world along with the usage and the meaning of words. In short, when a coding system is created, regardless of the means, it inherently matches the context it is created in. This background represents a massive challenge for the study of comparative policy agendas as no two contexts are ever exactly alike. As it turns out fisheries, policing, culture, and many other policy areas present interesting challenges for comparative public policy as how these policies are defined and addressed varies considerably from nation to nation. To that end, this research note openly discusses the challenges of the CAP and introduces the CAP Master Codebook discussing its creation, intended use, and limitations. The chapter is a guide for those interested in the ever-growing volume of CAP-coded data that highlights the logic behind the CAP codes. It is my hope that this explication will lead to a better understanding of what can be done with CAP codes, how they can be iterated on, and the wider use of CAP coded data as well as new projects that value the approach.

The rest of this chapter takes the following form. First, I discuss the creation of the CAP from its roots in the US Policy Agendas Project to its guiding principles of a limited coding system focused on coding policies, not targets. I next move onto the Master Codebook process explaining its necessity and the process of creating it. I further discuss some of the more difficult-to-address issues cross-nationally and present a discussion of external validity. I conclude with an overview of the value and the limitations of CAP data for current and future research. In addition, several appendices are tied to this chapter including a set of basic coding rules, the continuing Master Codebook process for new and existing projects, and a brief introduction as well as guidelines for starting new projects. Up-to-date versions of these appendixes are maintained at https://www.comparativeagendas.net/.

2.1 The Comparative Agendas Project: A Philosophy and a Beginning

The CAP was built on the shoulders and limitations of the US Policy Agendas Project (US PAP) created by Frank Baumgartner and Bryan Jones. Widely used by political scientists, practitioners, and students the US PAP data represents a key achievement for public policy research in the United States. The project's goal was to create a series of commonly coded databases focused on the policy content of government and public agendas since World War II. To achieve this goal the US PAP codebook was created based on the development of the project's congressional hearings dataset with major and subtopic codes, the method for classifying data employed by the CAP, reflecting the policy attention of the US Congress. As good planning, luck, and/or serendipity would have it hearings are in fact a highly representative government agenda leading to the creation of a robust and lasting codebook for US government agendas (see Jones and Baumgartner, 2005).

The codebook did, however, go through several revisions since the project was first started in 1993, such as the folding of family issues into law, order, and family issues[2] and the development of several new subtopic codes in the major topic of health. It has also been modified to fit new datasets. Even before the development of comparative projects challenges have routinely presented themselves such as how to address randomly sampled media data with stories on the weather, fires, and obituaries presenting new topics not present in government datasets. Voluntary associations presented another problem with not all associations interested in policy such as Bob's International an association of people named Bob with awards for, among other things, the best Shiska-Bob (Bevan et al., 2013). To deal with these issues new, non-policy codes were developed and introduced uniquely for the datasets that required them.

Each of these changes followed the "prime directive," to quote Bryan Jones, of the CAP if you will, which states that existing codes may never be combined, but that new codes can be created either to match truly new concerns or through the further separation of existing codes. For example, sports, specifically sports scores and news unrelated to the business aspect of sports, warranted a new code when the media data was first coded in the United States. Moving beyond the United States, immigration, an existing subtopic code in the original US codebook, warranted an extensive separation into a detailed major and subtopic structure in the majority of European nations where the policy area receives extensive attention in relation to the European Union (see Guiraudon, 2000). By following the "prime directive" these and other changes to the original codebook were in theory easily reverted in order to create a harmonized, common codebook for comparative analyses. In practice the process of harmonization was more involved and led to several revisions to the original codebook discussed in section 2.2 "Coding through Compromise."

2.1.1 But What Is CAP Data?

Up until April 2016 and the launch of the CAP website CAP data has been defined quite broadly, namely as any dataset using a version of the CAP codebook in order to capture the policy attention of different government and public datasets based on their textual content. Policy attention meaning the substantive focus of the policy used, proposed, or discussed for each observation. These observations can vary, from individual laws or news stories, for example, to aggregated measures such as with "most important problem" type measures that capture the general policy attention of the public (e.g., Bevan and Jennings, 2014). Regardless of the unit of analysis each observation is coded based on a common set of rules for that dataset aimed at capturing the primary policy focus of the observation. For example, coding newspaper stories based on their introductory paragraph or secondary legislation based on their explanatory notes that summarize highly technical legislation. In general CAP datasets are coded over a long time frame and as comprehensively as possible, including all known bills or executive speeches over several decades for example. The datasets themselves include as much information as possible, including links and/or identifying information for each case as well as the text or other information used to code the case when such information is available and legally shareable. CAP data is therefore also as transparent, replicable, and contestable as possible.

This broad definition of what CAP data is has been refined to a new gold standard based on the criteria for data included on the common CAP website, namely, the ability for data to be matched to the CAP Master Codebook. This standard exists to ensure the CAP can live up to the first part of its acronym, comparative, well into the future.

2.1.2 Coding Limited by Design

Despite the scale of the data gathering across the CAP, the effort put into the Master Codebook and the unprecedented level of detail and access to raw data, the CAP is limited by design. The CAP community includes a wealth of researchers from political science, sociology, communication, and computer science amongst other disciplines. That says nothing for the wealth of subfields represented and research questions being asked by the members of CAP projects. In short, while everyone involved in the CAP is concerned with attention in some manner or another, why and how they look at attention almost always differs. Building such a diverse and differently motivated group of scholars led to the limited, but robust coding system it employs. After all, attention is the sine qua non of policymaking as a change in framing, preferences, and/or direction requires that a policy is first attended to. While this focus limits how CAP-coded data can be directly used, the transparency and inherent replicability of the CAP datasets allows for more detailed work on the framing, preferences, and other factors beyond policy attention that make up each case. Whenever possible CAP datasets include both a means of linking to the original documents and importantly whatever text or information that was used to code each observation. This allows the users of the data to locate policies related to specific problems or countries, to build on or further refine the CAP coding by adding frames or more specific breakdowns of policy, and importantly to challenge how a case or cases have been coded. Like any dataset, CAP data has errors, but by limiting the coding's focus to a common interest in attention and making the data as transparent as possible the quality of the data and its continued quality is as robust as the communities resources can allow for.

2.1.3 *Policy Not Targets? Terrorism and the Economic Crisis*

Targets and policies are not the same. Whether or not solutions search for policy windows (Kingdon, 1995), the policies aimed at targets often come from several places and often need to. Terrorism is one target for policy that often requires many different policies to address. Terrorism is a problem that can highlight issues with specific policy areas such as military intelligence, airline safety, immigration, and a host of other areas. Moreover, the responsibility for directly addressing acts of terrorism can fall to the police, the military, or a combination of both depending on the system of government and the source of terrorism itself. The CAP codes the policies that address the problem of terrorism according to their substantive policy focus rather than simply terrorism as a target for policy.

The CAP coding system's emphasis on the substantive focus of policy is perhaps its most common criticism (e.g., Dowding et al., 2016). Clearly based on the description above a complete look at terrorism using CAP data would require additional work to identify the policies that were aimed at addressing the problem, but the same is true for other problems as well. How the CAP coding system addresses an economic crisis is another important example of the difference between targets and policies. The economic crisis that occurred in the late naughts, and that has had continued effects for a number of years since, was a problem of banking, consumer confidence, unemployment, and more. In short, it was a macroeconomic problem. However, the policy solutions to this macroeconomic problem did not just focus on changing interest rates, lowered taxes, and other macroeconomic tools, but also focused on creating jobs, supporting new businesses, and addressing social welfare issues in order to combat increasing unemployment numbers. In fact, the politics of austerity pushed by many nations meant that addressing the economic crisis included policies, however contentious, that touched on nearly every policy area government deals with from healthcare to public lands at least when it came to government spending. Ultimately, the economic crisis was a shock, a large shock that affected many policy areas that the government dealt with for a considerable time.

Problems no matter where they come from can lead to many different policies in many different areas with targets for policy such as terrorism or the economic crisis of the naughts driving new policies in the majority of policy areas. This is not a flaw of the CAP system of coding, but a choice to focus on policies and not targets. However, different targets as well as different problems, like countries and regions, can easily be identified through a search of the raw CAP data.

2.2 Coding through Compromise: The CAP Master Codebook

Each project and often each dataset requires specific adaptations of the codebook to address observations and topics that do not exist in other contexts. More often than not these changes include the adaptation of existing codes to match the context of the project or dataset in question. However, with the number of projects having grown to nearly two dozen as of July 2014, the lack of a hierarchical CAP leadership and various levels of resources created a noticeable level of codebook drift. Much of this drift was of course necessary as projects needed to adapt the original American codebook to fit different contexts, while still keeping the key goal of comparison in mind. While each project does an excellent job of coding and reconciliation with initial coding agreements ranging between 75 percent and 90 percent before cleaning, each of these activities were completed independently for each project. Only the determined focus and collegial nature of the CAP community led to generally comparable datasets that have already led to several noteworthy findings, such as the general effect of core issues on government attention (e.g., Jennings et al., 2011) and truly general patterns of public policy (e.g., Jones et al., 2009).

Nevertheless, these analyses were not without their flaws due to cross-national codebook incompatibilities. Some clear incompatibilities such as how immigration was included in the codebook were obvious. For the yet unknown differences robustness checks performed by the authors of this early research such as the jack-knifing of topics to search for any influential issues (e.g., Jennings et al., 2011) means that while these codebook issues were not severe enough to change the inferences gained from these analyses future work without a truly comparative coding system might not be so lucky. As of July 2014, more than 450 subtopics existed across fifteen projects with complete or draft crosswalks from an initial list of 225 subtopics. While most of these revised subtopics introduced minor alternations of existing codes in order to deal with minor differences between projects, a clear need for a common, comparative Master Codebook existed.

The process of developing the CAP Master Codebook started early on in the CAP's life and has had various members of the CAP community involved with Herschel F. Thomas III and Jeroen Joly having acted as previous heads, laying the groundwork through an independent assessment of each team's national language codebook. This partial crosswalk was used as a basis for comparison in several comparative papers (e.g., Baumgartner et al., 2011), but a great deal of work was left to be done, especially on the subtopic level where many errors and incompatibilities were left to be addressed. The rest of this section describes the logic and history of the Master Codebook. Our website includes the Master Codebook itself as well as full documentation about how it came about and examples of how to apply the Master Codebook crosswalk to project-coded data. It is designed to be useful both to users of the data as well as to anyone thinking of creating a new project for a political system that does not already have one.

2.2.1 *The Master Codebook Process*

In the summer of 2012 I was informally elected by a group of project PIs to act as the Topic Coding Coordinator for the CAP with the goal of finalizing the process through a true Master Codebook. The objectives of this effort were outlined in a memo to all teams explaining the concept and the process of creating the CAP Master Codebook and were as follows: (1) create a common Master Codebook that allows for accurate comparisons across all CAP datasets; (2) minimize the overall amount of work by seeking a common middle ground between projects rather than asking any project to use a particular country's codebook; (3) whenever possible avoid the need for recoding with appropriate aggregations.

Objective 1 was a clear-cut goal to not exclude any project from the Master Codebook as the power and ideal of the CAP is its comparative nature. The second Objective, to create a new Master Codebook, was both practical and diplomatic in that my other work in the community did not drive the process. While I have and continue to work on the US and UK projects neither of their codebooks were appropriate as a basis for comparative Master Codebook. This is not just because the United States is one of the only countries with a secondary mortgage market and the United Kingdom still has a monarchy either. In reality, like all project codebooks, they were adapted to a specific case and could not fit policy cross-nationally in general. Finally, considering the immense amount of work conducted by each team by the summer of 2012 Objectives 2 and 3 further proved essential with many teams low or lacking any additional resources in order to conduct this work. These objectives reduced the workload through a least common denominator Master Codebook that maintained a balance of detail and feasibility splitting the distribution of work between projects.

With these objectives in mind and through the support of the Mannheim Centre of European Social Research (MZES), alongside the various projects I picked up where the previous efforts had left off by asking each team to create an English language codebook and arranging face-to-face meetings with projects over the next year. Prior to each meeting teams completed a common coding exercise on a selected set of UK Acts of Parliament intended to highlight common issues and difficult cases and which was graded and discussed in detail in the meeting. Also prior to each meeting I read each English language codebook in its entirety to identify possible drift and new interpretations of codes to be discussed in the face-to-face meetings. Finally, before my first meeting I created a draft Master Codebook with twenty-one major topics and roughly 230 subtopics as a point of reference based on the previous Master Codebook efforts.

With a list of issues and the "graded" coding exercises in hand I visited each team to discuss their codebook and coding efforts in detail over the course of two days. Using my notes and the draft Master Codebook as a guide we discussed how to deal with any drift and inconsistencies either through the need for the project to recode the data or through the use of a crosswalk that often combined topics that were difficult to bound cross-nationally, such as policing.[3] I left each team with a brief list of issues for the team to directly address along with many notes concerning my draft Master Codebook and how to rebuild the crosswalk. After my last face-to-face meeting in the late spring of 2013 I cross-referenced these notes to build a second version of the Master Codebook with twenty-one major topics and 213 subtopics.

With a memo outlining the major differences between the Master Codebook and many national project codebooks and the draft Master Codebook sent to all teams, I presented and sought comments at the largest coding meeting yet at the 2013 CAP conference in Antwerp, Belgium. Following a difficult discussion at the meeting and several revisions to the explanation of the changes and the process of recoding the data the first crosswalks between the Master Codebook and each project were completed and sent to national teams for further comments. This process led to several small changes concerning the crosswalks, but ultimately resulted in a final version of the Master Codebook with twenty-one major topic codes and 213 subtopic codes although significant revisions to the names of these topics were made to make them more generally applicable across projects. Crosswalks based on this final version of the Master Codebook continue to be produced, revised, and proofed based on individual project feedback. When a proofed version of a project crosswalk is produced it is added to the Master Codebook crosswalk and the project adds the Master Codebook major and subtopic codes to their data.

Major topic codes and names for the CAP Master Codebook are presented in Table 2.1. A complete list of all subtopic codes is available at the CAP website along with an up-to-date version of Appendix B that outlines the process of matching project-coded data to the CAP Master Codebook.

2.2.2 The Devil in the Details

Despite this rather straightforward, but intensive process for creating the Master Codebook the effort was far from easy. In order to create a truly comparable Master Codebook the devil was absolutely in the details with seemingly easy-to-understand issues like fisheries and culture creating some

Table 2.1. CAP Master Codebook major topic codes

Major Topic	Title
1	Domestic Macroeconomic Issues
2	Civil Rights, Minority Issues, and Civil Liberties
3	Health
4	Agriculture
5	Labor and Employment
6	Education
7	Environment
8	Energy
9	Immigration and Refugee Issues
10	Transportation
12	Law, Crime, and Family Issues
13	Social Welfare
14	Community Development and Housing Issues
15	Banking, Finance, and Domestic Commerce
16	Defense
17	Space, Science, Technology, and Communications
18	Foreign Trade
19	International Affairs and Foreign Aid
20	Government Operations
21	Public Lands, Water Management, and Territorial Issues
23	Cultural Policy Issues

Source: CAP Master Codebook

of the most intense debates possible concerning the coding system. Policy, after all, differs based on context and with a variety of different political and temporal contexts to address a common understanding of policy across projects was a difficult task. As of July 2014 a total of more than 450 different subtopics existed across fifteen projects with completed or draft crosswalks. The majority of these subtopics offered slight revisions in order to cover some unique aspect of the political system in question. Others were more unique, highlighting the importance of specific religions in a country's policymaking or chose to split existing codes like freedom of speech and religion into its component parts. Some new codes like fishing and culture, however, had no true analog in the original US codebook and served as a source for debate since before I first started working with the CAP in 2007.

Fishing, a primary means for agribusiness in many European nations, fell in a mixture of the original US codes loosely tied to agriculture and was never an issue in landlocked countries like Switzerland. Comparatively, however, fishing is at least as important as ranching in the United States or food safety in the United Kingdom.[4] Based on the importance of the policy area, fishing was added as a new subtopic under agriculture in the Master Codebook.

No less important were the newly created immigration and culture major topic codes employed by a large number of projects. Immigration, while a common issue in many countries has often focused on civil rights or, in

25

countries with seasonal and/or illegal workers, on labor issues. Yet, as most EU scholars would argue immigration is a policy area unto itself having played a major role in the creation of the European Union (Guiraudon, 2000) and as a continued source of debate and policymaking in many EU member states exemplifying its importance. Culture, namely the preservation and promotion of culture and language also plays an important role in many countries. Concerns over EU, US, and other international influences on nations like France and Italy has led to the production of a large volume of cultural policy. While countries like the United States produce far less cultural policy, the importance of cultural policy in many systems is clear. The United States' broad influence on culture internationally through its entertainment and business industries in fact adds to the external validity of culture as a policy area with little concern or need to maintain US culture compared to a strong focus by countries like France focused on the preservation of its culture and language. Due to the importance of culture and immigration cross-nationally they too were added to the Master Codebook as new major topic codes.

Ultimately the Master Codebook addresses each of these and many other seemingly minor issues by assuring that each team addresses the related policy area in the same manor in relation to the Master Codebook through each team's use of the Master Codebook crosswalk. By employing a common Master Codebook with a common and established way of coding the CAP data is internally valid cross-nationally.

2.2.3 A Cold War Mentality: Addressing the Country and Regional Subtopics

Created in the 1990s in reference to the US policy since World War II the original US codebook, like the policy it focused on, maintained a Cold War mentality and view of the world when introducing country and regional subtopics. Intended as a category of last resort, the regional and country subtopic codes under international affairs were used on items with a broad, non-specific focus on a country or region that could not be coded elsewhere. The purpose of these codes is an extremely important one though, as they allow for a separation of foreign and domestic items especially in media and other similar agendas that are likely to mention other parts of the world without producing policy implications back at home.

However, the choice of which regions and countries to focus on reflected a transitory view of the world with subtopics like Soviet Union and Former Republics based on how countries and regions were discussed in the US Congress historically rather than based on theory or geography. As a result, the country and especially the regional subtopic codes were used inconsistently between projects with no common agreement or rule on where to place countries like Turkey and Egypt. Moreover, many projects recognized this shortcoming and chose to forgo the original system altogether and instead introduced a dummy variable system that indicated the countries present in each item with the most extensive usage occurring in media agendas. This produced one of the biggest practical and potentially financial problems for the Master Codebook. Completing an additional level of coding for all projects that did not originally use the new dummy variable system was cost prohibitive, but the usage of the dated, Soviet-era country and regional codes of yore would be wasteful. Similarly, the creation of a new system based on geography or current geopolitical standings would also be wasteful and eventually just as dated. Instead, a compromise to combine these historically dated subtopic codes into a single specific country or region subtopic code was decided upon. The exception to this rule is the code for the European Union and Western Europe due to the inability for many projects to separate these two items. This process involved the combination of all regional and country subtopics in the countries that have them, and the crosswalk to the new code when the country dummy coding system indicated a focus on another nation without a focus on the project's own country. In other words, when the item was purely international affairs, such as the election of a new foreign president, it should be coded in this general specific country or region subtopic code. While the general specific region or country subtopic code is a loss of information from both sides, the transparency of the CAP data allows for much more directed and theory-driven country and regional focuses based on a search of the data.

2.3 The Validity of Policy Differences

The process of creating the CAP Master Codebook focused on the comparability of policies and the terms/concepts that construct them. Across languages, time, and various institutional forms the system is designed so that policies governing everything from the angle of vehicle headlights to the legality of a certain election campaign receives the same major and subtopic code regardless of the time, institutions, or translations that need to take place from one data point to another. However, it is easy to forget that comparative research and a comparative design for research is about both similarity and differences. Many of the discussions and much of the feedback I received during the process of creating the Master Codebook concerned policy areas that received very little if any attention in a context or country. However, I saw these concerns as good, qualitative affirmations of validity. While the CAP Master Codebook had to be completely uniform, the applicability of CAP coding did not, in fact it should not be. For example, fishing is an important if not fundamental issue for certain countries like Denmark, but at best a very limited issue for a landlocked country such as Switzerland. Being a landlocked or an oceangoing nation does not mean potential policy areas differ, only that their applicability and level of use does. In order for CAP data to be valid representations of policy areas variation is essential.

This section considers the validity of policy differences between projects, institutions, and time periods. It makes use of the publicly available tools on the CAP website as of January 2018 in order to promote the free investigation and interpretation of these differences by readers and other scholars. The policy differences presented here are both in no particular order and based on no particular theory or world view. Instead, they simply represent some of the most common targets of the "we don't" and "is not a policy here" comments I received while working on the CAP Master Codebook.

2.3.1 Defense Policy: The United States vs Switzerland

In some ways the major topic defense was made for the United States. Not only has the US military been involved in a large number of military actions since World War II, but spending on defense far outstrips every other CAP country.[5] That spending creates many points for policymaking as well, from procurement procedures to bases and much, much more.

Switzerland on the other hand is quite different in this regard. Despite being a country with mandatory military service it is also a neutral country that has not taken a major military action since 1815 with spending generally less than one third of that spent by the United States as measured as a percentage of GDP. Overall this leads to less of a need to attend to defense from a policy perspective than in the United States as demonstrated in Figure 2.1, which shows the number of Reports/Bills and Legislation for both countries from 1978 to 2008.

Clearly there is a vast disparity in legislative activity on defense between the United States and Switzerland. Nevertheless, not everything in the dataset follows this same pattern. A comparison of the front page of the *Neue Zürcher Zeitung* and the *New York Times* Index from 1995 to 2003 (see Figure 2.2) where data is currently available through CAP shows a noticeably higher level of attention to defense issues in the Swiss media owing to its more external and international media viewpoint.

2.3.2 Culture: Something France Has and the United Kingdom Does Not?

If someone was to overhear many of the discussions concerning culture within the CAP over the years it would seem as if half of policy scholars

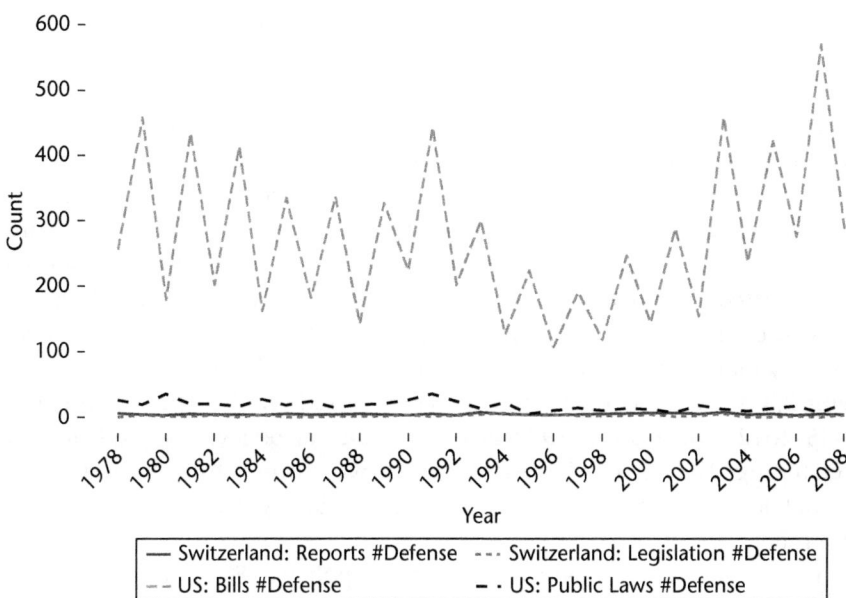

Figure 2.1. Bills and laws—United States vs. Switzerland on defense
Source: Comparative Agendas Project

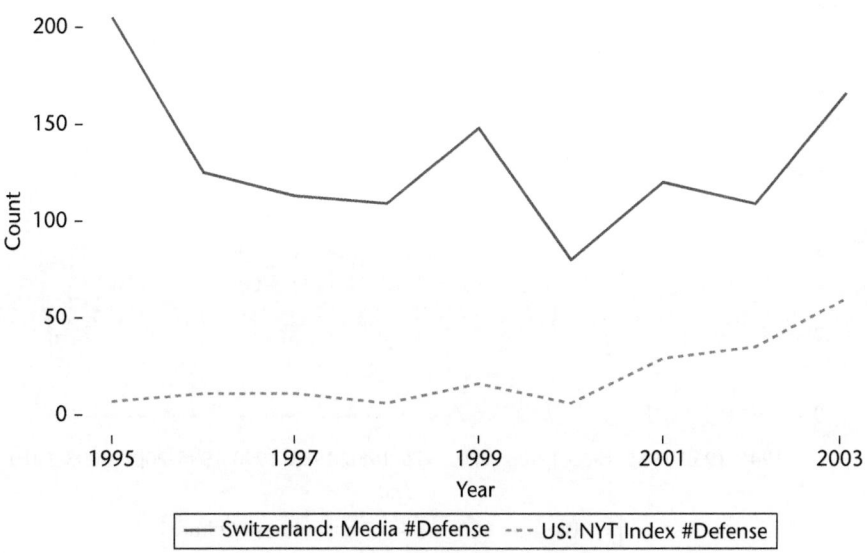

Figure 2.2. Media—United States vs. Switzerland on defense
Source: Comparative Agendas Project

thought culture was merely a fictional concept. In reality much of the debate in the network over culture has been focused on whether or not cultural policy exists. Perhaps unsurprisingly several countries simply do not have cultural policies as the desire to promote their national language, protect cultural industries like film, theatre and more is not strong enough or central enough for the government to take notice. In others the importance of these sorts of items is strong enough to lead to government policies, sometimes very many policies. The CAP Master Codebook treats culture as a topic for policy, but one that admittedly is not attended to equally by all nations. In fact the differences between countries like the United Kingdom and France are so pronounced that they make the comparison for defense in Figures 2.1 and 2.2 look strong. Figure 2.3 shows the percentage of laws passed in the United Kingdom (1945–2012) and France (1979–2012) on cultural policy. A period of non-overlapping data for the United Kingdom was chosen to show that while cultural policy in the United Kingdom is rare, it did regularly receive attention for a time.

The difference in the production of cultural policy in France and the United Kingdom is quite clear to see. For the overlapping period almost no cultural laws are made in the United Kingdom while as much as 7.4 percent of the laws passed by France are cultural in a year. While France shows a higher average compared to the United Kingdom outright it is noteworthy that the passage of

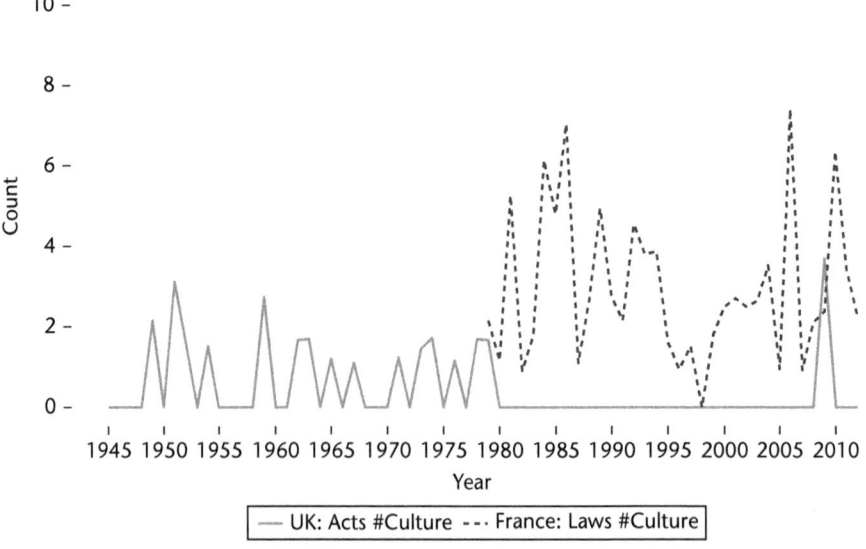

Figure 2.3. Culture across the Chanel—cultural laws in the United Kingdom and France
Source: Comparative Agendas Project

cultural laws was at one time far more regular in the United Kingdom. However, the production of cultural laws all but died after Thatcher became Prime Minister, not only for her and her party, but for the administrations that came after, showing a distinct and lasting impact on policymaking.

2.3.3 *Universal Health: Policy Attention*

Not all policy areas are created unequally. Perhaps one of the most surprising early comparisons born out of the emerging CAP network was the comparison of policymaking attention to health in Denmark and the United States (Green-Pedersen and Wilkerson, 2006). Green-Pedersen and Wilkerson's (2006) work showed that despite fundamental differences in each country's approach to healthcare, a general rise in the amount and complexity of legislative attention (bills, hearings, debates, and questions) from the 1950s to the early 2000s occurred in both countries. Factors like new technologies and aging populations suggest that if a country is producing healthcare policy it must continue to attend to health. Figure 2.4 extends this work presenting the percentage of hearings, questions and prime minister's questions on health in the United States, Denmark, Spain, and the United Kingdom from 1982 to 2002 (or for as long as data is available).

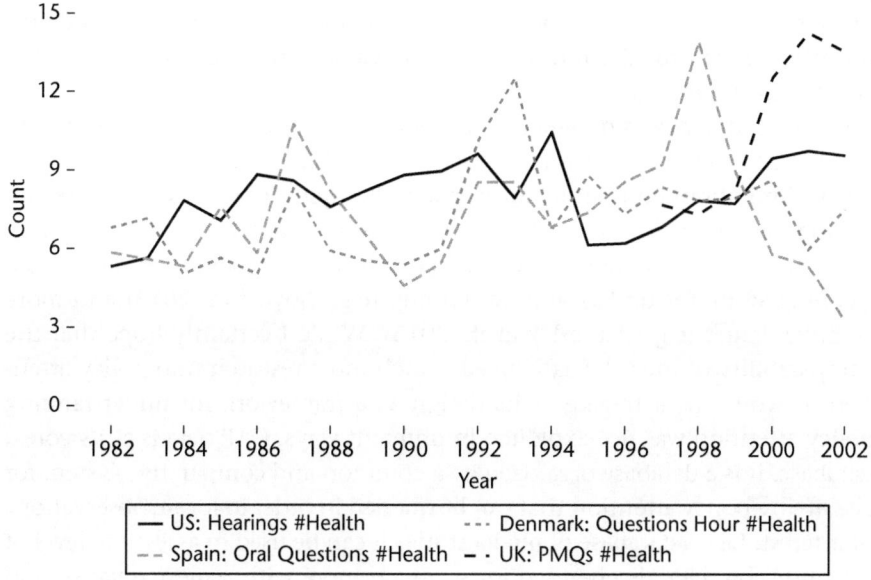

Figure 2.4. Questioning health—legislative questions cross-nationally
Source: Comparative Agendas Project

While not as strikingly similar nor clearly trending as in the previous work, questions related to health in each of these countries have fairly steady levels of attention marked by peaks in activity. This both demonstrates the general importance of health across these four countries and likely much more broadly across most CAP countries, but also that national variation especially relating to higher patterns of attention do exist. In fact, the same can be said for many of the major topic and subtopic comparisons made across countries, not just those for health. Given the generally similar concerns of most governments general patterns of attention across countries and datasets are to be expected though and adds to validity of CAP data.

2.4 Conclusion

Through the creation of the CAP Master Codebook and associated crosswalks CAP data allows for an unparalleled level of comparison on policy between nations. It is my sincere hope that the CAP data and the efforts the community have made at harmonizing it spurs a host of new comparative research never before possible. As the work from the CAP community has already shown, several original insights can be gained through truly comparative cross-national data such as the common law of punctuated budgets (Jones et al., 2009) or the general effect of core issues on government agendas (Jennings et al., 2011). The ever-growing volume of CAP data is a resource not just for public policy scholars or even scholars in general, but students, practitioners, the media, and elected officials alike if the success of the US PAP is any indication.

CAP-coded data was designed as a tool for understanding policy attention, but can be used as a basis for so much more. While CAP data obviously has several limitations and cannot answer all policy questions, the framework and datasets are intended not just for analyses as they stand, but to be built upon. A great deal of work already demonstrates how CAP coded data provides a stepping stone for understanding framing (e.g., Boydstun, 2013) and more complex issues (e.g., Annesley et al., 2015). While I certainly hope that the comparability of the CAP data breeds much more research into policy attention, it would be a tragedy if its design as a framework for understanding policy attention was not exploited in different ways. CAP data is at its core a database. It is a database organized by a common and comparative system for classifying policy attention that can be queried in order to locate observations of interest. Like a database of media stories it can be used to assess the level of attention, but can also be used for so much more with a more detailed and importantly directed investigation of the data. The CAP community agrees on the importance of attention in all of our research, but work on framing, preferences, and more can and is being done based on this data. I think I am safe to say that as a community we only hope that the users of this database are able to add to and manipulate it in order to answer detailed and comparative questions on policy in a way that was never before possible. If you are interested starting a project of your own and joining the CAP community please refer to the advice for new projects contained on our website.

Acknowledgements

Thanks go to the members of the CAP community for their hard work and hospitality. Particular thanks go to Christoffer Green-Pedersen, Stefaan Walgrave, Frank Baumgartner, and Bryan Jones for their additional support and for originally suggesting and organizing this effort.

Special thanks go to the Mannheim Centre for European Social Research (MZES) at the University of Mannheim for allowing me to conduct this work as part of my research fellowship. Without their support, the CAP Master Codebook would still only be just an idea.

Notes

1. My advisor is more of a tennis man actually.
2. The folding of immigration into labor and employment, and family issues into law and order is the reason for the missing major topic numbers 9 and 11 respectively in the original US codebook. The decision to combine these topics in the very early days of the project was based on how government addressed these issues in practice. For example, the US government purposefully avoids most family issues, but when it does it tends to address legal issues like child custody and illegal acts such as domestic violence. The advantage of the old, non-sequential coding system was that the missing major topics used to provide a quick indication of someone's familiarity with the codebook when asked how many major topic codes existed with the uninformed, modal answer being 21 with the correct answer being 19. Tragically, the CAP Master Codebook makes the old uninformed answer of 21 correct with the introduction of two new major topic codes removing the applicability of this informal heuristic.
3. Policing primarily varies in its structure with national and local or subnational police operating in unique ways from country to country.
4. The United Kingdom's scandal concerning the presence of horsemeat in frozen food in early 2013 did little to ease the number of jokes told concerning British cuisine.
5. Based on October 2016 data.

References

Annesley, C., Engeli, I., and Gains, F. (2015). The Profile of Gender Equality Issue Attention in Western Europe. *European Journal of Political Research*, 54(3): 525–42.

Baumgartner, F. R., Brouard, S., Green-Pedersen, C. et al. (2011). The Dynamics of Policy Change in Comparative Perspective. *Comparative Political Studies*, 44(8): 947–72.

Bevan, S., Baumgartner F., Johnson, E., and McCarthy, J. (2013). Understanding Selection Bias, Time-Lags and Measurement Bias in Secondary Data Sources: Putting the Encyclopedia of Associations Database in Broader Context. *Social Science Research*, 42(6): 1750–64.

Bevan, S. and Jennings, W. (2014). Representation, Agendas and Institutions. *European Journal of Political Research*, 53(1): 37–56.

Boydstun, A. E. (2013). *Making the News: Politics, the Media, and Agenda Setting*. Chicago: University of Chicago Press.

Dowding, K., Hindmoor, A., and Martin, A. (2016). The Comparative Policy Agendas Project: Theory, Measurement and Findings. *Journal of Public Policy*, 36(1): 3–25.

Green-Pedersen, C., and Wilkerson, J. (2006). How Agenda-Setting Attributes Shape Politics: Basic Dilemmas, Problem Attention and Health Politics Developments in Denmark and the US. *Journal of European Public Policy*, 13(7): 1039–52.

Guiraudon, V. (2000). European Integration and Migration Policy: Vertical Policy Making as Venue Shopping. *Journal of Common Market Studies*, 38(2): 251–71.

Jennings, W., Shaun B., Timmermans, A. et al. (2011). Effects of the Core Functions of Government on the Diversity of Executive Agendas. *Comparative Political Studies*, 44(8): 1001–30.

Jones, B. D., and Baumgartner, F. R. (2005). *The Politics of Attention: How Government Prioritizes Problems*. Chicago: University of Chicago Press.

Jones, B. D., Baumgartner, F. R., Breunig, C. et al. (2009) A General Empirical Law of Public Budgets: A Comparative Analysis. *American Journal of Political Science*, 53(4): 855–73.

Kingdon, J. W. (1995). *Agendas, Alternatives, and Public Policies*. 2nd ed. New York: HarperCollins.

Klüver, H. (2009). Measuring Interest Group Influence Using Quantitative Text Analysis. *European Union Politics*, 10(4): 535–49.

3

The Comparative Agendas Project

The Evolving Research Interests and Designs of the CAP Scholarly Community

Stefaan Walgrave and Amber E. Boydstun

This book describes and presents the evidence gathered in the framework of the Comparative Agendas Project (CAP). In this chapter, we adopt a slightly different approach. Instead of presenting the countries and the evidence they've gathered, and instead of showing what *can* be done with the agenda data, we shift our attention to what *has* been done with the agenda data during the last dozen years or so. We examine the evolving research interests of the scholars participating in the CAP community and the designs they used for their work. We then discuss what these past trends may suggest for the future of CAP research—a future that is very bright, indeed.

At the heart of the CAP community are conferences, organized since 2006, that occur each year in changing venues. The first conference was organized in Aarhus in 2006, the last so far in Edinburgh in 2017. In the years between, the CAP community met in Paris (2007), Barcelona (2008), Den Hague (2009), Seattle (2010), Catania (2011), Reims (2012), Antwerp (2013), Konstanz (2014), Lisbon (2015), and Geneva (2016). The work presented at these yearly events no doubt grasps the gist of the work undertaken with CAP data. All country teams have been represented at nearly every CAP conference, and as soon as a new CAP project starts in a new country, the team is invited to attend the next year's conference in order to formally present the new country's project, its aims and data. As a consequence, the number of participants in the CAP conference has increased considerably, from only thirteen in 2006 to seventy-nine in 2017. The greatest increase in participants and papers took place in 2009, in Den Hague, when the number of participants nearly doubled from the previous year (up from 32 in Barcelona in 2008 to 60). The Netherlands are, after all, lovely in June. Since Reims (2012), the number of participants has more or less stayed the same and there is no more growth to be noted. Looking at the work that has been presented at these yearly conferences gives us a good overview of what CAP scholars have been up to with the agenda data they've collected.

This chapter presents simple and descriptive analyses of the abstracts of papers that were presented at one of eleven CAP conferences—there have been twelve CAP conferences but the data from Paris in 2007 are missing (we blame the excellent French wine). In total, our analysis draws upon exactly 398 papers presented/co-authored by more than two hundred different individuals. We, the authors of this chapter, in line with the CAP content analysis approach, coded the abstracts on a number of variables. We did not implement any inter-coder reliability procedures but agreed on the variables and how to code them before we started our work. Some of the paper abstracts were unclear, vague or sometimes even entirely missing.[1] As a consequence, the total number of conference papers in the tables and figures below varies, as missing data varies across variables. Note that in most cases we content-analyzed the abstracts that were submitted *before* the conference in order to be accepted to present a paper. The actual paper that was eventually presented later at the conference (and that was published even much later in a journal or book, if at all) could have been different; our experience is that even among the excellent CAP community, there can often be some slippage between promises and delivery.

3.1 What CAP Scholars Are Interested in

The essence of the CAP is attention to issues. Political attention is a scarce resource as politicians have limited time, energy, money, staff, etc. to deal with all the problems in a society. At the same time, and maybe exactly because it is scarce, political attention is consequential; it is an absolute precondition for policy change. So, CAP scholars investigate the causes and consequences and dynamics of political attention to issues. Political agendas are manifold, though. All political actors and institutions more or less have their own agenda, their own prioritized list of issues they devote more or less attention to. *The* political agenda does not exist. Over the years, CAP scholars have addressed issue attention with regards to a wide variety of political agendas, broadly defined. Figure 3.1 lists the number of CAP conference papers examining each major agenda, noting that many papers examine more than one agenda and thus might be included multiple times.

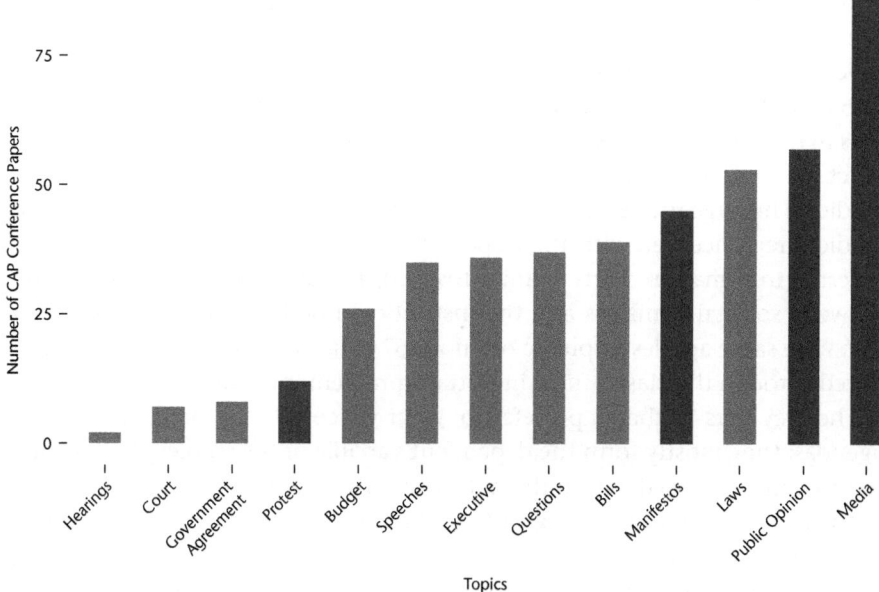

Figure 3.1. Number of CAP conference (2006–17) papers containing attention data for the listed agendas

Notes: N = 398 papers; 459 instances of an agenda studied.

Source: Authors

The figure shows that the policy agendas approach has been applied to no less than thirteen different agendas, ranging from congressional hearings to street protests, from parliamentary questions to law making and budgeting. CAP scholars used all these agendas to take quantitative measure of the amount of attention paid to a given issue or issues. This was mostly done by counting the number of individual items (e.g., laws, street demonstrations) per time unit devoted to one of the CAP codebook issues, but sometimes also by counting money (e.g., budgets) or sentences or quasi-sentences (e.g., manifestos, State of the Union addresses) spent on issues. The figure underpins the versatility of the agenda approach that has been applied to a very wide variety of political attention venues.

The graph indicates that the media agenda is by far the most examined agenda in the CAP network. Of all 398 papers presented at CAP conferences, eighty-seven contained media data (22 percent). This is a remarkable result, since the media cannot be considered as a *pure sang* policy agenda. Rather, the media are often used as an indicator of societal demands and of incoming signals. In a way, the media are supposed to capture the external information that is injected into the political system. As a consequence, the mass media are mostly an independent variable in agenda research; only in rare cases are they the dependent variable.

Further, the graph shows that the media are definitely not the only 'societal' agenda in the body of work that CAP has produced over the years. The darker bars in the figure refer to societal agendas—these are not policy agendas in the strict sense—that are mostly used as alternative independent variables in some studies. The large interest in societal agendas suggests that a good deal of CAP studies are concerned with the responsiveness of the core policy agendas to external information. Party manifestos (45), parties forming the prime link between societal demands and the institutional political system, score high also. The same applies to public opinion (57) that was most often operationalized through the classic most important problem measure.

The grey bars in the graph refer to, what we could call, 'hard core' policy agendas; they mostly form the dependent variable of the studies. The agenda most commonly used within this category is the agenda of laws (53). Agenda scholars have also shown a large interest in bills (39), parliamentary questions (37), executive orders (36), and executive speeches (35). What we could call the most viscose and most consequential agenda of them all, the yearly budget (Baumgartner et al., 2009), appears in twenty-six studies.

Thus, our analysis of what CAP scholars are interested in shows a notable interest in agendas that go beyond what one would spontaneously mention when thinking about policy agendas. Or, in other words, the CAP community's take on politics and policymaking is broad and does not remain confined to the classic, institutional policy agendas situated at the end of the policy cycle. Figure 3.1 is thus a first indicator of the fact that the CAP network produces mainstream political science research examining the political *process* and is not just interested in policy output.

This observation can be put in a longitudinal perspective, as well. Figure 3.2 shows—as an example of the attention to societal signals—the percentage and number of papers in which the media agenda was coded. The bars are labeled with the absolute number while the size of the bar is proportional to the number of papers presented that year. The graph shows a general rise in work including the media from 2012 onwards in absolute numbers; in percentages, the media agenda seems to have received a little less attention during the most recent years. In 2017 in Edinburgh, our last observation, seven of the in total forty-eight papers deal, among others, with the mass media (16 percent).

Apart from the question of which agendas CAP scholars are interested in, a second important distinction between studies is whether scholars try to *explain* the attention for issues on a given agenda. In fact, a large share of the initial agenda work as inspired by Frank Baumgartner and Bryan Jones (1993; 2005) was, at least empirically, *descriptive* in nature. Its aim was to show

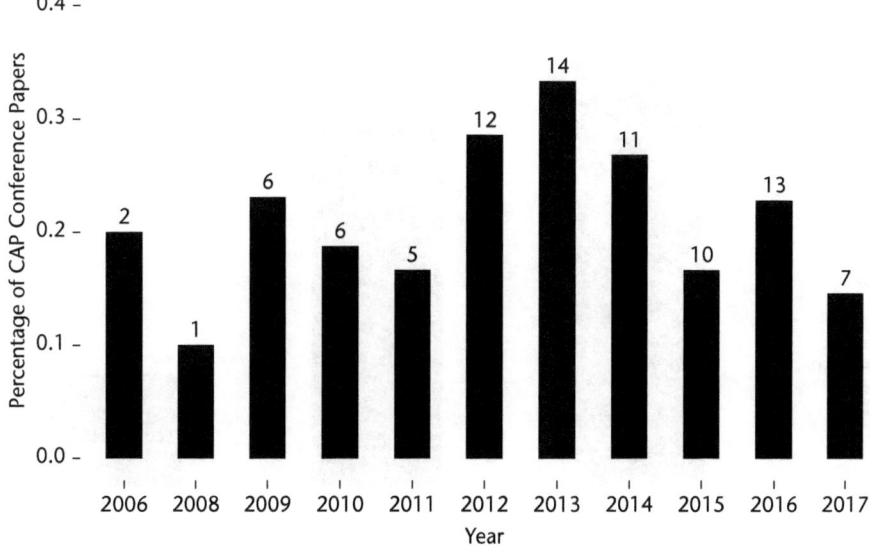

Figure 3.2. Percentage of CAP conference (2006–17) papers containing media agenda data

Notes: N = 398 papers.

Source: Authors

that political attention is stochastic and spiked with long periods of stasis alternating with short bursts of attention. It is difficult to conclude based on short abstracts whether the (to be written) paper is descriptive or rather explanatory. As a simple solution, we coded the abstracts for whether they mention the fact that the paper will assess the impact from one agenda on another. We can be reasonably confident that these inter-agenda papers are explanatory in nature. Figure 3.3 contains the evidence.

A large group of papers (198) assesses the impact of one agenda on another. Incorporating at least two agendas, these papers are basically interested in how attention for an issue jumps from one agenda to another. Prime examples here are studies dealing with how media attention leads to parliamentary questions or how executive speeches foreshadow legislation. Other CAP papers (152) do not tackle inter-agenda effects. These papers study one agenda only, sometimes seeking to explain variance in that one agenda as a function of other variables in a given country (e.g., economic conditions), and other times in a comparative perspective. Examples are studies dealing with legislation in two countries finding that the same issues become the object of legislation in the two countries at about the same time.

Yet again, we see quite a dramatic change over time. Figure 3.4 shows the number of inter-agenda papers over time and displays a secular increase.

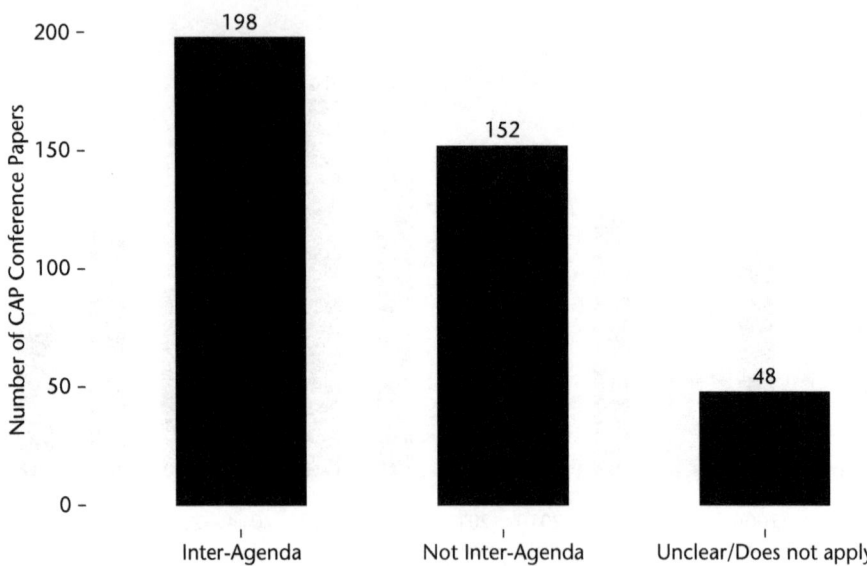

Figure 3.3. Percentage of CAP conference (2006–17) papers dealing with inter-agenda impact

Notes: N = 398 papers.
Source: Authors

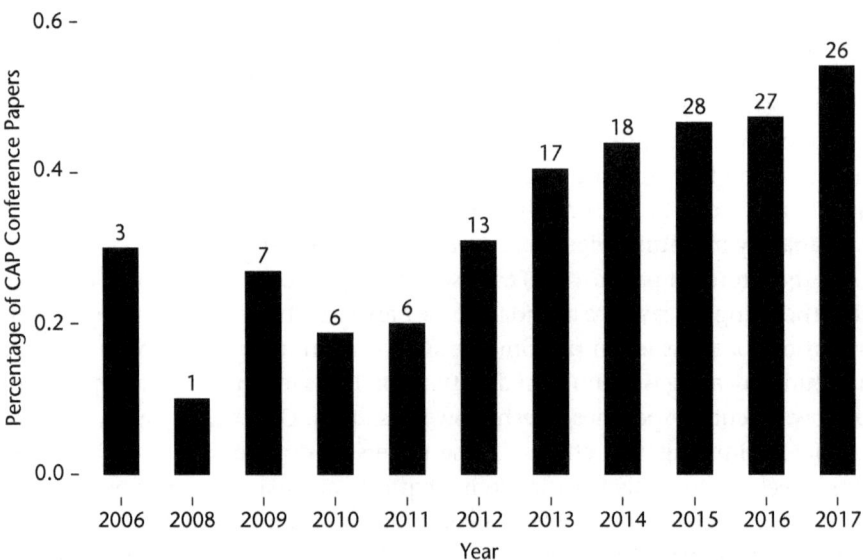

Figure 3.4. Percentage of CAP conference papers over time dealing with inter-agenda impact

Notes: N = 398 papers.
Source: Authors

More and more, CAP scholars have become interested in the *dynamics* of agenda-setting by examining how agendas influence each other. At the last conference in 2017 (Edinburgh), twenty-six of the forty-eight papers were somehow looking into inter-agenda effects (54 percent) while the average for the entire period is 36 percent. This clear trend reflects the increasing value CAP scholars have put on explaining why issue attention goes up or down over time. We've known for a while that attention for issues is irregular and punctuated, and increasingly the CAP community has turned to explaining why this could be the case. Inter-agenda influence is one of the prime candidates.

3.2 Designs Used by CAP Scholars

The previous section explored the evolving interest of the CAP community over time: the agendas under study and the increasingly explanatory take on the agenda process. But what designs have students of agenda-setting been using?

To start with, to what extent has CAP work been comparative? The network of CAP scholars has been growing organically, with country teams gradually joining the common endeavor but (intentionally) without strong centralized efforts and (unintentionally) without consistent funding to integrate the country data in a common comparative dataset. Prior to the coordinated effort among all participating projects to edit their data in accordance with the common CAP codebook (Bevan, 2017) and then the launch in 2016 of the www.comparativeagendas.net website, comparative work depended on the willingness of country teams to share data and on their ability to put together integrated databases. This challenge has seriously hampered the pace of development of comparative work in the CAP community. Indeed, most studies deal with evidence from one country only. We found only eighty comparative studies; that is, studies containing evidence of more than one country (20 percent). A majority of work in the CAP community is not comparative in nature (58 percent). Figure 3.5 has the evidence.

Figure 3.6 shows that the structural shift towards comparative work has not occurred yet. Despite the concerted efforts of the CAP community to unify a central coding scheme and the strong professional relationships between researchers of different countries, there is simply no increase in comparative work over time. On the contrary, the percentage of CAP conference papers examining comparative evidence has gone down over time. That said, as we will elaborate in the conclusion, we expect a major shift towards comparative agenda work in the years to come.

Although a good deal of the CAP work is not comparative, the community is highly international, with scholars from many different countries gathering

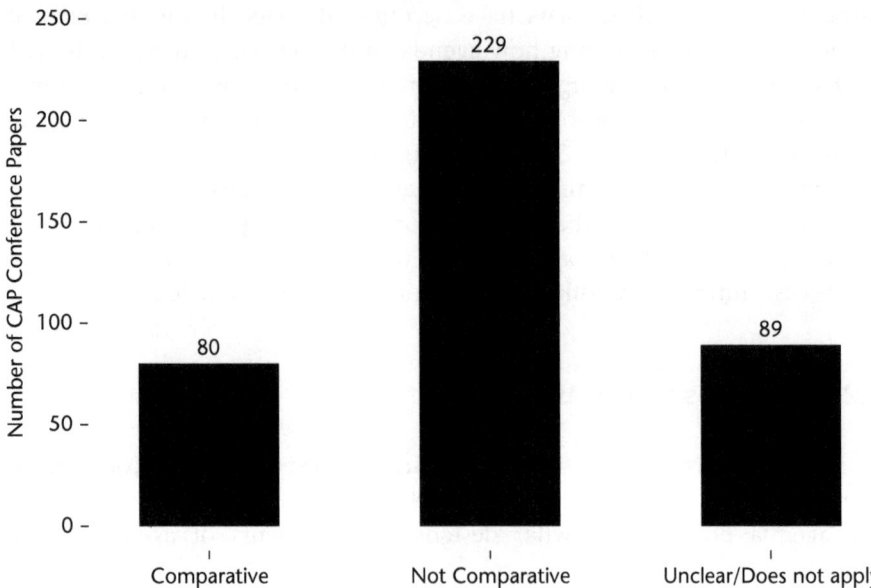

Figure 3.5. Number of CAP conference (2006–17) papers with comparative evidence
Notes: N = 398 papers.
Source: Authors

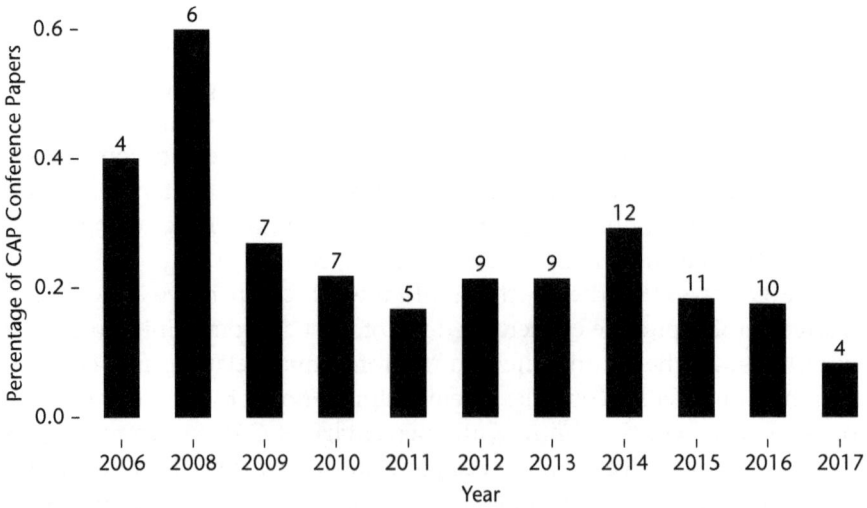

Figure 3.6. Percentage of CAP conference papers over time with comparative evidence
Notes: N = 398 papers.
Source: Authors

agenda data according to CAP standards, attending CAP conferences, and publishing about their own or other countries. Still, the country project triggering the whole CAP undertaking has been the US Policy Agendas Project, which has been ongoing from the 1990s onwards. CAP has been spreading to other countries, but exactly how international is the work produced by CAP? Instead of coding the nationality of CAP attendees, we simply coded the abstracts for which country (or countries) the paper examined, including two US states: Florida and Pennsylvania. Note that comparative papers are double (or triple, quadruple, etc.) counted. Figure 3.7 summarizes the evidence.

The data show that US evidence dominates the CAP community. Over the years, ninety-one out of 398 papers have used (at least) US evidence (23 percent); nearly one-quarter of all papers deal with US data. All in all, this is not an extremely large share, knowing the head start of the US country team with its project dating back at least ten years compared to the second country's project. A number of European countries with early-starting and long-lasting agenda projects are also well represented in the country list: United Kingdom (41), Belgium (38), Denmark (32), Spain (32), the Netherlands (28), Switzerland (26), and France (24). Together with the Americans, these (Western) European countries have formed the core of the CAP community for many years. These results strongly underpin the US-European bias in

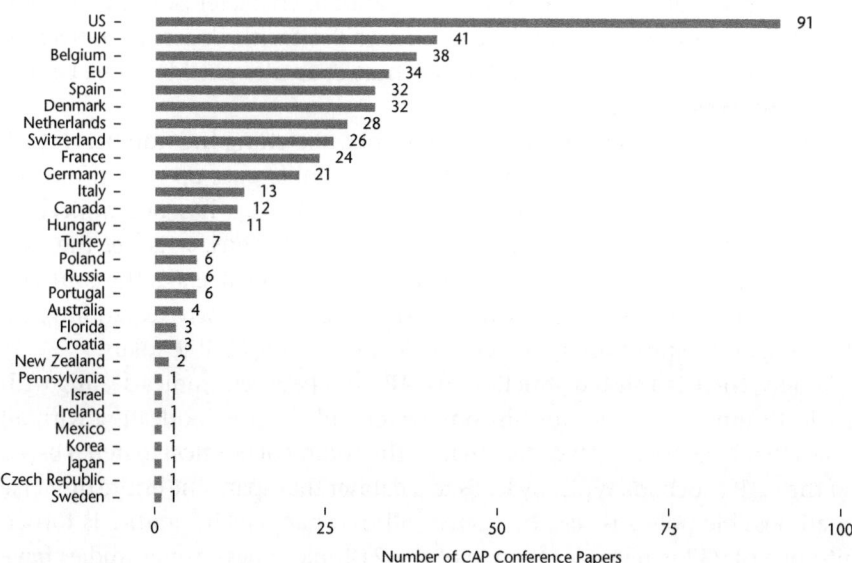

Figure 3.7. Number of CAP conference (2006–17) papers containing evidence on various countries (and two US states)

Notes: N = 398 papers.

Source: Authors

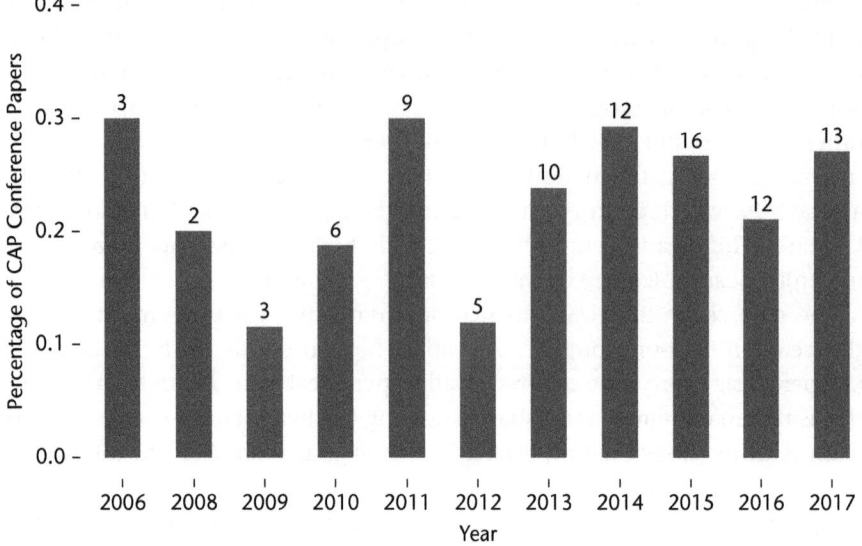

Figure 3.8. Percentage of CAP Conference Papers over Time with US Evidence
Notes: N = 398 papers.
Source: Authors

agenda work. Still, testifying to the international character of the CAP community, papers presented at CAP conferences dealt with no less than twenty-nine distinct countries, with thirteen of these countries outside of the United States and Western Europe.

Figure 3.8 focuses on the United States only, sketching the number of CAP papers with US evidence over time. The raw number goes up with the years, but in fact as a percentage of all papers the US focus has not noticeably increased. But neither has it noticeably decreased. Thus, it is *not* the case that CAP scholars are slowly turning away from US evidence. On the contrary, while the number of countries with CAP evidence is slowly expanding, US data remain the most used sources of evidence among CAP scholars.

Finally, there is a clear distinction in CAP work between studies dealing with a select number of issues (or just one issue) and other work dealing with all issues that have been CAP-coded. In fact, the coding of political material based on the CAP codebook typically leads to a dataset that spans the entire universe of all possible policy issues. In a sense, all that happens in politics is turned into one of 233 issue codes (or one of the 21 topic codes). Some studies have taken this entire dataset and have looked at all issues. These typically are studies looking for an overall pattern of agenda-setting across issues. Other studies have, in contrast, looked at a single issue or a small number of issues. These studies were more interested in a specific policy domain because of its

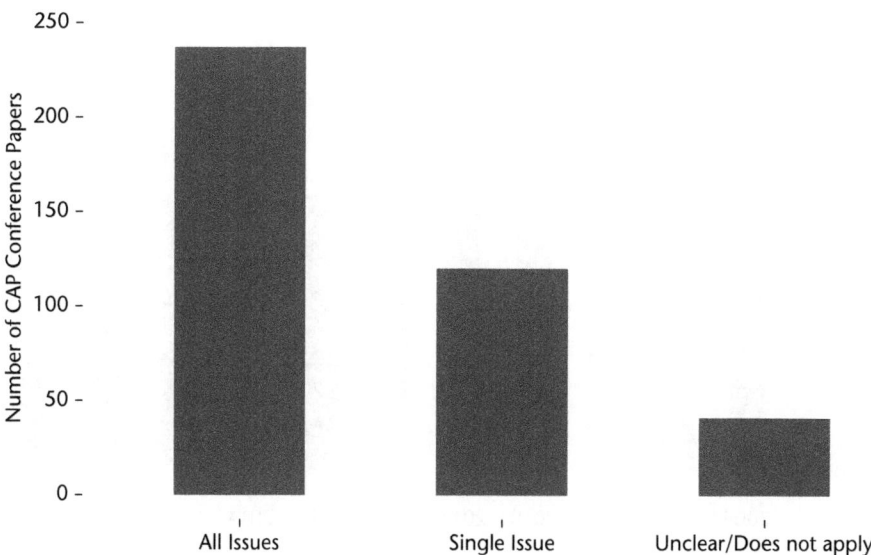

Figure 3.9. Number of CAP conference (2006–17) papers using evidence on all issues or on selected issues

Notes: N = 398 papers.

Source: Authors

substantial interest or they selected a smaller number of issues because of theoretical reasons. The former strategy of examining all issues can be considered to be typical for political scientists more generally; they are less interested in specific policies but more in the general political process. The latter strategy of focusing on only one or a few issues is typical for policy scholars who are mostly interested in the output of the political system and who care about some specific issue(s) for substantial reasons. So, is CAP more of a general political science or rather more of a specific policy science community? Figure 3.9 has the evidence.

The studies using the full dataset including all issues are clearly prevailing. No less than 60 percent of all papers presented at CAP conferences encompass all issues. This pattern suggests that the CAP community may be more of a political science than of a policy science group. There is less interest in substantive issues but more in how issues in general are processed in the political system. Issues are mostly just cases that are used to track the political process. Still, a sizable minority of studies (30 percent) focus on one or only a few issues.

Again, we looked over time at the difference between papers that did and did not encompass all issues to see whether there is an evolution through the years. There are some indications of a trend, but it is definitely not secular, as

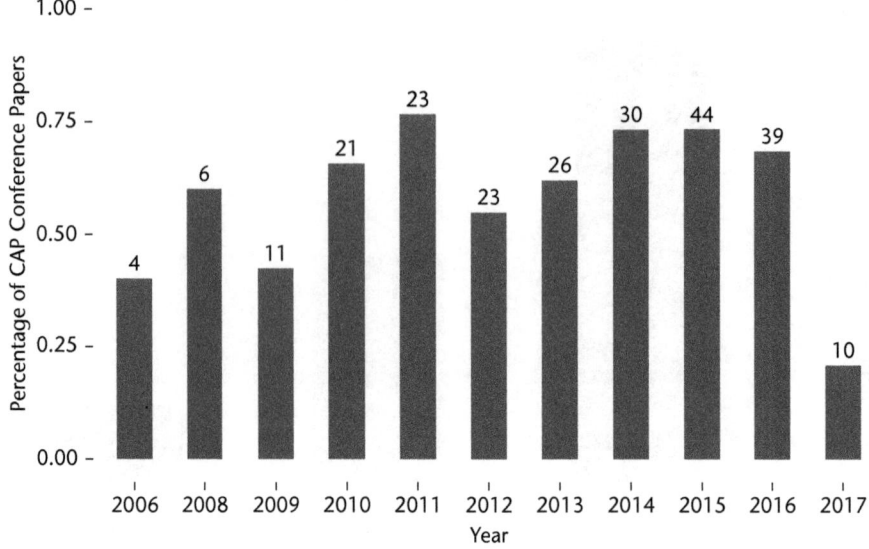

Figure 3.10. Percentage of CAP conference papers over time using evidence spanning all CAP issues

Notes: N = 398 papers.

Source: Authors

Figure 3.10 shows. The last Edinburgh conference in 2017 seems to be an outlier, with exceptionally few all-issue papers (21 percent). Looking at the whole series suggests that the trend has been generally upward, though, especially compared to the early years. This finding suggests that, over time, the CAP community may have evolved even more into a mainstream political science group. The interest in specific issues was never very high but it appears even to have decreased over the years.

3.3 Conclusion: Past and Future of the Comparative Agendas Project

Our data suggest that the scholars of the Comparative Agendas Project are mainly interested in the political process and less in public policy. The interest in the political process has been present from the very beginning of the project but seems to have become even stronger over the years. Indeed, CAP has become mainstream political science. Moreover, the agenda data are increasingly used to analyze how agendas influence each other and, thus, to track political power. Arguably the most central research agenda within the CAP community is dealing with the responsiveness of political institutions (and their agendas) to societal signals coming from outside the political system, *sensu stricto*. So, ultimately, what drives much of the agenda work seems to be a concern about democratic representation. The main weakness of the network is its relatively limited attention for comparison. By far most of what has been done with CAP data is single-country only and does not compare across countries; there is no trend towards more comparative work. Further, while the number of countries with agenda data is definitely growing, the original American and Western European countries are still dominating the CAP conferences.

This chapter looked back and sketched the (short) history of CAP by examining the papers presented at the yearly conferences. Can we draw conclusions about the future development of CAP from it? It is of course most simple to predict that the next years will bring more of the same and that the tendencies witnessed in previous years will continue to manifest themselves in the years to come. Yet, there are some signs that the next few years will also bring structural changes to CAP—we could call them 'punctuations' (although CAP scholars have never been very good at predicting when exactly the spike of change is going to occur, not even afterwards).

The most important crucial new thing is the data website launched in the summer of 2016. While before the CAP data were not centralized and could only be collected by asking each country responsible for its data and then by following by a painstaking exercise to construct a comparative and comparable dataset, the free availability of all CAP data in a standardized format is expected to strongly boost the comparative use of the CAP data in the years to come. Indeed, the collected dataset is so vast that it likely is the biggest dataset available in the whole of political science (with millions of observations). It is not hard to predict that these data will be used for non-strictly agenda-setting purposes as well. So, the variety of research questions, designs, and purposes for which CAP data will be used is surely about to increase further.

The increased centralization and standardization of the dataset could have an impact on the functioning of the CAP network as well. The network grew organically, as new country teams popped up and sought connection with people already doing agendas work. A hallmark of the CAP conferences has been an openness to newcomers. Also, despite some key senior researchers responsible for the development of the CAP community, these researchers were careful not to take dictatorial charge, fostering instead a rotating set of temporary leaderships coupled with a tradition of the conferences moving from one venue to another. It remains to be seen whether such an informal structure without formal leadership or central funding can survive in the long term, especially when a common dataset has to be maintained. The maintenance and updating of the common dataset is the most obvious main challenge for the years to come. At present, there is a core of comparable data covering many years, but this evidence will soon be outdated. Shall country teams find the energy and the funding to update their datasets? This challenge might prove daunting. At the same time, as more and more scholars use the now easy-to-access CAP data, the need and will to regularly update these datasets will be felt even more acutely. And by any measure, the quality and commitment (and likeability) of the CAP community is superb. We are optimistic about its future.

Note

1. For various reasons, not all papers that were presented at conferences over the years had their abstracts archived. The data we present here captures available abstracts, thus underrepresenting the total number of papers presented (but not, to the best of our knowledge, in any biased way).

References

Baumgartner, F., Breunig, C., Green-Pedersen, C. et al. (2009). Punctuated Equilibrium in Comparative Perspective. *American Journal of Political Science*, 53(3): 603–20.

Baumgartner, F., and Jones, B. D. (1993). *Agendas and Instability in American Politics*. Chicago: University of Chicago Press.

Bevan, S. (2017). Gone Fishing: The Creation of the Comparative Agendas Project Master Codebook. Available at: http://sbevan.com/cap-master-codebook.html [Accessed 24 Apr. 2018].

Jones, B., and Baumgartner, F. (2005). *The Politics of Attention: How Government Prioritizes Attention*. Chicago: University of Chicago Press.

Part II
Country Projects

4

The Australian Policy Agendas Project

Keith Dowding, Aaron Martin, and Rhonda L. Evans

4.1 The Australian Political System

The Commonwealth of Australia was formed in 1901 when the six self-governing colonies federated under a popularly sanctioned Constitution. Australia's position with regard to the United Kingdom progressed thereafter as the country's independence was recognized and most of the elements of its colonial status were removed. The federal structure was driven in part by pragmatism. Given the size of the continent and the sparseness of the population, which included a significant rural population, it made sense that the federal government take responsibility for certain policy areas. While the founders envisioned a relatively minimal role for the federal government, its reach has expanded over time, stimulated to some extent by the exigencies of war. In particular, since 1942 the federal government has collected income tax and, since 2000, a consumption tax, the Goods and Service Tax (GST), bearing out the first half of Hackett's 1891 prophecy that 'either responsible government will kill federation, or federation . . . will kill responsible government' (cited in Fenna, 2009: 152). Today, Australia has six states and two territories, each with its own government and public service.

Australia's Constitution enumerates the limited law-making powers of the Federal Parliament, allocating residual powers to the states and territories.[1] The Federal Parliament possesses exclusive power over an array of areas such as regulation of immigration and management of 'external affairs';[2] and the states possess exclusive authority in areas not expressly given to the Commonwealth. Both levels of government share concurrent powers in some policy areas (such as health and education), but the Constitution provides that federal law prevails in the event of conflicting legislation.[3] Over time, the Commonwealth has acquired greater power at the expense of the states, and the system has developed into a more cooperative form of federalism than the Constitution would suggest.

The Federal Parliament consists of a House of Representatives and Senate, with the government formed from the majority controlling the House. The House's 150 members are elected by the Alternative Vote from single-member constituencies. Elections are required within three years with the precise date chosen by the prime minister. Senators have six-year terms with half-Senate elections every three years. Government consists of a prime minister (PM) and a cabinet that must maintain confidence of its party room. The British Queen, styled Queen of Australia, is head of state, although the governor-general, appointed by the Australian government, actually performs the office's largely ceremonial functions. Because the PM and cabinet dominate legislative agenda-setting, policies that do not align with the House majority's preferences are unlikely to be enacted. Disciplined political parties ensure that legislative votes almost always follow strict party lines. Private Members (all Members of the House except the PM, Speaker, ministers, and parliamentary secretaries) may introduce bills, but without government support such measures rarely become law—only twenty-five have been enacted since Federation.

Australia melds parts of the federal structure of politics in the United States with aspects of the Westminster system in the United Kingdom. Where it comes closest to the Westminster system and least resembles the US system is the location and power of the executive. The executive sits in and derives its power from parliament. The executive also derives its power from being the party that won the majority of votes in the House of Representatives. If we think of a chain of responsibility, we could think of the PM as chair of the executive, which derives its power from being the party in control of parliament, but which is ultimately accountable to the entire parliament. The role of the opposition is a key element of Westminster systems. Rather than a legislature with floating coalitions partly held together by party loyalty, the Australian parliament, like other Westminster systems, historically comprises a governing majority party faced by a unified opposition.

A few other points should be noted. Australia's contemporary party system features three major political parties: the Australian Labor Party (ALP), the Liberal Party of Australia, and the much smaller National Party, whose stronghold is rural and regional Australia. The latter two parties, both conservative, operate together and are known simply as 'the Coalition'. In the post-World-War-II era, government has alternated between the ALP and the Coalition. Voting in Australia has been compulsory since 1924. Australia has an independent judiciary with policymaking capabilities. It can invalidate legislation that breaches its understanding of the Constitution. These decisions can only be overturned through an onerous referendum process. Judges can influence public policy through their development of the common law, statutory interpretation, and constitutional judicial review. A system of national courts overlays separate systems of courts in each of the states and territories.

Australia's bicameral legislature, system of courts, and federal division of power thus afford multiple policymaking venues. The political system also features two key 'veto points': a Senate that can obstruct the law-making process and a High Court that can invalidate legislation and disallow executive actions of governments.

4.2 Datasets of the Australian Policy Agendas Project

One helpful way to think about what we have coded is in terms of agendas developed within formal institutions (governor-general speeches, legislation, and opposition questions) and those that are constituted outside these institutions (media and public opinion) (see Dowding and Martin, 2017).

Table 4.1 outlines what we coded and over what time span. Coding work was conducted at the ANU, the University of Melbourne, and the University of Texas (Austin) by numerous research assistants. We coded six key areas.

4.2.1 *Legislation*

All legislation is coded according to the Policy Agendas Project (PAP) framework (slightly modified for the Australian context). The data starts with the prime ministership of Holt in 1966 and goes up to the end 2015. Details of legislation are available at the Australasian Legal Information Institute (AustLII). We coded over seven thousand pieces of legislation.

4.2.2 *Governor-General's Speeches (1945–2013)*

These constitute our measure of the executive agenda. The governor-general's speech is given at the beginning of each government's term on behalf of the PM. In the absence of formal party manifestos, these constitute the single best

Table 4.1. Datasets of the Australian Policy Agendas Project

Dataset	Period Covered	N
Federal legislation	1966–2015	7,860
Governor–general's speeches	1945–2013	36
Opposition questions	1980–2013	31,668
Media: *The Australian*	1996–2013	3,913
Media: *Sydney Morning Herald*	1990–2015 every 5th year	6,127
Public opinion	1992–2013	14
High Court of Australia decisions	1903–2016	7,462

Source: Comparative Agendas Project—Australia

indicator of governmental intent. They can be considered governmental 'pre-commitments' and we examine whether they correspond with legislative attention (see Dowding et al., 2010; Dowding et al., 2012; Dowding and Martin, 2017: Ch. 5).

4.2.3 Opposition Questions

The Australian parliament has formal questions addressed to the PM and we code those questions from opposition MPs from 1980 to 2013 (over 30,000). While often used for political point scoring, opposition questions reflect important and controversial issues of the day.

4.2.4 The Media

Almost four thousand front-page stories in the *Australian* newspaper (the only truly national popular newspaper) were coded from 1996 (when electronic copies of the front page first became available) and these are analyzed in Dowding and Martin (2017). In addition, the *Sydney Morning Herald* (*SMH*) dataset contains information on each article published on the newspaper's front page for each day in the years 1990, 1995, 2000, 2005, 2010, and 2015. Work is underway to create a complete dataset for every year between 1950 and 2016. Although not a national newspaper, the *SMH* is a leading Australian newspaper published by Fairfax Media and located in the country's largest city. As such, it complements the data collected from *The Australian*, a News Corp publication, and has the added benefit of offering a nearly comprehensive online archive that facilitates data collection. Following the protocol of the US Agendas Project's *New York Times* dataset, subtopic codes were not assigned.

4.2.5 Public Opinion

Public opinion, as measured by Roy Morgan Research (the respected Australian market research and polling company), was coded by the issues identified by the public as the most important. This dataset begins in 1992 when Roy Morgan began collecting and reporting these data.

4.2.6 The High Court of Australia

The dataset (coded under the auspices of the Edward A. Clark Center) contains information on every decision reported by the Court in the *Commonwealth Law Reports* and published online by the AustLII for the years 1903 to 2015. Decisions serve as the unit of analysis. Each decision was coded in terms of its policy content and several other variables.

4.3 An Example

Figure 4.1 (reprinted from Dowding and Martin, 2017) illustrates some of the many interesting patterns uncovered by the coding of agendas in different domains. It shows legislative, opposition, and media attention to the economy (1980–2013). We can see that government is always paying a moderate amount of attention to the economy. This is to be expected; but PAP allows us to understand the bounds of this attention. The opposition, on the other hand (most notably in 1992 and 1993), pays a disproportionate amount of attention to the economy. This has implications for accountability, because it means the opposition is probably ignoring other important policy issues such as social welfare and defence. We might expect to find the same pattern in media attention, but in fact we see that media attention more closely follows legislative patterns. These data reveal much about the allocation of attention in different agenda domains and the implications for political accountability in Australia, and underscores the value of a consistent coding scheme across time and space. Furthermore, such data allow for the type of international comparisons included in Dowding and Martin (2017) and numerous other publications that have arisen out of CAP.

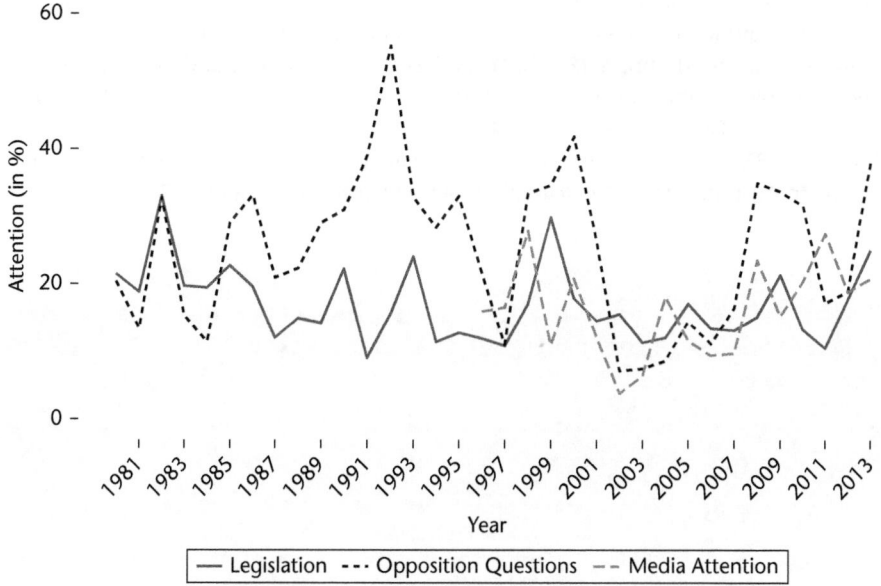

Figure 4.1. Attention across domains: economy
Source: Comparative Agendas Project—Australia

Notes

1. *Constitution of Australia*, ss. 51–2, 109 (enumerated powers); s. 107, 109 (residual powers).
2. Section 51.
3. Section 109.

References

Dowding, K., Faulkner, N., Hindmoor, A., and Martin, A. (2012). Change and Continuity in the Ideology of Australian Prime Ministers: The Governor-General's Speeches, 1946–2010. *Australian Journal of Political Science*, 47(3): 455–72.

Dowding, K., Hindmoor, A., Ile, R., and John, P. (2010). Policy Agendas in Australian Politics: The Governor-General's Speeches, 1945–2008. *Australian Journal of Political Science*, 45(4): 533–57.

Dowding, K., Hindmoor, A., and Martin, A. (2013a). Australian Public Policy: Attention, Content and Style. *Australian Journal of Public Administration*, 72(2): 82–8.

Dowding, K., Hindmoor, A., and Martin, A. (2013b). Causes, Content and Party Influence on the Australian Policy Agenda. *Australian Journal of Public Administration*, 72(4): 481–4.

Dowding, K., Hindmoor, A., and Martin, A. (2016a). The Comparative Policy Agendas Project: Theory, Measurement, and Findings. *Journal of Public Policy*, 36(1): 3–25.

Dowding, K., Hindmoor, A., and Martin, A. (2016b). Attention, Content and Measurement: Rejoinder to Jones and Adams. *Journal of Public Policy*, 36(1): 46–50.

Dowding, K., and Martin, A. (2017). *Policy Agendas in Australia*. London: Palgrave.

Fenna, A. (2009). Federalism. In *The Australian Study of Politics*, ed. R. A. W. Rhodes. Basingstoke: Palgrave Macmillan, 146–59.

Martin, A., Dowding, K., Hindmoor, A., and Gibbons, A. (2014). The Opinion-Policy Link in Australia. *Australian Journal of Political Science*, 49(3): 499–517.

5

The Belgian Agendas Project

Stefaan Walgrave, Jeroen Joly, and Julie Sevenans

5.1 The Belgian Agendas Project

The Belgian Agendas Project started in 2001 when professor Stefaan Walgrave from the University of Antwerp (UA) acquired a grant (2001–3) from the Belgian government (Federal Science Policy) to code political agendas for issue content. The initial project was co-sponsored by the Université Catholique de Louvain (UCL), and more specifically by professors Lieven De Winter, Benoît Rihoux, and Frederic Varone. The project covered the 1991–2000 period and involved the coding of media, laws, questions, and budgets at the federal level. Yet, unconnected to the work being conducted in the United States and Denmark at that time, the issue codebook was not the same as the present CAP codebook—this is why all the old data have been recoded afterwards using the common CAP issue codebook. A second grant (2005–8) was acquired by Walgrave from the UA research council (BOF) and the decision was taken to restart the coding process using the common CAP codebook, as there was now an emerging CAP community and an international network with whom arrangements could be made. Some of the older data were recoded automatically (e.g., the questions dataset because this dataset was originally coded using the very detailed EUROVOC system) but most of the material had to be coded from scratch. New data were added, so that the full research period now ran from 1991 to 2008—and for some agendas, even older and more recent data were gathered. The third and fourth grant came from the UA research council (BOF) and from the European Science Foundation (ESF) and covered the same period (2008–12). Finally, a grant specifically focusing on the agenda-setting power of protest was awarded by the Flemish Science Foundation (FWO) and ran from 2011 to 2014. Through these five grants, the present Belgian agenda data were coded. More than half a dozen research assistants (Knut De Swert, Michiel Nuytemans, Jeroen Joly, Brandon Zicha, Tobias Van Assche, Anne Hardy, Julie Sevenans, and Régis Dandoy) coordinated data gathering and a few dozen student coders did the actual coding. Note that the bulk of the Belgian data have been coded manually. Some of the media data have been coded using computer learning procedures for which the team has been assisted by Wouter van Atteveldt from the Free University of Amsterdam (VU).

5.2 The Belgian Political System

Belgium is divided by a linguistic fault line (Deschouwer, 2009). During the post-war period, Belgium was characterized by three cleavages—a religious, a socio-economic and a linguistic one. While the religious conflict has withered and the socio-economic remained constant, the linguistic conflict has been acerbated during the last decade. Belgium is decentralized in regions and communities that have adopted a good deal of the competences from the central level over the years in a conflictual process of state reform in which mostly the Flemish, Dutch-speaking, northern region has asked for more power and autonomy. Although Flemings outnumber Francophones, the Belgian government constitutionally consists of an equal number of Dutch- and French-speaking ministers. The country is a parliamentary democracy with a monarch without any real power. The government needs a constant majority in parliament and heavily dominates the legislative branch of government. Due to the splitting up of all former unitary parties into two linguistically homogenous parties and due to the proportional system and the success of green, nationalist, and populist radical right parties, the polity is extremely fragmented, with a lot of parties sitting in Parliament and none of the parties really outnumbering the others. National governments generally consist of four to six parties. Apart from its decentralized system and its fragmentation, the Belgian polity is characterized by the strength of its parties. Belgium is considered as a textbook example of a partitocracy with parties, and their leaders, dominating policymaking and administrating (De Winter et al., 1996).

5.3 Belgian Datasets Description

The Belgian Agendas Project (BAP) includes a wide variety of datasets from different political actors. Note that the focus of BAP lies on the federal level. All political agendas that were collected and coded—for instance, parliamentary and governmental agendas—are federal agendas. Regional political actors (from the Flemish, Walloon, and Brussels region; and from the Flemish,

French, and German-speaking community) are not included in the project. This means that after the three first state reforms, political attention for the few issue domains for which the regional level received exclusive authority, such as agriculture, education, housing, spatial planning, or culture, is rare in the political datasets (for more information about the state reforms, see Section 5.5). Also, with regards to political parties—an agenda in which the Belgian team invested a lot—we coded the party manifestos preceding federal elections. It is not uncommon, however, for political parties to elaborate on regional issues in their federal manifestos.

The most notable absence is that of the public opinion agenda. There is no tradition in Belgium to ask for the most important problem (MIP) and, thus, simply no longitudinal public opinion data are available. The Belgian team has alternatively invested a lot in two agendas that may serve as a proxy for public opinion: mass media and protest. Of course, these datasets contain federal, regional, and international issues alike. Furthermore, in the first generation agenda project, the budgetary agenda was also coded, but these data have not been updated or recoded according to the common CAP issue codebook.

The aim of the data collection was to obtain data from different actors at different stages of the policymaking process over an extended period of time. This allows us to examine how policy priorities evolve throughout the policy process, from expressed party priorities during the electoral campaign to the priorities of the newly installed government and their ensuing policy outcomes. This vast data collection also allows us to assess how different actors are able to affect these priorities at different moments and understand how they influence the policy priorities over time. The datasets were collected and constructed in a way that would allow for both quantitative and qualitative approaches to studying policy agendas and how issues evolve over time.

The Belgian datasets (see Table 5.1) have been coded in accordance with the prevailing international CAP methods and standards on how to code agendas. The Belgian agendas topical codebook was originally based on the US version and included some of the changes made by the Danish, British, and Dutch teams. We included a major topic code (9) to capture policies related to immigration, integration, and refugees, as well as a minor topic code to capture policies related to federalization (state reform), the distribution of competences, and relations between different levels of government within the main 'government operations' category (20). All datasets have recently been updated to correspond to the harmonized master CAP codebook matching standards.

From the outset, the Belgian Agendas Project has invested in the collection of news media priorities, in part to compensate for the lack of available public opinion data to obtain input on what is going on in society. Hence, we coded ten years of the front section of *De Standaard*, a Flemish quality newspaper, comparable to *The New York Times* in the United States, or *Le Monde* in France.

Table 5.1. Belgian Agendas data

Agenda	Data source	Unit of analysis	Period	Number of observations
Media—Newspaper	De Standaard	Individual front-section articles	1999–2008	20,963
Media—Television news	VRT and VTM RTBf and RTL	Individual news items	2000–8	135,582
Political Parties	Manifestos	(Quasi-)sentences	1978–2008	174,994
Protest	Police archive	Individual demonstrations	2001–10	5,328
Government	Coalition agreements	(Quasi-)sentences	1978–2008	12,936
Government	State of the Union	(Quasi-)sentences	1992–2008	
Government	Ministerial Council press releases	Individual decisions	1992–2008	11,021
Parliament	Bills (including laws, which are accepted bills)	Individual bills	1988–2010	8,737
Parliament	Questions and interpellations	Individual oral parliamentary questions and interpellations	1988–2010	48,381

Source: Comparative Agendas Project—Belgium

From 1999 until 2004, we coded the front page and after a change in format, we coded the front section, called "Vooraan" ("Up Front"). These are the first three pages of the paper and, on average, contain the same number of news stories as the front page did before 2004. Additionally, we also coded the individual news items from the main 7 o'clock evening television news for the public and commercial Flemish broadcasters (Flemish VRT and VTM and Francophone RTBF and RTL, resp.) for that same period (1999–2008). Data were hand-coded by students and each news item received one topical CAP code.

Given the central position and role of political parties in the Belgian political system, coding policy priorities of each party for every federal election campaign was a crucial ambition of the Belgian Agendas Project. Hence, the manifestos of every party holding at least one seat in parliament have been coded[1] from 1978 to 2008. All manifestos were coded using a similar approach to that of the Manifestos Research Group (now MARPOR) whereby each (quasi-)sentence was coded on its topical policy content, with the possibility of attributing up to three codes per unit. Using the same procedure, we also hand coded every coalition agreement from 1978 to 2008, as well as yearly state of the union speeches by the prime minister.

To measure governmental priorities in a more dynamic way and on a more frequent basis, we also coded press statements of the weekly ministerial councils. Each decision or statement was coded individually on its policy content, providing us with an insight into the decisions that have been made and the issues that have been discussed by the government on a regular basis. Data was only available in a reliable and consistent format from 1995 onwards, first through a magazine called *Feiten* ("Facts") and published by the government, then, from 2001 through weekly online press briefings.

Additionally, bills and laws provide a more regular measurement of governmental priorities. Here, we make a distinction between governmental bills (wetsontwerp/projet de loi) and parliamentary bills (wetsvoorstel/proposition de loi) submitted by Members of Parliament. These data were available from 1988 to 2010 and were coded by the parliamentary services according to the elaborate European EUROVOC coding system and automatically recoded into our Agendas coding scheme using a matching codebook. The same recoding approach was used for all parliamentary data, including oral and written parliamentary questions and interpellations.

Finally, the Belgian Agendas Project has coded protest data that were collected by Ruud Wouters directly from the Brussels police archive. The data are an alternative way to look at public opinion, giving an indication of the issues that make people take to the streets. All individual demonstrations taking place between 2001 and 2010 were coded according to an extensive coding scheme, including CAP codes, but also, for instance, protest size, degree of disruptiveness of the protest, and so on.

5.4 Focus of the Belgian Project

In terms of content, the Belgian project has had three distinct substantive foci over the years. First, and most importantly, the Belgian project has dealt extensively with the impact of the media agenda on the political agenda. Drawing on the agendas data, numerous publications on that topic have been published, mostly by the Antwerp team, often co-authored with Rens Vliegenthart from the University of Amsterdam (UvA) (Walgrave and Van Aelst, 2006; Walgrave et al., 2008; Vliegenthart and Walgrave, 2011; Vliegenthart et al., 2013; Sevenans and Vliegenthart, 2015; Vliegenthart and Walgrave, 2008, 2010; Vliegenthart et al., 2016a; Joly, 2014, 2016). A second line of research has focused on the political parties that play such a central role in the Belgian political system. We asked the question: To what extent the party agendas are influenced by and are influencing other agendas (Vliegenthart et al., 2011; Joly and Dandoy, 2016; Joly, 2013)? A third aspect of the UA's research program has been the interest for protest and its agenda effect: Do the issues that get protested about subsequently get more attention on the political agenda? Results have been presented in several publications (Vliegenthart and Walgrave, 2012; Walgrave and Vliegenthart, 2012;

Vliegenthart et al., 2016b). A constant in all the work done by the Belgian CAP team so far is that the interest has been in assessing the effect of one agenda on another. Departing from the idea that observing how issue salience "jumps" from one agenda to the other is an important way to measure power in a political system. Actors who manage to let their issue attention affect other actors' agendas exert power.

5.5 Example: State Reform

To show how our agenda-setting data allow us to track attention to a specific issue over time, but also how attention from one actor influences that of another, we focus on the specific case of Belgian state reform. Belgian has had six major state reforms, the last one following the 'Butterfly agreement' of 2011. After two first state reforms of 1970 and 1980, Flemish demands for further reform continued and increased. While each language community was now in charge of its own cultural and language policies, Flemish parties wanted to expand their institutions and policy competences. In 1987, as a result of much attention from both Flemish and Francophone parties, almost 10 percent of the government agreement was dedicated to reforming the Belgian constitutional setup and redistributing policies from the national level to the language communities. The result was a third, major, state reform that delegated educational policies to the communities and created a separate decentralized entity—region—for Brussels in 1989.

In 1992, an agreement was made for a fourth state reform, which radically changed the institutional setup by transforming the unitary Belgium to a federal state with separate regions and communities and proper legislative assemblies. Once the Francophone parties had obtained a number of competences they wanted, it is clear from Figure 5.1 that their attention to state reform and community issues dropped, reflecting their preference for the status quo position. For Flemish parties, however, demands for further reforms and more competencies kept arising slowly but steadily after 1995, suggesting that the Flemish and Francophone parties have become increasingly out of sync with each other on this issue.

A closer look at the attention of each individual party per language community in Figures 5.2 and 5.3[2] shows that neither Flemish nor Francophone parties operate as a monolithic voice, and that differences in attention to state reform greatly vary within each language community and over time—even within a given party. Looking at the Flemish parties on the left side of the ideological spectrum, it is clear that the major gap in attention between Flemish and Francophone parties is mostly driven by one or two nationalist parties—VU/N-VA and Vlaams Blok/Vlaams Belang. This also explains the

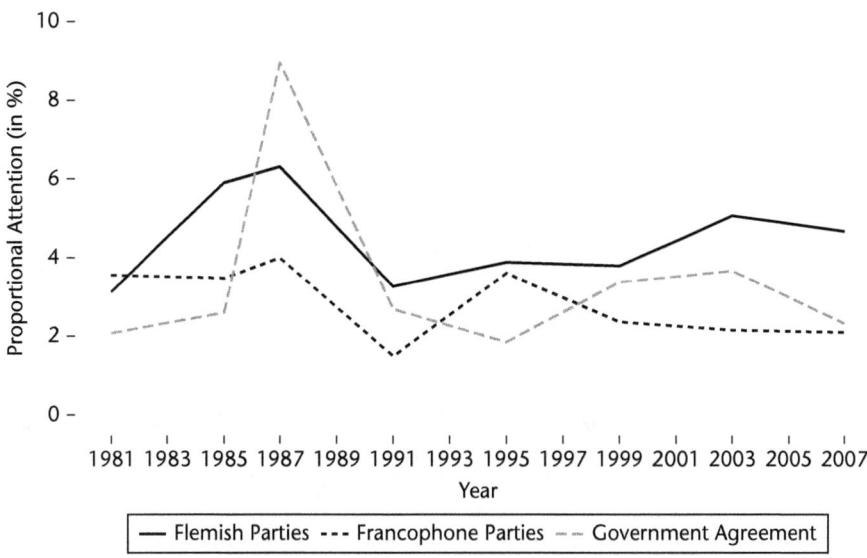

Figure 5.1. Proportional attention to state reform by Flemish and Francophone parties and the government (agreement)
Source: Comparative Agendas Project—Belgium

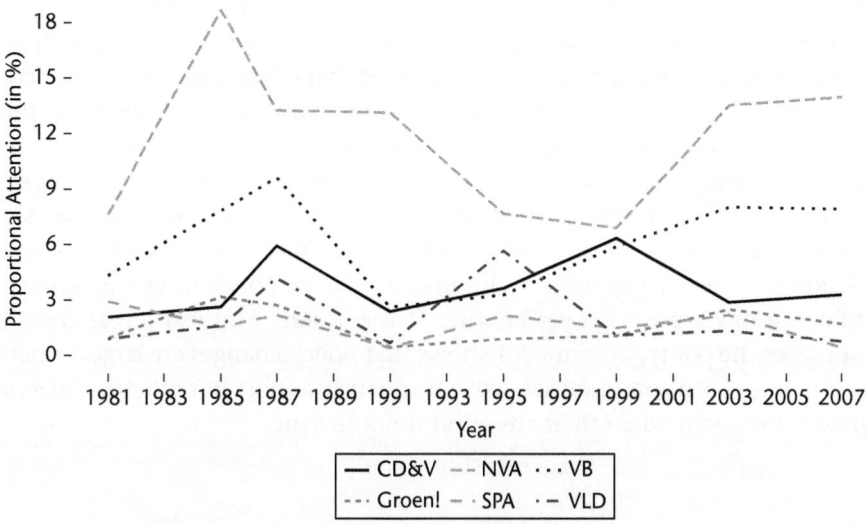

Figure 5.2. Proportional attention to state reform by Flemish parties
Source: Comparative Agendas Project—Belgium

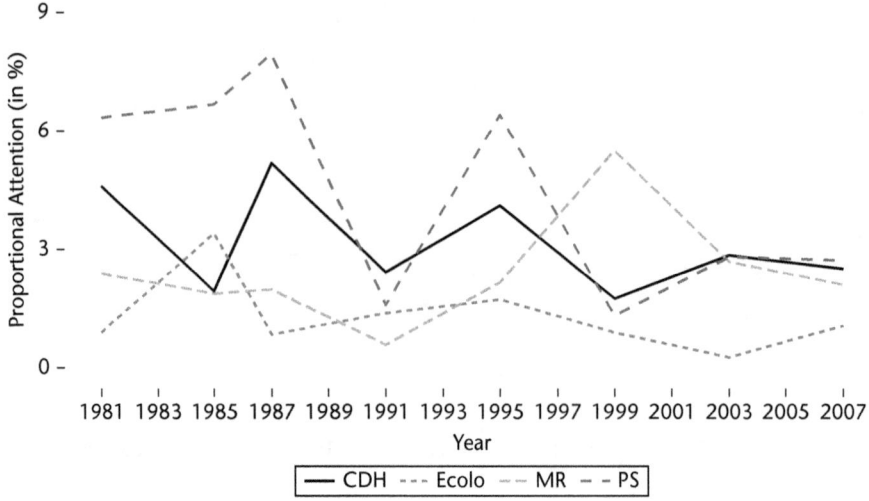

Figure 5.3. Proportional attention to state reform by Francophone parties
Source: Comparative Agendas Project—Belgium

lower levels of attention to state reform in the government agreements in Figure 5.1, given that they were not part of the government and given the VU/N-VA's modest electoral performances in the period under study.

Hence, this example shows how our agenda-setting approach and data can be used as a useful tool to examine how an issue evolves on the agenda of a specific actor over time, compare attention from different actors, and how attention from one (set of) actor(s) influences that of another. In this particular example, as elections precede the formation of a new government and the drafting of a coalition agreement, we know that the correspondence in attention between partisan and governmental attention (r=.66, p<.1 for both Francophone and Flemish parties) reflects a causal relationship. Such analyses can be carried out—qualitatively as well as quantitatively—for a wide variety of policy issues, separately or simultaneously, demonstrating the general influence one actor has over another. These results can also reveal certain aspects of the polity, as Figure 5.1 shows that policy changes are largest when parties from both communities dedicate much attention, but much smaller or almost inexistent when their attention is not in sync.

Notes

1. Except for the manifesto of ROSSEM in 1992, which was unavailable, and for the Flemish Greens in 2003, who were included in our dataset despite not having a seat in the federal parliament.

2. FDF and FN were not included in Figure 5.2, as they did not issue an electoral manifesto at each election. The available manifestos were, however, included in Figure 5.1, as part of the Francophone party agenda.

References

De Winter, L., della Porta, D., and Deschouwer, K. (1996). Comparing Similar Countries: Italy and Belgium. *Res Publica*, 38: 215–36.

Deschouwer, K. (2009). *The Politics of Belgium*. Basingstoke: Palgrave.

Joly, J. K. (2013). *The Impact of Domestic Forces on Foreign Policies: A Study of Party and Media Influences in Belgium*. Antwerp: Universiteit Antwerpen.

Joly, J. K. (2014). Do the Media Influence Foreign Aid Because or in Spite of the Bureaucracy? A Case Study of Belgian Aid Determinants. *Political Communication*, 31: 584–603.

Joly, J. K. (2016). Disentangling Media Effects: The Impact of Short-Term and Long-Term News Coverage on Belgian Emergency Assistance. *Cooperation and Conflict*, 51: 428–46.

Joly, J. K., and Dandoy, R. (2016). Beyond the Water's Edge: How Political Parties Influence Foreign Policy Formulation in Belgium. *Foreign Policy Analysis*, 14: 512–35.

Sevenans, J., and Vliegenthart, R. (2015). Political Agenda-Setting in Belgium and the Netherlands: The Moderating Role of Conflict Framing. *Journalism & Communication Quarterly*, 93: 187–203.

Vliegenthart, R., and Walgrave, S. (2008). The Contingency of Intermedia Agenda-Setting: A Longitudinal Study in Belgium. *Journalism & Mass Communication Quarterly*, 85: 860–77.

Vliegenthart, R., and Walgrave, S. (2010). When Media Matter for Politics: Partisan Moderators of Mass Media's Agenda-Setting Influence on Parliament in Belgium. *Party Politics*, 17: 321–42.

Vliegenthart, R., and Walgrave, S. (2011). Content Matters: The Dynamics of Parliamentary Questioning in Belgium and Denmark. *Comparative Political Studies*, 44: 1031–59.

Vliegenthart, R., and Walgrave, S. (2012). The Interdependency of Mass Media and Social Movements. In *The Sage Handbook of Political Communication*, ed. H. A. Semetko and M. Scammell. London: Sage Publications, 387–98.

Vliegenthart, R., Walgrave, S., Baumgartner, F. R. et al. (2016a). Do the Media Set the Parliamentary Agenda? A Comparative Study in Seven Countries. *European Journal of Political Research*, 55: 283–301.

Vliegenthart, R., Walgrave, S., and Meppelink, C. (2011). Inter-Party Agenda-Setting in the Belgian Parliament: The Contingent Role of Party Characteristics and Competition. *Political Studies*, 59: 368–88.

Vliegenthart, R., Walgrave, S., Wouters, R. et al. (2016b). The Media as a Dual Mediator of the Political Agenda–Setting Effect of Protest: A Longitudinal Study in Six Western European Countries. *Social Forces*, 95(2): 837–59.

Vliegenthart, R., Walgrave, S., and Zicha, B. (2013). How Preferences, Information and Institutions Interactively Drive Agenda-Setting: Questions in the Belgian Parliament, 1993–2000. *European Journal of Political Research*, 52: 390–418.

Walgrave, S., Soroka, S., and Nuytemans, M. (2008). The Mass Media's Political Agenda-Setting Power: A Longitudinal Analysis of Media, Parliament and Government in Belgium (1993–2000). *Comparative Political Studies*, 41: 814–36.

Walgrave, S., and Van Aelst, P. (2006). The Contingency of the Mass Media's Political Agenda-Setting Power: Towards a Preliminary Theory. *Journal of Communication*, 56: 88–109.

Walgrave, S., and Vliegenthart, R. (2012). The Complex Agenda-Setting Power of Protest: Demonstrations, Media, Parliament, Government, and Legislation in Belgium (1993–2000). *Mobilization: An International Quarterly*, 17(2): 29–156.

6

The Canadian Agendas Project

Jean-Philippe Gauvin and Éric Montpetit

The Canadian Agendas Project was instigated in 2004 by Stuart Soroka, who sought to measure legislative activity and government responsiveness to public opinion by adapting the codebook of the US Policy Agendas Project. Since then, many researchers have contributed to the project, multiplying datasets on a diversity of agendas. Most datasets were produced with documents that highlight governmental activity and include oral questions, Speeches from the Throne, and governmental bills among others.

6.1 The Canadian Political System

Canada's political system combines British parliamentarism with federalism, giving rise to unique patterns of policymaking. As in the United Kingdom, Canada is a constitutional monarchy, with Queen Elizabeth II acting as symbolic head of state. Her majesty's representative in Canada is the governor general, who mostly has a ceremonial role. Canada also has a Westminster-style parliament, with a prime minister as head of government. Finally, Canada has a federal system, comprised of ten provinces and three territories.

This specific combination of Westminster parliamentarism and federalism grants intergovernmental relations some importance for policymaking. On the one hand, the Westminster type of parliamentarism concentrates powers in the hands of the executive branch. In other words, the prime minister and cabinet exert considerable control over the policy agenda (Savoie, 1999). The principle of responsible government in fact requires government to define policy priorities, present budgets, and introduce most bills while keeping the confidence of the House of Commons. Party discipline ascertains confidence and therefore the government's control of the agenda diminishes only on the rare occasions when the governing party cannot count on a majority of seats in the House of Commons. On the other hand, federalism divides powers territorially, among the provinces and territories. In their exclusive spheres of jurisdiction, provinces are free to prioritize whichever issues they choose. In a context of policymaking complexity, however, intergovernmental relations among the members of the federal and provincial's executive branches have gained in importance, in some cases at the expense of federal and provincial legislative assemblies.

Owing to the decentralization of the Canadian federation, provinces now play a large role in governance and policymaking (Atkinson et al., 2013). Many policy innovations come from provinces, before diffusing across the country. In the last decade, the provinces have also demonstrated more leadership in specific domains, such as the environment, given the relative disengagement of the federal government. Textbooks point to an era of collaborative federalism (Simeon et al., 2014), in which intergovernmental relations become a way of improving policy through learning from each other's experience, even in policy domains where the federal government is relatively absent. These relations between sub-federal units (as well as federal–provincial relations) typically occur during sectoral meetings of ministers and deputy ministers, often prescheduled to happen once a year. During these meetings, priorities are negotiated and agreements are made. Between these meetings, civil servants from various governments interact with a view to implementing these priorities and agreements.

Federal politics in Canada revolves around three main parties, as well as a regional party limited to Quebec. Since 1921, governments have alternated between the right-wing Conservative Party of Canada and the Liberal Party of Canada, which stands in the centre. The left spectrum of politics is occupied by the New Democratic Party, as well as by the Bloc Québécois, which only presents candidates in the province of Quebec. Provinces have their own party systems. As a result, most provincial parties are independent from their federal counterpart. While most provinces have Liberal, Conservative, and New Democratic parties, several of them are independent from their federal cousin. To illustrate, the Liberal Party of British Columbia is closer to the federal Conservative Party than it is to the Liberal Party of Canada. There are also several province-specific parties, notably the Wild Rose in Alberta and the Parti Québécois in Québec. In fact, Quebec's party system is the most distinct of all provinces owing to the importance of the independence issue in the province's politics since the end of the 1960s.

The federal government and the ten provinces use the same plurality voting system. Candidates compete in constituencies and the winner becomes a member of parliament (MP). The legislative branch in Canada is comprised of these elected MPs. The party that wins the most seats becomes the governing party and its leader becomes prime minister. The prime minister and cabinet form the executive branch.

At the pinnacle of the judicial branch is the Supreme Court of Canada. It is the highest court in the country and has been the final court of appeal since 1949. Prior to this date, final appeals were given by the Judicial Committee of the Privy Council in London. The role of courts in Canadian politics has increased since the adoption of the Charter of Rights and Freedoms in 1982. Since then, courts are authorized to overturn governmental and legislative decisions that interfere with some basic rights, adding to the court's role to settle jurisdictional disputes between the federal and provincial governments. The Supreme Court can also be called upon by government to provide opinions, so-called reference cases.

6.2 Canadian Political Agendas

The Canadian project covers some, but not all of the particularities of Canadian politics just presented (see Table 6.1). For instance, it has so far covered executive priorities as presented in Speeches from the Throne, some legislative activities, some Court decisions, and public opinion.

Like many other CAP projects, public opinion data are produced from survey questions on the most important problem (MIP). The question asks respondents: What is the most important problem facing Canadians today?; it was asked in Environics Focus Canada quarterly omnibus surveys from 1987 to 2009. These data exist both in quarterly periods and yearly averages. They are coded for main topics only.

The project initially aimed to measure how legislative activity in the Canadian House of Common reflected changes in public opinion. Two time series were thus created. One was a database of governmental bills that spanned the period 1968 to 2004 (Soroka and Blidook, 2005). This series included 1,852 observations and was coded for topic and subtopic, including multiple subtopics when necessary. This series is currently being expanded from 1960 to 2010. A second series was produced using oral questions. While

Table 6.1. Canadian Political Agendas datasets

	Indicator	Period covered	CAP ready	N
Public	Most important problem	1987–2009	2018	1,322
Legislative	Oral questions	1982–2004	2018	43,426
	Government bills	1960–2010	Expected 2019	3,646
Executive	Speeches from the Throne (federal)	1960–2009	2018	8,147
	Speeches from the Throne (provinces)	1960–2009	Expected 2019	108,606
	Intergovernmental meetings	1969–2015	Expected 2019	3,468
Judiciary	Supreme Court decisions	1960–2010	Expected 2020	4,875
	Leave to appeal	1990–2010	Expected 2020	10,835

Source: Comparative Agendas Project—Canada

formal rules were established and codified in 1964, the practice of the Question Period exists since the beginning of the Confederation in 1867 and provides the opportunity for the opposition to hold government accountable by criticizing its policies and administration. A total of 43,426 questions and answers were coded between 1982 and 2004 for topic, subtopic, date, length, and which MPs asked and answered the questions (Soroka, 2005).

A second phase of the project focused on executive priorities. The Speeches from the Throne were chosen as the main indicator of such priorities. Such Speeches are delivered at the beginning of every legislative session and typically serve to announce the government's plans for the coming year. Using multiple trained coders, the federal and provincial Speeches were coded from 1960 to 2009. In total, 117,146 quasi-sentences were coded for topic and subtopic. The main objective of this research was to study federalism in Canada, comparing federal and provincial priorities (Montpetit, 2012). Following this research, Gauvin et al. (2014) looked at how intergovernmental meetings in Canada shaped these executive priorities. Meetings between ministers and deputy ministers typically occur each year in a variety of policy sectors. These meetings serve to decide upon common nationwide priorities and to harmonize policies. The Canadian Intergovernmental Conference Secretariat (CICS) maintains a registry of these conferences. Each meeting file was coded for topic, as well as multiple variables such as presence of federal government, location of meeting, presence of a press release, etc. A total of 3,468 meeting files that span the years 1969 to 2014 are included in the dataset.

The Canadian project is currently investigating the work of the Supreme Court of Canada. Decisions of the Court are being coded for both topic and subtopic over the period of 1960 to 2010. Looking at distributions of judiciary attention can lead to insightful conclusions about courts' involvement in policy decisions. Furthermore, in the Canadian judiciary system, appellants can apply for leave to appeal, which if granted will allow them to go plead their case in a higher court. Granted motions for leave to appeal in the Supreme Court are currently being coded for the period 1990–2010. By looking at both inputs and outputs of the judiciary system, it will be possible to see if the Supreme Court is actually responsive to citizens' demands for the revision of government policy.

6.3 Contributions of the Project and Perspectives

Since its beginning, the Canadian CAP's primary objective has been to collect data on policy agendas in order to analyze possible interactions between them. As mentioned earlier, Canadian policymaking is heavily influenced by a key feature of its political system: the combination of Westminster parliamentarism, federalism, and judiciary.

To get a better understanding of policymaking as conditioned by these features of the Canadian system, the project first looked at the relationship between legislative attention and public opinion through the study of oral questions. Using oral question and public opinion data, Soroka et al. (2006) asked whether federal legislators were responsive to the public's agenda. The authors find that when focusing on four major topics, namely health, education, debt, and taxes, parties' agendas vary in ways that reflect public opinion. Going even further into the analysis of oral questions, Soroka et al. (2009) found that individual MP's questions were driven by specific constituency characteristics, suggesting the existence of a dyadic representation in the Canadian parliamentary system.

Second, the project looked at the impact of federalism on executive priorities. It asked the following question: Since federal systems multiply actors and potential veto points, does it lead to more stalemates than found in unitary systems? When comparing Canadian priorities as expressed in Speeches from the Throne with those of the United Kingdom, Montpetit and Foucault (2012) found that while federal systems do lead to constrained policy changes immediately after a government change, the following years present opportunities for larger changes in policy attention than found in the United Kingdom. Further study of these documents looked at correlations of attention between federal and sub-federal units and found interprovincial correlations to be stronger than federal–provincial correlations (Montpetit, 2012; Montpetit and Foucault, 2014). Figure 6.1 shows the correlations in attention from the federal to the provincial level (vertical), and across the provinces (horizontal).

Figure 6.1 shows that interprovincial priorities steadily have been growing in similarity since 1970, while correlations of federal-provincial priorities go in cycles. This suggests that interprovincial collaboration grows steadily while federal–provincial relations go through periods of increases and decreases in similarity. Montpetit and Foucault (2014) speculated that these patterns affect policymaking in Canada. Gauvin et al. (2014) expanded on this research and looked at the precise impact of intergovernmental relations on policy priorities. Combining data on IGR meetings with both public opinion data and Speeches from the Throne, analyses show that executive priorities are heavily influenced by both IGR meetings and public opinion. These results further support the idea that intergovernmental relations in Canada shape policy agendas in significant ways.

Studying the interactions between different political agendas in Canada remains the main objective of the project for the years to come. Existing datasets will be updated and other sources of data are to be coded. However, the project's current datasets already provide interesting insights into the Canadian policymaking process. For instance, Figure 6.2 presents attention to the environment in four distinct agendas.

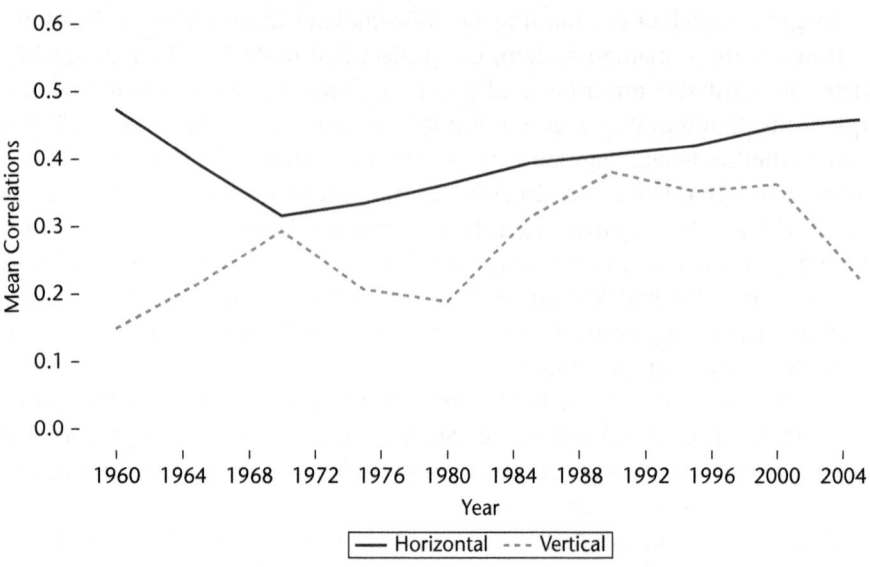

Figure 6.1. Federal-provincial and interprovincial correlations in issue attention
Source: Comparative Agendas Project—Canada

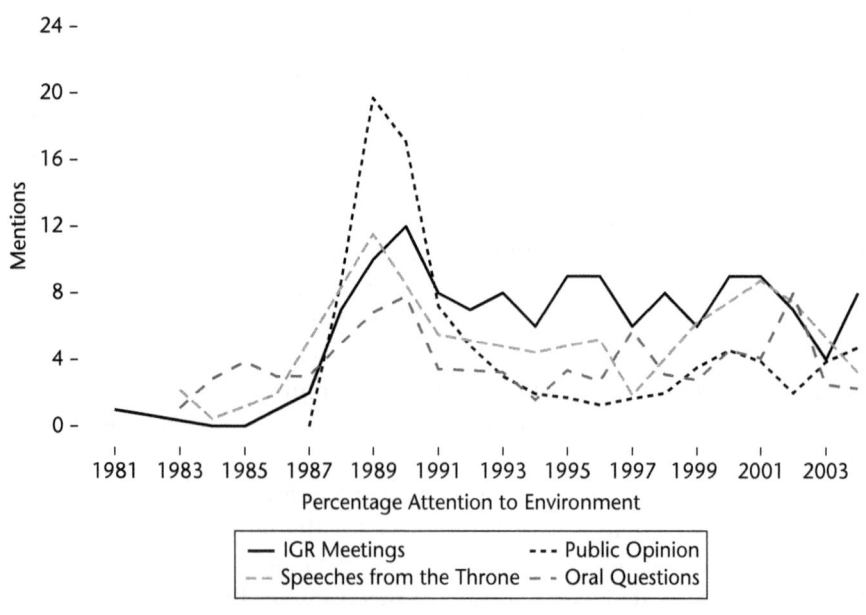

Figure 6.2. Attention to environment across series
Source: Comparative Agendas Project—Canada

Figure 6.2 shows that attention to this topic seems to follow a similar pattern over time and across the different agendas. The Canadian data are rich in observations of this sort that have yet to be investigated. The availability of similar data collected by the other projects also offer ample opportunities for comparative analyses. In short, the Canadian Agendas Project promises to make a significant contribution to the understanding of the country's policy-making process.

References

Atkinson, M. M., Béland, D., Marchilson, G. P. et al. (2013). *Governance and Public Policy in Canada: A View from the Provinces*. Toronto: University of Toronto Press.

Gauvin, Jean-P., Montpetit, É., and Foucault, M. (2014). Intergovernmental Meetings and the Politics of Attention in Canada. Presented at the CAP conference, Lisbon, June 23.

Montpetit, É. (2012). Are Interprovincial Relations Becoming More Important than Federal-Provincial Ones. *Federal News*, 3: 1–6.

Montpetit, É., and Foucault, M. (2012). Canadian Federalism and Change in Policy Attention: A Comparison with the United Kingdom. *Canadian Journal of Political Science*, 45(3): 635–56.

Montpetit É., and Foucault, M. (2014). On the Relative Neglect of Horizontal Intergovernmental Relations in Canada. In *The Changing Federal Environment: Rebalancing Roles?* ed. N. Verrelli. Kingston: McGill-Queen's University Press, 195–214.

Savoie, D. J. (1999). *Governing from the Center: The Concentration of Political Power in Canada*. Toronto: University of Toronto Press.

Simeon, R., Robinson, I., and Wallner, J. (2014). The Dynamics of Canadian Federalism. In *Canadian Politics*, ed. J. Bickerton and Alain-G. Gagnon, 6th ed. Toronto: University of Toronto Press, 65–92.

Soroka, S. N., Penner, E., and Blidook, K. (2006). Legislative Priorities and Public Opinion: The Representation of Partisan Agendas in the Canadian House of Commons. *Journal of European Public Policy*, 13(7): 1006–20.

Soroka, S. N., Penner, E., and Blidook, K. (2009). Constituency Representation in Parliament. *Canadian Journal of Political Science*, 42(3): 563–91.

7

Croatian Political Agendas

Daniela Širinić and Dario Nikić Čakar

7.1 Introduction

The Croatian Agendas Project is the newest member of the Comparative Agendas network. It was initiated in 2015 by a group of researchers from the Faculty of Political Science at the University of Zagreb and lead by Daniela Širinić. The project was financed by the Operational Program 2014–16 of the European Social Fund. The initial goals of the project were twofold. First, as is the case with the other projects in the group, we aimed to collect data on the activities of political institutions and second, to contribute to the agendas literature by expanding the universe of cases to new democracies.

7.2 The Croatian Political System

Croatian transition to democracy started in 1990 when the first multiparty elections were held under the provision of a two-round electoral system. Those elections marked the end of a long period of communist rule and a start of the transformation of political and economic systems towards democracy and free market economy. The Croatian Democratic Union (HDZ), as the new ruling party, soon began to shape democratic institutions in accordance with the preferences of its leader Franjo Tuđman, whose charismatic appeal was institutionalized within the framework of a semi-presidential system. Institutional features that facilitated the concentration of powers in the hands of a strong president, backed by absolute parliamentary majorities, very soon started to display authoritarian tendencies, making the HDZ's regime one of a defective and illiberal democracy (Dolenec, 2013). During the first half of the 1990s the new leadership was also faced with the threat of the

Croatian War of Independence, which had prevented full-scale progress of economic, social, and political transition to democracy and market economy. However, the HDZ made the most of the ongoing war and military operations. The party aimed at maximizing its electoral performance by introducing a mixed-member electoral system before the 1992 parliamentary elections, and creating strong ties with numerous war veteran and refugee groups that became its steady electoral base.

By the end of the 1990s, when the state-building program was successfully completed, the HDZ's legitimacy started to deteriorate under the pressure of a social and economic crisis. Facing a growing disaffection by voters and imminent decline of electoral support, the ruling party once again changed the electoral rules by means of institutionalizing proportional representation. Nonetheless, the HDZ's predominant party rule ended soon after Tuđman's death, when the party lost power in the parliamentary and presidential elections in early 2000. The new center-left government led by the Social Democratic Party (SDP) pursued an agenda of comprehensive constitutional reforms in order to prevent any future concentration of powers in the hands of one person. Governing coalition established functional checks and balances between the different branches of government. By way of the new constitutional rules, the president of the Republic had been stripped of most previous powers in an attempt to establish a parliamentary system with a balance of power between the executive and the parliament. The electoral reform and the subsequent constitutional changes also set the pattern for future cabinet formation since coalition-building became the norm for all successive governments. Moreover, the center-left government initiated a comprehensive reform of foreign and internal policies, insisting on a broad all-party consensus over Croatia's NATO and EU membership.

Over the last fifteen years, the parliamentary system of government proved to be quite stable. Although presidents are still elected directly, they have been subdued to a symbolic and ceremonial role and left with only limited prerogative powers in defense and foreign affairs. The government took over the leading executive role with the prime minister acting as the effective head of the executive branch. The government dominates over the parliament in the legislative process due to the strong discipline which party leaders and prime ministers enforce upon their parliamentary party groups. As a result, and similar to other parliamentary democracies, Croatia has a comparatively weak parliament, which is best exemplified by the fact that more than 90 percent of all laws originate from the government.

Up until parliamentary elections in 2015, most coalition governments were stable and internally cohesive, and managed to end their terms without any serious ideological or organizational disruptions. The stability of coalition governments had mostly emanated from rather stable and predictable patterns of party competition characterized by significant centripetal tendencies that induced a gradual reduction in the party system polarization (Henjak, Zakošek, and Čular, 2013). In contrast to the predominant party system developed in the 1990s, following the 2000 elections, the party system may best described as moderate pluralism. Both the HDZ and the SDP advanced their vote-seeking strategies in an attempt to approach the median voter, whereas smaller parties employed office-seeking strategies and were inclined to change coalition camps between election cycles, thus participating in both center-left and center-right governments. Since the beginning of the 2010s, the two main parties have started to build large pre-electoral coalition blocs. Thereby they reduce the potential for smaller parties to cross the floor and change coalition ranks. This pattern of coalition building was especially evident in the parliamentary, presidential, and European elections over the course of the last five years. Parliamentary elections in 2015 and 2016 have shaped a new political landscape in Croatia. Since the elections did not produce a clear-cut winner, neither the left nor the right coalition block could form the government by themselves. The keys to government formation were in the hands of the MOST, a newly created anti-establishment party that managed to secure significant parliamentary representation and thus became the first genuinely pivotal party in Croatian politics.

7.3 Datasets

The Croatian Agendas Project was set up to investigate agenda-setting of the main political institutions and organizations—political parties, the parliament, the government, and the president—in the last twenty-five years (see Table 7.1). Since the agenda-setting process is best understood as a "bottleneck of attention," we sought to study which and how many issues make it through all of the echelons and reach decision-level agenda (Green-Pedersen and Walgrave, 2014: 6). To accomplish this, we have decided to collect data on systemic, institutional, and decision-based levels of agenda (Birkland, 2001). The systemic agenda includes a dataset on all election platforms and a sample of front pages of the daily newspaper *Večernji list*, representing the media agenda. The institutional agenda includes a dataset covering all agenda items from parliamentary sessions (bills and other types of motions), a dataset on parliamentary questions and all items from the agendas of weekly government meetings. The decision-level agenda includes laws and other decisions adopted by the parliament and all decisions of the executive bodies (the government and the president) published in the *Official Gazette of the Republic of Croatia*. All datasets were prepared according to the latest version of the CAP Master Codebook (Bevan, 2014) and coded at the level of subtopics.

Table 7.1. Datasets of the Croatian Agendas Project

	Dataset name	Description	Period/Elections	N
Systematic Agenda	Election platforms	Election platforms	1990, 1992, 1995, 2000, 2003, 2007, 2011, 2015	27,716 quasi-sentences; 62 platforms
	Večernji list front-pages	Structured sample of front-pages from the *Večernji list* daily	1/1/1990–31/12/2015	2,128 front pages 18,317 headlines
Institutional Agenda	Parliamentary plenary session	Agenda items from plenary sessions (bills and all other types of motions)	1/1/1990–31/12/2015	12,892
	Government weekly sessions	Agenda items from weekly government meetings	1/1/1990–31/12/2015	48,157
	Parliamentary questions	Oral parliamentary questions	14/10/1992–31/12/2015	4,989
Decision Agenda	Parliamentary Acts	Laws and other decisions	1/1/1990–31/12/2015	8,535
	Government decisions	Decisions	1/1/1990–31/12/2015	18,384
	Presidential Acts	Decisions	1/1/1990–31/12/2015	5,195

Source: Comparative Agendas Project—Croatia

Election platforms dataset, coded using quasi-sentences, includes the platforms of twenty-seven parties that won parliamentary seats in the course of eight election cycles.

A decision to collect the front pages of *Večernji list* was made with regard to two individual criteria: this daily has a broad spectrum of readers at the national level (it has dominated the Croatian press scene until 1998) and it has been published continually throughout the observed period. The reasons behind using the sample rather than coding the entire collection were merely practical, as the idea was to capture the entire twenty-five-year period instead of comprehensively coding all front pages. Timing of government or parliament sessions in Croatia is not set to a specific day in the week and we did not have any prior expectations on the domination of policy topics in the newspaper regarding weekdays. To ensure that the final sample consists of twelve weeks for each year in the observed period, front pages were selected by using a quota sample. The final sample consists of 2,128 front pages and includes one non-consecutive week for each month in the period.

The parliamentary sessions dataset includes all items appearing in the minutes of the parliament plenary sessions during the 1990–2015 period. The dataset also covers the period in which the country was at war and presents a rare opportunity to study wartime agenda-setting. This dataset is not limited to discussions on bills alone, as items also include all other parliamentary acts such as the Constitution, declarations, resolutions, recommendations, the state budget, rules of procedure, or declarations. Every discussion, such as the ratification of international treaty or a yearly report from the Central Bank is treated as a single item.

The possibility of asking parliamentary questions was first introduced in 1992. Since then MP's can ask written and oral questions directed at the government or individual cabinet members. Written questions must be submitted directly to the Speaker of the parliament and they are not publicly available, as well as answers to oral questions as they are not recorded in official session minutes. This is why the dataset on parliamentary questions includes only oral questions posed at the beginning of each session during the so-called Morning Question Time.

Until recently, government session agendas were not publicly available as many of the items pertaining to defence or privatization were classified as confidential—a classification then automatically applied to the entire meeting agenda. However, all agendas were declassified for the purposes of the project and we have been able to collect all items appearing at cabinet weekly meetings from 1990 until the end of 2015.

The parliamentary acts dataset includes all laws and other acts published by the parliament in the *Official Gazette*. Similarly, the government decisions dataset includes all government decisions published in the *Official Gazette*.

Since the year 2000, the Croatian president no longer has broad jurisdiction. Presidential powers are limited to procedural duties during the elections, referendums, and government appointment, and presidential acts are limited to decisions, regulations, orders, and decrees. This dataset was prepared mainly to analyze the break in the agenda-setting power of the president as Croatia transitioned from a semi-presidential system to a parliamentary one.

7.4 Specificities

Broad coverage of agenda levels in the Croatian datasets provides an opportunity to analyze the "bottleneck of attention" process. Moreover, datasets coverage of the entire life span of a new democracy enables the comparison of an agenda-setting between different stages of regime change, but also between large institutional changes such as the change from a semi-presidential to a parliamentary system of government. However, these are not the only distinctive characteristics of the Croatian Project.

7.5 Automated Classification Procedure

Only two of the presented datasets were prepared exclusively by human coders—newspaper front pages and party platforms. All other datasets were compiled using an automated topic classification procedure (ATC), as we have developed a new topic classification module for the purposes of the project. Supervised topic classification requires a high-quality manually coded dataset with a sufficiently large coverage. In this respect, and aside from the mere training sessions, additional measures were taken to ensure reliability during manual coding. Firstly, a random sample of all document titles was prepared for manual coding. To ensure sufficient variation across subtopics, stratified random sampling was selected, accounting for the source of the document (the *Official Gazette*, parliamentary sessions agenda, government weekly meetings agenda, or parliamentary questions). This introduced a variance across topics and document types, which differ greatly in vocabulary and title form. Secondly, the main coding session was carried out in four phases. In the first phase, each document title was coded independently by two out of thirteen coders who were asked to take notes and tag the examples they consider problematic. In the second phase, thirteen coders were assigned to four groups and coded the titles over which coders disagreed in the first coding phases, as well as titles tagged as problematic by at least one of the coders (even if they agreed on the code). In the third coding phase, three experts coded all titles independently, whereby the codes by the two groups differed. Finally, the disagreements remaining after the third coding phase were discussed and resolved by consensus by the three experts (see Table 7.2).

Table 7.2. Intercoder reliability

		Subtopic level (223[b] categories)			Topic level (21 category)		
	Measure	Phase 1	Phase 2	Phase 3	Phase 1	Phase 2	Phase 3
Decision agenda	Percent agreement	51.2	79.7	83	72.9	88.9	89.5
Institutional agenda	Cohen's kappa	0.50	0.79	–	0.78	0.87	–
	Fleiss' kappa[a]	–	–	0.87	–	–	0.92
Večernji list front-pages	Percent agreement	66.9	–	76	79	–	91
	Cohen's kappa	0.65	–	0.74	0.77	–	0.90
Election platforms	Percent agreement	–	–	78.8	–	–	88
	Cohen's kappa	–	–	0.78	–	–	0.86

Note: [a] Fleiss' kappa is an extension of Cohen's kappa, which is applicable for tests with more than two coders. [b] Number of categories differs, media and party programs have several additional categories.
Source: Comparative Agendas Project—Croatia

In addition, and following the example set by Purpura and Hillard (2006), we have experimented with a number of design choices (different machine-learning algorithms, multi-class classification schemes, and methods to handle topic and subtopic hierarchy) in order to find an appropriate supervised topic classification method. We hope that lessons learned from these experiments will be useful to others working on the same or similar task for other languages; a detailed description on the ATC can be found in Karan et al. (2016). Lastly, the prepared dataset was fed into the APC module. Not all codes produced by the module were equally accurate. In some cases, mainly for subtopics, the number of manually coded items was too small to enable efficient "learning" and for some documents titles were very short and uninformative so they could not be used for common feature detection. The module provided a measure of confidence of classifier decisions for each individual title and also a second and third best topic and subtopic prediction. We have used those measures to develop several rejection threshold strategies and selected all those items where thresholds were not reached for additional manual coding. A subset of titles for which the decision confidence was low or a difference between the best and second best prediction small, was checked by experts. For instance, a code was checked by experts if a prediction had low confidence at the major topic level (under 0.95), (2) if subtopic confidence was less than 0.90, and if (3) the difference to the second-highest confidence subtopic was less than 0.05.

7.6 Example: Government Confidentiality Policies

Because the aforementioned dataset on the government session agenda was constructed of declassified original documents we had received, it also contained information on the type and level of classification for each item. We used this information to supplement the CAP topic codes with information on the levels and types of secrecy for each of the classified meeting agenda items. These additional pieces of information have enabled us to study the change in government confidentiality policies. As an example, Figure 7.1 shows the share of closed government meeting items by main CAP topics. Almost half of the government discussions in the last twenty-five years regarding international affairs and foreign aid, government operations (most notably government property management), domestic macroeconomics and—unsurprisingly—defense, were classified under the secrecy acts. This finding implies that most decisions regarding Croatia's accession to the European Union were discussed behind closed doors and without public discussion.

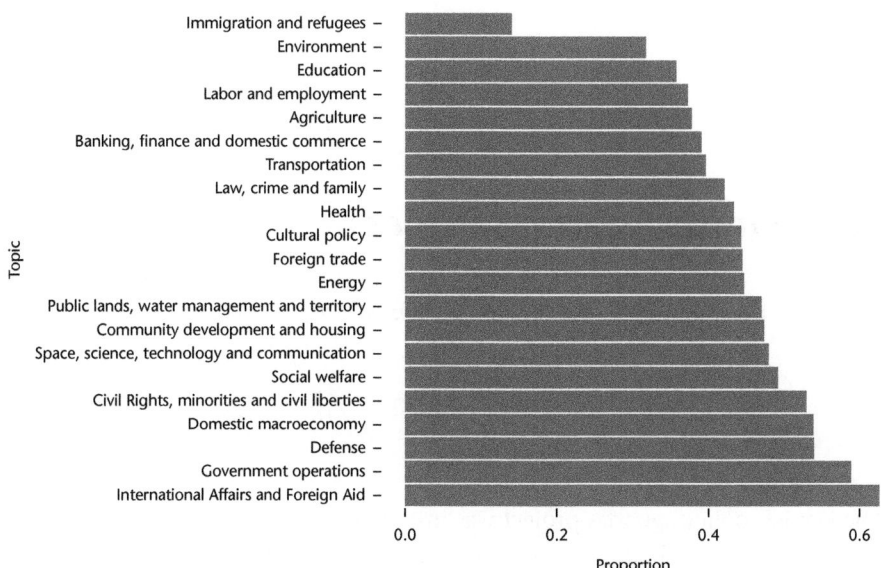

Figure 7.1. Share of closed agenda by CAP topics
Source: Comparative Agendas Project—Croatia

References

Bevan, S. (2014). Gone Fishing: The Creation of the Comparative Agendas Project Master Codebook. Technical report. Mannheim: MZES.

Birkland, T. (2001). *An Introduction to the Policy Process: Theories, Concepts, and Models of Public Policy Making.* Armonk: M. E. Sharpe.

Dolenec, D. (2013). *Democratic Institutions and Authoritarian Rule in Southeast Europe.* Colchester: ECPR Press.

Green-Pedersen, C., and Walgrave, S. (2014). *Agenda Setting, Policies, and Political Systems.* Chicago: University of Chicago Press.

Henjak, A., Zakošek, N., and Čular, G. (2013). Croatia. In *Handbook of Political Change in Eastern Europe,* ed. S. Berglund, J. Ekman, K. Deegan-Krause, and T. Knutsen. Cheltenham: Edward Elgar, 443–80.

Karan, M., Šnajder, J., Širinić, D., and Glavaš, G. (2016). Analysis of Policy Agendas: Lessons Learned from Automatic Topic Classification of Croatian Political Texts. Proceedings of the 10th Workshop on Language Technology for Cultural Heritage, Social Sciences, and Humanities (LaTeCH 2016), ACL 2016, Berlin.

Purpura, S., and Hillard, D. (2006). Automated Classification of Congressional Legislation. In *Proceedings of the 2006 International Conference on Digital Government Research.* Digital Government Society of North America, 219–25.

8

The Danish Agendas Project

Christoffer Green-Pedersen and Peter B. Mortensen

The Danish policy agendas project was initiated by Christoffer Green-Pedersen in 2002. With much inspiration and generous support from Bryan D. Jones, Frank R. Baumgartner, and John Wilkerson, the aim of the project was a double one: First to use a policy agenda-setting approach to better understand the Danish political system. Second, to introduce a comparative perspective into the policy agenda-setting literature to foster its further theoretical development. Based on a grant from the Danish Social Science Research Council, a Danish version of the US codebook was developed and the first parliamentary time series were developed.

Later, Peter B. Mortensen joined the project, which made it possible first to add further datasets on executive speeches and party platforms and later on also to expand the project into local government, see Section 8.4. Rune Stubager has also been involved in developing the media dataset of the project. Further grants from the Danish Social Science Research Council and from the Research Foundation of Aarhus University have made the data collection possible.

8.1 The Danish Political System

To understand the idea behind the datasets that have been developed, the functioning of the Danish political system must be taken into account. The Danish political system can in many ways be characterized as a "single venue system" (Green-Pedersen and Wolfe, 2009). To understand Danish politics, one must focus on parliamentary party politics. In practice, Denmark in general has no other central political venues at the national level of policy-making. There is no presidency, no second chamber, and no constitutional court. The constitution (§42) allows for extensive use of referendums, but in reality referendums only take place with regard to European integration.

The Danish parliament, Folketinget, is strongly structured around party lines as party cohesion is comparatively very strong (Skjæveland, 2001). Furthermore, Denmark has no strong separation between the executive and the legislative branch. This means that parliamentary politics is structured as competition between the parties holding government power and those being in opposition. The Danish PR electoral system allows many political parties to gain representation, which, together with the principle of negative parliamentarism, makes majority governments the exception. Almost all governments since the early 1970s have been minority governments. This constellation implies that the political parties in parliament can be divided into three groups, namely those holding government power, those supporting the minority government and the "real opposition" wanting another government (Green-Pedersen and Thomsen, 2005).

One final aspect of the Danish political system which is important to be aware of is that despite Denmark being a central state and not a federation, Denmark is in fact quite decentralized. Thus many policy aspects especially of the extensive Danish welfare state are actually managed by local government, which opens the door for considerable local influence. The decentralized nature of the Danish state is also reflected in the constitution (§82).

8.2 Datasets

The nature of the Danish political system has of course strongly influenced the dataset collected. Table 8.1 presents an overview of the datasets.[1]

All the data in Danish datasets, with the exception of the media data, were originally coded according to the Danish version of the policy agendas codebook, which was developed when the project started. This first version of the Danish codebook generally stayed close to the original US one, including categories for different country groups under the main topic of international affairs (topic 19). However, some additional subtopics referring to cultural issues and fishing were added.

When the comparative Master Codebook was developed (see Chapter 2), a new version of the Danish codebook was developed. This is fully compatible with the Master Codebook, but has some additional subtopics. For instance, it has a subtopic (210) for attention to the Danish national church, which is a subtopic of 207 in the Master Codebook (freedom of speech and religion). Compared to the original Danish codebook, the differences are minor. The introduction of the 1227 subtopic (domestic response to terrorism) is the most significant difference.[2]

Table 8.1. Datasets of the Danish Agendas Project

Policymaking level	Dataset	Period	Unit of analysis	N
National	Bills	1953–2013	Individual bill	14,333
	Accounts	1953–2013	Individual account	779
	Interpellations	1953–2013	Individual interpellation	1,794
	Motions	1953–2013	Individual motion	6,176
	Parliamentary Questions (§20)	1953–2013	Individual question	106,911
	Opening speeches	1953–2013	Natural sentences	16,220
	Closing speeches	1979–2013	Natural sentences	7,459
	Party manifestos	1953–2011	Natural sentences	30,165
	Radio news	1984–2003	News feature	196,831
Local	Local council meeting agendas (from all 98 Danish municipalities)	2007–13	Items on the council agendas	188,897
	Local council meeting agendas (from 23 Danish municipalities)	1990–2006	Items on the council agendas	76,164
	Local standing committee meeting agendas (from 14 municipalities)	2007–13	Items on committee agendas	97,598

Source: Comparative Agendas Project—Denmark

One of the special subtopics in the Danish codebook compared to the Master Codebook is the existence of a special subtopic to capture attention paid to European integration.[3] This subtopic captures questions relating substantially to the European Union, such as enlargement and institutional questions. At the same time, a dummy variable has been added to capture all references to the European Union, thus also including for instance, a directive on environmental affairs that is coded under the main topic 7. This coding thus reflects whether European integration is *about* European integration or about policies *through* the European Union (Senninger, 2016).

Most national-level time series go back to 1953 when Denmark had a constitutional reform, which among other things abolished the second chamber.

8.3 Parliamentary Data Series

The first time series to be constructed were various outputs from the working of the Danish parliament. All bills back to 1953 have been coded. In the Danish context almost all bills are presented by the government and almost all bills are passed.[4] Accounts are another government-initiated output presented to parliament by a specific minister often based on a prior parliamentary decision. They are quite few in number and are only sometimes followed by a parliamentary debate.

Motions and interpellations are important instruments of the opposition. Interpellations can be asked for by any party and generate a debate in the plenary of the Danish parliament. A resolution can be passed in the end by a simple majority, but this is rarely the case. Motions resemble laws in as much as they can in principle ask the government to do certain things. However, in most cases motions like interpellations only generate a parliamentary debate.

Parliamentary questions are regulated by §20 of the standing order of the Danish Folketing. Unlike the other activities coded, which are party based, parliamentary questions are asked by individual MPs without much coordination. The main type of §20 questions are written and generally also answered in writing, though a small number of questions are answered during weekly question time. From 1997, a question hour was also introduced where MPs can ask questions to the minister without any prior notice and receive an answer right away. Both types of questions are coded. In the Danish context, the vast number of questions are asked by opposition MPs. MPs from the government parties ask very few questions, reflecting their loyalty to the government. This distinction is another indication of the lack of clear executive/legislative division.

Since the number of bills and accounts is relatively low, measuring the issue priorities of the executive is difficult simply based on the parliamentary outputs. Therefore, two types of executive speeches delivered by the Danish prime minister (PM) were also coded with natural sentences as the coding unit. The most important one is the one given at the opening of parliament each year in October as specified in the constitution (§38). Since 1979, the PM has also given a speech at the end of each parliamentary session, which has also been coded.

All the data series based on the parliamentary behavior of the parties are strongly colored by whether a party is in government or in opposition. This means that comparing agendas across different parties can be challenging based on parliamentary outputs. Comparing issue priorities as expressed in parliamentary speeches directly to an agenda expressed in parliamentary questions involves problems of comparability.

The party manifesto data series provide opportunities for comparing directly across parties. In the Danish context, identifying party manifestos can, however, be challenging as Denmark has no real tradition for producing party manifestos (cf. Hansen, 2008). However, parties almost always produce some sort of document presenting their issue priorities when an election is called. Such documents were identified by the CMP project and the same documents have been coded in Denmark based on the agendas coding scheme.

For the period, 1984–2003, a media time series has been coded based on Danish radio news. Radio news has been used to capture the entire media agenda because in the period radio news was shown to provide an important link between the bigger Danish morning newspapers and the news broadcast of the television in the evening (Lund, 2000). In the period, the noon radio news had up to a million listeners out of a population of around 5 million. The coding of the radio news was based on summaries of the individual news features. The coding scheme used for the issue codes was a simplified version of the original Danish policy agendas coding scheme with 58 subtopics.

All coding of the time series has been done by student coders who first went through intensive training and who were then subjected to intercoder reliability tests, which all showed acceptable or high levels of intercoder reliability. Details about the coding are provided in the data-reports of the different time series and their update, available at www.agendasetting.dk.

8.4 Local Government Agendas

Based on a four-year grant from the Danish Social Science Research Council, the CAPCAS[5] project was initiated in January 2014. A central part of the project is collection and content coding of Danish local government agendas. Originally, agenda-setting research grew out of the local US community power studies, and a main motivation of the CAPCAS project is to show how the local level of government can provide new insights into the causes and consequences of policy agenda-setting.

After a major structural reform in 2007, the number of Danish municipalities was reduced from 275 to ninety-eight. Compared to many other countries, the ninety-eight Danish municipalities are quite large with an average of about 55,000 inhabitants. The municipalities are also multipurpose political units with significant policy responsibilities within areas such as primary and secondary education, daycare, elderly care, unemployment, health, environmental protection, traffic and roads, immigration, and culture.

The main units of analysis in these datasets are items appearing on the local council meeting agendas. Given the structural reform of 2007, the time series cover the period January 1, 2007 to December 31, 2013. In this period all council meeting agendas have been content coded based on a coding scheme that is consistent with the Comparative Agendas coding scheme. Some of the major topics have been expanded in order to better capture local government variation, whereas others have been simplified, reflecting, for instance, that the Danish municipalities do not have any responsibilities with respect to defense, and international affairs.[6]

The items appearing on the local council meeting agendas are coded based on the heading under which they appear. Various tests have indicated that this heading is very informative about the content of the item on the agenda. The total number of agenda items coded adds up to more than 200,000. The meeting agendas have been coded in a collaboration between human coders and new computerized tools (see Loftis and Mortensen, 2018). The latter has made it possible to extend the local government data in two ways. First, for a set of fifteen municipalities it has been possible to collect and content code council meeting agendas back to 1990. This addition makes it possible to trace more long-term developments in the local government agendas. Furthermore, given the structural reform of 2007, the longer time series make it possible to investigate what happens to the policy agenda when one or more political units are merged into one. Second, a large number of meeting agendas from local standing committees have been collected and content coded. The question about the interplay between the committee system and the central assembly is a classic one, and the multiple local government units makes it possible to approach this question from a new perspective using statistical tools of analysis.

8.5 Major Findings from the Danish Project

The data series developed in the Danish project have been used to investigate a series of questions relating both to the Danish political system and to comparative questions. A few are worth highlighting here.

Whereas most research on political parties takes its point of departure from whether parties are left or right, the Danish project has drawn attention to the difference between opposition and government parties. Green-Pedersen and Mortensen (2010) show how the opposition parties are able to influence the government agenda by influencing what Green-Pedersen and Mortensen call the party system agenda. The agenda-setting game between government and opposition and the fact that the opposition often seems to have the upper hand was further developed by Thesen (2013), who focused on the interaction between media and party competition. Seeberg (2013) shows how this dynamic also has important policy consequences.

One of the examples of opposition influence is the growth of immigration on the party system agenda, which is shown in Figure 8.1. The right-wing opposition from 1993 to 2001 used its issue-ownership of immigration to generate increasing party system attention to immigration. This issue expansion was based on claims about the need for a much stricter immigration policy (Green-Pedersen and Krogstrup 2008). When the right-wing parties then gained government power in 2001, they implemented exactly that and this makes Denmark stand out as a country with a very strict immigration policy (cf. Akkerman, 2012: 518–20).

The idea of a party system agenda has also been utilized in other publications from the Danish project. The theoretical idea is that parties through party competition influence each other so a common perception is formed of

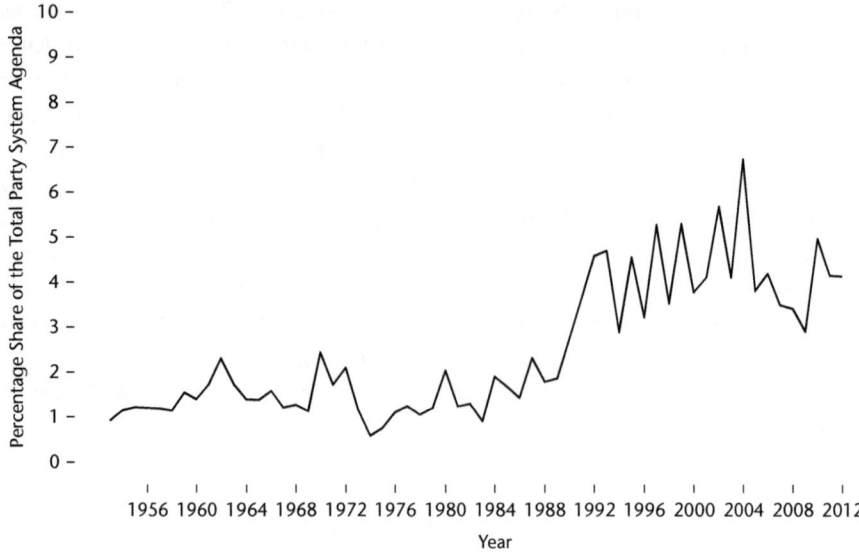

Figure 8.1. Immigration issue in the total party system agenda
Source: Comparative Agendas Project—Denmark

which issues it is necessary to pay attention to. The party system agenda is thus both constraining for political parties and something they can influence. In Green-Pedersen and Mortensen (2010), the party system agenda was measured through the length of debates about bills, accounts, motions, and interpellations in the Danish parliament.

Publications from the project have shown how the party system agenda can explain whether governments pay attention to the spending preferences of the electorate (Mortensen, 2010) and the development of the Danish ministerial structure (Mortensen and Green-Pedersen, 2015). These findings thus underline the importance of understanding how the party system agenda is formed.

Notes

1. A new version of the parliamentary data and the party manifestos will have been available in the spring of 2019.
2. This made it possible to recode the original Danish data, so a version now exists that is fully compatible over time and fully compatible with the Master Codebook. This version of the data is available at comparativeagenda.net.
3. The subtopic 1910 in the Master Codebook is divided into European Integration (1910) and Western Europe (1913).
4. In the case of an election, bills not yet passed are withdrawn, but then often passed after the election.

5. CAPCAS is an acronym for Causes and Policy Consequences of Agenda Setting. Other participants in the CAPCAS project are Henrik Bech Seeberg, Carsten Jensen, Matt Loftis, and Martin Bækgaard.
6. The adjusted codebooks can be found here: http://ps.au.dk/forskning/ forskningsprojekter/capcas/data-and-codebooks/.

References

Akkerman, T. (2012). Comparing Radical Right Parties in Government: Immigration and Integration Policies in Nine Countries (1996–2010). *West European Politics*, 35(3): 511–29.

Green-Pedersen, C., and Krogstrup, J. (2008). Immigration as a Political Issue in Denmark and Sweden: How Party Competition Shapes Political Agendas. *European Journal of Political Research*, 47(5): 610–34.

Green-Pedersen, C., and Mortensen, P. B. (2010). Who Sets the Agenda and Who Responds to It in the Danish Parliament? *European Journal of Political Research*, 49(2): 257–81.

Green-Pedersen, C., and Thomsen, L. H. (2005). Bloc Politics vs. Broad Cooperation: The Functioning of Danish Minority Parliamentarism. *The Journal of Legislative Studies*, 11(2): 153–69.

Green-Pedersen, C., and Wolfe, M. (2009). The Hare and the Tortoise Once Again: The Institutionalization of Environmental Attention in the US and Denmark. *Governance*, 22(4): 625–46.

Hansen, M. E. (2008). Back to the Archives? A Critique of the Danish Part of the Manifesto Database. *Scandinavian Political Studies*, 31(2): 201–16.

Loftis, M. W., and Mortensen, P. B. (2018). Collaborating with the Machines: A Hybrid Method for Coding Policy Agendas, *Policy Studies Journal*. https://doi.org/10.1111/ psj.12245

Lund, A. B. (2000). De journalistiske fødekæder. In *Først med det sidste: En nyhedsuge i Danmark*, ed. Anker Brink Lund. Århus: Ajour, 143–52.

Mortensen, P. B. (2010). Political Attention and Public Policy: A Study of How Agenda Setting Matters. *Scandinavian Political Studies*, 33(4): 356–80.

Mortensen, P. B., and Green-Pedersen, C. (2015). Institutional Effects of Changes in Political Attention: Explaining Organizational Changes in the Top Bureaucracy. *Journal of Public Administration Research and Theory*, 25(1): 165–89.

Seeberg, H. (2013). The Opposition's Policy Influence through Issue Politicisation. *Journal of Public Policy*, 33(1): 89–107.

Senninger, R. (2016). Issue Expansion and Selective Scrutiny—How Opposition Parties Used Parliamentary Questions about the European Union in the National Arena from 1973 to 2013. *European Union Politics*, 18(2): 283–306.

Skjæveland, A. (2001). Party Cohesion in the Danish Parliament. *The Journal of Legislative Studies*, 7(2): 35–56.

Thesen, G. (2013). When Good News Is Scarce and Bad News Is Good. *European Journal of Political Research*, 52(3): 364–89.

9

The French Agendas Project

Emiliano Grossman

The French Agendas Project (FAP) was initiated in 2005 by Sylvain Brouard and Emiliano Grossman. Frank Baumgartner was closely associated with the project from the beginning. The main motivation for the project was the will to remedy to the lack of quantitative series concerning the activity and relations of political institutions in France. The US Policy Agendas Project appeared as a rather original way of filling this void, while engaging in innovative research and joining a nascent international network of scholars engaged in comparable projects in other countries. The project has evolved strongly since, and the two initiators continue to work on the project.

9.1 The French Political System

France is famous for its semi-presidential political system. This essentially boils down to a system with separate presidential and parliamentary elections, much like in a classical presidential system. Unlike in the latter, however, there is also a prime minister, who is the effective head of government. However, the prime minister is not only responsible to the lower chamber, but also to the president. Under this "presidential" version of semi-presidential government (cf. Duverger et al., 1997), the president, while usually not dealing with day-to-day government business, is the effective head of the executive. The prime minister submits all major decisions to the president's scrutiny and all ministers are approved by the president. While the extent of presidential involvement has varied, it has usually been extensive and the president's role in day-to-day politics has rather increased over time.

Under "divided government" or "cohabitation" (in French), the system reverts to a more classical version of parliamentary government with a prime minister who is the effective head of government and a president who is confined to more representational functions, while continuing to monitor closely the "reserved areas", i.e., foreign policy and defense. This has often led to tensions, especially as the next presidential election approaches. Cohabitation had become quite common since 1986 with three major periods of divided government. Following a constitutional reform in 2000, bringing the presidential term in line with the parliamentary term, however, cohabitation has become less likely, as the presidential and the parliamentary elections take place only about six weeks apart. In the three presidential/legislative elections that have taken place since the reform, newly elected presidents have confirmed their majority in subsequent legislative elections.

Beyond intra-executive relations, France features a comparatively weak parliament (Kerrouche, 2006), despite some reinforcements introduced in 2008. The executive, usually based on a multiparty coalition, mostly controls the parliamentary agenda, especially in the more important lower chamber. The vast majority of laws originate in government bills and even the few member bills that are adopted every year usually imply prior government approval to stand a chance on the floor. The Senate can be overruled by the lower chamber, following article 45. This leads de facto to a suspensive veto, even if open conflict between the two chambers is rare.

Until recently, the party system was dominated by a left-wing and a right-wing block. The former was dominated by the Socialist Party, but also included the Greens, the Communist Party and, more recently, the Parti de gauche. The conservative block was made up of the Union pour un mouvement populaire, recently rebranded Les Républicains, and the centrists. Both blocks usually conclude pre-electoral agreements regarding candidacies in the 577 constituencies. The 2017 election upset the classical pattern, leading to a substantial weakening of both blocs, but more particularly of the Socialist Party, significantly diminished electorally. It has been all but replaced by the new party created by Emmanuel Macron, La République en marche, which obtained an absolute majority of seats in the 2017 legislative elections, following Macron's victorious presidential bid.

The electoral system, a two-round plurality system with a threshold to reach the second round, favors pre-electoral arrangements, though negotiations between the rounds are not uncommon. This has usually excluded the far-right party Front national from representation at the national level. Despite its leaders' historical results at the 2017 presidential election, the party only obtained eight seats at the legislative elections a few weeks later.

Finally, there is a highly active Constitutional Council that has the particularity of mainly deciding on the constitutionality of laws *before* they come into force. This has changed recently, but continues apply to the vast majority of decisions. In terms of constitutional review, it is among the more interventionist courts in Europe (Brouard, 2009).

9.2 Datasets

Today there is a variety of datasets available that have been coded using the harmonized CAP codebook (see Table 9.1). These datasets have been collected over a long period starting in 2005. While the most important coding operations are completed, there is an effort to regularly update already existing datasets.

The heart of CAP are laws. Data concerning laws have been the first data collected for most national projects and this is where the first comparisons were possible. And, finally, this is where we tested and consolidated our coding techniques. Generally speaking, we preferred human coding for all "small" datasets, i.e., all those that could reasonably be coded manually. Like other projects, we developed a consolidated training dataset where coders had to achieve a minimum of correct codes (85 percent). All manually coded datasets, moreover, were comprehensively checked by one of the two principal investigators. The laws dataset moreover includes a variety of qualitative information regarding the context of adoption.

A second major source of data was the weekly government council meeting summaries. These documents have been systematically published, probably since the beginning of the Fifth Republic. Thanks to the support of government information services, we were able establish a consolidated database that goes back to 1974. Government councils include the president, the prime minister, and all plenary ministries, as well as other cabinet members if requested. Council meetings include four categories of agenda items: government bills, communications, governmental decrees, and appointments. Government bills provide

Table 9.1. Datasets of the French Agendas Project

Dataset	Period covered	N
Laws	1978–2017	3,069
Government bills	1974–2013	2,904
Government communications	1974–2013	6,447
Government decrees ('ordonnances')	1974–2013	1,118
Presidential New Year's speech	1981–2017	3,523
Prime minister speeches at the Assemblée nationale	1981–2012	6,538 (sentences)
Constitutional Council Decisions	1951–2009	3,612
Parliamentary questions	1996–2010	334,247
Party programs	1981–2012	24,467 (sentences)
Le Monde (national quality newspaper)	1981–2013	55,768
8pm news shows for the two major broadcasting networks	1986–2008	302,962

Source: Comparative Agendas Project—France

the list of all important government bills, but exclude a certain number of bills, such as bills ratifying bilateral agreements. The constitution stipulates that the latter have to be ratified by law, and make up a very substantial share of adopted laws (up to 40 percent in certain parliamentary sessions), but are de facto waved through parliament in fast-track mode. Communications are a rather heterogeneous category that includes government statements on some issue of current concern, as well as presentations of long-term programs in some policy areas or an expertise on the effects and problems of a particular policy program. Government decrees are a classical decree-law device that requires a prior delegation vote by the assembly (art. 38 of the constitution). This has been of varying importance: historically quite rare, decree-laws became very common between 2000 and 2005, but their importance diminished again thereafter. We did not code appointments, which include a very long series of official appointments that have to be ratified by the Government Council.

A third series of datasets are the speeches. The only regular speech is the New Year's speech of the president. Unlike the Queen's Speech in the United Kingdom or the US State of the Union speech, it has a lot of non-political content that limits its usefulness. We have therefore also coded the prime minister's speeches in the lower chamber of parliament. These speeches often contain general policy declarations, but may sometimes focus on just one major issue of concern. Moreover, those speeches are not very regular, as they follow an initiative on behalf of the prime minister herself or a no-confidence motion. Speeches were divided into quasi-sentences, double-coded and cross-checked by one of the two principal investigators.

The French team has been among the first to code party programs using the CAP codebook for France (Brouard et al., 2014) and other countries. Like before, this has been done using quasi-sentences, double-coding, and systematic cross-checks.

Media contents, finally, have been coded using automatic coding, rather than manual coding, and, in particular, RTexttools, the coding package developed within CAP (Jurka et al., 2013). Three independent datasets are available in this area. We coded the front page of the quality newspaper *Le Monde* over a period of twenty-eight years. This amounts to close to sixty thousand news items. The datasets include the 8pm news shows in the two major French networks between 1986 and 2008. This amounts to several hundred thousand news items. Machine learning and automatized coding thus represented the only way to code this amount of data. A disadvantage of this procedure, however, is that "rare" codes are very hard and often impossible to predict. We have therefore restricted coding to "major topics" only: media data thus only distinguishes about twenty different topics. For these we have calculated the quality of prediction. Whenever this quality fell below the human "gold standard", i.e. 85 percent of correct predictions, we conducted a systematic rereading of the coded items. For those codes that reached the expected standard, only samples were controlled.

9.3 Specificities and Perspectives

From the beginning, the main goal of the French Agendas Project was to improve our understanding of the institutional setup and practices of the French political system. The study of the latter had been dominated by lawyers and was strongly focused on institutional history and rules. The members of the team felt a resolutely empirical approach to French politics and institutions was necessary. In particular, it seemed necessary to test some long-established hypotheses about law-making, executive pre-eminence or the behavior of the Constitutional Council. Given the weakness of quantitative research in French political science, institutions and policymaking were mainly studied through case studies, allowing for very limited inference and generalization. The goal was therefore to provide an infrastructure for the empirical study of institutions and policymaking in France.

A related objective was to put France back on the map of comparative political science. The absence of comparative data for France, maybe excluding large surveys, such as the European Electoral Survey or the World Value Survey, has led over time to a true anti-comparative bias in case studies on France. As is often the case, one-case specialists tend to stress the unique traits of their case, deliberately limiting and sometimes even preventing comparison. The thesis of "French exceptionalism" was part of the long-established dogmas that the French Agendas Project aims to contradict.

These goals were partially achieved a few years later with two edited volumes that included many empirical studies on France's fifth Republic, though only some of the chapters and articles relied on Agendas data (Brouard et al., 2009; Grossman and Sauger, 2009). The study of French institutions became more and more developed as a consequence of these studies.

Increasingly other goals emerged as the possibilities linked to the new data became apparent. Early on members of the project focused on the evolution and possibility of partisan government in France (Baumgartner, Brouard, and Grossman, 2009; Baumgartner, Foucault, and François, 2009; Froio et al., 2012). The coding of party programs has allowed for a novel approach to party issue profiles and issue competition in France (Brouard et al., 2014) and beyond (ongoing). Other work focused on the institutional constraints and the consequences of divided government, comparing France to the United States (Baumgartner et al., 2014). These contributions have adopted often novel perspectives, either by introducing the French case into comparative studies

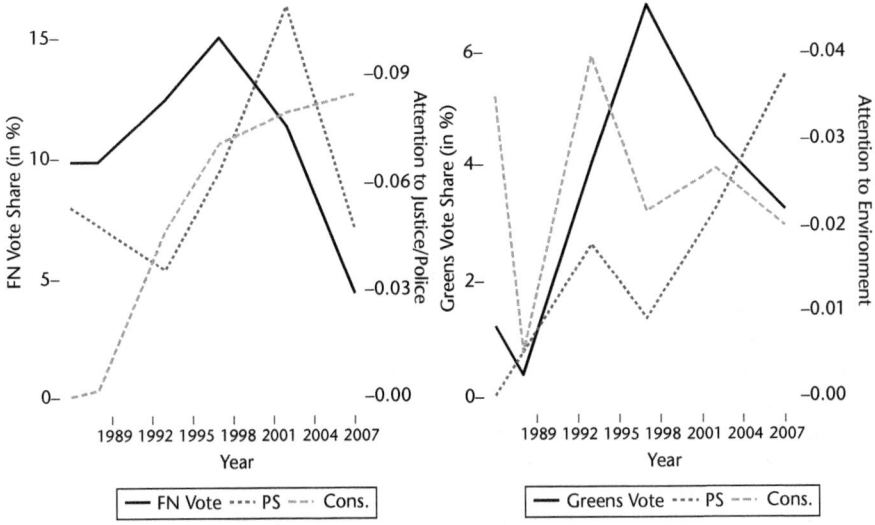

Figure 9.1. The impact of niche party vote on issue attention
Source: Comparative Agendas Project—France

or, simply, by allowing a new analysis of the French case to develop. A good case in point is the study of cap-coded French party programs. As CAP codes attention, rather than direction, this has allowed for interesting analyses concerning the evolution of political debate in France, as Figure 9.1 illustrates.

Figure 9.1, inspired by the work in Brouard et al. (2014), presents the results of the vote for niche parties with a strong issue focus on attention to those topics in the other parties' programs over time. In both cases, the results or the anticipated results of niche parties in general elections have a strong impact on attention to those parties' pet issues among government parties. Here we include the two main government parties, i.e., the Socialist Party and the Conservatives (Cons.), who have run under two different names over the period considered (RPR, UMP).[1]

A lot of other issues lie ahead. Many of the series, especially concerning the media or speeches by the prime minister, remain, so far, under-exploited. Related projects concerning parties are currently comparing issue attention with specific pledges. Moreover, a paper devoted to the specific contributions of CAP to the understanding of French politics is under way.

Note

1. They changed their name again after the 2012 general election to "Les Républicains."

References

Baumgartner, F., Brouard, S., and Grossman, E. (2009). Agenda-Setting Dynamics in France: Revisiting the 'Partisan Hypothesis'. *French Politics*, 7(2): 75–95.

Baumgartner, F. R., Brouard, S., Grossman, E. et al. (2014). Divided Government, Legislative Productivity, and Policy Change in the USA and France. *Governance*, 27(3): 423–47.

Baumgartner, F. R., Foucault, M., and François, A. (2009). Public Budgeting in the French Fifth Republic: The End of La Republique des partis? *West European Politics*, 32(2): 404–22.

Brouard, S. (2009). The Politics of Constitutional Veto in France: Constitutional Council, Legislative Majority and Electoral Competition. *West European Politics*, 32(2): 384–403.

Brouard, S., Appleton, A. M., and Mazur, A. G. (2009). *The French Fifth Republic at Fifty: Beyond Stereotypes*. London: Palgrave.

Brouard, S., Grossman, E., and Guinaudeau, I. (2014). The Evolution of the French Political Space Revisited. In *Agenda Setting, Policies, and Political Systems: A Comparative Approach*, ed. C. Green-Pedersen, and S. Walgrave. Chicago: University of Chicago Press, 53–68.

Duverger, M., Lijphart, A., and Pasquino, G. (1997). A New Political System. *European Journal of Political Research*, 31(1–2): 125–46.

Froio, C., Guinaudeau, I., and Persico, S. (2012). Action publique et partis politique. *Gouvernement et action publique*, 1(1): 11–35.

Grossman, E., and Sauger, N. (2009). The Fifth Republic at Fifty (Special Issue). *West European Politics*, 32(2).

Jurka, T. P., Collingwood, L., Boydstun, A. E. et al. (2013). RTextTools: A Supervised Learning Package for Text Classification. *The R Journal*, 5(1): 6–12.

Kerrouche, E. (2006). The French Assemblée nationale: The Case of a Weak Legislature? *The Journal of Legislative Studies*, 12(3–4): 336–65.

10

Political Agendas in Germany

Christian Breunig and Tinette Schnatterer

10.1 The German Political System

In textbooks on German politics (Rudzio, 2015; Schmidt, 2003), the post-World-War-II political system typically is described in terms of stability and moderation. Several institutional features foster cooperation and consensus. A proportional electoral system paired with competition among a modest number of parties produces broad-based two-party coalition governments. Party competition is dominated by two large parties—Christian Democratic Union and Social Democratic Party—with relatively similar policy stances. The Germany political system is also characterized by the high degree of federalism, a strong upper chamber, and the existence of several other relatively independent institutions, such as the central bank and the Federal Constitutional Court. Because industrial conflict is highly institutionalized among interest groups and government, the term "policy of the middle way" is commonly used. As Schmidt (1987: 138) states: "The policy of the middle way marks a third way between the extreme poles of Scandinavian social democratic welfare capitalism and political economies in which bourgeois tendencies dominate." Classical studies of comparative politics therefore categorize Germany a consensus democracy (Lijphart, 1999) or a semi-sovereign state (Katzenstein, 1987).

During the last decades however, two large-scale transformations—Europeanization and reunification—contributed to a restructuring of the political system (Breunig, 2014). As for the other member states, one of the main challenges of Europeanization is coordinating public policy at the domestic level with actions taken at the European level. European influence in politics and in legislation has grown steadily over the last three decades. However, this trend typically remains concentrated in some policy domains, such as agriculture. In contrast to the creeping influence of Europeanization, German reunification in 1990 led to a sudden and lasting reconfiguration of the political system. The addition of five new *Länder* changed the composition of the upper chamber. The inclusion of a new left-wing party (former PDS, now Die Linke) with strong support among the former East German states created strategic dilemmas within the party system.

Institutional transformations often spur changes in the wider political environment, ranging from how citizens understand political issues to public policymaking. In this chapter, we describe a data set on political activities in Germany that enables researchers and the lay public to investigate how German politics has evolved since the 1970s. Utilizing the presented data, we can inquire into core questions about the German polity. Is policymaking really characterized by deliberation and incremental adjustments? Did the institutional ruptures occurring in the last thirty years lead to a different style of policymaking? Does Europeanization remove some issues out of national public and parliamentary attention and relegate them to less visible supra-national decision-making? Are policymakers responding to public concerns and what institutional tools do they use in their response?

The chapter first introduces each political agenda, ranging from policy inputs to government outputs. We describe data sources and their coding, including a discussion on intercoder reliability. Following a discussion on coding procedures, a brief application that examines the German reunification process highlights the potential of the database and concludes the chapter.

10.2 German Political Agendas

Individual political agendas, especially for particular policy domains, have been the subject of research in German politics: the legislative agenda, parliamentary questions, government speeches and public opinion as measured by the most important problem question. What is missing is a comprehensive dataset that covers different political agendas over a long period of time. We examine all political activities within each agenda and code each item thematically. Doing so, our effort—the German Agendas Project—offers a database that is exhaustive, consistent, and comparable across time and agendas. In the following description, we split out the policy cycle into input (public opinion and party platforms), policy processes (government speeches, parliamentary questions, and bills), and outputs (laws). The time span of the database covers the years from 1986 to 2005 for the answers to the most important problem (MIP) question and 1976 to 2005 for all the other documents. Unless otherwise noted, all data are based on the Dokumentations—und Informationssystem für Parlamentarische Vorgänge (Parliamentary Material Information System [DIP]).

We characterize the public's agenda using public opinion data and concentrate on answers to the most important problem (MIP) question: An open-ended question asks respondents what they consider to be the most important problem in Germany. The exact wording of the question is: "According to you, what is the most important problem in Germany at the moment." The most important problem database is compiled from yearly survey databases for both West and East Germany provided by the Politbarometer survey. Conducted by the Forschungsgruppe Wahlen e.V. (the German Institute for Election Research) in mostly yearly intervals since 1977, the Politbarometer survey has become the major representative survey of German society. The GESIS Leibniz Institute for the Social Sciences makes the data publicly available through its ZACAT data portal. A large number of respondents are included in each survey wave: 11,000 to 25,000 respondents for the yearly waves in the old Bundesländer, and 11,000 on average in the new Bundesländer. Instead of using the cumulated dataset provided by GESIS, we compiled and recoded the variables of interest of all individual waves. Doing so enables more fine-grained coding. The most-important-problem question was first asked in 1980. It appeared in the surveys consistently and with the same wording from 1986. The data can be broken down to the monthly level and are not weighted. The answers to the open-ended questions have been grouped in more general categories by the Politbarometer team. All answer categories have been CAP-coded on the basis of the yearly databases.

The input series is complemented by the content of the party platforms for the eight legislative elections between 1980 and 2005. Party platforms of the five German parties represented in the Bundestag (CDU/CSU, FDP, Grüne, Linke/PDS and SPD) have been coded on the level of natural sentences under the direction of Christoffer Green-Pedersen (Aarhus University) and Isabelle Guinaudeau (Sciences Po, Bordeaux) with the identical coding-scheme and protocol.

Government speeches (*Regierungserklärungen*) can be used as indicator of the government's agenda. Government speeches are not codified in parliamentary law or the German Constitution. The federal government (Bundesregierung) employs government speeches for explaining its political principles and past actions as well as emphasizing its legislative intentions. The government cannot be compelled to make a government policy statement by the Bundestag. At the start of a legislative period, the chancellor gives a "major" government policy statement (Korte, 2002: 13) in which policy goals of the newly elected government are presented. Since the late 1960s, most governments also deliver a "state of the union speech," which is typically held early in the year and presents specific policy ideas for the subsequent sessions. Speeches generally concentrate on the policy packages of the current coalition and aim to display the chancellor's power to determine broad policy principles

(Art. 55, Grundgesetz (GG)). The chancellor as well as other members of the government are able to offer a government policy statement in order to explain the government's perspective on current political topics or in the course of political events (e.g., meetings of the European Council). These statements are shorter in length, less comprehensive, and their number has increased over time. For our database, we only considered major speeches given by the chancellor and if several government speeches where held by the chancellor the same year, the most important speech was identified. Speeches covering several topics were privileged over one-issue speeches and longer speeches over shorter ones. We split each speech into quasi-sentences and then coded each quasi-sentence thematically.

Parliamentary questions (Große Anfragen/Kleine Anfragen—minor and major interpellations) are a parliamentary process that is typically used by opposition parties and MPs. Technically, every parliamentary group or 5 percent of all MPs can ask a parliamentary question in Germany (rule 75–76, GODB). Empirically, this instrument is mainly used by the opposition parties and among them the Green party and the Left party/former PDS. For instance, 62 percent of the Kleine Anfragen in the 14th legislature originate from members of the Left party. Minor and major interpellations have to be answered in written form by the federal government. While major interpellations might be discussed in the plenum, this is generally not the case for minor interpellations. Minor interpellations are mostly used to monitor government action by requesting information about "specifically designated issues" (rule 104, GODB). Major interpellations can be described as the "most important instrument of the opposition to initiate major plenary debates about political issues" (Ismayer, 2007: 183) and as a form of political control (Rudzio, 2015: 234). We coded each parliamentary question according to CAP and relied on title, key words, and the summary of the questions provided by the Dokumentations—und Informationssystem für Parlamentarische Vorgänge (Parliamentary Material Information System [DIP]). In case of doubt we additionally relied on the text for the whole question.

The agenda of the parliament as a whole finds its expression in legislative bills. Bills can be submitted by the government, the Bundesrat or by 5 percent of all MPs (Art. 76, GG). Bills from the government are usually prepared by a division within the ministry responsible for the respective policy area. These so-called draft bills are revised several times and reviewed by the Ministry of Justice. Before a draft bill becomes a federal government bill it has to meet the approval of the cabinet. Federal government bills have to be sent up to the Bundesrat, which can comment on such bills within six weeks (in exceptions within three or nine weeks) (Art. 76 (2), GG). The government initiates more than half of all bills. Bills from the Bundesrat can be introduced by one or several federal states. An absolute majority of all members of the Bundesrat have to support the initiated bill. Bundesrat bills are sent to the Bundestag, which can comment on such bills within six weeks (in exceptions within three or nine weeks) (Art. 76 (3), GG). Bills from the floor of the Bundestag must be signed by 5 percent of the members of the Bundestag or a parliamentary group (a parliamentary group must also consist of a minimum of 5 percent of the members of the German Bundestag) (rule 75 and 76, GODB). Bills from the floor of the Bundestag constitute about one third of all legislative initiatives introduced.

Federal laws are passed by the Bundestag. A distinction can be drawn between approval laws and objection laws. Approval laws need to be passed by the Bundestag and the Bundesrat, objection laws can be passed by the Bundestag without the support of the Bundesrat. Approval laws are laws that make amendments to the constitution (Art. 97 (2), GG) or affect the finances of the Länder (Art. 104a (4) GG) or whose implementation would interfere with the Länder's administrative sovereignty (Art 84 (1), GG). Before a bill is put up for a vote in the Bundestag, it usually has to pass three readings and be discussed in a committee. In the third reading amendments can only be requested by parliamentary groups or groups of at least 5 percent of the members of the Bundestag. At the end of the third reading the bill is put to final vote. Most laws need a simple majority to be passed (Art. 24 (2), GG). Laws that make amendments to the constitution need a two-thirds majority (Art.79. (2), GG). If the bill has passed the Bundestag, it is assigned to the Bundesrat. Approval laws need to be passed by the Bundesrat, objection laws can come into force without the approval of the Bundesrat. In case of conflict between the two chambers the Mediation Committee can become active on the basis of a request from the Bundesrat, the Bundestag, or the Federal Government. For each bill or law we used the title, the key words, summary, and the whole content of the text provided by the DIP as well as the ministry assignment of the document in order to place it into a particular policy category.

10.3 Coding Procedure and Data Description

Following the Comparative Agendas Project coding scheme, the data are coded into twenty-one major and 232 minor topic areas. Unique to the German codebook is a separate category for issues related to reunification. Documents are coded under reunification if the item directly mentions unification or clearly links to the consequences of reunification. We opted for this restrictive approach as a balance between capturing this unique historical incident and recognizing the political challenges of new Germany.

All documents have been coded by at least two well-trained coders, looked through by a third person and in case of divergent classifications discussed collectively and then placed in a policy category. For all parliamentary documents (questions, bills, and laws) we coded the title, the key words and

Table 10.1. German political agendas

	Indicator	Actors	Unit of analysis	No. of observations	Intercoder reliability
Input	Most important problem (*Wichtigstes Problem*)	Respondents of representative survey	Answer to open survey question	379,820	90.6
	Party platforms (*Parteiprogramme*)	Political parties	Sentences	39,603	97.7
Policy process	Most important government speech for each year (*Regierungserklärungen*)	German Chancellor	Quasi-sentences	13,566	87.2
	Parliamentary questions (*Große und kleine Anfragen*)	Every parliamentary group or 5 percent of all MPs	Text of the question	10,029	81.9
	Bills (*Gesetzesentwürfe*)	The government, the Bundesrat or 5 percent of all MPs	Text of the legislative activity	5,801	82.6
Output	Laws (*Verabschiedete Gesetze*)	Parliament voting the laws	Text of the law	3,137	79.8

Source: Comparative Agendas Project—Germany

the summary of the text provided by the DIP. In case of doubt we additionally opened the document itself. The parliamentary questions of the (11–15 legislature) have been coded semi-automatically with the help of RTextTools. The algorithms were trained to classify texts using previously manually coded texts and the results verified following our normal coding procedure (by at least two well-trained coders, looked through by a third person, and in case of divergent classifications discussed collectively and then placed in a policy category). In the case of the semi-automatically coded texts, the original documents were not opened.

Table 10.1 summarizes the databases. Overall our database consists of six data series. For inputs, we classified 379,820 answers on the most important problem question and 39,603 quasi-sentences in party manifestos. Intercoder reliability is 90.6 percent for MIPs and 97.9 percent for party platforms. For policy processes, we coded 13,566 quasi-sentences in government speeches, 10,029 parliamentary questions and 5,801 bills with an intercoder reliability of 87.2 percent for government speeches, 81.9 for parliamentary questions and 82.6 percent for bills. On the output side, we coded 3,137 laws with an intercoder reliability of 79.8 percent.

10.4 A First Look at the Database: Reunification in Political Agendas

The reunification of East and West Germany transformed the German polity. We briefly describe how this process unfolded across different political

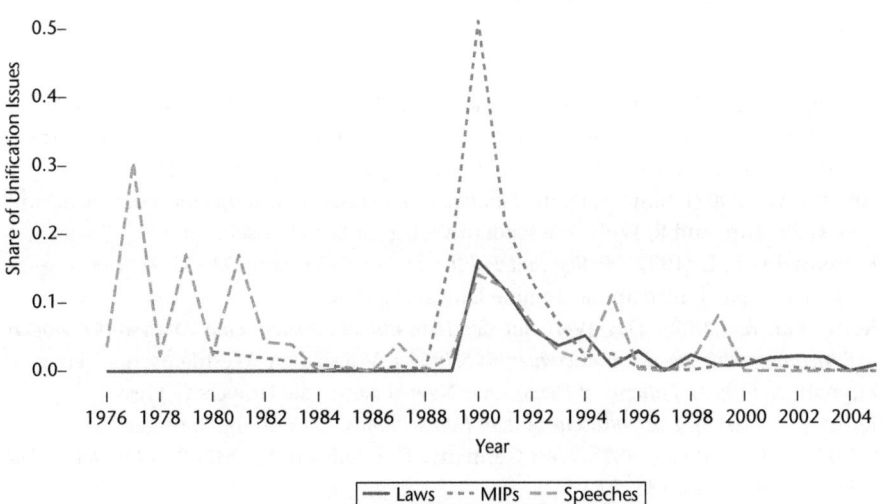

Figure 10.1. Reunification issue in Germany

Source: Comparative Agendas Project—Germany

agendas and thereby offer a quick glimpse into the power of our database. Figure 10.1 displays the percentage share of the reunification topic over time across three policy series: public opinion, government speeches and laws.

Public opinion, captured by the most important problem question, changes most dramatically. This seesaw pattern confirms the ephemeral nature of public opinion. Government speeches display three noticeable peaks in attention in the 1970s and 1980s. These peaks are a consequence of the new eastern policy (*Ostpolitk*) that was initiated during Brandt's chancellery. German chancellors regularly discuss reunification issues in the state of the union speech. The discussions often conclude speeches and are expressed in a propitiatory tone. Laws on reunification are concentrated in a short period in the early 1990s. In the years of the fall of the Berlin Wall (1989) and reunification (1990), we observe an increase in attention on reunification issues across all political agendas. This finding is unsurprising but delivers some clear validity for our data. What is more interesting are the clear differences between political agendas over time. Reunification issues have seldom been aired in party platforms before an election and in parliamentary questions during the legislative session (and therefore we didn't plot them). This inattention shows that reunification has neither been an important issue in electoral competition, nor has it been an issue for the opposition. The issue has not really been politicized and has predominantly been driven by speech-making and legislation. Our conviction is that the database can be fruitfully employed not only for disentangling the reunification process but also for other broad questions on German politics and public policy.

References

Breunig, C. (2014). Content and Dynamics of Legislative Agendas in Germany. In *Agenda Setting, Policies, and Political Systems: A Comparative Approach*, ed. C. Green-Pedersen, and S. Walgrave. Chicago: University of Chicago Press, 125–44.

Ismayer, W. (2007). Bundestag. In *Handbuch zur deutschen Außenpolitik*, ed. S. Schmidt, G. Hellmann, and R. Wolf. Wiesbaden: Verlag für Sozialwissenschaften, 175–91.

Katzenstein, P. J. (1987). *Policy and Politics in West Germany: The Growth of a Semisovereign State*. Philadelphia: Temple University Press.

Korte, Karl-R. (2002). *Das Wort hat der Herr Bundeskanzler: Eine Analyse der großen Regierungserklärungen von Adenauer bis Schröder*. Wiesbaden: Westdeutscher Verlag.

Lijphart, A. (1999). *Patterns of Democracy*. New Haven: Yale University Press.

Rudzio, W. (2015). *Das politische System Deutschlands*. Oldenburg: Springer VS.

Schmidt, Manfred G. (1987). West Germany: The Policy of the Middle Way. *Journal of Public Policy*, 7(2): 135–77.

Schmidt, Manfred G. (2003). *Political Institutions in the Federal Republic of Germany*. Oxford: Oxford University Press.

11

The Hungarian Agendas Project

Zsolt Boda and Miklós Sebők

The Hungarian Policy Agendas Project was established in 2013. It was initiated and has been led by Zsolt Boda and Miklós Sebők, both researchers at the Institute for Political Science, Centre for Social Sciences of the Hungarian Academy of Sciences. It forms part of the Institute's endeavor to contribute to the development of policy studies, a much neglected part of political science in Hungary.

The Comparative Agendas Project, and the underlying paradigm of Punctuated Equilibrium Theory (PET), served as a natural starting point for conducting policy research in a Central Eastern European country with no deep traditions in policy research for at least two reasons. First, because it involves the creation of large-scale databases that can be used in different kinds of empirical analyses pursuing research questions unrelated to PET in the future. In this, our project not only contributes to the growing research community of CAP, but also to Hungarian political science in general.

Second, the general PET framework directly links policy to politics: policy topics and issues to political actors and institutions. This approach promotes the emancipation of policy studies within political science in Hungary where policy issues are most often discussed along field-specific, technical or expert logics. From our perspective, one of the biggest strengths of PET is that it highlights the profoundly political nature of policymaking.

11.1 The Hungarian Political System

Hungary became a democracy after the regime change of 1990, in the "third wave" of democratization (Huntington, 1991), along with other countries in the region. However, the legacy of the *ancien régime* is still haunting

Hungary in many respects. The pre-1989, socialist system was characterized by the overwhelming role of the state in both the economy and politics. Governance and policymaking was extremely centralized, closed, and dominated by the Socialist party, with few policy venues and very sparse participatory opportunities. Independent civil society was virtually nonexistent, except for some small opposition circles with a limited outreach to the larger society and a few semi-legal movements in less politicized fields like culture or nature conservation. As a result, the transition process to a democratic system was ushered in by changes in global politics and it was orchestrated by the political and cultural elite rather than by mass mobilization from below.

Hungary is a unicameral parliamentary democracy with a relatively strongly institutionalized division of power and a system of checks and balances. MPs have been elected through a mixed electoral system ever since 1990. The prime minister is elected by the National Assembly with a simple majority. The president of the Republic is elected by the National Assembly for a period of five years, which creates a shifted overlap between the presidential and the governmental cycles. The president must sign each piece of legislation and has the right to either send them back to the National Assembly for further consideration or ask the Constitutional Court to review them. Local municipalities have had relatively high political autonomy and a wide range of responsibilities from education to healthcare.

Despite the high social costs of the transition process, the decade of the 1990s brought about a consolidation in both economic and political terms. Hungary experienced an intensive influx of foreign direct investment; GDP started to grow; the country applied for membership of the European Union, which resulted in EU accession in 2004. In politics the two-block system stabilized with the Hungarian Socialist Party as the leading force of the left and Fidesz as the strongest party of the right. Although political polarization increased significantly, the political system appeared to be strong enough to provide the needed stability. However, the second half of the 2000s was marked by a series of political and economic crises, which led to a landslide in Hungarian politics at the 2010 elections. Two new parties, a radical right and a green party, gained seats in the National Assembly, the Socialist party collapsed, while Fidesz won a two-thirds majority.

Using its power, Fidesz initiated large-scale institutional reforms, including the passing of a new constitution, the "Basic Law," in 2011. These reforms have certainly weakened the system of checks and balances: laws requiring a two-thirds majority (which, most of the time, would require a consensus among the governing parties and the opposition) were reduced in number; the rights of the Constitutional Court were curtailed and the possibility of popular motions was eliminated; the Office of the Commissioner for

Fundamental Rights was weakened; a wave of centralization reduced the autonomy of local municipalities.

The extent to which the Fidesz reforms have modified the political system in Hungary is still a matter of debate for political scientists. András Bozóki (2015: 3) argues that Fidesz "has significantly altered the country's legal, social and political infrastructure." While not denying the significance and the scope of the changes, András Körösényi (2015) suggests that the reforms are less important in terms of the formal or legal elements of the political system. The institutions of checks and balances, although weakened, are still in place. The novelty of the Fidesz approach is that it has managed to control or appease these institutions through politically loyal appointees. Körösényi argues that Fidesz imposed a new style of governance and a new political culture, characterized by extremely centralized decision-making, a rejection of the culture of consensus, and a unilateral use of power. In other words, democratic backsliding is less a consequence of institutional changes, but of informal practices.

The political style of Fidesz has had an effect on governance and policy-making as well. The executive branch of government dominates the legislative branch to a large extent (Korkut, 2012). This is hardly a new trend in Hungary, however, Fidesz has further disciplined its MPs through formal and informal norms. Bills originating from the opposition have had practically no chance to be approved since 2010. The speed of the legislation process has further accelerated. According to our own calculations, during the period of 2010–14 the average time between the submission of a bill and the final vote was thirty-four days, the shortest since 1990. Before 2010, the yearly number of adopted laws never surpassed 150. Since 2010, the average number of laws approved per year was more than two hundred, the highest number since 1990.

11.2 Datasets

The Hungarian Policy Agendas Project started in 2013 with the support of the Hungarian Scientific Research Fund (OTKA).[1] Adopting the coding system of the Comparative Agendas Project, our country project released a wide range of databases up until the second quarter of 2017 (see Table 11.1).

We put special emphasis on collecting data for each major phase of the policy process: inputs (media, public opinion, party platforms), policy processes (interpellations, laws, executive decrees, and speeches) and outputs (final accounts). We also prioritized modules that may be of wider interest for social scientists such as newspaper front pages (communication studies), laws (legal studies), and budgets (economics).

Table 11.1. Datasets of the Hungarian Policy Agendas Project

Module	Number of observations	Method of policy coding	Time frame	Coding level
Media	20,992	Hand-coded and automated text classification	2010–14	Whole text of individual front-page articles
Party platforms	12,857	Hand-coded	1990; 1994; 1998; 2002; 2006; 2010	Quasi-sentence
Interpellations	4907	Hand-coded	1990–2014	Whole text
Laws	3407	Hand-coded	1990–2014	Whole text
Executive speeches	6687	Hand-coded	1990–2014	Paragraphs
Executive decrees	16,418	Hand-coded	1990–2015	Whole text (excluding appendices)
Budgets and Final Accounts	51,667	Automated text classification	1868–2013	Line items

Source: Comparative Agendas Project—Hungary

Our approach evolved in terms of the underlying methodology of coding. We started out with what is considered to be the gold standard for such endeavors: double-blind hand-coding. Over time we have initiated a process of adopting automated text classification for most of our modules. This evolution is best illustrated by the history of our media database. Our first dataset (for the period 2010–14) was hand-coded, and yielded over 20,000 observations. A switch to automated text classification (which is under way in 2017 for the period 1990–2010) presented itself as an inevitable choice. In light of these experiences our budgets and final accounts datasets were prepared with the help of a dictionary-based classifier algorithm by design.

Turning now to the specifics of each module, our party platform database was compiled from various online and library sources for thirty-five party platforms of eight different parties with a parliamentary group for the period between 1990 and 2014. Here we followed the conventions of manifesto research by coding quasi-sentences. Media data was obtained from the coding of front pages of two major Hungarian daily newspapers, *Magyar Nemzet* and *Népszabadság* for the period 2010–14. Both of these were papers of record in this period, representing the political right and left, respectively. (As of 2016, *Népszabadság* was discontinued by its new, right-wing, publishers.)

The interpellations database contains interpellations, a form of parliamentary question, performed in parliament from the 1990–4 electoral cycle through the 2010–14 electoral cycle (Sebők et al., 2017). All MPs are eligible to submit written forms of interpellations. Plenary agenda access for oral presentations, however, is limited by institutional constraints (limited debate time and parliamentary group by-laws). Our database concerning laws covers the same period. Individual MPs, committees, and the government are all entitled to introduce bills. Nevertheless, plenary access is usually tightly controlled by government parties through committees, which results in governing majority dominance in adopting laws in the unicameral legislature. For both interpellations and laws, the underlying raw databases were downloaded from the Hungarian National Assembly website.

Executive decrees regulate the minutiae of policy subsystems and are adopted by the cabinet, its individual members or by the prime minister himself/herself. They are usually prepared by the ministries and in some cases also reflect the impact of lobbyists and the results of societal consultations. Executive speeches in our database are confined to plenary speeches of the incumbent prime minister in parliament. This is the only "process stage" (Baumgartner et al., 2009: 604) database for which the unit of analysis is not the whole text (of the interpellation, law, decree). In this case, in line with the structural characteristics of executive speeches, the coding level was set at the paragraph level. In most cases, paragraphs are the smallest units for which separate policy topic codes could be assigned.

Finally, our dataset concerning adopted budgets and final accounts (containing information on both appropriations and actual outlays) was compiled from electronic and paper-based official documents. The database covers over 150 years of budgetary history. Coding was carried out by relying on automated content analysis (dictionary-based scripts) on the line item level (for more technical details, see Sebők and Berki (2017)). All databases mentioned above include a wide variety of additional variables beyond policy topic coding. They can be downloaded after free registration from the Hungarian Project's website (cap.tk.mta.hu), and they are also available at the joint comparative website of CAP.

11.3 Specificities of the Hungarian Project

Due to the post-communist political development of Hungary our country project shows some specificities vis-à-vis more established projects in Western Europe and the United States. Three areas are worth mentioning: the codebook, the specific list of datasets and the availability of data for non-democratic periods.

First, our codebook accounts for some peculiarities of post-regime-change Hungarian policy development. While it remains perfectly compatible with the Master Codebook, it also adopts the terminology used in Hungarian policy sciences. Examples of such rephrasing include the reference to the state instead of government in multiple instances; the inclusion of EU funds for farm subsidies; or competition policy for antitrust regulation. Nevertheless, none of these terminological changes affect coding comparability as they only serve as an aid for local coders to correctly select the policy code pertinent to the given subject.

In some cases new substantial minor topic codes were also introduced in the Hungarian codebook, which describe policy topics that are not relevant for countries that have no post-communist past. Full comparability was maintained since all these subtopics were nested under an internationally recognized major topic and a direct reference to the relevant minor topic codes was also inserted in the comparative crosswalk. For instance, Hungary has a centralized healthcare system that makes the differentiation of public and private health insurance and healthcare necessary (in comparative work, however, both were listed under health insurance). Similarly, matters related to the millions of "Hungarians beyond the borders" and the diaspora were justified in getting a separate minor topic code. The same holds for issues related to restitution and the crimes of the non-democratic regimes in Hungarian history (we return to this topic in the concluding section).

Second, the relative underdevelopment of Hungarian quantitative social sciences also shaped our research agenda to a large extent. Even basic research questions—such as the role the mandate source (party list or single member district) of individual MPs plays in their legislative activities—required extensive data collection on behalf of our team. In the case of interpellations it was the Hungarian CAP that digitalized the paper-based collection for the first democratic government cycle of 1990–4 for the first time. Similarly, our colleagues scanned and cleaned data for budgets from the 1860s onward as they were not published in any format suitable for data analysis. A further problem is the unavailability of public agenda data from most important questions type surveys. In the event our project provided funding for a limited set of surveys.

The Hungarian CAP published a number of additional databases that were required to address our research questions. These include, inter alia, a complete database equipped with multiple dozens of variables of all MPs and similar datasets for the committees, parties, and parliamentary group leadership of the National Assembly as well as data on governments or the geographical composition of single-member districts.

Third, the turbulent political history of Hungary allows for the comparison of policy agendas of various subsequent regimes. Therefore, our current efforts are focused on the extension of our datasets to the decades—or, in some cases, centuries—preceding the regime change of 1990. The wide variety of particular regime forms in Hungarian history offer a fertile ground for the testing of hypotheses related to the role of regime type in shaping policy agendas (see e.g., Baumgartner et al., 2017). Accordingly, we have started new modules on historical data with the first new datasets covering interpellations (1945–90) and budgets (1868–1990).

11.4 Perspectives: The Politics of Communism and Restitution

One example of the aforementioned political system-specific coding problems is related to restitution and crimes committed during the various types of authoritarian regimes in Hungarian history. For natural reasons, of all these systems of government, at the time of the regime change of 1990 it was the communist regime—and its office-holders—who received most of the attention of the public, the media, and the political elite. Nevertheless, subsequent debates similarly highlighted the crimes of right-wing authoritarian and Nazi regimes of the period preceding 1945. In fact, these debates related to crimes and justice, remembrance and restitution, and in general the role of Hungarian leaders and the nation itself in twentieth-century world politics served as the basis for some of the most persistent political cleavages in post-regime change Hungarian politics and policymaking.

In light of these considerations the project introduced a specific minor topic code for issues concerning pre-1990 political history, with topics covered such as restitution and compensation for nationalized property, the prosecution of former office-holders and secret police agents, and policy issues related to the politics of remembrance in general. This addition to the codebook enabled researchers associated with the Hungarian CAP to compile case studies related to the interplay of high-octane political issues and policy agendas while maintaining the comparability of our results (as we discussed in Section 11.3).

One such case was related to Béla Biszku, one of the last living communist leaders as former Minister of the Interior after the anti-communist revolution of 1956 (Boda and Patkós, 2015). While a hot topic during the transition period, the role of Biszku in crimes committed against opposition figures and ordinary citizens during the communist era was less of a major agenda item for more than two decades following regime change. Eventually this topic re-emerged in the media in June 2010, with the release of a documentary film about Biszku, in which he adopted a permissive tone when speaking about the sanctions after the 1956 revolution and the execution of prime minister Imre Nagy. His statements in the film provoked indignation and lawyers in the media suggested that he should be tried for crimes against humanity.

Some months later an opposition party MP asked the attorney general about the case in an interpellation. Eventually, in January 2011, Biszku was formally accused of denial of crimes of communist totalitarianism. In October 2011, a governing party politician from the Fidesz party introduced a bill on crimes of the communist era that was approved in December the same year, and, as a consequence, Béla Biszku was charged with war crimes and crimes against humanity in October 2013. Although media coverage was continuous after the release of the documentary, as we can see in Figure 11.1, political and

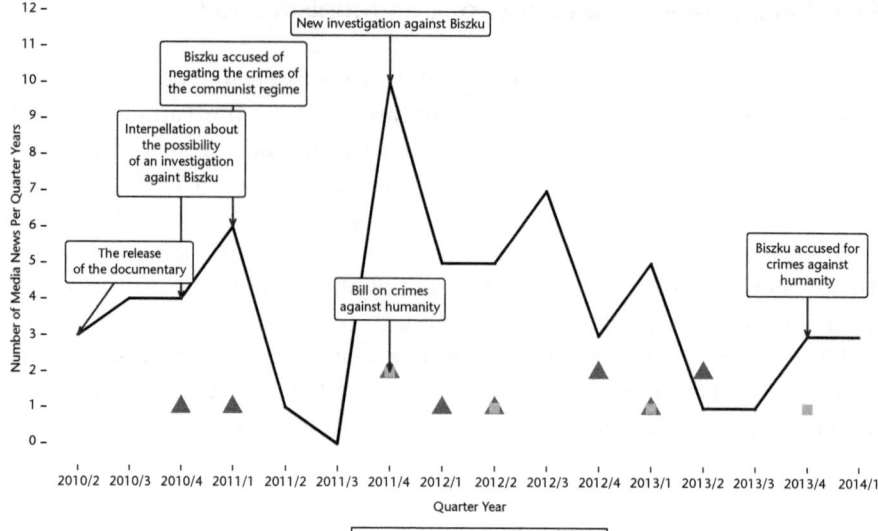

Figure 11.1. Béla Biszku's case

Source: Comparative Agendas Project—Hungary

government actors (notably, prosecutors) were quick to react and elevate the issue to the macro-political level.

Media attention only surged after these actors had taken up the issue and (re-)presented it as part of the national discourse (see the point in the media time series in the 4th quarter of 2011). In other words, the independent agenda-setting power of the media is not verified in this case. At best, media and politics "co-produced" a major agenda item in domestic political discourse.

Note

1. See the website of the project at http://cap.tk.mta.hu/en.

References

Baumgartner, F. R., Breunig, C., Green-Pedersen, C. et al. (2009). Punctuated Equilibrium in Comparative Perspective. *American Journal of Political Science,* 53: 603–20.

Baumgartner, F. R., Carammia, M., Epp, D. A. et al. (2017). Budgetary Change in Authoritarian and Democratic Regimes. *Journal of European Public Policy,* 24 (6): 792–808.

Boda, Z. and Patkós, V. (2015). Driven by Politics: Agenda Setting and Policy-Making in Hungary, 2010–2014. In *8th Annual CAP Conference.* Lisbon.

Bozóki, A. (2015). Broken Democracy, Predatory State, and Nationalist Populism. In *The Hungarian Patient: Social Opposition to an Illiberal Democracy*, ed. P. Krasztev and J. Van Til. Budapest: The CEU Press, 3–36.

Huntington, S. P. (1991). Democracy's Third Wave. *Journal of Democracy*, 2: 12–34.

Korkut, U. (2012). *Liberalization Challenges in Hungary: Elitism, Progressivism, and Populism*. Basingstoke: Palgrave Macmillan.

Körösényi, A. (2015). A magyar demokrácia három szakasza és az Orbán-rezsim (The Three Phases of Hungarian Democracy and the Orbán Regime). In *A magyar politikai rendszer—negyedszázad után (The Hungarian Political System—A Reappraisal after Twenty-Five Years)*, ed. A. Körösényi. Budapest: Osiris and MTA TK PTI, 401–22.

Sebők, M. and Berki, T. (2017). Incrementalism and Punctuated Equilibrium in Hungarian Budgeting (1991–2013). *Journal of Public Budgeting, Accounting and Financial Management*, 29: 151–80.

Sebők, M., Kubik, B., and Molnár, C. (2017). Exercising Control and Gathering Information: The Functions of Interpellations in Hungary (1990–2014). *Journal of Legislative Studies*, 23(4): 465–83.

12

The Israeli Agendas Project

Nir Kosti, Ilana Shpaizman, and David Levi-Faur

12.1 Introduction

The Israeli Agendas Project was launched in 2012 at the Hebrew University of Jerusalem in order to contribute to the analysis of issue attention and policy dynamics from a regulatory governance perspective. The Project's main aim is to understand how and why regulations and primary law vary in number, content, and purpose over time and across issues and countries. This should help to better understand the conditions under which there is an increase in regulatory output. Regulation has become a core concept of governments in the last few decades, yet too little attention has been paid to the questions of how, when, and where regulatory output is growing. By shedding light on longitudinal and cross-national analyses of the study of regulations, as assessed quantitatively via official gazettes, we aim to open a new research agenda on the different national patterns of regulations. We seek to understand whether national dynamics and clear national differences exist across different countries regarding the bureaucratic activity and agenda. Since 2014, the Project's aim has been expanded to examine changes in the Israeli agenda in the executive branch, focusing on cabinet decisions.

12.2 The Israeli Political System

Israel was established in 1948 as a parliamentary democracy. It is a unitary system, and the unicameral parliament is composed of 120 members. The president is the official head of state and his role is mainly symbolic, without substantive executive responsibilities. On the constitutional level, Israel does not have a formal written constitution. However, although it does not have an official constitution, it has several constitutional laws that are known as "basic laws." Their superior status over ordinary laws gives the Supreme Court the right to act in any case where ordinary law conflicts with what follows from basic laws.

One of the basic laws ("The Knesset" 1958) that holds special standing in the Israeli legal framework is the law that provides for general, free, equal, discrete, direct, and proportional elections to be held every four years. In Israel, every Israeli citizen over age 18 is eligible to vote in the general elections. Members of the Knesset (Israeli parliament) are elected by national and proportional elections with a 3.25 percent electoral threshold.

The party system is composed of left-wing, right-wing, and center-wing parties as well as sectoral parties representing various segments of the population, such as immigrants from the former Soviet Union, ultraorthodox Jews and Arabs. Until the mid-1970s, the party system was dominated by the Labor Party. Since then leadership for most of the period has transferred to the right and to the Likud Party. At the same time the effective number of parties has grown significantly since the 1990s, as the number of parliamentary seats held by the first- and second-biggest parties has declined steadily. During the Israeli legislative election in 2015, the Likud and the Zionist Union (a center-left political alliance of the Labor Party and two other parties), the two biggest parties, won nearly 40 percent of the votes. Thus, in the Israeli party system, the power of small parties is greater than their actual size. As a result, the size of the left/right blocs determine the ability of a prime minister to compose a coalition, rather than the size of his/her own party.

12.3 Datasets

Table 12.1 presents the various datasets of the Israeli Agendas Project. As shown, it consists of both the regulatory and legislative agenda in Israel over long periods.

Table 12.1. Datasets of the Israeli Agendas Project

Dataset	Period covered	Main topic/subtopic	N
Laws	1948–2014	Main topic	6,841
Arrangement laws	1985–2013	Main topic and subtopic	1,375
Regulations	1948–2014	Main topic	49,396
Cabinet decisions	2003–2016	Main topic and subtopic	3,985

Source: Comparative Agendas Project—Israel

12.3.1 Laws and Regulations

The datasets of laws and regulations provide a longitudinal perspective on the Israeli regulatory and legislative agenda, and provide us with a better understanding of corresponding legislature and bureaucratic agendas. The former dataset includes the numbered list of primary laws that the Knesset (i.e., Israeli parliament) legislated annually over sixty-seven years. It provides a comprehensive glance at the legislative production of the Knesset, which has risen significantly since the 1990s. The dataset includes both new legislation and amending acts that were published in the "Sefer Hahukim" ("Book of Laws"). It also contains laws that are in force together with laws that were canceled or expired. Moreover, all types of primary laws—whether initiated by the government (government bills), members of Knesset (private members' bills), or by a Knesset committee—are included.

A complimentary dataset of the Israeli legislative agenda covers all arrangement laws ("Hesderim Laws") that were enacted between 1985 and 2013. The arrangement law is an omnibus legislation package that was first enacted in 1985 as part of the Economic Stabilization Plan. Since then, the arrangement law has been reenacted annually along with the annual budget. It includes many amendments to existing legislation in various policy fields. It is a tool that the cabinet uses in order to promote rapid policy changes. Our dataset includes 1,375 articles of all the arrangement laws.

The secondary legislation ("Takanot Mishene") dataset includes regulations, by-laws, orders, instructions, proclamations, notices, and rules that were published annually in the "Kovetz Hatakanot" (Collection of Regulations) since 1948. It provides a thorough perspective on the regulatory output of the Israeli bureaucracy, as it includes almost 50,000 regulations. Unlike the previous dataset, it was not coded entirely. Two blind coders coded a random sample of 8,231 regulations between 1948 and 2014 out of 49,396 regulations systematically (k = 6), ensuring coverage of the whole period.

12.3.2 Cabinet Decisions

Cabinet decisions are made in all parliamentary democracies. They contain proposals approved by the cabinet as a whole during the weekly cabinet meetings. Once the proposal is approved, it becomes binding. In Israel, each year the cabinet makes about five hundred decisions. In these decisions, the cabinet uses a broad policy tool kit. It can set up a new program, for example, a program encouraging the return of Israelis who emigrated from Israel. It may change regulations, for example, a decision to reduce the regulatory burden on businesses. It may allocate funding, for example, a decision to allocate funding to the municipality of Tel Aviv to support day care for immigrant children.

It may also appoint committees, such as a committee for the investigation of the fire on Mount Carmel in 2010. The decisions are made during the entire cabinet term—even when the Knesset is dismissed due to elections—and they involve all policy fields.

The cabinet decision dataset includes decisions made from 2003 through 2016. Besides information on the policy topic, the data includes information on the policy tools suggested in the decision (i.e., new program, budget appropriation, omnibus legislation, change in authority, and others). It also includes information about the relationship of each decision to previous decisions (for example, amending or expanding previous decisions), as well as to legislation and Supreme Court ruling. Lastly, in each decision, one or more responsible ministries are specified. This way we can examine not only the change in the policy agendas but also the change in the policy tools and the responsible institutions.

12.4 An Example: The Arrangement Law (The Hesderim Law)

The arrangement law has become one of the Israeli government's most powerful policy tools in recent decades, allowing the promotion of extensive reforms and decisions every year. Originally, it was presented as an emergency measure to supplement the Economic Stabilization Program in 1985. Since then it has become a permanent component of the budget law, comprising various bills and amendments that are needed in order to achieve the government's economic policy. As an omnibus law, each law consists of varying amounts of new legislation and amendments that are presented to the Knesset within the framework of single law. By relying on its majority and discipline among coalition members, the law has become a governmental device that enables the expediting of the legislative process while being subject to limited parliamentary and public supervision due to its size and complexity.

Since Israel's multiparty coalition's instability and fragility have been on the rise in recent decades, the use of the law has become a vital tool to promote the government's goals and agendas. Bills and amendments regarding various issues that were clearly non-economic have been included in the laws, and a fierce criticism within the Knesset and among the public has been raised. Academic researchers have not systemically investigated this trend. Many researchers applied a conventional method to assess the expansion of the laws by observing the number of articles per laws. However, we argued that a better understanding can be attained by taking an agenda-setting perspective. In other words, rather than focusing on the scope of

Figure 12.1. Arrangement laws by the number of topics and subtopics, 1985–2013
Source: Comparative Agendas Project—Israel

each law, we suggested investigating the expansion of the laws by observing the amount of topics each law contains.

Figure 12.1 shows the number of policy issues included within each arrangement law that were enacted based on the codification of each article by main topic and subtopic. The figure suggests that over the years a significant fluctuation has occurred in the laws' agenda—from four and five main topics and corresponding subtopics in 1985 to a peak of sixteen main topics and forty subtopics in 2003. It also reveals 1997 to be the turning point in the expansion of the laws. Before 1997, most of the articles in the laws dealt with macroeconomic issues. Since 1997, the laws have included less macroeconomic issues and have expanded to other issues. This can be seen by observing the expansion of main topics and subtopics in Figure 12.1.

12.5 Unique Features of the Israeli Coding Procedure

The coding of the Israeli agendas creates several challenges that are unique to the Israeli politics: state and religion, diaspora Jews, the Holocaust, and the occupied territories.

First, in Israel there is no formal and full separation between state and religion. Consequently, religion plays a significant role in Israeli politics, policy, and society. From an institutional perspective, this results in a special ministry for religious affairs, local religious councils and rabbis appointed by the state, and religious courts that have exclusive authority over marriage and divorce. In addition, the government intervenes in individuals' religious affairs—for example, by regulating kosher food, subsidizing religious institutions, and regulating the conversion-to-Judaism process. Despite this uniqueness, we decided that all of these issues can be coded using the CAP scheme once the policy content is examined, regardless of its religious context. For example, religious marriages will be coded under family issues, and the administration of religious councils will be coded under government affairs. Yet one should remember that applying CAP coding to issues of state and religion only allows us to trace changes in issue attention, not changes in the power of religious institutions in Israeli politics. This shortcoming is by no means unique to Israel, since the CAP coding scheme addresses the policy content and not the policy tools or target population.

Second, Israel is defined as the national home of Jewish people, and as such it sees itself as a home to all Jews around the world. As a result, the Israeli government makes policy regarding diaspora Jews. For example, the Israeli government makes programs for increasing the connection of Jewish youth to Israel and increasing efforts to encourage Jews to immigrate to Israel. Since "Diaspora Jews" are the target population, we coded these issues based on the content. For example, immigration encouragement programs are coded under immigration and programs for Diaspora Jews are coded under tourism. In addition, we also added a separate subtopic of Jewish immigration under the immigration topic to reflect the uniqueness of this issue in Israeli politics.

Third, the Holocaust is a defining issue in Israeli society. During the first few decades following the establishment of the state of Israel, the Holocaust played an important role in Israeli politics. For example, in the 1950s, the reparations agreement between Israel and West Germany sparked one of the most controversial disputes that Israeli politics has ever known. Today, while the Holocaust receives less attention from Israeli politicians, we decided to follow the topic by adding a dummy variable.

Fourth, the West Bank has a special legal status and is not officially appended to the state of Israel. As such, there are special policies that are made regarding this area and its population. Due to this fact we decided that policies dealing specifically with the West Bank will be coded under topic 2105.

Reference

"Basic Laws: 'The Knesset'" Knesset official website: www.knesset.gov.il/description/eng/eng-mimshal_yesod1.htm (English).

13

The Italian Agendas Project

Enrico Borghetto, Marcello Carammia, and Federico Russo

Because of its particular features and for its capacity to alternate stability and radical transformations, the Italian political system has traditionally been a source of interest for researchers and practitioners alike. This chapter provides a brief overview of the main characteristics and turning points of the Italian Republic, illustrates the Italian datasets contributed to the CAP database so far, and provides a simple illustration of how CAP data can be used to investigate key aspects of the Italian political system.

13.1 The Italian Political System

In 1946, after the end of World War II, Italian citizens voted in a popular referendum to replace the monarchy with a republican democracy. In 1948 the new Italian Constitution entered into force, designing a parliamentary form of government with a rather weak executive and a redundant bicameral system. One of the main peculiarities of this system was the necessity for governments to win a confirmatory confidence vote in both the Chamber of Deputies and in the Senate before taking full powers (Russo, 2015). With regard to the electoral system, a proportional rule with preference votes was adopted for both chambers.

From 1948 to 1993, the Italian party system did not experience major changes: Christian-Democracy (DC) was always the leader of the governing coalitions, and the Communist Party (PCI) the main opposition party. However, Italian membership of the North Atlantic Treaty Organization (NATO) was not compatible with a governing role of the communists: accordingly, all other parties formed coalitions to prevent that possibility. The medium-sized Socialist Party (PSI) remained in opposition until the early 1960s, but then joined forces with the DC and entered the governing

coalitions. A set of smaller parties (from left to right: social democrats, republicans, liberals) alternated in government as junior partners of the Christian
Democrats. Finally, the small neo-fascist party (MSI) was always excluded
from the governing coalitions because its democratic credentials were not
trusted by the other parties.

To understand the pre-1993 Italian political system it is essential to consider
that, although pivotal to the system, the DC was an extremely factionalized
party in which factions were united by their anti-communism but ideologic-
ally distant on the left–right axis. In summary, both the constitutional design
and the fragmentation of the party system dispersed power among several
actors and institutional veto-players to form what has been defined as a
system of "bargained pluralism" (Hine, 1993). It is worth noting that in this
period the average cabinet duration was about eleven months.

The post-war party system collapsed at the beginning of the 1990s due to
the combined effect of the disappearance of the communist threat, the disclosure of a pervasive network of corrupt exchanges between the main political parties and the business community (the Clean Hands investigation), and
a severe economic crisis that undermined the capacity of governing parties to
distribute particular benefits (Cotta and Isernia, 1996). By 1994, all three
major Italian parties (DC, PCI, PSI) had disappeared or changed name, while
new parties emerged to contest the status quo, most notably the regionalist
anti-immigration Northern League and "Go Italy" founded by the media
tycoon Silvio Berlusconi.

In the same years, the idea that the proportional electoral rule was partly
responsible for maintaining fragmentation and instability in the Italian political system gained increasing popularity (Katz, 2001). After two referenda
held in 1991 and 1993 to repeal parts of the existing electoral system, the
parliament introduced a mixed-member system in which 75 percent of the
seats were allocated in Single-Member Districts with plurality vote and 25
percent through proportional representation. In 2005 this system was
replaced by a proportional representation system with a majority bonus cor-
rection for both the Chamber of Deputies and the Senate. Both systems
strongly encouraged the formation of pre-electoral coalitions.

From 1994 to 2013, Italy experienced alternation in government between
centre-left and centre-right coalitions (for a comprehensive account see
Almagisti et al., 2014). In the six general elections that were held in this period,
several leaders alternated at the helm of the centre-left coalition, while the centre-
right was always led by Silvio Berlusconi. The average duration of governments
increased from eleven to nineteen months, and executive agenda-setting
powers became stronger vis-à-vis other institutions. Although the Constitution
remained largely unaltered, commentators refer to the post-1994 period as the
"Second Republic."

Other features of the "First Republic," however, proved more resilient. The legislative process remained dysfunctional, as evidenced by the executive's abnormal reliance on decree laws, delegated legislation, and confidence motions to implement its legislative agenda (Kreppel, 2009). Furthermore, the party system continued to be polarized and fragmented. Moreover, party switching became endemic as parties did not prove to be capable of consolidating their organizational machine.

The unfinished transition (Morlino, 2013) from the First to the Second Republic was exposed, once again, at the beginning of the 2010s by the joint occurrence of a financial crisis, corruption scandals, and international instability. The 2013 elections following the technocratic government led by Mario Monti saw the unexpected success of the anti-establishment Five Star Movement, and crisis in the mainstream parties such as the Democratic Party and Go Italy as they struggled to redefine their leadership and ideological profile.

13.2 Codebook and Datasets

All Italian datasets have been coded using both the CAP Master Codebook and the Italian agendas codebook (which contains 21 major and 239 minor topics). The latter includes a few additional minor topic codes to take into account some specificities of the Italian case. These country-specific codes capture issues related to freedom of religion (and more general matters related to relationships between the state and religious organizations) or references to criminal organizations (such as the Sicilian Mafia or the Camorra of Naples). Moreover, a number of immigration-related and culture-specific minor topics were created under major topics 9 and 23, respectively.

All documents were coded by two trained coders. Cases where the coders disagreed were discussed and solved jointly with one of the three principal investigators. At present, the Italian Policy Agendas Project includes six datasets (see Table 13.1). In four cases, the time span of the datasets encompasses the last legislative terms of the First and about two decades of the Second Republic.[1] This time frame allows us to inspect, through the lenses of issue attention, to what extent this transition resulted in change or continuity in party competition and policymaking processes.

Party manifestos represent our indicator of party priorities.[2] In total, forty-nine manifesto documents were analyzed covering all the significant parties that contested Italian parliamentary elections between 1983 and 2008 (the parliamentary term ending in 2013). The text of each manifesto was broken down into quasi-sentences (logically autonomous sections of a sentence),

Table 13.1. Datasets of the Italian Agendas Project

Dataset (unit of analysis)	Period covered	No. of observations	Source
Party manifestos (quasi-sentences)	1983–2008 (9th–16th legislature)	39,268	Every electoral manifesto available in an election
Investiture speeches (quasi-sentences)	1979–2014 (8th–17th legislature)	12,910	Every speech made by a candidate prime minister before the investiture vote
Parliamentary questions (every tabled question)	1997–2014 (13th–17th legislature)	4,317	Every oral question to the cabinet asked on the floor
Primary laws (every adopted act)	1983–2013 (9th–16th legislature)	4,555	Italian Law-Making Archive
Legislative decrees (every adopted act)	1988–2013 (10th–16th legislature)	1,267	Italian Law-Making Archive
Budget (yearly spending per category)	1990–2012	897	Eurostat

Source: Comparative Agendas Project—Italy

which were taken as the unit of analysis and assigned content-specific codes. This resulted in a dataset of more than 42,000 quasi-sentences, about 39,000 of which were coded by policy content.

The cabinet agenda is captured through the quasi-sentence coding of Italian investiture speeches (Borghetto et al., 2017).[3] After being appointed by the president of the Republic, every candidate prime minister is required to deliver a speech in front of both houses and to secure a vote of confidence on both occasions before officially taking office. In part, these declarations contain a political analysis of the events leading to the cabinet investiture; in part they set officially and publicly (these are highly mediatized events) the cabinet agenda for the rest of the mandate. The time horizon of cabinets can vary and this affects the content of speeches. Some are delivered at the beginning of the five-year parliamentary term (first government formation after the elections) and are normally longer and wider in scope. Others follow a coalition crisis and the withdrawal of confidence by the parliament. In such circumstances, the Constitution allows the president of the Republic to explore the feasibility of new parliamentary coalitions before calling for early elections. Historically, political forces often preferred these "parliamentary" solutions, so it has been rather common to have cabinet reshuffles and new investiture votes during the same legislative term. The agenda scope and diversity of the cabinet agendas is affected by the time frame.

Among the many available documents apt for measuring the parliamentary agenda, we opted for the Italian question time,[4] officially referred to as "parliamentary questions with immediate answer" (*interrogazioni a risposta immediata*).[5]

The question time is generally held once a week on Wednesdays and, depending on the topic of the tabled questions, it envisages the intervention of either the president/vice-president of the Council or the minister/s in charge of the portfolio under debate. Each parliamentary group is allowed one question per session, so this can be considered a party-driven activity. The questioner has the obligation to submit the question in writing one day in advance through the president of his/her parliamentary group. Questions are expected to be concise (less than a minute) and to address a topic of general interest. The cabinet representative is allowed a three-minute answer, followed by a two-minute response from the questioner.

Similarly to other CAP teams, primary laws were among the first documents to be coded.[6] Two types of legislative acts were considered. First, we coded all primary laws adopted by the Italian parliament. Bills can be introduced by the cabinet, any MP, at least 50,000 voters, the National Council of the Economy and Labor or by Regional Councils. In order for a bill to become law, both Chambers have to agree on an identically worded text. Bills can be adopted either on the floor plenary (ordinary procedure) or at the committee level (abbreviated procedure). The second procedure cannot be invoked for specific categories of laws[7] and can be called off by the government, by 10 percent of deputies, or by a fifth of committee members, which results in the bill going back to the ordinary legislative procedure. The president of the Republic has to sign each adopted law before it can enter into force. In case of presidential veto, the act has to go through a new parliamentary review and adoption process. If the bill is approved a second time, the president is obliged to promulgate it. Ordinary acts vary extensively in terms of content and political saliency. Laws ratifying international treaties are usually adopted without generating much debate in parliament. Other acts present themselves as complex and heterogeneous texts regulating a variety of policy areas (they are also referred to as "omnibus laws"). In these cases—representing a small proportion of the totality—we scanned the whole text and selected the code capturing the most prominent policy area regulated by the act.

According to article 76 of the Constitution, the parliament can decide to authorize the cabinet to legislate in a particular area for a defined period. These delegating acts are adopted through the ordinary procedure and can contain more than one delegation (Borghetto 2018). The decrees passed by the cabinet (legislative decrees) have the force of primary laws and do not need formal approval from parliament before being submitted to the attention of the president for their promulgation. Because of their sheer number and importance (primarily as instruments used for the legal adaptation to EU law and for passing important structural reforms), we opted for the codification of all legislative decrees issued since 1988.[8] Besides those acts adopted through the ordinary legislative procedure, the dataset comprises three other categories of "special" legislation: laws converting decree-laws,[9] Constitutional laws,[10] and budget laws.[11]

With regard to budgetary data, at present the Italian team relies on public expenditure data collected by Eurostat (1990–2012), the official statistical office of the European Union.[12] These figures are communicated on a yearly basis from the Italian Statistical Institute and harmonized to be comparable at the European level. The dataset contains yearly data on public expenditure at the general government level (defined as total payments recorded in the annual final balance of payments) categorized according to the COFOG system (classification of the functions of government) developed in 1999 by the Organisation for Economic Co-operation and Development. Data are expressed at current prices but a deflator is reported to adjust for inflation. The COFOG scheme classifies expenditures on the basis of their objective: it is a three-level classification with ten divisions at the first level and sixty groups at the second level. Levels are further divided into multiple classes, but these data are not available for the Italian case. The ten divisions are: general public services; defense; public order and safety; economic affairs; environment protection; housing and community amenities; health; recreation, culture, and religion; education; social protection.

13.3 Specificities and Perspectives

The Italian political system is sometimes regarded as eccentric, if not fully chaotic. And yet, it has attracted the attention of a wide international scholarship and has been the subject of studies that have developed seminal notions—for example, on political cultures (Banfield, 1967) or social capital (Putnam et al., 1994). The intrinsic relevance of the Italian case is certainly due to the complexity of its political and social history, but also to the Italian tendency to anticipate certain patterns and changes. Take—just to mention some recent examples—the mediatization and personalization of politics, the crisis of mainstream parties, and the advent of anti-establishment and populist parties as key actors in the political game.

In addition to its intrinsic interest, the developments of the last few decades made the Italian case particularly relevant to the understanding of the consequences of broad processes of political change. Few established democracies have recently experienced a comparable radical change in political institutions and party systems. Although not codified in a constitutional revision (and arguably unfinished, see Morlino, 2013 and Russo, 2015) the experience of within-democracy transition from the "First" to the "Second" Republic is a real laboratory of political change. In this respect CAP data are uniquely well placed to analyze the quasi-experimental Italian context and empirically observe the effects of political change (see Borghetto et al., 2018).

Drawing on the Italian CAP dataset, recent studies have started addressing questions about the effect of the introduction of alternation in power on the congruence between party electoral priorities and government legislative outputs (Borghetto et al., 2014); the consequences of the shift from post- to pre-electoral coalitions on the composition of the priorities of the coalition (Borghetto and Carammia, 2015); the policy content of the question time (Russo and Cavalieri, 2016), and the relation between party priorities and public-spending changes (Russo and Verzichelli, 2016). Drawing on Borghetto et al. (2014), Figure 13.1 provides a simplified illustration of a possible application of CAP data to the study of Italy. The bar graph shows the correlation between the policy agendas declared by political parties during election campaigns (based on party manifesto data) and the legislative agendas implemented by those parties during their term in government; and it observes such correlations over the last two terms of the First Republic and the first two terms of the Second Republic.

As Figure 13.1 shows, such correlation is consistently higher during the Second Republic terms observed, which seems to indicate an increased agenda effect of the policy priorities declared during election campaigns. This would

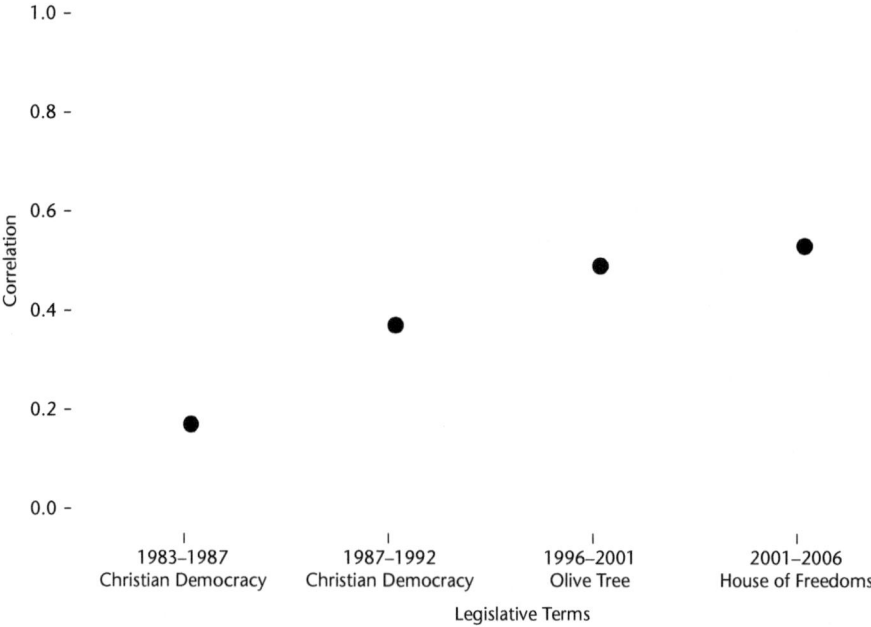

Figure 13.1. Correlation between electoral manifestos and legislative agendas
Source: Comparative Agendas Project—Italy

be consistent with the changed incentives provided by the introduction of alternation in government. Things are probably more complicated than that. It is questionable whether the degree of correlation reached in the Second Republic marks a clear shift toward "mandate politics" (Borghetto et al., 2014); and a focus on opposition parties shows that their agenda-setting power also increased (Carammia et al., 2018). This, however, only shows a need for further research, and the potential contribution of CAP data to provide new answers to old questions about Italian politics and comparative politics at large.

Notes

1. Oral questions to the cabinet have been institutionalized since 1993. A major reform occurred in 1997, so for the sake of longitudinal comparability we started coding questions only since this date.
2. Manifestos were coded at the University of Catania under the supervision of Marcello Carammia.
3. Speeches were jointly coded by Enrico Borghetto, Francesco Visconti, and Marco Michieli.
4. Data were retrieved from dati.camera.it and coded under the supervision of Federico Russo at the University of Siena.
5. Only question time in the lower house (Chamber of Deputies) was coded and examined. The Rules of Procedure of the Senate introduced a procedure named in the same way, but the content of the questions is predetermined by the conference of party group leaders.
6. The coding was carried out at the University of Milan as part of a wider project named "Italian Law-Making Archive" (ILMA). ILMA is a web database facilitating access to Italian legislative data for research purposes (Borghetto et al., 2012).
7. These include electoral laws, constitutional laws, laws ratifying international treaties, budget laws, and delegating legislation.
8. Law 400/1988 disciplined their adoption procedure and distinguished them from other executive acts.
9. Decree-laws can be adopted by the executive in case of "extraordinary urgency" (Article 77 Constitution). They enter into force on the day of their issuance. Their validity expires after sixty days if, in this interval, they are not converted into law by the parliament through an executive-sponsored act.
10. Laws amending the Constitution have to be passed through an aggravated procedure (Article 138 Constitution).
11. Budget laws are presented by the executive and discussed, amended, and approved in the autumn of each year by the parliament according to a tight schedule (Article 81 Constitution).
12. An alternative dataset covering a longer period (1948–2009), but with much less detailed categories, is available form Russo and Verzichelli (2016).

References

Almagisti, M., Lanzalaco, L., and Verzichelli, L. (eds) (2014). *La transizione politica italiana: Da Tangentopoli a oggi*. Rome: Carocci editore.

Banfield, E. C. (1967). *Moral Basis of a Backward Society*. New York: Free Press.

Borghetto, E., and Carammia, M. (2015). Party Priorities, Government Formation and the Making of The Executive Agenda. In *The Challenge of Coalition Government: The Italian Case*, ed. N. Conti and F. Marangoni. Abingdon: Routledge, 36–57.

Borghetto, E., Carammia, M., and Russo, F. (2018). Policy agendas in Italy. Special issue of the *Italian Political Science Review*, 3, 48.

Borghetto, E., Carammia, M., and Zucchini, F. (2014). The Impact of Party Policy Priorities on Italian Lawmaking: From the First to the Second Republic, 1983–2006. In *Agenda Setting, Policies, and Political Systems: A Comparative Approach.*, ed. C. Green-Pedersen and S. Walgrave. Chicago: University of Chicago Press, 164–82.

Borghetto, E., Curini, L., Giuliani, M. et al. (2012). Italian Law-Making Archive: A New Tool for the Analysis of the Italian Legislative Process. *Rivista italiana di scienza politica*, 42(3): 481–502.

Borghetto, E., Visconti, F., and Michieli, M. (2017). Government Agenda-Setting in Italian Coalitions: Testing the "Partisan Hypothesis" Using Italian Investiture Speeches 1979–2014. *Rivista Italiana Di Politiche Pubbliche*, 2: 193–220.

Carammia, M., Borghetto, E., and Bevan, S. (2018). Changing the Transmission Belt. The Programme-to-Policy Link in Italy between the First and Second Republic. *Italian Political Science Review* 48, 3: 275–288.

Cotta, M., and Isernia, P. (1996). *Il Gigante dai piedi di argilla: la crisi del regime partitocratico in Italia*. Bologna: Il Mulino.

Hine, D. (1993). *Governing Italy: The Politics of Bargained Pluralism*. Oxford: Clarendon Press.

Katz, R. S. (2001). Reforming the Italian Electoral Law, 1993. In *Mixed-Member Electoral Systems: The Best of Both Worlds*, ed. M. Soberg Shugart and M. P. Wattenberg. Oxford: Oxford University Press, 96–122.

Kreppel, A. (2009). Executive-Legislative Relations and Legislative Agenda Setting in Italy: From Leggine to Decreti and Deleghe. *Bullettin of Italian Politics*, 1(2): 183–209.

Morlino, L. (2013). The Impossible Transition and the Unstable New Mix: Italy 1992–2012. *Comparative European Politics*, 11(3): 337–59.

Putnam, R. D., Leonardi, R., and Nanetti, R. Y. (1994). *Making Democracy Work: Civic Traditions in Modern Italy*. Princeton: Princeton University Press.

Russo, F. (2015). Bicameral Investiture: Parliament and Government Formation in Italy. In *Parliaments and Government Formation: Unpacking Investiture Rules*, ed. J. A. Cheibub, M. Shane, and B. E. Rasch. Oxford: Oxford University Press, 136–52.

Russo, F., and Cavalieri, A. (2016). The Policy Content of the Italian Question Time: A New Dataset to Study Party Competition. *Rivista Italiana Di Politiche Pubbliche*, (2): 197–222.

Russo, F., and Verzichelli, L. (2016). Government Ideology and Party Priorities: The Determinants of Public Spending Changes in Italy. *Italian Political Science Review*, 46(3): 269–90.

14

The Dutch Policy Agendas Project

Arco Timmermans and Gerard Breeman

The Dutch Policy Agendas Project was initiated in the summer of 2006, shortly after an ECPR workshop on agenda-setting organized by Christoffer Green-Pedersen and Arco Timmermans in April 2006 in Nicosia, Cyprus. Since then, the project has been directed by Gerard Breeman and Arco Timmermans, and it moved from coding national executive agendas to the agendas of political parties, the legislature, the media, local executives, and party think tanks.

A central characteristic of the Dutch Agendas Project's approach is its explicit combination of quantitative and qualitative methods. Besides quantitatively mapping and explaining the up-and-down patterns of the policy agendas over time, we want to put meaning to these patterns for both academics and practitioners. As we will illustrate at the end of this chapter, we analyzed, for instance, how the development of attention to security issues in the past twenty-five years revealed that the securitization agenda is the result of both proactive long-term policy investment and short-term reactive policy decisions with a crisis element in them.

14.1 The Dutch Political System and Agenda-Setting

The Dutch parliament (Staten-Generaal) consists of a first and a second chamber. The 150 members of the second chamber are directly elected based on proportional representation. There is just one national electoral district and there is practically no electoral threshold, which means that small parties can easily enter the second chamber. After the general elections of 2017, there were thirteen parties in the second chamber. The seventy-five members of the first chamber, the Senate, are elected indirectly. Contrary to senates in many other countries, the Dutch Senate cannot formally propose or amend legislation, but only accept or reject.

Thus far it has always been necessary to form a coalition government, which typically works with a written coalition agreement that forms the political agenda of the government, and which usually also commits the supporting parties in the second chamber. Traditionally, the three large parties are the center-left PvdA (Labor; social-democrat), the centrist CDA (Christian-democrat) and the center-right VVD (liberal-conservative). Since 2000 new parties have entered the stage, of which most notably are the party for the elderly, the animal rights party ("Partij voor de Dieren"), and the provocative anti-Muslim and anti-EU party PVV (party of freedom) led by Geert Wilders.

The traditional Dutch model of consensus (Lijphart, 1968) has come under pressure. Despite mechanisms of coalition governance such as written coalition policy agreements and arenas for political conflict management, the branches of parties in government have become more exposed to leadership battles. Traditional political parties experience function loss, and the politicization of issues such as immigration and the European Union has turned out to be a fruitful activity for populist parties. In this development, new institutional mechanisms of representation and interest representation are employed, such as referenda and negotiations with social and economic stakeholders in order to extend the basis of societal support for government policies.

14.2 Datasets and Coding Procedures

In the Netherlands, institutional friction plays an important part in coalition politics, and the Dutch Policy Agendas' datasets cover all the "stages," of the policy cycle, from input agendas to output. Table 14.1 presents the datasets developed in the Netherlands.

In 2016, the codebook and Dutch datasets were adjusted to come into line with the international CAP coding scheme. The Dutch codebook thus contains twenty major topic categories and each of these is further subdivided into more detailed subtopics, in total 226 subtopics. All datasets are constructed with historically consistent topic categories that do not change over time. We paid attention to coding items consistently in terms of the framing of the policy topics at the time they appeared on the agenda.

The datasets were constructed by trained human coders applying consistent definitions of the content categories across the entire historical period and across all the data sources. Coding was done by at least two coders independently and checked for intercoder reliability (minimal 95 percent on main topic and 80 percent on subtopic level). After the training phase we had weekly or

Table 14.1. Overview of datasets of the Dutch Agenda-Setting Projects

Dataset	Period covered	Unit of analysis	N
Speeches from the throne	1945–2015	Quasi-sentence	9,855
Coalition agreements	1963–2012	Paragraph	5,391
Bills (legislative proposals)	1981–2009	Bill	6,574
Laws (adopted in parliament)	1981–2009	Law	6,574
Media:		Article (keywords)	
–Safety topics NRC	1990–2008		38,572
–Safety topics Telegraaf	1999–2008		9,723
–Environmental topics NRC	1990–2008		13,485
Publications of the Environmental and Nature Planning Agency (MNP) and the National Institute for Health and Environment (RIVM) (Both are scientific advisory agencies on the environment (topic 7)).	1990–2006	Publications	848
Local executive policy agendas (local coalition agreements)	1986–2014	Paragraphs	8,657
Election programs of national political parties	1981–2012	Paragraphs	45,528
Policy agendas of think tanks related to political parties	2000–2011	Reports and articles	3,612
Questions from parliament to the government (*vragenuurtje*)	1984–2009	Question	1,507
Interpellation debates (*spoeddebatten*)	2004–2009*	Topic of the issue	247
Introductory section to the budget of the minister of the interior	1985–2008	Paragraph	4,972

Note: *1 April 2004–31 March 2009.
Source: Comparative Agendas Project—Netherlands

bi-weekly meetings to discuss the problematic cases. Consistency with other Agendas Projects was achieved through frequent contact with other project leaders (especially Denmark, France, and Spain).

14.3 Description of Datasets

Questions from parliament to a minister (vragenuurtje). Every Tuesday afternoon at 2 p.m., individual members of parliament invite ministers to the parliament to question them about a certain topic. Usually the MPs refer in their question to an issue that obtained media attention, which is a variable in the dataset. Please refer to Timmermans and Breeman (2010) when using this dataset.

Interpellation debates (spoeddebatten). This small dataset contains all extraordinary debates considered urgent, for which endorsement of at least thirty members of the second chamber is required.

Coalition agreements. Coalition agreements between the political parties who won the general elections are important policy agendas in the Netherlands. They contain the most important policy priorities and intentions of the coalition partners for the coming term in office. The discipline and enforcement when implementing items in the coalition agreement can be quite strong. Please refer to Timmermans and Breeman (2014) when using this dataset.

Local coalition agreements. This dataset contains local coalition agreement of six municipalities of different sizes in the Netherlands between 1986 and 2014. Refer to Breeman, Scholten, and Timmermans (2015) when using this dataset.

Speeches from the throne. The speech from the throne is delivered by the King (since 2013, before then the head of state was a Queen) on the third Tuesday of September at the opening of the budgetary year. The speech contains policy plans of the government (and it is written by the government) for the coming year, as well as a "state of the nation." The dataset includes variables for policy intentions (versus general statement about problems) also for references to the European Union or the international environment. For the use of this dataset, refer to Breeman et al. (2009).

Introductory section to the budget of the minister of the interior. This database was developed for the safety policy project described further below. It consists of the introductory paragraphs of government budgets, and thus can be seen as an indicator of more specific policy plans in the domain. Refer to Breeman, Timmermans, and Van Dalfsen (2011) when using this database.

Bills and laws dataset. This dataset contains all bills (*wetsvoorstel*) sent to parliament by the government and bills drafted by MPs (*initiatiefwet*). More than 95 percent of all bills are drafted by the government. Since agenda-setting is about raising attention to topics, we considered the date that a bill is sent to parliament as the agenda-setting moment. Separately available is a dataset containing all voting dates (in the second chamber) from 1995 to 2009. The dataset also contains the number of amendments per bill. For use of this dataset please refer to Timmermans and Breeman (2014).

Media datasets. The media datasets were constructed for two specific projects. One about the politics of attention of safety issues (commissioned by the Ministry of Internal Affairs) and the other about agenda-setting on environmental issues (commissioned by the Dutch parliament). The data are based on keywords searches in LexisNexis. The safety dataset contains thirteen different subtopics covering a variety of safety and security related issues—from juvenile delinquency to flooding. The environment dataset covers all subtopics of main topic category 7 (the environment). When using the safety database, refer to Breeman, Timmermans, and Dalfsen (2011), when using the environment database refer to Breeman, Dewulf, Pot, and Timmermans (2009).

Publications of the MNP and RIVM scientific agencies on the environment (topic 7). This small dataset includes all publications of two important advisory agencies to the government on the environment. It was developed for the project commissioned by the parliament. For this project we also subdivided some of the subcodes into more detailed subcodes. Refer to Breeman and Timmermans (2008) when using this dataset.

Election programs of national political parties. The electoral programs of the national political parties were content coded by Simon Otjes. The dataset contains over 45,000 observations for twenty-two parties in total that participated in ten successive parliamentary elections.

Policy agendas of think tanks affiliated to political parties. Party think tanks (*wetenschappelijke instituten*) advise party elites on strategic political decisions. We collected data for the four main party think tanks connected to parties with a governmental track record, namely CDA, PvdA, VVD, and D66 for the period 2000–11. Our measure for the agenda of party think tanks are articles included in their house journals (N=3,612). These journals are a main channel of expression of attention to policy themes and present views on them. We added a special code for capturing items addressing ideology and party principles rather than specific policy problems (refer to Timmermans, Van Rooyen, and Voerman (2015)).

14.4 Example: The Policy Agenda of Safety Issues

Our data collection was in part funded by public organizations that requested that we should carry out commissioned research on attention patterns and their underlying mechanisms. In 2012, the Ministry of Internal Affairs asked us to look at how and why the attention to safety issues diversified in the past decades. As our graphs of two coalition agreements show, the variety of topics the governments linked to safety issues increased considerably between 1977 and 2010 (Figure 14.1).

An important finding in our study was that attention to safety-related events and incidents only leads to major policy plans if politicians and policymakers link these events and incidents to longer-term trends. In this way, we were able to distinguish two types of cascading effects: a short-term cascading effect over incidents and a long-term cascading effect resulting in long-term policy plans.

In the first type, cascading occurs when different actors such as journalists, politicians, and experts respond quickly to each other about an incident. Characteristic of this type is that incidents are considered as a "stand-alone" event with no link to other phenomena. When the incident is cleared, the media and all other actors lose interest and shift their attention to other matters. Thus in this process, attention is temporal.

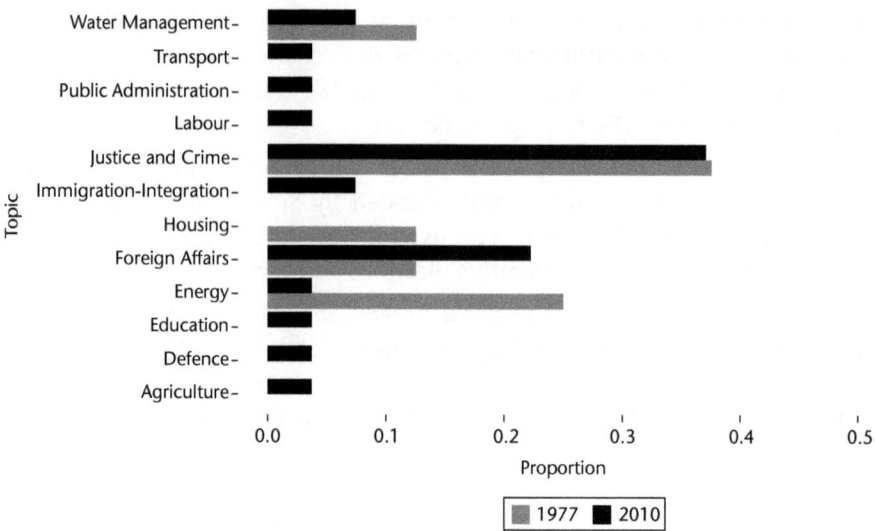

Figure 14.1. Attention to safety in policy domains—coalition agreement in 1977 and 2010

Source: Comparative Agendas Project—the Netherlands

The second type occurs when policymakers link different incidents with each other and consider these as part of a trend. A single incident does not usually lead to a major policy change. In our case studies of specific safety related issues we observed for instance how several youth crime incidents were linked to each other and were followed by a substantive policy program on immigrant integration. Once this policy program was put in place, incidents were more quickly connected to the observed trend and, as a self-reinforcing mechanism, these new incidents legitimized and strengthened the policy program. Thus, in this process, problem signals reinforced policy development.

References

Breeman, G., Dewulf, A., Pot, W., and Timmermans, A. (2009). Evolutie van het klimaatvraagstuk: agendadynamiek en framing van het klimaatprobleem in de media. Bestuurskunde, 18(4): 27–37.

Breeman, G., Scholten, P., and Timmermans, A. (2015). Analysing Local Policy Agendas: How Dutch Municipal Executive Coalitions Allocate Attention. *Local Government Studies*, 41(1): 20–43.

Breeman, G., and Timmermans, A. (2008). *Politiek van de aandacht voor milieubeleid*. Wageningen: Wot-rapport.

Breeman, G., Timmermans, A., and van Dalfsen, F. (2011). *Politiek van de aandacht voor het Nederlandse veiligheidsbeleid. Een onderzoek naar maatschappelijke dynamiek, politieke agendavorming en prioriteren in het Nederlandse veiligheidsstelsel*: Wageningen: Wageningen University Press.

Lijphart, A. (1968). *The Politics of Accommodation: Pluralism and Democracy in the Netherlands*. Berkeley: University of California Press.

Timmermans, A., and Breeman, G. (2014). The Policy Agenda in Multiparty Government: Coalition Agreements and Legislative Activity in the Netherlands. In *Agenda Setting, Policies and Political Systems: A Comparative Approach.*, ed. C. Green-Pedersen and S. Walgrave. Chicago: Chicago University Press, 86–104.

Timmermans, A., and Breeman, G. E. (2010). Politieke waarheid en dynamiek van de agenda in coalitiekabinetten. In *Jaarboek parlementaire Geschiedenis 2010: Waarheidsvinding en Waarheidsbeleving*, ed. C. v. Baalen, W. Breedveld, M. Leenders et al. Amsterdam: Boom, 47–62.

Timmermans, A., Rooyen, E. v., and Voerman, G. (2015). Policy Analysis and Political Party Think Tanks. In *Policy Analysis in The Netherlands*, ed. F. v. Nispen and P. Scholten. Chicago: University of Chicago Press.

15

The New Zealand Policy Agendas Project

Rhonda L. Evans

15.1 New Zealand's Political System

New Zealand comprises a set of small and geographically remote islands in the South Pacific. Today it has a population of nearly 4.7 million, with roughly 30 percent residing in and around the city of Auckland located on the North Island. Human habitation likely began around 1300 AD when people from Eastern Polynesia first reached the islands (Smith, 2012: 6–7). Their descendants, the Māori, know the country as *Aotearoa*, "land of the long white cloud." British colonization formally began in 1840 when the Crown and various Māori representatives signed the Treaty of Waitangi. Over the course of the twentieth century, New Zealand's position with respect to the United Kingdom evolved as the country's independence was recognized and most vestiges of its colonial status were removed. New Zealand has experienced profound political, economic, and societal change in recent decades. Electoral reforms have tempered its strongly majoritarian political system, neoliberal reforms have revolutionized its once highly protected and regulated economy, and immigration from Asian countries is leading New Zealand to consider how it will reconcile its bicultural identity with an increasingly multicultural society.

New Zealand followed the British example and adopted a Westminster system of representative government in 1852. Three key features of this system endure to this day. First, the country remains one of only three in the world to lack a written constitution, despite periodic calls that one should be adopted (Joseph, 2007: 135).[1] Second, the British monarch continues to serve as New Zealand's head of state, though the governor-general performs the largely ceremonial duties of the office, doing so on the advice of the country's democratically elected government in all but the most extraordinary circumstances. It seems unlikely that New Zealand will decide to adopt a republican form of government anytime soon. In 2011, 53.2 percent of those polled expressed support for the monarchy's retention (NZES, 2002–11). And finally, notwithstanding local government innovations to accommodate the burgeoning Auckland metropolitan area, New Zealand remains a unitary state in which local governments possess a "limited range of functions" and operate under "tight external and fiscal constraints" (Miller, 2015: 32).

As a result of electoral reform in the mid-1990s, New Zealand, once described as the world's "purest" Westminster system (Lijphart, 1984: 97), experienced "a radical shift away from the Westminster model" (Lijphart, 1999: 9–47). From 1914 to 1996, the country used a first-past-the-post (FPP) electoral system to elect members to its unicameral (since 1951) parliament.[2] This generated single-party governments with strong majorities. At a 1993 referendum, voters approved a proposal to replace FPP with a mixed-member proportional (MMP) system that affords voters two ballots, one for a single representative from the geographic electorate in which they reside (as under FPP) and another for a political party according to a closed party list (Vowles, 1998: 12–27). Using the Saint-Laguë method, the system operates to ensure that parties are allocated seats "roughly equivalent to their share of the party vote" (Miller, 2015: 88–94). In conjunction with the switch to MMP, the size of parliament was increased from 99 to 120 seats. The use of separate Māori-designated seats, a practice that dates from 1867, was retained. These seats have been gradually increased in number (Geddis, 2006), and today there are seven.

Since the first MMP election was held in 1996, two main consequences have followed. First, New Zealand's two-party system has evolved into a multi-party system, and second, no single party has won enough seats to form a majority government, though the center-right National Party came close in 2014. Scholars debate the magnitude of the change in New Zealand's party system. On one hand, Alan Ware (2009: 15) claims that the two-party system has "collapsed." Clearly, a wider range of political parties—among them the Green Party, Māori Party, and New Zealand First—routinely win parliamentary seats and play important roles in government. On the other hand, however, Raymond Miller (2015: 159) emphasizes the resiliency of the two major parties and characterizes the new multi-party system as "moderate" in nature. Consider that together the National Party and center-left Labour Party have, on average, received 71.3 percent of votes cast at the seven post-MMP elections. They have thus dominated the coalition and minority governments that have governed since 1996, and as a result, they continue to exert considerable control over the political agenda. Even so, the switch to MMP effected a significant change, depriving the executive of the "unbridled power" that it had once possessed (Palmer, 1979; Palmer and Palmer, 2004).

Two additional reforms merit mention. First, in 1990, New Zealand enacted a statutory bill of rights. The *New Zealand Bill of Rights Act* (NZBORA)

137

does not permit judges to invalidate contrary legislation, but rather judges are charged with interpreting laws in accordance with the Act's provisions.[3] In addition, the NZBORA requires the attorney-general (AG) to report to parliament on any bill that contains provisions that appear to be inconsistent with the Act's terms.[4] Such bills may nevertheless be enacted into law. As of March 2016, the AG has filed seventy such reports. A second reform was implemented in 2004 when the New Zealand Parliament abolished appeals to the Judicial Committee of the Privy Council, a London-based body and remnant of colonial governance, and established the New Zealand Supreme Court (NZSC) to serve as the country's final appellate tribunal. The NZSC sits in Wellington, the national capital, and is comprised of a chief justice and four to five other judges that are appointed by the AG (as are all other judges) through a consultative and largely non-partisan process. Although both reforms were very controversial at their inceptions, both the NZBORA and the NZSC have become accepted features of New Zealand's political system.

In the last decades of the twentieth century, New Zealand also revolutionized its economy. The Labour Party came to power at the 1984 election. It embarked on a program of dramatic economic reform that included deregulating the financial markets, dismantling trade barriers, discontinuing subsidies, instituting a goods and services tax, restructuring the public service, and transforming state assets into state-owned enterprises tasked with earning a profit (Smith, 2012: 218; Kelsey, 1997). As Jonathan Boston and Chris Eichbaum (2014: 374) observe, "few, if any, democratic countries have witnessed such widespread policy changes in such a short period of time." Subsequent governments have remained committed to the general contours of these reforms.

Finally, New Zealand society also changed significantly in recent decades. The Treaty of Waitangi attained new political salience in the 1970s as a "Māori renaissance" flourished (Fleras and Spoonley, 1999). The government responded by establishing a process through which Māori grievances concerning land and resources could be resolved (Ward, 2015), officially acknowledging New Zealand as a bicultural society comprised of Māori and Pākehā (as New Zealanders of European ancestry are commonly known), and recognizing Māori as an official language. Although Māori remain New Zealand's largest minority group, comprising 14.9 percent of the population in 2013, New Zealand society is growing more diverse as a result of immigration from Asia (Spoonley, 2015). The proportion of the population that identifies as Asian nearly doubled between 2001 and 2013, rising from 6.6 to 11.8 percent.[5] With projections that Asians will overtake Māori to become the second largest minority group in two decades, some Māori leaders worry that New Zealand's commitment to biculturalism will wane.[6]

15.2 Datasets of the New Zealand Policy Agendas Project

Two datasets exist. One includes decisions issued by the New Zealand Supreme Court (2004–15) and the other includes all Questions for Oral Answer ("Question Time") asked during the 49th Parliament (2008–11). Every decision and oral question was coded at the document level according to the CAP coding scheme by a number of specially trained undergraduate research assistants who worked under close supervision. For policy content, two students coded each observation at the major topic and subtopic levels. For each observation where the original coders disagreed on their CAP code, a team of coders, led by a research supervisor, collectively examined and assigned a final code. Coding discrepancies were resolved by a team of undergraduate researchers and at least one research supervisor. Thereafter, research supervisors reviewed the data by major topic code to assess coding consistency.

15.2.1 *New Zealand Supreme Court*

This dataset includes all "leave" and "merits" decisions issued by the NZSC from its inception on 1 July 2004 through 31 December 2015 as reported online by the Ministry of Justice and the New Zealand Legal Information Institute.[7] The NZSC sets its own agenda. Parties must apply to the Court for leave to appeal, and the justices evaluate these applications in light of criteria set forth in the *Supreme Court Act 2003*.[8] Only when the Court decides to *deny* leave to appeal is it required to issue a written decision in response to an application. We call these "leave decisions." The dataset contains 558 of them. Cases for which leave is granted result in written decisions on their merits, and we call these "merits decisions." The dataset contains 215 of them. In addition to coding each decision's policy content, we also recorded the date of the decision, the outcome of the decision (i.e., whether the appellant of respondent prevailed), the names of the parties and their lawyers, and the names of the participating judges.

15.2.2 *Parliament—Oral Questions*

This dataset includes all 3,004 Oral Questions asked during the 49th Parliament (2008–11). In addition to coding each question's policy content, we also recorded personal characteristics of the MPs who asked and answered the questions, including their political parties, genders, ethnicities, and seat-types (electorate versus list). "Question Time," as it is colloquially known, operates differently across the Westminster world. In New Zealand (since 1996), up to twelve oral questions are asked at 2 p.m. on each day that parliament sits. These questions are allocated among the political parties in proportion to the size of their parliamentary delegations. The parties decide which of their members will ask questions as well as the content of those questions. They must lodge their questions with the Office of the Clerk in the morning of the day on which they are to be asked. A list of each day's questions is published prior to Question Time.

15.3 An Example

To the extent that datasets of judicial decisions exist, they tend to focus on legal issues as opposed to policy content (Spaeth et al., 2017; Haynie et al., 2007). CAP datasets, thus, represent an innovative development that promises new insights into the political and policymaking roles of courts. They not only afford us a view of a court's policy agenda, but they also allow us to compare the that agenda with the policy agendas of other institutions. Here we offer an example.

Figures 15.1 and 15.2 show the proportion of the NZSC's agenda space devoted to major policy areas. By looking at the applications for leave to appeal, what we call the Court's "leave agenda," we see the types of policy areas that parties sought to litigate before the Court. In other words, it shows us, the agenda-setting efforts of societal forces. Figure 15.1 clearly shows that

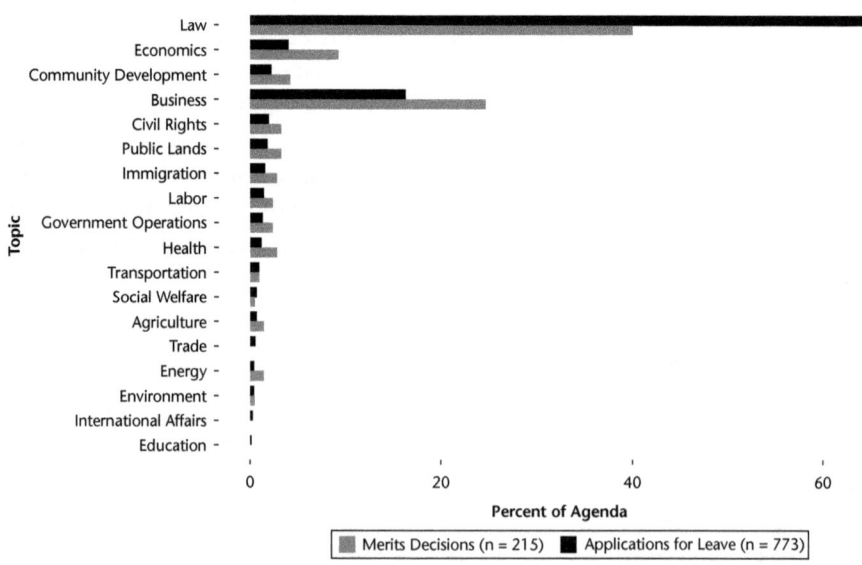

Figure 15.1. New Zealand Supreme Court agenda with law and business (May 2004–May 2013)

Source: Comparative Agendas Project—New Zealand

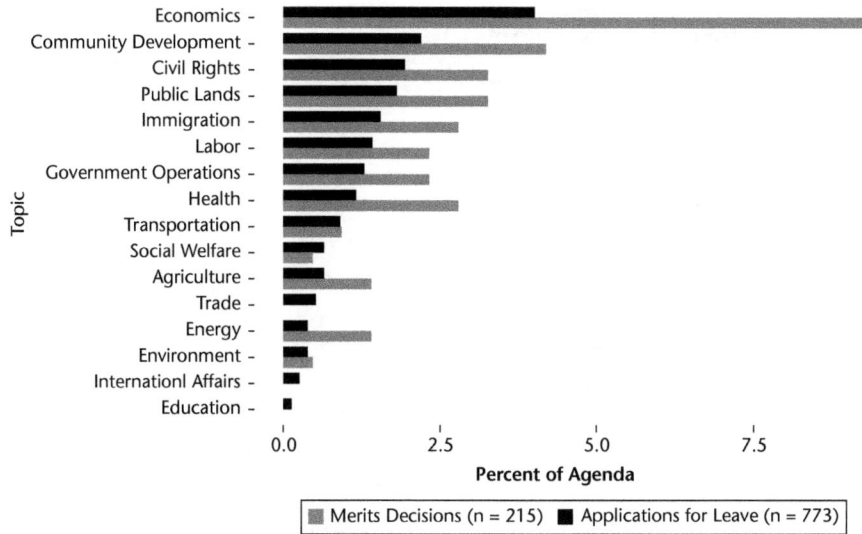

Figure 15.2. New Zealand Supreme Court agenda without law and business (May 2004–May 2013)

Source: Comparative Agendas Project—New Zealand

law and business cases predominate, with the former comprising 64 percent and the latter comprising 16 percent of all applications for leave. Criminal appeals account for most of the cases within the law category. Many of them are last-ditch efforts to avoid incarceration filed by indigent defendants operating without the benefit of legal representation. Notably, beyond law and business, no other policy area reaches 5 percent of the leave agenda.

Shifting our attention to the cases that the NZSC selects for review, what we call the "merits agenda," we see that the Court's agenda-setting process produces a relatively less concentrated policy agenda. Together, law and business cases still predominate, but law accounts for less than half (40 percent) of the merits agenda. Presumably, this reflects the justices' ability to sift the meritorious from the unmeritorious criminal appeals. By comparison, the Court affords a larger proportion of space on its merits agenda to business cases (24.7 percent). In fact, twelve of the remaining fourteen policy areas receive more attention from the Court as compared to the leave agenda (only social welfare and trade consume less agenda space); but, even so, none of these policy area crosses the threshold of 10 percent (see Figure 15.2). Thus, the policy content of the NZSC's merits agenda, as with its leave agenda, is skewed, making the difference between the two agendas a matter of degree rather than kind.

In political systems, courts can serve as forums for challenges to government policy. Comparison of the NZSC and Question Time data enable us to explore the extent to which this is true in New Zealand (see Figure 15.3).

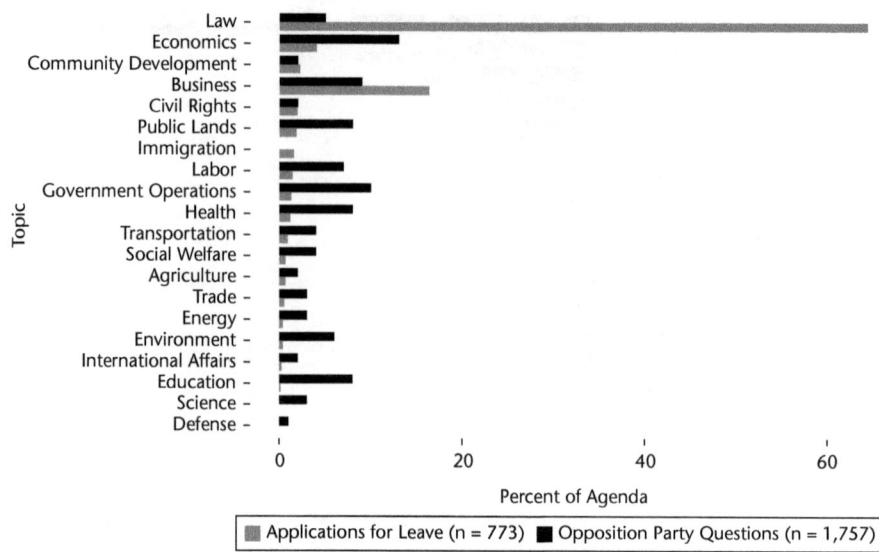

Figure 15.3. Comparing New Zealand Supreme Court agenda and opposition party question time agenda (Nov. 2009–Nov. 2011)

Source: Comparative Agendas Project—New Zealand

We use the rate of applications for leave by major policy area to measure the extent to which societal forces seek to use the NZSC to advance their policy interests. Figure 15.3 shows the rate of these applications relative to the policy content of questions asked by the Opposition parties during Question Time in the 49th Parliament.[9] It illustrates considerable disparity in the policy content of these two agendas. Most clearly, opposition MPs display far less concern than do litigants in law and business matters and far greater concern in a wider range of other policy areas. The disparity in these two agendas is most likely driven by the fact that New Zealand's legal system is more receptive to litigation pursued by persons seeking individualized redress, such as criminal defendants seeking to appeal their convictions or persons involved in civil disputes with other private persons, than it is to public interest litigation that seeks to challenge government policy writ large. As a unitary state that lacks a written constitution, New Zealand has historically not seen litigation as politics by other means, and hence, "judicial power is simply not part of New Zealand's constitutional culture" (Palmer, 2015: 159).

Notes

1. New Zealand's principal governing arrangements are codified in an ordinary statute, the Constitution Act 1986 that replaced and repealed the Constitution Act 1852.

2. In 1951, the upper house, known as the Legislative Council, was abolished, leaving the House of Representatives as the sole lawmaking body.
3. NZBORA 1990: ss. 4, 6.
4. NZBORA 1990: s. 7.
5. Statistics New Zealand "2013 Census QuickStats about Culture and Identity" <http://www.stats.govt.nz/Census/2013-census/profile-and-summary-reports/quickstats-culture-identity/asian.aspx.
6. 2013 Census QuickStats about national highlights.
7. http://www.courtsofnz.govt.nz/the-courts/supreme-court/judgments-supreme and http://www.nzlii.org/nz/cases/NZSC/.
8. *Supreme Court Act 2003* § 13.
9. For present purposes, we define Opposition parties to include Labour, the Green Party of Aotearoa New Zealand, and Jim Anderton's Progressive Party and thus exclude those parties that entered into confidence-and-supply agreements with the National Party Government (the ACT, the Māori Party, and United Future).

References

Boston, J. and Eichbaum, C. (2014). New Zealand's Neoliberal Reforms: Half a Revolution. *Governance*, 14(3): 373–6.

Evans, R. and Fern, S. (2015). From Applications to Appeals: A Political Science Perspective on the New Zealand Supreme Court's Docket. In *The Supreme Court of New Zealand 2004–2013*, ed. Mary-R. Russell and M. Barber. Wellington: Thomson Reuters, 33–60.

Fleras, A., and Spoonley, P. (1999). *Recalling Aotearoa: Indigeneity and Ethnic Politics in New Zealand*. Auckland: Oxford University Press.

Geddis, A. (2006). A Dual Track Democracy? The Symbolic Role of the Māori Seats in New Zealand's Electoral System. *Election Law Journal*, 5(4): 347–71.

Haynie, S. L., Sheehan, R. S., Songer, D. R., and Tate, C. N. (2007). *High Courts Judicial Database*. Accessed at the University of South Carolina Judicial Research Initiative (www.cas.sc.edu/poli/juri) on 25 April 2018.

Joseph, P. A. (2007). *Constitutional and Administrative Law in New Zealand*. 3rd ed. Auckland: Brookers.

Kelsey, J. (1997). *The New Zealand Experiment: A World Model for Structural Adjustment?* Auckland: Auckland University Press.

Lijphart, A. (1984). *Democracies: Patterns of Majoritarian and Consensus Government in Twenty-One Countries*. New Haven: Yale University Press.

Lijphart, A. (1999). *Patterns of Democracy: Government Forms and Performance in Thirty-Six Countries*. New Haven: Yale University Press.

Miller, R. (2015). *Democracy in New Zealand*. Auckland: Auckland University Press.

New Zealand Election Study (2002–11). Auckland: University of Auckland.

Palmer, G. W. R. (1979). *Unbridled Power? An Interpretation of New Zealand's Constitution and Government*. Wellington: Oxford University Press.

Palmer, G. W. R. and Palmer, M. (2004). *Bridled Power: New Zealand's Constitution and Government*. Wellington: Oxford University Press.

Palmer, M. (2015). Judicial Review. In *The Supreme Court of New Zealand 2004–2013*, ed. Mary-R. Russell and M. Barber. Wellington: Thomson Reuters, 158–70.

Smith, P. M. (2012). A Concise History of New Zealand, 2nd ed. Cambridge: Cambridge University Press.

Spaeth, H. J., Epstein, L., Martin, A. et al. (2017) Supreme Court Database, Version 2017 Release 01. http://Supremecourtdatabase.org.

Spoonley, P. (2015). New Diversity, Old Anxieties in New Zealand: The Complex Identity Politics and Engagement of a Settler Society. *Ethnic and Racial Studies*, 38(4): 650–61.

Vowles, J. (1998). Countdown to MMP. In *Voters Victory? New Zealand's First Election under Proportional Representation*, ed. J. Vowles, P. Aimer, S. Banducci, and J. Karp. Auckland: Auckland University Press, 12–27.

Ware, A. (2009). *The Dynamics of Two-Party Politics: Party Structures and the Management of Competition*. Oxford: Oxford University Press.

Ward, A. (2015). *An Unsettled History: Treaty Claims in New Zealand Today*. Wellington: Bridget Williams Books.

16

The Portuguese Policy Agendas Project

Ana Maria Belchior and Enrico Borghetto

The Portuguese Agendas Project was born out of the collaboration between two Portuguese universities, the University of Lisbon and the University Nova of Lisbon, and encompasses three different but complementary projects.[1] Part of the output of these projects was the creation of several datasets tracing the distribution of policy attention across the media, parliamentary, and governmental agendas. Depending on data availability, the data collection and coding went as far back in time as 1995 and stopped in 2015 (datasets will be kept updated). All the projects received the financial support of the Portuguese Foundation for Science and Technology (FCT).

16.1 The Portuguese Political System

Portugal does not perfectly fit into any of the classic regime types. Following Elgie (1999), recent scholarship (Neto and Lobo, 2009; Jalali, 2011) has tended to classify the Portuguese political system as semi-presidential, since the government is politically accountable towards both a president directly elected for a fixed term and the parliament. The president is endowed with legislative and non-legislative powers and has occasionally decided to use them (at times with success), but government leadership constitutionally and substantively rests in the hands of the prime minister (PM).

In its relationship with the unicameral parliament (the Assembleia da República) the government has the duty of keeping the 230 MPs informed about its cabinet and the public administration's decisions. To do so, PM and ministers participate in floor and committee debates on various occasions during the four-year legislative term. Either parliamentary groups or individual MPs can exert oversight or try to influence the agenda of the executive by either presenting a motion, by submitting interpellations, written and oral questions to the government, or by holding inquiries. Against the backdrop of a legislative function more and more dominated by the government over the years, the Portuguese parliament has seen its non-legislative functions reinforced (Leston-Bandeira, 2004; Norton and Leston-Bandeira, 2005).

All in all, the Portuguese parliamentary system has been described as highly cohesive and party-centered and, as a result, party discipline has generally been taken to be rather strong in Portugal (Leston-Bandeira, 2004, 2009; Lobo et al., 2012: 33–4). MPs, almost without exception, tend to follow the party line and parties mediate the relationship between MPs and voters (Leston-Bandeira, 2009: 698), so much so that, it has been shown, their perception of voters' political views does not necessarily influence their parliamentary behavior (Belchior, 2014). The closed-list proportional representation system (d'Hondt method) in force since 1976, two years after the Carnation Revolution that brought the authoritarian regime to an end, contributed to weakening a direct linkage between voters and elected representatives at the constituency level.

The configuration of the Portuguese party system was established soon after the revolution of April 25, 1974, and, apart from a few exceptions, has shown a considerable stability over time. The center-left Socialist Party (Partido Socialista—PS), founded in 1973, and the center-right Social Democratic Party (Partido Social Democrata—PSD, initially called PPD), founded in 1974, immediately became the country's largest parties. They are commonly considered catch-all parties or cartel parties and have alternated in government (either alone or in coalition) since 1987. With a few exceptions, the tendency has been for voting to be concentrated on these two centrist political parties: together they have consistently received around 70 percent of the votes.

To the right of the PSD is the Democratic and Social Center—People's Party (Partido do Centro Democrático e Social—Partido Popular—CDS-PP). Closest to a modern cadre type of party (e.g., Lopes, 2004: 33, 36–8), it represents mainly Christian-democratic values and conservative voters. Despite its small size in electoral terms (usually attracting less than 10 percent of the vote), the CDS-PP has been a government partner of the PSD on several occasions.

The radical left wing of the political spectrum is occupied by two parties. The Portuguese Communist Party (Partido Comunista Português—PCP), inspired by a Marxist-Leninist ideology, is the only one to approximate the classic definition of a mass party (e.g., Lopes, 2004: 79; Lisi, 2011). It was founded in 1921 and it is the only political formation that resisted the major hardships of the dictatorship period and had a concomitantly clandestine existence. Since 1987, the PCP has always run for election in coalition

(CDU—United Democratic Coalition) with the Greens (PEV—The Greens). The Left Block (Bloco de Esquerda—BE) is a left-libertarian party which gained its first parliamentary seats only in 1999. In the last ten years, the vote share for both parties in political elections has fluctuated between 5 and 10 percent.

16.2 Coding Issues and Data

The Portuguese codebook contains twenty-one major and 217 minor topic areas. Mostly, it follows the CAP Master Codebook, but for a few minor topic areas added to reflect the peculiarities of the Portuguese system and the specific research interests of the research team. Code 615 was added to track everything related to the career and training of school employees. All matters concerning social security and unemployment benefits were aggregated under 1309 to account for the fact that the same institution, the institute of Social Security (*Segurança Social*), is in charge of the two policies in Portugal. Finally, 2050 was added to capture matters related to former colonies and events leading to their independence. Coding activities started in 2011 and, so far, include six types of documents. In all cases the analysis was carried out by two trained coders working independently. Cases of intercoder disagreement were resolved in meetings with one of the principal investigators.

The parliamentary agenda (see Table 16.1) was measured by coding written parliamentary questions and oral questions put to the prime minister (PM) and ministers on the floor (also called "question time"). As far as written parliamentary questions are concerned, the 2007 reform discriminated between the debates with the PM and the ministers, and a new form of written questions, called *perguntas ao governo* (questions to the cabinet). There is no limit to the amount of *perguntas ao governo* an MP (or a group of MPs) can ask. Each question can be addressed to one administrative unit only (the same question has to be repeated for the number of addressees) and only addressed to senior or junior ministers (not to public officials or local administrations). When concerning different cities or geographical areas, it can be duplicated accordingly. There is an obligation for the government to answer questions within thirty days, and questions not getting an answer are published in a public list posted on the parliament's website.

The practice of questioning the cabinet on the floor goes back to the first years of the democracy (Borghetto and Russo, 2018). Yet, at least until the 2000s, it remained one of the "most criticized scrutiny devices." These sessions used to take place on Friday mornings and rarely managed to attract media attention. In the early phase, it was even possible for the government to choose which questions to answer and their order (Leston-Bandeira, 2004).

147

Table 16.1. Portuguese Policy Agendas

Dataset (unit of analysis)	Period covered	No. of Observations	Source
Oral parliamentary questions to the prime minister on the floor (every detected question)	2003–15 (9th–12th legislature)	2,385 oral questions	parlamento.pt
Oral parliamentary questions to the ministers on the floor (every detected question)	2003–15 (9th–12th legislature)	1,540 oral questions	parlamento.pt
Written parliamentary questions to the cabinet (every tabled question)	2007–15 (10th–12th legislature)	26,657 written questions	parlamento.pt
Party manifestos (every party pledge)	1995–2011 (7th–11th legislature)	5,630 pledges in manifestos	Electoral manifestos available in an election
PM speeches (every quasi-sentence referring to policy issues)	2002–11 (9th–11th legislature)	2,468 quasi-sentences	Prime ministers' speeches when taking office and other executive speeches
Media (every heading on newspaper's front page referring to policy issues)	1995–2015	34,810 headings	Mainstream newspaper *Público*

Source: Comparative Agendas Project—Portugal

Nowadays the debate receives considerable media coverage and it has become an important stage for the confrontation between opposition party front-benchers and the PM. The 2007 reform (and its partial revision in 2010) made the debate with the PM more frequent (from once to twice a month) and it enabled two debate formats: one allows the PM to speak first and then receive one round of questions on matters related to his/her intervention; the other leaves parliamentary groups free rein to ask one round of questions. In both cases, speakers have to communicate the general topic of their interventions at least 24-hours in advance. Time is allocated among parliamentary groups proportionally to their size and can be used all in one round or partitioned. Every minister has to appear on the floor at least once per legislative session (in line with art 225° of the Standing Orders reformed in 2007), in compliance with a schedule agreed by the Speaker, the cabinet and the Conference of Leaders (Filipe, 2009). In practice, these debates have rarely been scheduled.

Another major source of data on party agendas is electoral platforms. Unlike other CAP members, the unit of analysis in the Portuguese case is the party pledge. Using the definition and methodology developed by Royed (1996), we assessed to what extent each electoral pledge was converted into a political decision, searching many different sources, such as experts and journalists' reports, official websites, making direct phone calls to public departments, or legislation databases. Royed classifies a "pledge" as: "the commitment to carry out some action or produce some outcome, where an objective estimation can be made as to whether or not the action was indeed taken or the outcome produced" (1996: 79). Only precise and verifiable promises were included. Pledges have been coded as: fulfilled, unfulfilled, partially fulfilled, and no decision (if there is no available information). Each party pledge was simultaneously coded with the Party Pledges Group and the CAP coding systems. We included every party with parliamentary representation from 1995 until 2015.

To analyze the distribution of policy attention in the governmental agenda, we coded politically relevant PM speeches in the period between 2002 and 2011. These include: the PM speeches when taking office and at the moment of presenting the government's program (within ten days of his/her appointment); the yearly PM interventions during the parliamentary debate on the state of the nation (in one of the last ten meetings of the legislative session, the PM presents an account of salient decisions taken or to be taken by its executive, followed by questions from parliamentary groups); the discussion of the state budget; Christmas messages and speeches delivered in other relevant occasions, such as political crises.

Finally, our analysis of the media agenda relied on the coding of all the front-page article's headings of one mainstream Portuguese daily newspaper (*Público*, which is a leading quality newspaper). Newspapers in Portugal do not follow a party line and, for that reason, the analysis of media solely focused on a single newspaper. The dataset includes all available editions between 1995 and 2015, corresponding to a total of 7,260 front pages, and 34,810 articles/headings.

16.3 Party Pledges: Exemplifying on a Specificity

Figure 16.1 uses data on party pledges in electoral platforms to show that the distribution in issue attention differs across types of party. Extreme left-wing parties in Portugal (CDU and BE) present electoral platforms much more focused on macroeconomics, health, social policy, labor and employment issues, when compared to other parties. Catch-all parties (PS and PSD) exhibit a significant overlapping in terms of policy issue attention: they are more focused on education and culture, government issues and (to a lesser extent) to justice and internal affairs. Their policy attention is much more concentrated in comparison with the two left-most parties. In general, the thematic profile of the Portuguese conservatives (CDS-PP) resembles the catch-all parties', although they devote more attention to justice and internal affairs. It must be recalled that the CDS-PP has already been part of coalition governments with both catch-all parties, although more often with PSD.

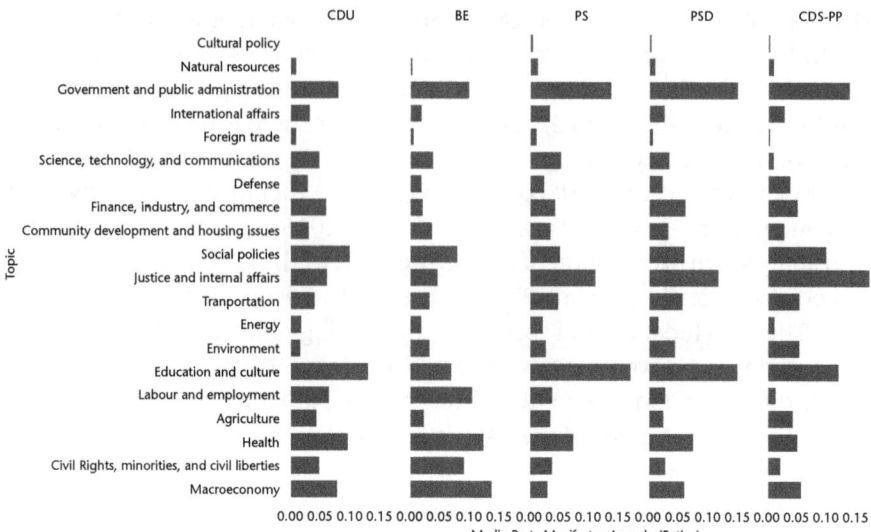

Figure 16.1. Party pledges in Portugal, 1995–2011(ratios)

Source: Comparative Agendas Project—Portugal

16.4 Final Remarks

The data collected and coded by the Portuguese policy agendas team represent a new and valuable resource for scholars interested in deepening their knowledge on media, parliamentary, and governmental policy attention in Portugal. Besides the current ongoing projects (Borghetto and Belchior, forthcoming), future efforts will be directed to either increase the data time span or to collect new data (for example, regarding legislative bills, the budget, and the press releases of the Council of Ministers).

Note

1. Party Pledge and Democratic Accountability: The Portuguese Case from a Comparative Perspective"—PTDC/CPJ-CPO/111915/2009 (2010 to 2014) coordinated by Catherine Moury; "Public Preferences and Policy Decision-Making: A Longitudinal and Comparative Analysis"—PTDC/IVC-CPO/3921/2012 (2013 to 2015) coordinated by Ana Maria Belchior; and "Portuguese Parliament: Agenda-Setting and Law-making"—IF/00382/2014 (2016 to 2020) coordinated by Enrico Borghetto.

References

Belchior, A. M. (2014). Explaining MPs' Perceptions of Voters' Positions in a Party-Mediated Representation System: Evidence from the Portuguese Case. *Party Politics*, 20(3): 403–15.

Borghetto, E. and Belchior, A. M. (forthcoming). Party manifestos, opposition and media as determinants of the cabinet agenda. *Political Studies*.

Borghetto, E. and Russo, F. (2018). The Determinants of Party Issue Attention in Times of Crisis: From Agenda Setters to Agenda Takers? *Party Politics*, 24(1): 65–77.

Elgie, R. (1999). The Politics of Semi-Presidentialism. In *Semi-Presidentialism in Europe.*, ed. R. Elgie Oxford: Oxford University Press, 1–20.

Filipe A. (2009). The 2007 Reform of the Portuguese Parliament: What Has Really Changed? *The Journal of Legislative Studies*, 15(1): 1–9.

Jalali, C. (2011). The President Is Not a Passenger. In *Semi-Presidentialism and Democracy*, ed. R. Elgie, S. Moestrup, and Yu-S. Wu. Basingstoke: Palgrave Macmillan, 156–73.

Leston-Bandeira, C. (2004). *From Legislation to Legitimation: The Role of the Portuguese Parliament*. London: Routledge.

Leston-Bandeira, C. (2009). Dissent in a Party-Based Parliament. *Party Politics* 15: 695–713.

Lisi, M. (2011). *Os Partidos Políticos em Portugal. Continuidade e Transformação*. Coimbra: Almedina.

Lobo, M. C., Pinto, A. C., and Magalhães, P. (2012). The Political Institutions of Portuguese Democracy. In *Portugal in the Twenty-First Century*, ed. S. Royo. Lanham: Lexington Books, 23–48.

Lopes, F. F. (2004). *Os Partidos Políticos: Modelos e Realidades na Europa Ocidental e em Portugal*. Lisbon: Celta Editora.

Neto, O. A., and Lobo, M. C. (2009). Portugal's Semi-Presidentialism (Re)considered: An Assessment of the President's Role in the Policy Process, 1976–2006. *European Journal of Political Research*, 48(2): 234–55.

Norton, P., and Leston-Bandeira, C. (2005). The Impact of Democratic Practice on the Parliaments of Southern Europe. In *Southern European Parliaments in Democracy*, ed. C. Leston-Bandeira. London: Routledge, 177–85.

Royed, T. (1996). Testing the Mandate Model in Britain and the United States: Evidence from the Reagan and Thatcher Eras. *British Journal of Political Science*, 26(1): 45–80.

17

Agenda Dynamics in Spain

Laura Chaqués-Bonafont, Anna M. Palau,
and Luz Muñoz Marquez

17.1 The Spanish Political System

The Spanish Constitution of 1978 defines Spain as a parliamentary monarchy, in which the *Presidente del Gobierno* (prime minister) leads the executive and the monarch is the head of state. Spain's political system is a multi-party system, but since the early 1980s two parties have been predominant in politics: the Spanish Socialist Workers' Party (PSOE) and the People's Party (PP). The majoritarian character of Spanish democracy generates a bias towards the formation of stable, single-party governments and the domination of the legislative process by the executive. Spain has been governed by majority governments for long periods of time (see Table 17.1 for a description). In this context, the governing party does not need to cooperate with opposition parties in order to legislate. However, minority governments have occurred several times (Table 17.1), increasing the chances for opposition parties to veto the introduction of particular issues onto the agenda, and/or to translate some of their policy priorities into final decisions. This was the case through the 1990s and late 2000s, when Spanish government formation depended on regional political parties. Under these circumstances, some regional governments (mainly Catalonia and the Basque Country) increased their capacity to generate shifts in political authority and to modify the Spanish polity towards increasing political decentralization (Chaqués-Bonafont and Palau, 2011a). From the late 2000s, there was a transformation in the Spanish party system with the emergence of Ciudadanos and Podemos as political parties that gained representation in the Spanish parliament in 2015. The increasing fragmentation of the party system is linked to the economic recession, and the crisis of legitimacy among political institutions

Table 17.1. Parliamentary legislatures, 1982–2017

Prime minister	Time in office	Duration in office (months)	Government vote	Votes (%)	Parliamentary seats (%)	Seats of the two main parties (%)	Investiture vote: support of parties**
González I	1982–6	43	PSOE	48	58	88	PCE, CDS, EE
González II	1986–9	40	PSOE	45	53	83	none
González III	1989–93	43	PSOE	40	50	81	none
González IV	1993–6	33	PSOE	39	45	86	CIU, PNV
Aznar I	1996–2000	45	PP	39	45	85	CIU, PNV, CC
Aznar II	2000–4	47	PP	45	52	88	none
Zapatero I	2004–8	47	PSOE	43	47	89	ERC, IU, BNG, CHA, CC
Zapatero II	2008–11	43	PSOE	44	48	92	none
Rajoy	2011–15	46	PP	45	53	85	UPN
Rajoy	2015–16	11	PP	27	32	54	UPN
Rajoy	2016–18	20	PP	31	36	58	Ciudadanos, CC

Note: PSOE (Partido Socialista Obrero Español), PP (Partido Popular), PCE (Partido Comunista de España), CDS (Centro Democrático y Social), EE (Euskadico Esquerra), CiU (Convergència I Unió), PNV (Partido Nacionalista Vasco), CC (Coalición Canaria), CHA (Chunta Aragonesa), ERC (Esquerra Republicana de Catalunya), IU (Izquierda Unida), BNG (Bloque Nacionalista Gallego).

Source: Own elaboration from electoral data available at *Ministerio del Interior* (www.infoelectoral.mir.es/min/); see also Chaqués-Bonafont, Palau, and Baumgartner (2015: 25)

in Spain. Despite this, in November 2016, the PP leader, Mariano Rajoy was, again, elected as prime minister of Spain with the support of Ciudadanos, and the abstention of the PSOE.

Another major feature of the Spanish political system is its "quasi-federal system" of distribution of territorial power, called the Estado de las Autonomías. After forty years of dictatorship, characterized by the centralization of power in a single level of governance, Spain gradually became a highly decentralized political system in which the Comunidades Autónomas have jurisdiction over a large range of issues. This process of devolution occurred gradually, as a result of intense negotiations, illustrating the ability of regional governments to influence Spanish policy through forceful, politicized bargaining, in which party preferences and the type of government play major roles (Chaqués-Bonafont and Palau, 2011b). The politics of decentralization have changed dramatically in recent decades, towards increasing radicalization and confrontation in and out of the parliamentary arena, as the secessionist movement in Catalonia illustrates. In contrast to previous decades, the debate is no longer led by minority governments of the PP or the PSOE allying with conservative regional parties, either CiU or the PNV, but rather by large social movements in alliance with political elites. By the same token, the debate has moved from one centered on the distribution of issue jurisdiction, to a debate centered on highly symbolic issues, such as the concept of nationhood (Chaqués-Bonafont et al., 2015). There is no other issue in Spanish politics today that so clearly shows the increasing polarization and lack of consensus that has characterized Spanish politics for the last decade.

This effect is the opposite of the pattern of Europeanization in Spanish politics. In 1986 Spain became a member state of the EEC (later European Union) and, in contrast to political decentralization, delegation to the European Union has generated a general agreement among political forces. This is so despite the fact that the European Union has imposed severe economic structural adjustments that have altered citizens' lives dramatically, and despite the fact that the European Union has forced Spanish leaders to amend the constitution in order to meet new goals relating to economic stabilization (Palau, 2018; Chaqués-Bonafont et al., 2015).

Finally, since the 1980s, the PSOE governments have committed to developing a Mediterranean corporatist welfare state (Esping-Andersen, 1999). Actually, Spanish public expenditure grew from 20 percent of GDP in the mid-1970s to about 50 percent by 1993, almost reaching the average public expenditure in social services of EU countries (Chaqués-Bonafont et al., 2015). Since the economic crisis, the Spanish governments of both the PSOE and PP have implemented policies oriented to curb spending and to control the public deficit, following the policy guidelines defined by EU institutions, with important consequences for the system of social provision. As Figure 17.1 illustrates, the crisis has resulted in a focus on macroeconomic issues in the symbolic agenda of the executive (speeches) reaching unprecedented levels. The economy is always a key issue in the agenda of the executive but attention

Figure 17.1. Attention on macroeconomic issues in Spain
Source: Chaqués-Bonafont, Palau, and Baumgartner (2015: 57)

declines when the economic situation is positive. Rodriguez Zapatero devoted less than 4 percent of his first speech in 2004 to talking about macroeconomics, and only 10 percent in his first speech of 2008. However, since 2009, Spanish presidents have devoted more than half of their total speech duration to talking about the topic, leaving other issues, such as rights and the environment, off the agenda (Chaqués-Bonafont et al., 2015: 59).

17.2 Databases

The Policy Agendas Project in Spain has developed comprehensive, reliable, and comparable datasets for analyzing the agendas of government and parliament, the electoral promises of political parties, the media, and public opinion. These databases cover the period 1982–2015, with the exceptions of the media and public opinion, which start in 1996 and 1993, respectively. In this section, we provide a description of these databases and details of the coding procedure (for further information see Chaqués-Bonafont et al., 2015).

The symbolic agenda of the executive is measured in our databases through information on two types of prime ministerial speeches: investiture speeches (*Discurso de Investidura*) and annual speeches (*Debate sobre Política General en torno al Estado de la Nación*). The substantive agenda of the executive is measured through records of executive bills and decree-laws. The supremacy of the executive in the Spanish political system is illustrated by the high percentage of decree-laws and by the pre-eminence of executive bills compared to parliamentary bills (Chaqués-Bonafont et al., 2015: 75). Decree-laws are provisional regulatory acts passed by the executive in cases of extraordinary and urgent need, when exceptional circumstances make it impossible to follow ordinary legislative procedure. However, the Spanish government is increasingly using this legislative instrument to take decisions about issues that have nothing to do with urgent necessities (Chaqués-Bonafont et al., 2015). Decree-laws represent 21 percent of total laws passed from 1982 to 2011, and more than 50 percent of those passed from 2011 to 2014. With regard to executive bills, these are the main source of legislative decisions in Spain, which means that the governing party has promoted more than 90 percent of the laws passed in Spain.

For analysis of the parliamentary agenda, we created a database including all the bills introduced by parliamentary groups. Because these are rarely acts oriented to generate legislation, parliamentary bills work mainly as an indicator of the symbolic agenda of parties in the parliamentary arena. We have also collected data about the scrutiny activity of parliamentary groups, including oral questions introduced in plenary meetings and in committees. Oral questions are presented by individual MPs, not parliamentary groups, at a fixed question time. The rules governing the introduction of questions have been subjected to different reforms over time (see Chaqués-Bonafont et al., 2015: 93) but generally the distribution of questions among parliamentary groups depends on the number of seats each group has in the chamber. The parliamentary databases also include data about organic and ordinary laws and legislative-decrees passed in the Spanish parliament, and laws passed in regional parliaments (Andalucía, the Basque Country, Catalonia, and Galicia).

Our databases also include information about the agendas of political parties in the electoral arena. We have created a database including information about the electoral promises of the governing party. This means having information about the issue priorities expressed in the party manifestos of the PSOE (Partido Socialista Obrero Español) and the PP (Partido Popular) for those elections prior to their incumbencies. Party manifestos, like speeches, have been coded at the quasi-sentence level.

For the study of the media agenda we created a database of the stories covered on the front pages of the two most-read Spanish newspapers in Spain (*El Pais* and *El Mundo*). As with the rest of the databases, this is a comprehensive dataset, not a sample, including information about all the stories published on the front pages of these two newspapers. We focused on front-page stories because they are important indicators of the prioritization of issues by media outlets, a quantifiable indicator of the relevance and newsworthiness of issues according to editors and journalists.

All the databases have been coded twice, by coders trained to obtain an in-depth understanding of the Spanish codebook. The first task we undertook, before starting the coding procedure, was to adapt the codebook to the peculiarities of the Spanish political system, to capture aspects that have no equivalent in other countries.

We have also adapted the codebook to the CAP Master Codebook, so that our databases are comparable with those created by other CAP teams. To control for the quality of databases we calculated reliability scores, counting as errors those cases where both coders disagreed. The result is a set of high-quality data sources that allow us to conduct longitudinal, cross-sectional and cross-country analyses of agenda dynamics.

17.3 Specificities: Multilevel Governance

From the transition to democracy to the present day, Spain has gradually been transformed into a multilevel system of governance, which implies an increasing delegation of political autonomy upwards to the European Union and downwards to the Comunidades Autonomas (CCAA). These two processes have taken place in parallel, following a gradual pattern, and neither has yet reached an end. First, in order to capture the importance of the process of political decentralization, we adopted the following criterion: all laws, bills, speeches, oral questions, party manifestos (sentences), and media stories dealing with the delegation of political autonomy to the regions in general terms, are coded as subtopic 2001. Further, we created a dummy variable to identify whether a law, bill, oral question, or media story dealing with a specific issue—from macroeconomics to family issues—was also related to the process of political decentralization. For example, a law transforming the fiscal autonomy of regional governments is coded as 1 (macroeconomics), subtopic 107 (taxes, tax policy, and tax reform), and a dummy variable (value 1), which identifies this law is related to political decentralization. Second, for the process of Europeanization we followed the same criterion. Any law, bill, oral question, speech, party manifesto (sentence), or media story related to the European Union, as a political and geographical unity, is coded as 1910 (Western Europe and Common Market issues). However, a law transposing an EU directive on recycling is coded as 707 (environmental issues: recycling), and a dummy variable (value 1) identifies its EU character.

17.4 Conclusions

Our research so far demonstrates that political responsiveness is declining over time. There is an increasing distance between the issues that are identified as most important by Spanish citizens and the issues that capture most of the attention of policymakers. Also, policymakers' capacity (and/or willingness) to fulfill policy promises, as defined during electoral campaigns, is declining over time, especially when parties are governing under a minority, in a context of economic crisis, and for those issues with shared jurisdiction. Regarding the consolidation of Spain into a multilevel system of governance, results illustrate that the Spanish legislative agenda is one of the most Europeanized within the European Union (Palau, 2018; Palau and Chaqués-Bonafont, 2012; Palau et al., 2015), with important differences across issues and time. Regarding the link between the media and political agendas, our results demonstrate that the media has a direct impact on citizens' perception of issues as political problems (Chaqués-Bonafont and Palau, 2009, 2012; Baumgartner and Chaqués-Bonafont 2013; Palau and Davesa, 2013; Chaqués-Bonafont and Muñoz, 2016; Guinaudeau and Palau 2016), and on policymakers' agendas, especially when they are in opposition (Chaqués-Bonafont and Baumgartner, 2015). One of our main goals in the future is to further analyze the extent to which the delegation of issue jurisdiction towards the European Union and regional governments affects the capacity and/or willingness of policymakers to respond to citizens' priorities, from a comparative perspective; and thus, to contribute to an intense theoretical debate about whether European integration and increasing regionalization have created a new political scenario in which governments are less responsive to the public.

Acknowledgements

We are especially grateful to Frank Baumgartner and John Wilkerson, whose collaboration has been crucial to developing the project in Spain. Also to Bryan Jones, for his invaluable support. Special thanks are also due to Shaun Bevan for all the work he has done to make the CAP Master Codebook a reality. Our research activity has been possible thanks to the support of several prestigious institutions, including the European Science Foundation, the Ministerio de Ciencia e Innovacion, the Agaur, ICREA Foundation, the Institut d'Estudis Autonómics, the University of Barcelona, and the Institut Barcelona d'Estudis Internacionals (IBEI). As a whole, the project has obtained six different competitive grants oriented to different approaches to the research topics.

References

Baumgartner, F., and Chaqués-Bonafont, L. (2013). Newspaper Attention and Policy Activities in Spain. *Journal of Public Policy*, 33: 65–88.

Chaqués-Bonafont, L. and Baumgartner, F. (2015). All News Is Bad News: Newspapers Coverage of Political Parties in Spain. *Political Communication*, 32(2): 268–91.

Chaqués Bonafont, L., and Muñoz, L. (2016). Explaining Interest Groups Access to the Parliamentary Arena. *West European Politics*, 39(6): 1276–98.

Chaqués-Bonafont, L., and Palau, A. M. (2009). The Dynamics of Policy Change: A Comparative Analysis of the Food Safety and Pharmaceutical Policy in Spain. *Journal of Public Policy*, 29(1): 103–26.

Chaqués-Bonafont, L., and Palau, A. M. (2011a). Assessing the Responsiveness of Spanish Policymakers to the Priorities of their Citizens. *West European Politics*, 34(4): 706–30.

Chaqués-Bonafont, L., and Palau, A. M. (2011b). Comparing Law-Making Activities in a Quasi-Federal System of Government: The Case of Spain. *Comparative Political Studies*, 44(8): 1089–119.

Chaqués-Bonafont, L., and Palau, A. M. (2012). From Prohibition to Permissiveness: A Two-Wave Change on Morality Issues in Spain. In *Morality Politics in Western Europe: Parties, Agendas and Policy Choices*, ed. I. Engeli, C. Green-Petersen, and L. T. Larsen. London: Palgrave, 62–87.

Chaqués-Bonafont, L., Palau, A. M., and Baumgartner, F. (2015). *Agenda Dynamics in Spain*. Basingstoke: Palgrave.

Esping-Andersen, G. (1999). *Social Foundations of Postindustrial Economies*. Oxford: Oxford University Press.

Guinaudeau, I., and Palau, A. M. (2016). A Matter of Conflict: How Events and Parties Shape the News Coverage of EU Affairs. *European Union Politics*, 17(4): 593–615.

Palau, A. M. (2018). *Catalunya en Europa: límites y oportunidades del proceso de integración.* Barcelona: IEA.

Palau, A. M., and Chaqués-Bonafont, L. (2012). Europeanization of Legislative Activity in Spain. In *The Europeanization of Domestic Legislatures: The Empirical Implications of the Delors' Myth in Nine Countries*, ed. S. Brouard, O. Costa, and T. Köning. New York: Springer, 173–97.

Palau, A. M., and Davesa, F. (2013). El impacto de la cobertura mediática de la corrupción en la opinión pública española (1996–2009). *Revista Española de Investigaciones Sociológicas*, 144: 97–125.

Palau, A. M., Muñoz, L., and Chaqués-Bonafont, L. (2015). Government-Opposition Dynamics in Spain under the Pressure of Economic Collapse and the Debt Crisis, *Journal of Legislative Studies*, 21(1): 75–95.

18

The Swiss Policy Agendas Project

Roy Gava, Pascal Sciarini, Anke Tresch, and Frédéric Varone

18.1 The Swiss Political System

The Swiss political system is peculiar in many respects (for an introduction see Kriesi and Trechsel, 2008). First, Switzerland stands apart regarding its form of government, which is neither parliamentary nor presidential. Second, direct democracy is a central element of Swiss politics. Third, Switzerland has often been characterized as a paradigmatic case of consensus democracy (Lijphart, 1999). Negotiation, compromise, and consensus-building have thus been traditionally considered a hallmark of policymaking.

The Swiss government, the Federal Council, is a seven-member executive body. Since 1959, it has integrated the four major political parties (i.e., Social Democrats, Liberals, Christian Democrats and the Swiss People's Party), systematically accounting for over 70 percent of the electorate. The government is consequently shared by all main parties, which receive a number of seats in the Federal Council that is roughly proportional to their parliamentary strength. Each federal councilor leads a ministry but shares otherwise the same governmental rights and duties. Moreover, the government operates under the collegiality principle. This means that the Federal Council speaks with a single voice: even if a federal councilor disagrees with a governmental decision, he or she is expected to endorse it and defend it vis-à-vis the parliament and the public. The governmental parties are, however, not bound by any coalition agreement. Therefore, governmental parties do not need to behave loyally towards the government and may even play the two-sided game of government and opposition.

The seven federal councilors are elected on an individual basis and for a mandate of four years, by the parliament. Unlike in a parliamentary system, however, they cannot be dismissed before the end of the legislature. The parliament and/or the people (by means of an ex post referendum) may well reject government policy proposals, but this does not have any effect on the composition of the Federal Council. Conversely, the government cannot dissolve the parliament or call for new parliamentary elections before the end of the legislature.

Direct democracy is a crucial arena in Switzerland. All popular votes are binding and citizens are called to the ballot box several times per year. Referenda are held either on constitutional amendments or on laws adopted by the parliament. In the former case, the referendum is mandatory and requires a double majority of both the people and the cantons. In the latter case, the referendum is optional, meaning that a vote only takes place if 50,000 citizens sign a referendum against a legislative act (federal laws and, under certain conditions, international treaties). The optional referendum requires only a simple majority of the people in order to succeed, i.e., to prevent the entry into force of the targeted law. Empirically, less than 10 percent of federal laws are challenged by a referendum—and submitted to the people (Sciarini and Tresch, 2014). Finally, citizens may launch a popular initiative to amend the Constitution, if they are able to collect 100,000 signatures. To be accepted, the initiatives also require a double majority of both the people and the twenty-six cantons. The parliament can propose a counter-proposal to the initiative on which the citizens also vote at the same time.

Switzerland has been often seen as the poster child of political stability and consensus democracy. The Swiss political system has nevertheless been through numerous readjustments since the early 1990s, leading scholars to critically revisit the functioning of the consensus model (Sciarini et al., 2015). Recent transformations include the polarization of politics during elections and in parliament, the strategic use of direct democracy by political parties, as well as the internationalization and mediatization of politics and policies. Beyond comparative endeavors, the tracing of issues across time and arenas provides insights into the changing nature of Swiss politics. For instance, such an approach has proven useful to investigate the transformation of the Swiss People's Party into a right-wing populist party (Varone et al., 2014), the impact of Europeanization on domestic politics and legislative production (Gava and Varone, 2012, 2014; Gava et al., 2017), the interaction between media and political agendas (Tresch et al., 2012, 2013; Vliegenthart et al., 2016a), and the interaction between protests, media, and political agendas (Vliegenthart et al., 2016b).

18.2 Datasets

Five datasets covering crucial agendas of the Swiss political system have been collected at the Department of Political Science and International Relations of the University of Geneva[1] following the CAP approach. These datasets allow

Table 18.1. Overview of Swiss Agendas datasets

Agenda	Source	Period	N
Parliament	Parliamentary interventions	1995–2003	9,949
Government	Legislative proposals	1978–2008	1,951
Legislation	Legislative acts	1978–2008	1,420
Direct democracy	Popular votes	1848–2014	605
Media	Newspaper front page	1995–2003	9,896

Source: Comparative Agendas Project—Switzerland

the study of parliamentary, governmental, legislative, direct democracy, and media agendas (see Table 18.1).

The Swiss parliament is composed of two chambers. The National Council represents the people (200 seats) and the Council of States represents the cantons (46 seats; two for each canton and one for half cantons). Parliamentary interventions materialize the agenda-setting power of the parliament, as well as the parliamentary oversight over the executive. Individual MPs or MPs organized in parliamentary groups and committees can introduce interventions, with no legal limitations in terms of number or scope. Nevertheless, MPs work part-time and usually meet four times a year for three-week sessions. Unlike parliamentary committees, individual MPs can only introduce parliamentary interventions during sessions.

Postulates, motions, and parliamentary initiatives allow MPs to initiate legislative processes. All these interventions are put to a vote, but their agenda-setting power varies considerably. *Postulates* require the approval of a single chamber. When a postulate is adopted, the government is required to prepare a report or to study whether legislation is required on a given topic. *Motions* are more constraining. If adopted by both chambers, the government is obliged to draft a bill on a given topic. The *parliamentary initiative* is the most powerful agenda-setting instrument at the disposal of MPs. Requiring the support of a parliamentary committee and a majority in both chambers, it allows the parliament to draft a bill and to control the decision-making process from start to finish, thus by-passing the executive.

Parliamentary *questions* and *interpellations* for the government fulfil a control function, but they also allow MPs to position themselves before the media and the public (Bailer 2011). Written questions can be introduced in both chambers by individual MPs. In addition, there is a parliamentary question hour in the National Council, which takes place at the beginning of the second and third week of each session, and is also used by MPs to draw attention to specific topics.

While MPs can draft legislation by means of a parliamentary initiative, the lion's share of Swiss legislation results from bills prepared and drafted by the executive (Sciarini et al., 2002; Sciarini, 2007). Government bills submitted to the parliament for its consideration are accompanied by an explanatory report (i.e., *Botschaft des Bundesrates* or *Message du Conseil fédéral*). These reports provide a way to capture substantial issue attention by the Swiss government and are published weekly in the *Federal Gazette*. The 2–3 page summaries at the beginning of each report were retained to assign CAP topics.

The legislation dataset focuses on primary legislation adopted by parliament and subject to either mandatory or optional referendum. These legislative acts consequently include amendments to the federal Constitution, federal laws, federal decrees, and ratification of international treaties.

The direct democracy dataset includes all direct democratic votes that were held since the creation of the modern federal state in 1848. That is, it includes all legislative acts submitted to the people as a result of mandatory referendum, optional referendum, or popular initiative.

The media dataset is based on the front page of the quality newspaper *Neue Zürcher Zeitung* (NZZ). The NZZ is considered to be the reference newspaper of the political and economic elites and is known for its complete and in-depth coverage of international and Swiss politics. The dataset includes, on an every-other-day basis, front-page articles, as well as all news articles on the first page of the national news section, and the main article(s) in the economy section referred to on the front page. CAP topics were assigned on the basis of the articles' full text. The data also provides information on whether articles focused on international, national or cantonal, and local news.

18.3 Direct Democracy and Agenda-Setting

Switzerland is often pointed out as the emblematic case of direct democracy. On the one hand, citizens may launch a popular initiative, introducing in this way a new policy proposal in the ballot. On the other hand, the referendum allows citizens to have the last say in relation to policies, since this instrument allows them to veto a constitutional amendment or a law adopted by the parliament. In other words, the direct democratic instruments can be activated in a top-down manner by political elites' decisions or, on the contrary, as a result of bottom-up pressure through the collection of citizens' signatures.

Since the 1990s, direct democracy has been increasingly activated. During the period 1990–2014, 234 policy proposals were placed on the ballot for the consideration of citizens. Roughly two-thirds of these policy proposals were the result of bottom-up pressure. These consisted of popular initiatives seeking policy change (42 percent) and optional referenda (32 percent) attempting to block policy change. The top-down agenda-setting by political elites was composed of mandatory referenda on constitutional amendments (20 percent) and counter-proposals (6 percent).

Figure 18.1 presents the share of policy domains on the direct democratic agenda, considering top-down and bottom-up votes separately. Given the relative low number of popular votes, the twenty-one major topics of the CAP have been regrouped into six domains.[2] Results show that the direct democratic arena has been activated the most frequently in relation to welfare and education issues (27 percent) and environment, energy, and transportation (21 percent). These two set of issues account for almost half of all the popular votes in the years 1990–2014.

Looking at the prioritization in terms of top-down and bottom-up agenda-setting shows similarities and differences across policy domains. Despite the difference in intensity, welfare and education remains at the top of both top-down (23 percent) and bottom-up (29 percent) popular votes. In contrast, two policy domains seem particularly desynchronized between the two direct democratic agendas. Government and macro-economy issues are relatively more prominent in the top-down agenda, while foreign policy and defense occupies a larger share of bottom-up popular votes.

In terms of policy implications of bottom-up agenda-setting, around 13 percent of the popular initiatives summoned to the ballot successfully translated into policy change. This relatively low rate of success contrasts with that of top-down policy reforms: 73 percent of the objects placed on

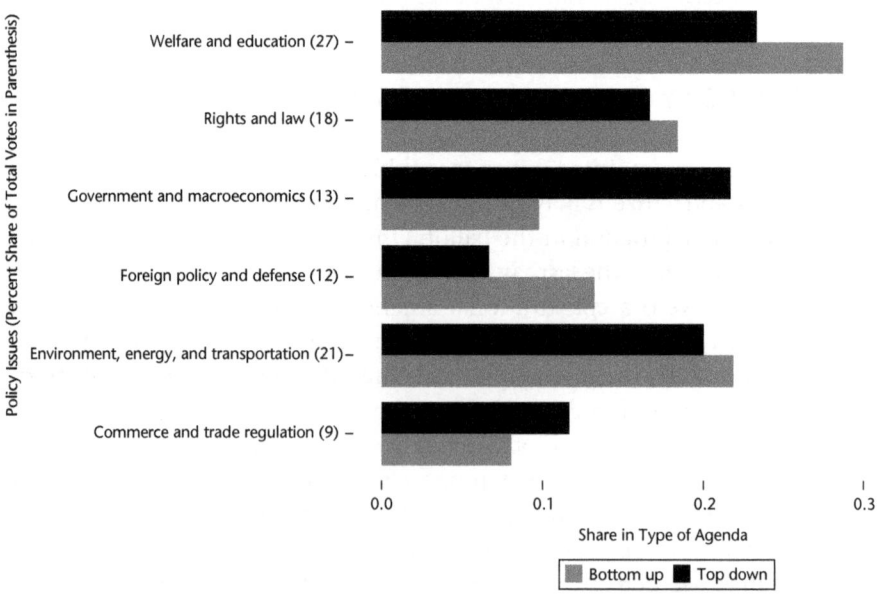

Figure 18.1. Policy issues of top-down and bottom-up direct democratic votes (1990–2014)

Source: Comparative Agendas Project—Switzerland

the ballot in the form of mandatory referendum and counter-proposals were accepted. In a similar vein, 71 percent of the legislative acts adopted by parliament and challenged by an optional referendum were accepted by citizens and therefore enacted (i.e., success for the political elite). In short, these bivariate figures suggest that while agenda-setting in direct democracy is fundamentally shaped by bottom-up pressure, policy change is still primarily top-down driven. However, this last statement needs some qualification, as Switzerland is also changing in that respect: over the last ten years the Swiss People's party has enjoyed an unusual rate of success with popular initiatives in the field of foreign and immigration policy (Varone et al., 2014).

Notes

1. The data was collected with the financial support of the Swiss National Science Foundation under the projects "Agenda-Setting in Switzerland" (grant number 105511-119245/1), sponsored as part of European Science Foundation EUROCORES "The Politics of Attention: West European Politics in Time of Change," and "The Mediatization of Political Decision Making," sponsored as part of the National Center of Competence in Research "Challenges to Democracy in the 21st Century."
2. The domains have been regrouped following the CAP major categories as follows: foreign policy and defense: 16, 19; energy, environment, and transportation: 7, 8, 10, 14, 21; government and macro-economy: 1, 20; welfare and education: 3, 5, 6, 13, 23; rights and law: 2, 9, 12; economic and trade regulation: 4, 15, 17, 18.

References

Bailer, S. (2011). People' s Voice or Information Pool? The Role of, and Reasons for, Parliamentary Questions in the Swiss Parliament. *The Journal of Legislative Studies*, 17(3): 302–14.

Gava, R., Sciarini, P., and Varone, F. (2017). Who Europeanizes Parliamentary Attention, on Which Issues and How? A Policy Agenda Perspective. *Journal of Legislative Studies*, 23(4): 566–93.

Gava, R., and Varone, F. (2012). So Close, Yet So Far? The EU's Footprint in Swiss Legislative Production. In *The Europeanization of Domestic Legislatures: The Empirical Implications of the Delors' Myth in Nine Countries*, ed. S. Brouard, O. Costa, and T. König. New York: Springer, 197–221.

Gava, R., and Varone, F. (2014). The EU's Footprint in Swiss Policy Change: A Quantitative Assessment of Primary and Secondary Legislation (1999–2012). *Swiss Political Science Review*, 20(2): 216–22.

Kriesi, H., and Trechsel, A. (2008). *The Politics of Switzerland: Continuity and Change in a Consensus Democracy*. Cambridge: Cambridge University Press.

Lijphart, A. (1999). *Patterns of Democracy: Government Forms and Performance in Thirty-Six Countries*. New Haven: Yale University Press.

Sciarini, P. (2007). The Decision-Making Process. In *Handbook of Swiss Politics*, ed. U. Klöti, P. Knoepfel, H. Kriesi et al. Zurich: NZZ, 465–99.

Sciarini, P., Fischer, M., and Traber, D. (2015). *Political Decision-Making in Switzerland: The Consensus Model under Pressure*. London: Palgrave Macmillan.

Sciarini, P., Nicolet, S., and Fischer, A. (2002). L'impact de l'internationalisation sur les processus de décision en Suisse: Une analyse quantitative des actes législatifs 1995–1999. *Swiss Political Science Review*, 8: 1–34.

Sciarini, P., and Tresch, A. (2014). Votations populaires. In *Manuel de la politique suisse*, ed. P. Knoepfel, Y. Papadopoulos, P. Sciarini et al. Zurich: NZZ, 497–524.

Tresch, A., Sciarini, P., and Varone, F. (2012). Media, Politics, and Policymaking: Lessons from Switzerland. *Perspectives on Europe*, 42(2): 29–34.

Tresch, A., Sciarini, P., and Varone, F. (2013). The Relationship between Media and Political Agendas: Variations across Decision-Making Phases. *West European Politics*, 36(5): 897–918.

Varone, F., Engeli, I., Sciarini, P., and Gava, R. (2014). Agenda-Setting and Direct Democracy: The Rise of the Swiss People's Party. In *Agenda Setting, Policies, and Political Systems: A Comparative Approach*, ed. C. Green-Pedersen and S. Walgrave. Chicago: University of Chicago Press, 105–22.

Vliegenthart, R., Walgrave, S., Wouters, R. et al. (2016a). Do the Media Set the Parliamentary Agenda? A Comparative Study in Seven Countries. *European Journal of Political Research*, 55(2): 283–301.

Vliegenthart, R., Walgrave, S., Wouters, R. et al. (2016b). The Media as a Dual Mediator of the Political Agenda–Setting Effect of Protest: A Longitudinal Study in Six Western European Countries. *Social Forces*, 95(2): 837–59.

19

The Turkish Policy Agendas Project

Alper Tolga Bulut and Tevfik Murat Yildirim

The Turkish Policy Agendas Project was launched in 2013 by Alper Tolga Bulut, Berna Yilmaz Maggione, and Tevfik Murat Yildirim. The project consists of three research units that are located in the University of Houston, University of Milan, and University of Missouri, each of which was assigned to code a particular set of policy agendas data. Although the Project does not have an official sponsor or a funding source, individual members of the Project have received financial support from the Kinder Institute on Constitutional Democracy at the University of Missouri and from the Association for the Study of the Middle East and Africa.

The main motivation behind the project is twofold. First, by providing scholars of Turkish politics with longitudinal datasets on policy and media agendas, the project sets out to encourage scholars of Turkish politics to focus on understudied topics in Turkey, such as agenda-setting and the link between policy, media, and public agendas. Second, the project aims to contribute to the Comparative Agendas Project (CAP) by bringing authoritarian politics into the study of agenda dynamics. Turkey, the first developing country to join the CAP, has experienced multiple military interventions, an authoritarian single-party regime and political scandals that hindered the health of democracy. This variation allows scholars of comparative public policy to explore agenda dynamics under democratic and authoritarian regimes. By so doing, scholars will get a chance to observe whether or not findings based on the Western democracies travel to the developing world.

19.1 Turkish Politics

Although the modern Turkish Republic was founded in 1923, the first multi-party fair elections were held in 1950. In this first free-and-fair election, the Republican People's Party (CHP), which had ruled the country over twenty-five years, suffered a stunning defeat against the center right Democratic Party (DP). The victory of the DP in the 1950 election marks the beginning of a new era of multiparty competition in Turkey. The period following the transition to democracy had also introduced several factors that eventually led to the weak party institutionalization, which still characterizes the country today. Sayari (2008) defines three non-electoral sources of weak party institutionalization in Turkey: military interventions, party closures by the constitutional court, and frequent party switching. Military interventions can be considered as one of the most significant sources of party system instability in Turkey. Since the transition to democracy in the late 1940s, Turkey has experienced several military interventions, (1960, 1971, and 1980) and two indirect interventions (1997 and 2007). Although electoral politics and party competition have survived these military interventions as none of the direct interventions lasted long, the party system became more unstable. Frequent elections, coalitions, and coalition breakdowns became an inherent characteristic of this period.

One of the most significant impacts of the military interventions on Turkish politics was the strengthening of political Islam (Çarkoğlu and Toprak, 2006). The governing Justice and Development Party (AKP)'s roots can be traced back to the Islamist National Order Party (MNP), which was formed by Necmettin Erbakan in 1970. After almost thirty years of struggle in politics and surviving coups and party closures, the AKP was established in 2001, by splitting from the Felicity Party and claiming to break ties with political Islam. Later, the party defined itself as a center-right party.

The 2002 parliamentary elections marked the beginning of a new era in the history of Turkish party politics. The AKP has benefitted greatly from the diminishing popularity of its rivals in the 2002 parliamentary elections. The party also inherited the strong grassroots organization of the pro-Islamic party tradition and had large numbers of dedicated party activists. Financially it had the support of a growing number of conservative businessmen. The electoral victory of the AKP coupled with the high election threshold, made it the dominant party in the Turkish party system. The consecutive electoral victories of the party not only strengthened its place in the Turkish party system but also increased its influence in governmental institutions. This inevitably enabled good access to political patronage, which is regarded as important to win elections in Turkey (Gumuscu, 2012; Sayari, 2007).

Studies on contemporary Turkish politics often make references to the clientelistic nature of elections in Turkey. The clientelistic behavior in Turkey shows itself in different shapes and forms. The nature and form of clientelism has changed significantly over time in Turkey. In early stages of the multiparty competition, it was largely confined to the rural population. However, rapid urbanization created a class of urban poor and combined with strengthened party organizations at the local and national level paved the way for large-scale clientelistic politics. In order to gain the votes of this large social class, parties had to offer goods that will mitigate their socioeconomic problems. In this respect, the pro-Islamist parties have been more successful than their rivals. According to Sayari (2011: 13), the success of these parties largely relies on the fact that they were able to replace vertical ties of clientelism with frequent face-to-face interaction between party workers and their neighbors. This strong base of party workers, coupled with state resources, created a new network of clientelism that played a major role in AKP's success.

Currently there are four parties in the Turkish parliament. According to the expert survey analysis conducted by Benoit and Laver (2006), BDP (the then pro-Kurdish party) and MHP are located at the opposite ends of the ideological left–right spectrum, with center right AKP and center left CHP in between. The period before AKP has been dominated by coalition governments and instabilities due to several factors as mentioned above. The post-AKP era, on the other hand, has shown less electoral volatility and more stability in terms of party competition, as the same party has been ruling the country for almost sixteen years and the same parties have entered the parliament in the last four elections. Finally, party politics in the last decade shows clear signs of an emerging dominant party system that is highly clientelistic.

19.2 Datasets

It is evident that scholars of the Middle East studying quantitative social sciences suffer greatly from the lack of data. Turkish sources, including from the period of the Ottoman Empire, constitute an important exception (Lewis, 1951). The collection of parliamentary speeches, recorded day by day since the founding of the Turkish parliament in 1920, consists of more than 150,000 oral statements made during parliamentary sessions. Additionally, parliamentary speeches from the Ottoman period (1908–18) are available online. Many other parliamentary activities were digitalized and made public, reachable on the website of the Grand National Assembly of Turkey (www.tbmm.gov.tr).

Data on budget allocations in Turkey, starting from the late Ottoman period in the 1840s, are available online in both Turkish and English. The budget documents have been preserved extraordinarily well (Shaw, 1975); there is no missing data even during the periods of military regimes. These documents consist of data on authorized spending and actual spending for each spending unit, along with total spending in each fiscal year. This dataset allows scholars to explore the government's longitudinal policy priorities and how they vary with changing political environments (e.g., under different governments and regimes).

Lastly, we content coded the front pages of a once-leading newspaper, *Milliyet*. *Milliyet* newspaper archives are public and available for the period of 1950–2007. According to the website of the archive, the archive will be expanded to 2016. Our dataset, currently covering the period of 1980–2005, consists of more than 41,000 news stories coded according to the CAP codebook. Fortunately, the period currently covered by the Turkish Agendas Project enables scholars to examine media attention under a military regime, and minority, coalition, and single party governments.

Extensive and detailed coding enables reliability in comparing issue attention across different decision-making venues and nations. While coding each item, our coders strictly followed the general guidelines of the CAP coding system. Each item in the dataset is coded according to the relevant issue area, giving a measure of aggregate issue attention of legislators and parties.

To code parliamentary questions and laws, we used their titles, which are usually long and detailed and therefore make coding relatively easy and straightforward. In those situations where the title was not enough to understand the content of the question, we have referred to the actual document (available in the parliament's website). For the parliamentary bills, we used their short summaries. The dataset was coded by the same four coders. These coders went through about a month of intensive training, where examples and problems were discussed. Several rounds of reliability tests were then conducted where the four coders coded the same documents. The training was stopped when the level of intercoder reliability reached 85 percent at the subtopic level.

We have also content coded the election platforms of the governing AKP and the main opposition CHP parties. Party platforms are widely used to measure the parties' policy stances on several issues; hence coding platform sentences enables us to measure party priorities before they enter the parliament. Together, this yielded more than 10,000 platform sentences to be coded. To code the platforms, we used the natural sentence rather than the quasi-sentence (QS), based on the findings of Daubler et al. (2012).

To measure the preferences of the public, we use the most important problem (MIP) survey question of the Eurobarometer Survey. The MIP question has been widely used in the literature to measure public preferences or the public's attention to the political agenda as well as the broader public salience of issues (see Jones and Baumgartner, 2004, 2005). The policy priorities of Turkish citizens are estimated on the basis of the survey question, "What do you think is the MIP facing our country today?" Since Turkish opinion surveys typically have not included this question, we rely on Eurobarometer Surveys, which have asked the MIP question in its surveys of Turkish citizens since 2003. To translate Eurobarometer polls into issue attention percentages, we followed three steps following Jones et al. (2009). First, we matched each

Table 19.1. Overview of Turkish Agendas datasets

Data type	Data source	Data availability	Period covered	No. of observations
Budget	Ministry of Finance	1841–2016	1841–2016	~ 6,800
Media (front-page coverage)	*Milliyet*	1950–2007	1980–2005	~ 41,000
Parl. questions	TBMM	1987–2016	1991–2011	~ 13,000
Parl. speeches	TBMM	1920–2016	1983–2007	~ 48,000
Laws	TBMM	1920–2016	2002–13	~ 1,700
Party platforms of CHP and AKP	TBMM	1960–2015	2002–11	10,403 sentences
Public opinion	Eurobarometer	2003–16	2003–13	40 surveys

Source: Comparative Agendas Project—Turkey

answer with the CAP main topics. Second, for each poll, we calculated the percentages of responses for every issue category. Finally, we aggregated the data annually by taking average values in those years where multiple polls were conducted (see Table 19.1).

19.3 Empirical Applications

Our dataset can be used to study several research questions. First, it can be used to trace and analyze issue attention at both the legislature level and the party level. Second, it can be used to analyze "opinion-policy responsiveness" or the responsiveness of political parties to the priorities of the public. Studies of opinion-policy responsiveness have been largely confined to Western democracies, mostly the United States and the United Kingdom. In this respect, analyses using this dataset have the potential to make significant contributions to the literature. Third, the dataset can be used to analyze the responsiveness of the parties to their party platforms (which is usually defined as program to policy linkage).

In this section, we will briefly illustrate two possible applications. First, we will look at the general congruence between the public priorities and legislative activities, more specifically parliamentary bills. Second, following the scholars of the Punctuated Equilibrium Theory, we will show the annual changes in annual budget allocations during Turkey's single-party government.

19.3.1 *Measuring Public Preferences and Government Responsiveness*

Figure 19.1 compares parliamentary bills with public priorities. It shows the proportion of bills introduced in a given topic area with the proportion of the public stating that that is the most important problem facing the country.

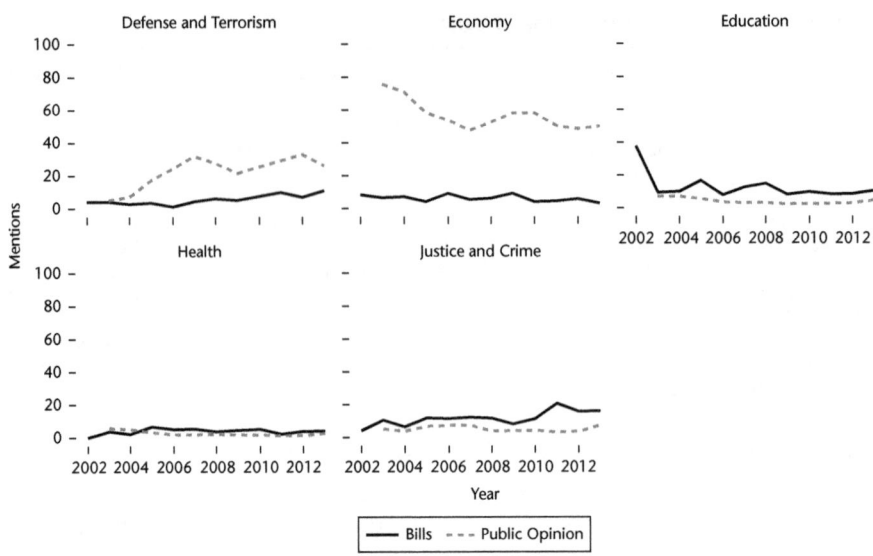

Figure 19.1. Public priorities (MIP) versus parliamentary bills (2002–13)
Source: Comparative Agendas Project—Turkey

Although the visual evidence seems to indicate a gap between public priorities and parliamentary bills, there is a directional correspondence. The gap between the public priorities and laws is most evident in the topic of economy. For other topics, there seem to be a better correlation between public priorities and laws. The legislative agenda seems to be particularly responsive in the domain of defense and terrorism. However, as in the other CAP datasets, we can see that MIP responses tend to be highly concentrated in the areas of economy and defense, whereas the policy activities of the government are widely dispersed across all the CAP topic areas.

19.3.2 Public Budgeting in Authoritarian Regimes

Punctuated Equilibrium Theory (PET) contends that public policies can best be described as long periods of stasis and brief but dramatic periods of change (Baumgartner and Jones, 2010; Jones and Baumgartner, 2005). Disproportionate information processing that stems from "cognitive" and "institutional friction" is at the core of PET. Evidence for PET comes mostly from Western democracies (Jones et al., 2009). Recent scholarship, however, expanded PET to authoritarian regimes. Lam and Chan (2015) find that authoritarian periods in Hong Kong are associated with more punctuated policy process. Chan and Zhao (2016) show that information restrictions lead to punctuated

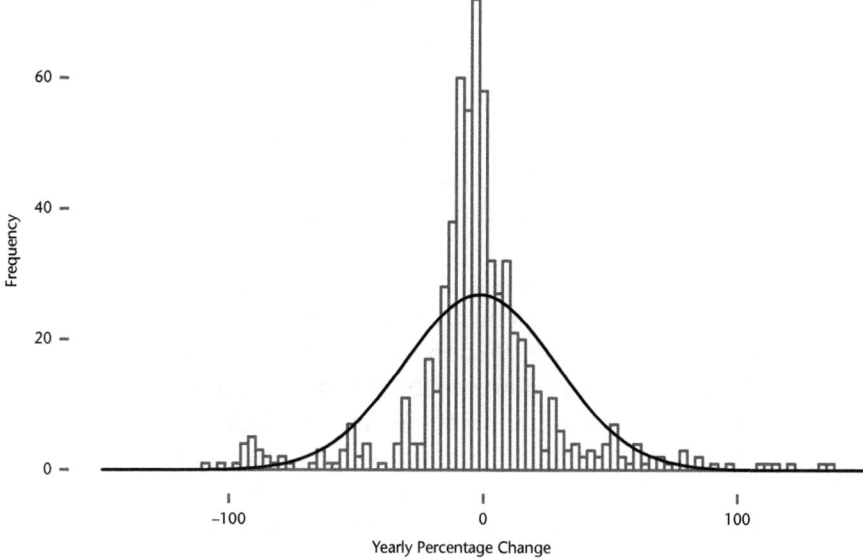

Figure 19.2. The distribution of annual budgetary changes during the one-party regime

Source: Comparative Agendas Project—Turkey

equilibrium in the policy process in China. In a more comprehensive study, Baumgartner et al. (2017) lend support to these studies, demonstrating that democratic transitions in Turkey, Malta, Russia, and Brazil are associated with lower policy punctuations. Starting from the 1840s, Turkish budget data allow for more comprehensive tests of PET in authoritarian regimes.

Figure 19.2 shows the distribution of annual changes in budget allocations. As seen in the figure, the distribution of budgetary changes during the one-party regime can be described as leptokurtic, showing the presence of punctuated equilibrium in the Turkish policy process. In other words, Turkish policy process during the authoritarian one-party government was dominated by forces protecting the status quo, and this trend was often disrupted by policy shocks and led to dramatic policy changes.

19.4 Concluding Remarks

The Turkish Policy Agendas Project produced massive datasets on media, public, and policy agendas in a limited time, thanks to the digitalized government sources that date back to the early 1900s. The fact that Turkey has experienced one-party and multiparty elections for decades, several military interventions and de-democratization during the period we cover indicates that scholars of comparative public policy can make use of the Turkish case to explore some previously unanswered questions. How do authoritarian regimes translate policy inputs into outputs and how is it different from that in democratic regimes? How does the link between political and media agenda vary with changing political environments? Were the Turkish military regimes different from others in Latin America or Africa in terms of policy-making (Demirel 2005)?

Finally, our dataset also enables us to broaden the study of opinion–policy and program–policy linkage to a highly clientelistic polity. Research on these topics is quite extensive in the Western context, and the literature's findings suggest a strong relationship. However, the dynamics of party politics in these two settings are quite distinct, as parties use different linkage mechanisms to connect with voters. Previous studies have argued that in clientelistic party systems, politicians lack the incentive to create coherent and well-structured party platforms on which to compete that inevitably leads to unresponsive parties (Epstein 2009; Hagopian 1990). In this respect, our dataset will enable researchers to investigate opinion–policy and program–policy nexus in a different setting. In short, we believe that the Turkish Agendas Project will help scholars explore the agenda dynamics in developing countries under various political settings.

References

Baumgartner, F. R., Carammia, M., Epp, D. A. et al. (2017). Budgetary Change in Authoritarian and Democratic Regimes. *Journal of European Public Policy*, 24(6): 1–17.

Baumgartner, F. R. and Jones, B. D. (2010). *Agendas and Instability in American Politics*. Chicago: University of Chicago Press.

Benoit, K., and Laver, M. (2006). *Party Policy in Modern Democracies*. London: Routledge.

Çarkoğlu, A., and Toprak, B. (2006). *Değişen Türkiye'de din, toplum ve siyaset*. TESEV.

Chan, K. N., and Zhao, S. (2016). Punctuated Equilibrium and the Information Disadvantage of Authoritarianism: Evidence from the People's Republic of China. *Policy Studies Journal*, 44(2): 134–55.

Däubler, T., Benoit, K., Mikhaylov, S., and Laver, M. (2012). Natural Sentences as Valid Units for Coded Political Texts. *British Journal of Political Science*, 42: 937–51.

Demirel, T. (2005). Lessons of Military Regimes and Democracy: The Turkish Case in a Comparative Perspective. *Armed Forces & Society*, 31(2): 245–71.

Epstein, D. J. (2009). Clientelism versus Ideology Problems of Party Development in Brazil. *Party Politics*, 15: 335–55.

Gumuscu, S. (2012). The Emerging Predominant Party System in Turkey. *Government and Opposition*, 48(2): 223–44.

Hagopian, F. (1990). Democracy by Undemocratic Means? Elites, Political Pacts, and Regime Transition in Brazil. *Comparative Political Studies*, 23(2): 147–70.

Jones, B. D. and Baumgartner, F. R. (2005). *The Politics of Attention: How Government Prioritizes Problems*. Chicago: University of Chicago Press.

Jones, B. D. and Baumgartner, F. R. (2004). Representation and Agenda Setting. *Policy Studies Journal*, 32(1): 1–24.

Jones, B. D., Larsen-Price, H., and Wilkerson, J. (2009). Representation in American Governing Institutions. *Journal of Politics*, 71: 277–90.

Lam, W. F., and Chan, K. W. (2015). How Authoritarianism Intensifies Punctuated Equilibrium: The Dynamics of Policy Attention in Hong Kong. *Governance*, 28(4): 549–70.

Lewis, B. (1951). The Ottoman Archives as a Source for the History of the Arab Lands. *Journal of the Royal Asiatic Society of Great Britain & Ireland (New Series)*, 83(3–4): 139–55.

Sayari, S. (2007). Towards a New Turkish Party System? *Turkish Studies*, 8(2): 197–210.

Sayari, S. (2008). Non-Electoral Sources of Party System Change in Turkey. In *Essays in Honor of Ergun Özbudun*, ed. S. Yazıcı, K. Gözler, F. Keyman et al. Istanbul: Yetkin Yayınları, 399–417.

Sayarı, S. (2011). Clientelism and Patronage in Turkish Politics and Society. In *The Post Modern Abyss and the New Politics of Islam*, ed. B. Toprak and F. Birtek. Istanbul: Bilgi University Press, 81–94.

Shaw, S. J. (1975). Ottoman Archival Materials for the Nineteenth and Early Twentieth Centuries: The Archives of Istanbul. *International Journal of Middle East Studies*, 6(1): 94–114.

20

The UK Policy Agendas Project

Shaun Bevan and Will Jennings

20.1 The UK Policy Agendas Project

Through a series of collaborations and research grants, the UK Policy Agendas Project has collected a wide range of data on the policy agendas of major institutional venues in British politics and on the public and media agendas. This began with a small grant from the British Academy to support coding the policy content of Speech from the Throne over the post-war period (John, 2005), along with the collection of historical Gallup poll data on public opinion about the most important problem (Jennings and John, 2009). The datasets were extended back in time and further datasets were added—including budgets, Acts of UK Parliament, front-page stories of *The Times of London*, Prime Minister's Questions, and bills and hearings of the Scottish Parliament—under a grant from the UK's Economic and Social Research Council (ESRC) (John et al., 2008). These data underpin the book *Policy Agendas in British Politics* (John et al., 2013), which summarized our key findings on policy stability and instability—developing a theory of "focused adaptation" to explain patterns of policy change, characterized by structural breaks in time series of issue attention. Since ESRC-funding ended in 2012, the UK Project has continued updating several of the datasets and generating new data sources through collaborations, such as on UK party manifestos (Froio et al., 2016), reports of parliamentary select committees (Bevan et al., 2018), and statutory instruments (Bevan, 2015).

20.2 The UK Political System and Agenda-Setting

The United Kingdom's political system takes the form of a majoritarian parliamentary democracy (influential as the Westminster model of parliamentary democracy adopted by many other countries). Members of the lower house of the legislature (the "House of Commons") are elected via a first-past-the-post electoral system in single-member districts, while members of the upper house (the "House of Lords") are largely political appointees alongside a small number of hereditary peers. The prime minister is the member of the House of Commons who is able to command the support of a majority of the Commons, forming the executive from members of both Houses and exercising executive powers on behalf of the monarch.

There are a range of institutional venues in which governments, parties, and legislators can set the agenda in the UK political system. Formally, UK governments set out their legislative and executive agenda in the Speech from the Throne (also known as the King's or Queen's Speech), which opens each session of Parliament (see Jennings et al., 2011a). This is typically done on an annual basis, though on occasion speeches have been presented more than once in a year (e.g., 1921, 1974) or skipped a year where the parliamentary session was extended (e.g., 2010–12). While the speech provides a high profile signal of the priorities of the executive, the government enacts its policy agenda via primary legislation (Acts of UK Parliament). In recent decades the number of acts passed by the UK government has declined—and it instead has made use of omnibus legislation that combines policy measures, expanded its use of secondary legislation and handed over decision-making authority to independent regulatory agencies and supranational bodies such as the European Union. The executive still maintains considerable discretionary power through statutory instruments—often empowered under the terms of previous legislation—though these typically are not a venue for symbolic agenda-setting.

Formal channels for the opposition to set the policy agenda in the UK Parliament are relatively limited, though "urgent questions" (granted by the Speaker of the House of Commons) and Opposition Day Debates give it opportunities to draw attention to specific issues. The most prominent parliamentary venue for holding UK government to account is the weekly Prime Minister's Questions (PMQs), where the opposition leader(s) and MPs have the opportunity to highlight issues or concerns—often impacting on the media agenda by setting the content of later news bulletins. In recent decades, development of the system of parliamentary select committees has created venues in which cross-party groups of legislators—independent of government or opposition—can set the policy agenda through their inquiries, hearings, and reports. This reflects the growing dispersion of agenda-setting power in formal institutional venues in the UK political system. Also integral to this is the process of devolution that the United Kingdom has undergone since the late 1990s, which has seen the creation of new venues for agenda-setting—the devolved legislatures in Scotland, Wales, and Northern Ireland—and given prominence to new actors, first ministers, as leaders of the devolved governments. Beyond the United Kingdom's patchwork of institutional rules and arrangements that create multiple formal venues for agenda-setting, there are of course many informal settings in which both elites, organized interests, and citizens can seek to shape the agenda—often funneled through traditional news media, and now increasingly via social media.

20.3 Project and Data

20.3.1 *The UK Coding System, Protocols, and Reliability*

The original coding system of the UK Project was directly adapted from the codebook of the US Policy Agendas Project, with very few adjustments. Most major and subtopics translate very well to UK public policy (and the public's issue agenda). For purposes of coding and data use, we developed a national codebook with additional instructions and UK-specific examples to aid coders and data users. All UK data has now been coded in line with the Comparative Agendas Project coding system. Notable coding practices that apply to the United Kingdom specifically relate to the use of 1627 for domestic terrorism and 1927 for international terrorism. Another quirk of the coding system for the United Kingdom is that the 2105 topic is used for dependent territories of the British Empire/Commonwealth (which are then coded under international affairs once independence is achieved) and for control of UK government over its countries (e.g., Wales, Scotland, and Northern Ireland), dependencies (e.g., the Isle of Man), territories (e.g., Bermuda, Falkland Islands), and for members of the Commonwealth where the Queen is head of state. One dataset where coding has had to break convention is for the Ipsos MORI "most important issue" series. The pollster's coding of survey responses groups together the issues of defence and international affairs, major topics 16 and 19 respectively in the CAP coding system. The decision was taken to code these responses as international affairs. This means that it may be advisable to merge topics 16 and 19 when using UK data on the public agenda.

The majority of the UK data was double-blind coded by postgraduate or postdoctoral students.[1] While levels of intercoder reliability varied somewhat across datasets it was generally consistent, typically in the region of 85 percent to 90 percent reliability at the major topic level. Following this initial phase, all coded data were subject to an intensive moderation process, led by one or more of the project leaders, which included the resolution of any coding disagreements, random checks of agreed codes, and targeted checks on identified problem areas. Importantly, our approach to coding classification is "open source," so wherever it is possible (i.e., when not constrained by copyright restrictions), the raw data needed to code each dataset (e.g., the long and short title of Acts of UK Parliament or the full text of the Speech from the Throne) is made publicly available. This enables other researchers to check, and provide feedback/corrections on, our coding. It also allows other researchers to add to or easily build on our work (e.g., Annesley et al., 2015).

20.3.2 Comparing Cross-Nationally

The UK data series have a high degree of comparability to those for other parliamentary systems and advanced democracies in general. This has been consistently demonstrated by comparative studies; which have used the Speech from the Throne and similar executive speeches (Breeman et al., 2009; Jennings et al., 2011b; Mortensen et al., 2011), Acts of UK Parliament and primary legislation (Brouard et al., 2009; Bevan and Jennings, 2014), and PMQs and parliamentary questions (Vliegenthart et al., 2016).

As with any comparative analysis, one must be aware of institutional differences when using the data. For example, the United Kingdom produces a relatively small number of pieces of primary legislation compared to legislatures in other countries across the Comparative Agendas Project, on average around fifty Acts of Parliament a year. This is due in part to the UK government's heavy use of delegated legislation, where "statutory instruments" (secondary legislation) are able to fulfill many tasks reserved for primary legislation in other systems (see Bevan, 2015). This means that level-differences must be controlled for when comparing with legislatures that produce far more pieces of legislation (such as US Congress). Similarly, the Speech from the Throne provides a formal statement of the intended programme of the government, read by the monarch, but does not typically seek to influence other political actors or groups through rhetoric and symbolism in the same way as the US president's State of the Union Address (which can be substantially longer than the UK speech). While the UK data is entirely appropriate for cross-national comparisons, slight differences in the institutional function or logic of equivalent agenda venues in other countries need to be understood before use.

20.3.3 Datasets

The data collected for the United Kingdom include measures of prominent institutional agendas of British politics and government (covering both the executive and the legislature), as well as measures of the public and media agenda. The timeline of when particular data was collected and updated/

Table 20.1. Timeline of data releases for the UK Policy Agendas Project

Phase	Pilot	Extension	Expansion	Current
Period	2005–6	2006–8	2008–12	2012–present
Team	John	John and Jennings	John, Jennings, Bevan, Halpin, and Bertelli	Bevan and Jennings
Funders	British Academy	LSE Manchester	ESRC Manchester	Mannheim Edinburgh Southampton
Speech from the Throne (King's and Queen's Speech)	1945–2005	1945–2005	1911–2010*	1911–2016
Acts of UK Parliament		1945–2008	1911–2008	1911–2016
Public opinion (the most important problem/issue)		1960–2001	1960–2008	1944–2016
Public expenditure by function of UK government			1911–2007	1911–2007
Media (front-page headlines of The Times of London)			1960–2008	1960–2008
Prime Minister's Questions			1998–2008	1998–2008
Public opinion, Scotland (the most important issue)			1998–2008	1998–2008
Bills/Acts of Scottish Parliament			1999–2008	1999–2008
Hearings of Committees of Scottish Parliament			1999–2007	1999–2007
Party election manifestos				1983–2008
Reports of Select Committees of UK Parliament				1997–2014
Statutory Instruments of UK Parliament				1987–2008
Prorogation speech				1975–2016

Note: * Recoding of the Speech data as part of ESRC project.
Source: Comparative Agendas Project—United Kingdom

extended is summarized in Table 20.1. This highlights the expansion of the number of venues covered by the project over the time period between 2005 and 2018.

20.4 Insights from the UK Policy Agendas Project Data

The UK Project has produced a wide range of outputs that draw on its data on policy, public and media agendas. Our data is introduced and described in most detail in *Policy Agendas in British Politics* (John et al., 2013), which traces attention of British government to different policy topics since 1945. This shows, for example, how crime has risen on the agenda since the 1950s, though dropped during the late 2000s around the time the global financial

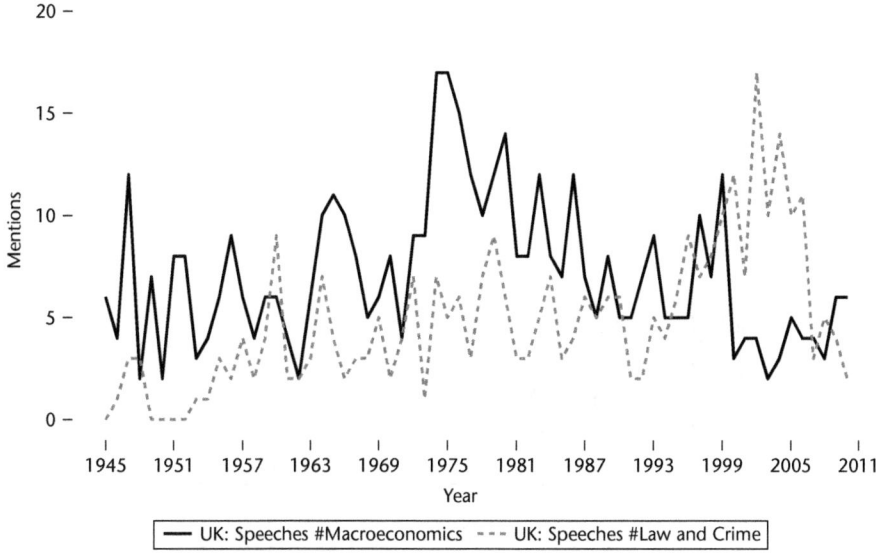

Figure 20.1. Frequency of mentions of the economy and law and crime in the Speech from the Throne, 1945–2012

Source: Comparative Agendas Project—United Kingdom

crisis hit. This is shown in Figure 20.1. The economy is notable for its "squeezing out" effect on other issues (Jennings et al., 2011a).

Broadly, publications from the project team have tended to focus on the themes of policy change and responsiveness to public opinion. Studies of policy stability have shown the uneven distribution of policy change (e.g., John and Jennings, 2010; John and Bevan, 2012), as depicted in Figure 20.2, with the dominant central peak indicating high levels of incrementalism in policymaking attention to issues and fat tails equated with occasional large and sudden shifts in attention.

Some work has looked at the transmission of attention from one venue to another, such as from Speeches to Acts of UK Parliament (Bevan et al., 2011) or from party manifestos to Acts (Froio et al., 2016). Other research has looked at the link between public opinion and policy agendas (Jennings and John, 2009; John et al., 2011; Bevan and Jennings, 2014; Bevan, 2015). Aside from core outputs related to the project, other scholars have used the UK data for their analyses, for example in studies of gender equality (Annesley et al., 2015) and crime (Miller 2016; also see Jennings et al., 2017). This UK Policy Agendas Project data therefore offers important insights into the issues that are attended to, or disregarded, by key political actors in and around British government, by the media and citizens more widely.

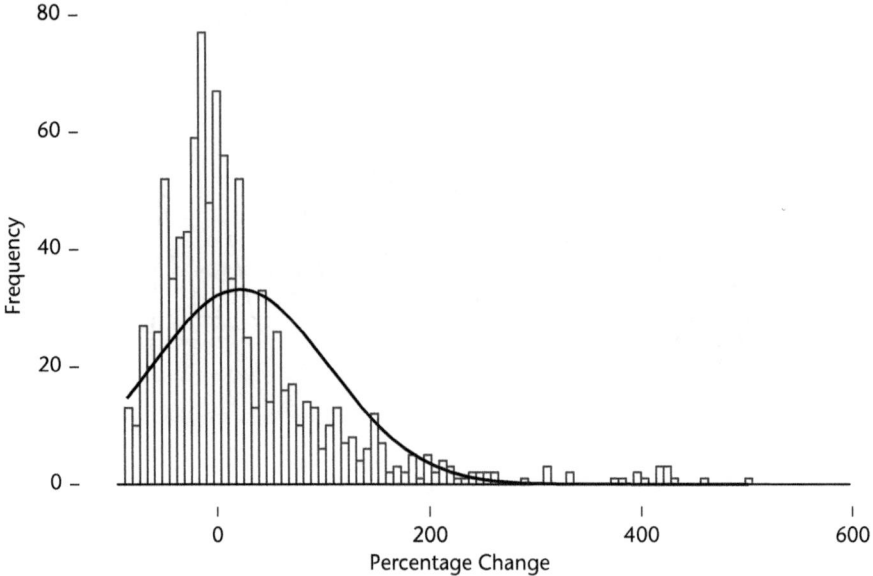

Figure 20.2. Distribution of percentage changes in attention to major policy topics in the Speech from the Throne, 1945–2012

Source: Comparative Agendas Project—United Kingdom

Note

1. There is one exception. Namely, the second coder for approximately 2/3rds of the PMQs dataset was a toolset now incorporated in RTextTools for supervised learning, which proved just as reliable as human coders despite difficulties often associated with oral questions.

References

Annesley, C., Engeli, I., and Gains, F. (2015). The Profile of Gender Equality Issue Attention in Western Europe. *European Journal of Political Research*, 54(3): 525–42.

Bevan, S. (2015). Bureaucratic Responsiveness: The Effects of Government, Public and European Attention on the UK Bureaucracy. *Public Administration*, 93(1): 139–58.

Bevan, S., and Jennings, W. (2014). Representation, Agendas and Institutions. *European Journal of Political Research*, 53(1): 37–56.

Bevan, S., Jennings, W., and Pickup, M. (2018). Problem Detection in Legislative Oversight: An Analysis of Legislative Committee Agendas in the U.K. and U.S. *Journal of European Public Policy*.

Bevan, S., John, P., and Jennings, W. (2011). Keeping Party Programmes on Track: The Transmission of the Policy Agendas of the Speech from the Throne to Acts of the UK Parliament. *European Political Science Review*, 3(3): 395–417.

Breeman, G., Chaqués, L., Green-Pedersen, C. et al. (2009). Comparer Les Agendas Gouvernementaux: les "discourse du trône" aux Pays-Bas, au Royaume-Uni, au Danemark et en Espagne. *Revue Internationale de Politique Comparée*, special issue "Les Agendas Politiques," 16(3): 405–21.

Brouard, S., Wilkerson, J., Baumgartner, F. R. et al. (2009). Comparer Les Productions Législatives: enjeux et méthodes. *Revue Internationale de Politique Comparée*, special issue "Les Agendas Politiques," 16(3): 381–404.

Froio, C., Bevan, S., and Jennings, W. (2016). Party Mandates and the Politics of Attention: Party Platforms, Public Priorities and the Policy Agenda in Britain. *Party Politics*, 23(6): 692–703.

Jennings, W., Bevan, S., and John, P. (2011a). The Agenda of British Government: The Speech from the Throne, 1911–2008. *Political Studies*, 59(1): 74–98.

Jennings, W., Bevan, S., Timmermans, A. et al. (2011b). Effects of the Core Functions of Government on the Diversity of Executive Agendas. *Comparative Political Studies*, 44(8): 1001–30.

Jennings, W., Farrall, S., Hay, C., and Gray, E. (2017). Moral Panics and Punctuated Equilibrium in Public Policy: An Analysis of the Criminal Justice Policy Agenda in Britain. *Policy Studies Journal*. DOI: 10.1111/psj.12239.

Jennings, W., and John, P. (2009). The Dynamics of Political Attention: Public Opinion and the Queen's Speech in the United Kingdom. *American Journal of Political Science*, 53(4): 838–54.

John, P. (2005). The Policy Priorities of UK Governments: A Content Analysis of King's and Queen's Speeches, 1945–2005. *British Academy award reference SG42076*.

John, P., Bertelli, A., Jennings, W. and Bevan, S. (2013). *Policy Agendas in British Politics*. Basingstoke: Palgrave Macmillan.

John, P., and Bevan, S. (2012). What Are Policy Punctuations? Large Changes in the Agenda of the UK Government, 1911–2008. *Policy Studies Journal*, 40(1): 89–108.

John, P., Bevan, S., and Jennings, W. (2011). The Policy-Opinion Link and Institutional Change: The Policy Agenda of the United Kingdom and Scottish Parliaments, 1977–2008. *Journal of European Public Policy*, 18(7): 1052–68.

John, P., and Jennings, W. (2010). Punctuations and Turning Points in British Politics: The Policy Agenda of the Queen's Speech, 1940–2005. *British Journal of Political Science*, 40(3): 561–86.

John, P., Jennings, W., Halpin, D. et al. (2008). Legislative Policy Agendas in the UK. *ESRC award reference R1059382008*.

Miller, L. (2016). *The Myth of Mob Rule: Violent Crime and Democratic Politics*. Oxford: Oxford University Press.

Mortensen, P. B., Green-Pedersen, C., Breeman, G. et al. (2011). Comparing Government Agendas: Executive Speeches in the Netherlands, United Kingdom, and Denmark. *Comparative Political Studies*, 44(8): 973–1000.

Vliegenthart, R., Walgrave, S., Bonafont, L. C. et al. (2016). Do the Media Set the Parliamentary Agenda? A Comparative Study in Seven Countries. *European Journal of Political Research*, 55(2): 283–301.

21

The US Policy Agendas Project

Rebecca Eissler and Bryan D. Jones

21.1 US Policy Agendas

Frank Baumgartner and Bryan D. Jones started the US Policy Agendas Project (PAP) in 1993 as a way to systematically measure government attention within and across specific policy areas and time. As the founding project of the Comparative Agenda Project (CAP) network, Baumgartner and Jones created the initial coding scheme that has since evolved into the common CAP coding scheme. One of the major aims of the initial work was to allow the creation of reliable time-series data on the policy topics scheduled for public debate. As such, a key criterion was backward compatibility—the need to adjust past policy categories if and when new categories were added in the future. This is necessary to make policy categories comparable across time. The model here was the National Income and Products Accounts, which established such a system to assess changes in various components of national economies (see Jones, 2016).

The development of the PAP coding scheme began as a pilot project at Texas A&M University while Baumgartner and Jones were studying US congressional hearings. Hearings were selected because they met a key criterion: hearings form a record of institutional attention at an early stage of the policy process. This characteristic was vital to their goal of understanding agenda-setting dynamics. By systematically collecting and coding data related to the activities of the federal government since 1947, the PAP has lead to political scientists being able to quantitatively understand dynamics that had previously only been explored via individual case studies (Eissler and Russell, 2016).

Over the past twenty years, the project has grown to examine a broader range of government activities. The project, currently located at the University of Texas at Austin's Department of Government, has expanded to include upwards of a dozen additional datasets, such as the New York Times Index, Roll Call Votes, Executive Orders, and State of the Union Addresses, as well as hosting datasets created and maintained by scholars outside the project that utilize the coding scheme. The quantity and variety of both in-house and affiliated datasets represent the collaborative and evolutionary nature of the project, as many of the current datasets started because of student researchers' interest in using the project's structure to advance their personal research (Eissler and Russell, 2016).

21.2 US Political System

The American national government has long been characterized by the separation of powers between the three branches. The legislative branch is made up of two chambers, the House of Representatives and the Senate, to which members are elected from single member districts using plurality rules. This structure has led to two-party domination of the political system. The Democratic party is traditionally a center-left party, while the Republican party is traditionally a center-right party, however in the past twenty years, both parties have moved away from the center towards their right and left extremes (Theriault, 2008). The House of Representatives is made up of 435 members and the distribution of seats is determined by the population in the states; with reapportionment occurring following the census, which happens once a decade in years ending in zero. The Senate is made up of 100 members, with each state permanently maintaining two seats. A president, who is both head of state and head of government, occupies the executive branch. His selection and powers operate separately from the legislative branch. As such, there is often competition between the two main policymaking branches of the federal government. The third branch, the judiciary, is made up of a system of courts that culminate in the Supreme Court, an institution that can weigh in only on "cases or controversies" that appeal to the Court for a decision. The modern Supreme Court is made up of nine justices who sit in one panel. They are appointed by the president and confirmed by the Senate. They have complete control over which cases they chose to hear.

21.3 Datasets

The PAP maintains and updates thirteen datasets covering the full range of government activities. Our legislative datasets include congressional hearings, public laws, and roll call votes. Our executive branch datasets include executive orders and State of the Union addresses. We code Supreme Court decisions to represent the activities of the judicial branch. We also code the policy content of the two main political parties via the party platforms datasets. The PAP tracks the budgetary activities of the federal government via the budget authority and budget outlays datasets. Our media datasets include the *CQ Almanac* and the New York Times Index. We track interest group activity via the Encyclopedia of Associations dataset. Finally, we track public opinion about policies using the MIP dataset (see Table 21.1).

All data is coded by hand, with each observation being assigned codes by two coders who work independently. Following coding, the two codes are reconciled to make a final determination. We strive for 90 percent agreement on major topic and 80 percent on minor topic following reconciliation. Additionally, all datasets contain the policy topic code according to the CAP coding scheme and the legacy PAP coding scheme. The legacy PAP code has been retained for replication and the continuation of research that is based solely in the US context. The differences between the two systems are minimal.

The primary differences between the CAP codes and the legacy PAP codes include: a separate subtopic within social welfare for food assistance, which gets incorporated into low-income assistance in the CAP codebook; arts and culture as a subtopic within education that gets moved to its own major topic

Table 21.1. PAP-maintained datasets

Dataset name	Type	No. of observations	Years	Unit of analysis
Congressional Hearings	Legislative	94,882	1947–2013	Description of hearing activity
Public Laws	Legislative	20,403	1948–2014	Title of each public law
Roll Call	Legislative	50,148	1947–2013	Description of vote
Executive Orders	Executive	4,190	1945–2015	Title of order
State of the Union	Executive	22,794	1946–2016	Quasi-sentence
Democratic Party Platform	Political parties	13,633	1948–2008	Quasi-sentence
Republican Party Platform	Political parties	19,836	1948–2016	Quasi-sentence
Supreme Court Cases	Judiciary	8,955	1945–2009	Summary of case
Budget Authority (Adjusted)	Budget	7,935	1947–2015	Dollars per OMB functions and sub-functions
Congressional Quarterly Almanac	Media	14,217	1948–2011	Articles in the publication
New York Times Index	Media	53,495	1946–2013	Random sample of index entries of newspaper content
Encyclopedia of Associations	Interest groups	972	1966–2001	Groups
Most important problem (MIP)	Public opinion	1,344	1947–2012	Answers to open-ended question

Source: Comparative Agendas Project—United States

in the CAP codebook; parental leave and child care is moves from labor in the PAP codebook to social welfare in the CAP codebook; a separate subtopic within health for other health benefits and procedures that gets incorporated into insurer providers in the CAP codebook; a separate subtopic for pollution and conservation in coastal and other navigable waterways within the environment that gets combined with drinking water in the CAP codebook; a separate subtopic for truck and automobile transportation and safety within transportation that gets incorporated with highways in the CAP codebook; a separate subtopic for police, fire, and weapons control within law and crime that gets moved into a single category for all law enforcement agencies in the CAP codebook; and a separate subtopic for military veterans within defense that gets combined with military personnel in the CAP codebook.

The congressional hearings dataset contains over ninety-four thousand observations, with each corresponding to a hearing held by Congress since 1947. Committees in both the House of Representatives and the Senate conduct hearings to accomplish a variety of tasks, which include investigating policy proposals and conducting oversight of bureaucratic agencies. Committees are organized according to task or policy area. These data were coded from the annual volumes published by the Congressional Information Service and, starting in the mid-2000s, from data available on the ProQuest Congressional database. In addition to basic identifying information, the dataset includes a number of variables containing additional information about the hearing purpose and the committee conducting the hearing.

The public laws dataset contains all public laws enacted since 1948. A public law is created by first being introduced as a bill into one of the two chambers of Congress, which then receives the approval of a majority in both chambers, before being signed into law by the president. The list of public laws was collected from the appendix of the annual editions of the *CQ Almanac*.

The roll call votes dataset records all the votes in the House and Senate in which the individual politicians' choices as either for or against the measure are recorded according to the CAP coding scheme since 1946. Many types of legislative action can be put to a roll call, such as votes for amendment to proposed legislation, as well as the vote for final passage of a bill. Although the data have come from multiple sources over time (more details in the data codebook), since the 107th congress, votes are obtained from Govtrack.us, an open-source, online database of congressional voting records.

The executive orders dataset contains the orders issued by a president to administrative agencies since 1945. These actions carry the force of law and do not require legislative approval. However, because presidents issue them unilaterally, they can be revoked unilaterally by a successor or over ruled by a public law. Observations are compiled from the Federal Register's Executive Orders "Disposition Table Index."

The State of the Union dataset provides information on the presidential State of the Union address since 1946. Although many of these are delivered orally in front of a joint session of Congress, occasionally these take the form of written documents. These speeches occur once a year in fulfillment of the constitutional requirement that the president "give to the Congress Information on the State of the Union, and recommend to their Consideration such Measures as he shall judge necessary and expedient." This dataset codes the text of the speech at the quasi-sentence level, which means that observation is the text between periods, semi-colons, and other punctuation marks.

Our party platforms datasets were originally compiled by Christina Wolbrecht and are maintained by the PAP. The datasets contain the Democratic Party and Republican Party platforms, which are written every four years during the presidential nominating conventions. The platforms are obtained from The American Presidency Project, an online database of presidential materials.

The Supreme Court case dataset contains all cases granted on certiorari or on appeal and argued before the Court since 1945. This dataset is the only publicly available dataset that examines the Court from a policy perspective. The Supreme Court has complete control over which cases it hears. Most years, the Court receives upwards of seven thousand petitions and, on average, only hears eighty cases, a number that has been on the decline for many years (Liptak, 2009).

The budget authority dataset is based on the Budget of the United States Government since fiscal year 1947. Originally compiled by James True, the dataset measures budget authority and provides an inflation-adjusted view of the budgetary process. The data is organized according to the functions and sub-functions of the federal government, rather than by the CAP policy topics.

The budget outlays dataset, compiled by Bryan D. Jones, Frank R. Baumgartner, and John Lovett, provides two "synthetic" series of annual, long-term budget outlays. No single series of expenditures (outlays) exist for the US federal government dating back to the founding of the republic, but two separate data series, compiled by the Treasury Department and the Office of Budget and Management allow for the construction of two "synthetic" datasets covering from 1791 to present. Outlays are noted for domestic and defense expenditures. The dataset includes both outlays and inflation-adjusted values.

The *Congressional Quarterly (CQ) Almanac* dataset contains information from all articles in the main chapters of the *CQ Almanac*. The *CQ Almanac* is published by CQ Press, which specializes in political news. Every year, they publish the *Almanac*, which highlights the important legislative events of the year. Each article usually covers one legislative initiative.

The New York Times (NYT) Index dataset is a sample of articles from *The New York Times* since 1946. *The New York Times* is a daily publication that is considered representative of the broader media agenda. The sample is generated by collecting information about the first entry on every odd numbered page of the NYT index volumes.

The *Encyclopedia of Associations* dataset tracks number of groups according to major topic policy areas since 1966 and is generated via the Gale Research, later Thomson/Gale, printed volume of the same name. We created a simple list of each group and coded the groups according to the PAP coding scheme. Complete data are available in five-year increments, as well as estimated annual counts for the whole time period.

The most important problem (MIP) dataset contains responses to Gallup's question "what do you think is the most important problem facing this country today?" Individual responses are aggregated at the annual level and coded according to major policy topic since 1947.

The PAP also acts as host to a number of datasets updated and maintained by other scholars, but that utilize the coding scheme. One such example is the Congressional Bills dataset, which is maintained by the Congressional Bills Project under the direction of E. Scott Adler and John Wilkerson, allows scholars to learn about the bills that are introduced into the US Congress. Another dataset the PAP hosts is a dataset assembled by Sam Kernell that examines presidential veto rhetoric offering insight into the threats that presidents make to veto legislation. On the public opinion side, the Project hosts the Policy Moods data, compiled by James A. Stimson and K. Elizabeth Coggins. This data allows users to study longitudinal measures of public opinion related to different policy issues. The PAP also hosts two media datasets. The New York Times Front Page dataset, by Amber Boydstun, examines articles that appear on the front page of *The New York Times* to measure the print media agenda, while the TV News Policy Agenda data, by Joe Uscinski, examines over sixty-five thousand TV news stories from the Vanderbilt archive. Finally, the PAP hosts the Tax Expenditure dataset, which was created and is maintained by Christopher Faricy. This data is based on the Congressional Joint Committee on Taxation's annual five-year estimates of federal tax expenditures. All of these datasets extend the efforts of the PAP to measure what government pays attention to over time.

21.4 A Look into the Data

Over the post-World-War-II period, health care policy has appeared repeatedly on the government agenda. The PAP datasets let us trace the attention to the issue over time and the many attempts to enact policy reforms. Figure 21.1 shows the percent of each dataset that is devoted to health. Prior to the late 1960s, healthcare was a small, but regular presence on the policy agenda across the legislative and executive branches, while barely registering on the

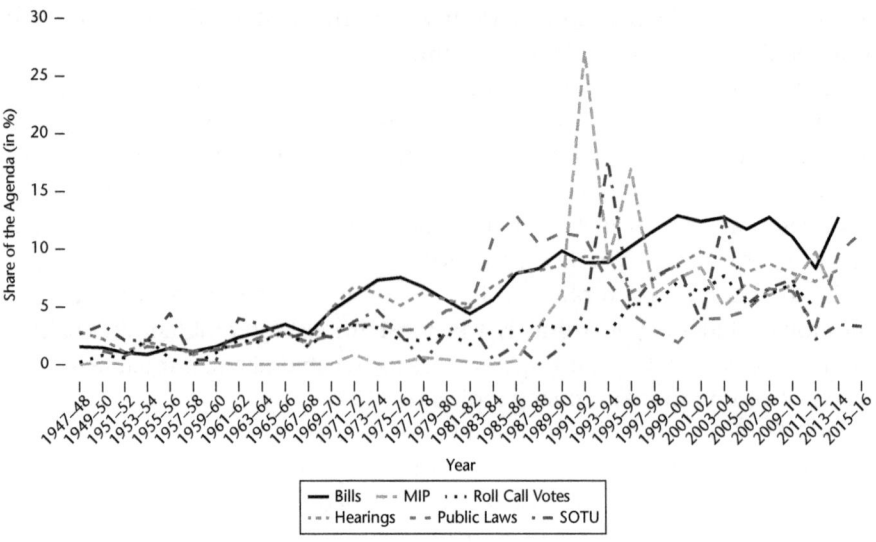

Figure 21.1. Attention to health across policy tools by Congress, 1947–2015
Source: Comparative Agendas Project—United States

mass public agenda. In the 1970s and 1980s, there was a steady increase in legislative activity, while the share of the president and public agenda stayed largely the same. Only in the 1990s and 2000s do we see healthcare become a significant portion of all agendas, particularly surrounding the Clinton healthcare reform attempt in the early 1990s and the successful passage of the Affordable Care Act during the Obama administration. This is merely one demonstration of how these data can be used understand attention to American policy over time and institutions.

References

Eissler, R., and Russell, A. (2016). The Policy Agendas Project. In *American Governance*, ed. S. Schechter. New York: Macmillan, 50–1.

Jones, B. D. (2016). The Comparative Policy Agendas Projects as Measurement Systems. *Journal of Public Policy*, 36: 31–46.

Liptak, A. (2009). The Case of the Plummeting Supreme Court Docket, *New York Times*, Sept. 28, 2009.

Theriault, S. M. (2008). *Party Polarization in Congress*. New York: Cambridge University Press.

22

The EU Policy Agendas Project

Petya Alexandrova

22.1 The EU Political System

The European Union traces its origin from the European Economic Community, established by the Treaty of Rome (1957). Integration began among six European countries in a narrow range of policy domains and has expanded tremendously over the last decades. At the time of writing, the Union encompasses twenty-eight member states and has competences in a wide spectrum of areas. The Treaty of Lisbon (2007) formally lists these competences distinguishing among exclusive jurisdictions, those shared with the member states, domains where the European Union ensures coordination, and actions to support, coordinate, or supplement those of the member states. Early scholars of European integration spent much time discussing the nature of the "beast" as the European Union is neither clearly a state nor just an international organization. Nowadays, there is a consensus that in terms of its political system the Union can serve as a case in comparative research (Hix and Høyland, 2011). Nevertheless, this system is distinct in some complex features designed to balance different interests and structure the flow of ideas.

The European Commission is a EU executive body with an administrative apparatus. It is led by a president and structured along thematic departments, called Directorates General. The Commission has multiple responsibilities, most notably it oversees compliance with EU treaties, implements EU policies, and prepares the drafts of legislative proposals. It is the only EU institution, which can officially table legislative proposals but informally other actors can exercise influence over this process. Therefore, the Commission needs to consider the views of the other core institutions in order to ensure the feasibility of adoption. The Commission also launches different non-legislative initiatives, coming out in the form of Green Papers, White Papers, reports, etc.

Once a legislative proposal is drafted, it is placed on the agenda of the Council of Ministers and the European Parliament. The Parliament originates from the Treaty of Rome but its members began to be directly elected in 1979. In the earlier years of European integration, the powers of the Parliament were limited both in terms of level of engagement (more often a consultative than a decision-maker role) and scope of policy areas in which it had a say. This changed substantively with the introduction and subsequent expansion of the co-legislative procedure, where the Council and the Parliament share equal powers. Therefore, these two institutions are seen as representing a bicameral legislature. The members of the European Parliament (MEPs) are elected from party lists at the member-state level with each country having a designated seat quota. However, most of these parties belong to EU-wide party federations and MEPs generally vote along party lines (e.g., Hix and Høyland, 2011).

The Council of Ministers has different thematic formations. The ten configurations, which currently exist, meet regularly but the number of meetings differs in accordance with the topics that need to be discussed and decided upon. Each formation consists of the twenty-eight responsible ministers for the respective topic in the member states. Today, the standard voting rule in the Council is qualified majority voting though some domains still require unanimity. Besides its legislative function, the Council is also responsible for coordinating member states' policies in several fields, including economic and fiscal policies, education, culture, sport, youth and employment policy. The preparation and chairing of Council meetings is a task of the rotating six-month country presidency.[1]

The European Council originated in the 1970s as an informal body, where the heads of state and government of all member states could discuss in a closed environment any matter of European integration. Nowadays, it is formally responsible for defining the overall priorities and directions for development of the European Union, thereby having a crucial role in agenda-setting. Over the course of its existence, the European Council has intensified both the regularity of its summits and the degree of engagement with specific policy issues. Until the Treaty of Lisbon entered into force the rotating country presidency used to be in charge of coordinating and chairing the European Council meetings. Ever since, this role has been taken up by a President of the European Council, appointed for a two-and-half year term with a possible single extension.

As the EU competencies vary across policy areas, so do some arrangements for policymaking. Particularly important in this respect is the domain of foreign and security policy, where the European Council provides guidelines based on which the Council of Ministers develops specific policies. The differentiated level of integration in some areas, most notably the Economic and Monetary Union has also triggered special institutional arrangements. Launched in 1998, an equivalent of the Economic and Financial Affairs (Eco-Fin) Council but consisting only of Eurozone member states' ministers—the Eurogroup—gathers informally before EcoFin meetings. Following two sporadic events in the aftermath of the global economic and financial crisis, since 2011 the European Council has also been meeting in a configuration consisting only of the Eurozone Heads of State or Government, known as the Euro Summit.

22.2 EU Policy Agendas Datasets

The first and so far only complete and released dataset of the EUPAP covers the agenda of the European Council. It includes all Conclusions (as well as statements and declarations) issued following meetings of the body between the first summit in 1975 and the end of 2014. The Conclusions are the only document produced by the European Council. They are published after all formal and often also after informal summits. The coding unit of the dataset is quasi-sentence, identifying the lowest possible level of issue attention. Policy issues are classified using the EUPAP codebook. Besides the policy issue variable, the dataset covers a range of "demographic" identifiers, such as the place and closing date of the meeting as well as multiple dummy variables. The coding was performed manually by pairs of trained students. Disagreements were discussed and resolved by the project leaders, working together in cases of more complex issues. As this was the first EUPAP dataset, the codebook was refined during the coding process (for a detailed description of the dataset see Alexandrova et al., 2014).

Currently, there are several more datasets in preparation within the EUPAP or following the EUPAP agenda classification approach. One of them focuses on the other core executive body—the European Commission. The project aims to categorize the topics on the agenda of this institution in the period 1995–2014 (a partial version of the dataset has been used in Alexandrova, 2017). The unit of analysis are documents issued by the Commission and the dataset allows distinguishing between the legislative and the non-legislative branches of the agenda. The coding is done manually by pairs of trained students, and all disagreements are settled in a discussion with the project leader. Each document receives a single main topic code but a secondary coding approach is also pursued, whereby all substantially relevant further codes are identified. The data is derived from EurLex and includes different variables on the time and context of each document (e.g., date of submission to the Council, responsible Directorate General, decision procedure in the College, etc.).

Another dataset (funded through the Europolix and Legipar ANR projects) aims to categorize the agenda of the European Parliament, focusing on questions for written answer submitted to the European Commission and the Council by MEPs. It contains all 84,170 such questions submitted between September 1, 1994 and October 1, 2011. The coding of issue attention via the EUPAP codebook is done manually for a large subsample and the remaining part is coded automatically via RTextTools (Jurka et al., 2012) using the question headlines. The dataset also includes information on the date of submission, the official registration number, and the name of the question author as well as his/her affiliation to a political group and nationality. In the case of multiple authors, a dummy variable is included and the assignment of nationality and political group is applied to the first author mentioned.

The EUPAP project has evolved into a decentralized network and the popularity of the coding approach has inspired the development of new datasets by scholars not directly linked to the project. One such example is a dataset on the Council working party meetings, which are organized by the rotating presidency. These working parties prepare the agendas for the different Council formation meetings and in many cases make decisions, which are subsequently only approved by the Council. The dataset takes a different perspective from the standard one in the agendas community, where the topics of attention are deduced from statements in policy documents. The topics here represent the thematic focus of the working party and the level of attention is captured via the meeting duration. The dataset covers over seventy thousand meetings in the period 1995–2014 (Häge, 2016).

Beyond the study of institutional agendas, attempts have been made to disentangle the public agenda in the European Union. Capturing the public agenda is a complex task, considering that the European Union does not have a common public sphere. One way around this problem is to consider the aggregate expression of public concerns among the citizens in all EU member states. Such data is available in the Standard Eurobarometer (EB) surveys issued by the European Commission. Since 2003 these surveys have regularly reported on the question of which (up to two) most important issues are facing the respondent's country at the moment of enquiry. Although the list of issues, which could be selected by the participants is not comprehensive and has changed over time, this data source represents the best existing longitudinal measure of EU public opinion (Alexandrova, Rasmussen, and Toshkov, 2016). The EUPAP project has compiled a small dataset of all aggregate EU data on the most important issues question from the Standard EB, and linked it to the applicable issue codes.

The research interest in the study of citizen priorities often focuses on the overall prioritization of problems, whereby scholars rely on data compiled by governing institutions. However, the questions on which opinion is being

Table 22.1. Datasets using the EUPAP approach

Policy venue	Data type	Unit of coding	No.	Period	State of dataset	Responsible scholar
European Council	Conclusions	Quasi-sentence	50,580	1975–mid- 2017	Available	Petya Alexandrova
European Commission	All issued documents	Document	Over 11,800	1995–2014	In preparation	Petya Alexandrova
European Parliament	MEP questions for written answer to the Commission and the Council	Question	84,170	01.09.1994–01.10.2011	In preparation	Sylvain Brouard
Council working groups	Meetings	Meeting duration	72,277	1995–2014	Available	Frank Häge
Public opinion	Most important issue question in Standard Eurobarometer (EB) surveys	Issue on the list of possible issues (EU aggregate prioritization)	395*	2003–mid-2017	Available	Petya Alexandrova
Production of public opinion by the Commission	Special EB surveys	Special EB survey	303	1970–2014	In preparation	Markus Haverland

Note: * The time series is unbalanced and incomplete because the list of issues from which citizens could select has been changing over time.

Source: Comparative Agendas Project—European Union

collected are determined by the policy venue seeking this information (even if its collection is commissioned to third parties). Therefore, the study of public opinion has a further dimension. The issues on which the expression of opinion is sought constitute an agenda themselves. Such is the case with the Special EB surveys released by the European Commission. Currently, a dataset on all special EBs produced between 1970 and 2014 is in development. The main topic of each EB report is coded manually by two researchers working independently and using the EUPAP codebook. The dataset includes further information, such as the Directorate General commissioning the survey (Haverland, de Ruiter, and Van de Walle, 2018).

Table 22.1 list all datasets using the EUPAP approach that have been developed or are currently in preparation, together with dataset specification, contact persons, and references (where applicable).

22.3 Specificities

The codebook of the EUPAP has been designed following the examples of other country projects in the Comparative Agendas Project (CAP) network. This means that the codebook is not organized around policy area distinctions determined by the EU competence catalogue. Rather than being a limitation, this approach has two important advantages. First, it allows for comparisons with other political systems irrespective of the scope and distribution of jurisdictional authority. Second, it provides the opportunity to measure the lack of attention to policy issues, which constitutes a very important aspect of agenda-setting, referred to as "non-decisions" (Bachrach and Baratz, 1962). In other words, the codebook features a list of topics that could only vaguely if at all be associated with EU competences. The fact that a particular institution avoids such issues would provide evidence for jurisdictional authority from an agenda-setting perspective. This would then also reflect the changing scope and extent of EU competences over the course of European integration. However, EU institutions do not engage only with issues within their jurisdictional capacity and the boundaries of the latter are often vague. The main reason for this is that in the European Union issues often need to be framed in a way that indicates their "Europeanness" in order to be successful in gaining the attention of policymakers (Princen, 2009). Therefore, a broader perspective to the range of potential issues is pertinent to understanding agenda-setting processes in the European Union.

Furthermore, the EUPAP codebook contains a set of specific sub-codes, relevant for the EU context such as the single market, common organization of agricultural markets, or cohesion and structural funds. In the Master Codebook these issue codes are clustered with the "general" codes in the corresponding category (business and finance, agriculture, and regional policy for the three examples above respectively). Other sub-codes represent split versions of sub-codes in the Master Codebook. For example, the EU codebook contains three separate issue codes for relations between the European Union and national, regional, and local authorities, which appear under a single sub-code for intergovernmental relations in the Master Codebook. For two of the EU-specific topics—enlargement and cohesion policy—dummies allow us to consider broader references to these domains whenever the coded topic is only a specific aspect of it (for an example on the European Council see Alexandrova et al., 2014).

Additionally, the EUPAP has a particular approach to foreign affairs (adopted in only some of the CAP country projects). Here dummy variables allow us to classify broad references to relations between the European Union and third countries in specific policy areas (e.g., visa liberalization towards Ukraine), discussions of developments within specific policy domains in third countries (e.g., healthcare reform in Russia) and EU positions on issues within global governance (e.g., international measures against climate change). A similar approach is taken to categorizing internal policy aspects of a specific member state (e.g., adoption of the Euro currency by Slovenia).

22.4 An Example

Figure 22.1 presents an example of EUPAP data. It shows a comparison between three datasets on the issue of terrorism (both domestic and international terrorism, which fall under major topics law and crime, and international affairs respectively). The figure covers the period 2003–13, on which data from all three sources is available. The plot is on biannual basis and presents attention by the European Council as proportion of all quasi-sentences in the Conclusions, attention by the Commission as share of all documents issued, and the segment of the EU population that considers the issue to be one of the two most important ones facing their country at the moment of enquiry. It is clear that terrorism is an issue that the European Commission hardly deals with as it occupies up to 1 percent of its agenda. This is in line with jurisdictional divisions in the European Union. For the European Council, this issue is more salient but attention is episodic, which seems to suggest that specific terrorist attacks within the European Union and abroad trigger reactions. However, the pattern in European Council attention and the issue prioritization by the public appear to be strongly associated. In fact, research has demonstrated tentative evidence of a responsiveness effect in this institution when controlling for the number of terrorist attacks within a given period (Alexandrova, Rasmussen, and Toshkov, 2016).

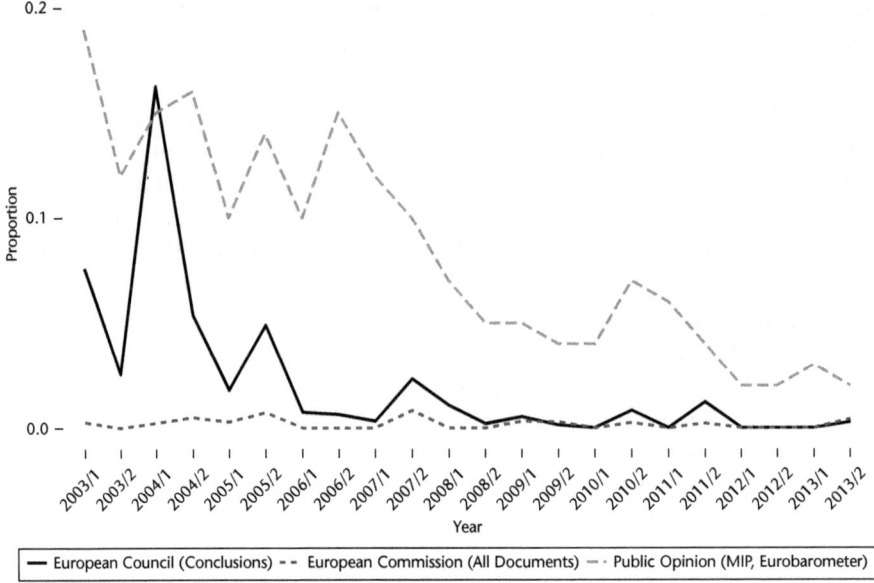

Figure 22.1. Relative attention to terrorism on the agendas of the European Council, European Commission, and EU citizens

Source: Comparative Agendas Project—European Union

Note

1. The only exception is the Foreign Affairs Council, which is chaired by the High Representative for Foreign Affairs and Security Policy (who since the Treaty of Lisbon is also a Vice-President of the European Commission).

References

Alexandrova, P. (2017). Institutional Issue Proclivity in the EU: The European Council vs the Commission. *Journal of European Public Policy*, 24(5): 755–74.

Alexandrova, P., Carammia, M., Princen, S., and Timmermans, A. (2014). Measuring the European Council Agenda: Introducing a New Approach and Dataset. *European Union Politics*, 15(1): 152–67.

Alexandrova, P., Rasmussen, A., and Toshkov, D. (2016). Agenda Responsiveness in the European Council: Public Priorities, Policy Problems and Political Attention. *West European Politics*, 39(4): 605–27.

Bachrach, P., and Baratz, M. S. (1962). Two Faces of Power. *American Political Science Review*, 56(4): 947–52.

Häge, F. M. (2016). Political Attention in the Council of the European Union: A New Dataset of Working Party Meetings, 1995–2014. *European Union Politics*, 17(4): 683–703.

Haverland, M., de Ruiter, M., and Van de Walle, S. (2018). Agenda–Setting by the Commission: Seeking Public Opinion? *Journal of European Public Policy*, 25(3): 327–45.

Hix, S., and Høyland, B. (2011). *The Political System of the European Union,* 3rd ed. Basingstoke: Palgrave Macmillan.

Jurka, T. P., Collingwood, L., Boydstun, A. E. et al. (2012). *RTextTools: Automatic Text Classification via Supervised Learning. R package version 1.3.9.*

Princen, S. (2009). *Agenda-Setting in the European Union.* Basingstoke: Palgrave Macmillan.

23

Agenda-Setting in the Florida Legislature

Kevin Fahey, Patrick Merle, Teresa Cornacchione, and Carol Weissert

Florida is the nation's third largest state and among the most racially, socio-economically, and politically diverse. Approximately 60 percent of the population is White, with Blacks and Latinos accounting for 16 and 17 percent of the population respectively. Nearly 20 percent of the population speaks Spanish, owning in large part to the Cuban and Caribbean diaspora. Florida's median income is slightly below the national average, but its income is among the most unequally distributed in the Union.

The Project is actively collecting and coding several datasets. The first and largest consists of approximately ten thousand bills, sponsored by members of the Florida House of Representatives in odd-numbered years, 1989–2015. The second dataset consists of media articles from the online aggregator Sayfie Review, which is widely read by members of the Florida state legislature and other policymakers. The third dataset uses policy-agendas codes to categorize biographical information of state legislators.

23.1 Florida

Florida is a rapidly growing diverse state whose political institutions are adapting to meet new realities and manage new challenges. The state's population has nearly doubled between 1989 and 2015, and several major metropolitan areas (Orlando, Jacksonville, Tampa, Miami-Ft. Lauderdale) reflect the growing diversity of its people. At the same time, the state's governing institutions have undergone significant changes in recent decades, including legislative term limits, revisions to the state constitution, and a shift in partisan control from Democratic to Republican.

The state legislature is part-time and semi-professionalized with 120 members in the lower chamber and forty in the upper chamber. Members of the House are elected every two years; Senators every four years. They meet sixty days each year and oversee a budget of approximately $83 billion. Florida's budget and appropriations process is handled through a single omnibus package. Relative to the US Congress, the Florida speaker of the house and Senate majority leader exercise substantial formal power in assigning members to committees, and control over the chamber rules. The governor is elected for a maximum of two four-year terms, and has seen his institutional powers grow as the state has taken on additional administrative tasks. From managing the state's economic growth, shaping the state judiciary, or mitigating the risks of climate change facing many of Florida's coastal cities, the governor has taken an increasing role in the affairs of the state.

The state's media environment has slowly adapted to the decline of print newspapers and the explosion of Internet media. Online aggregators such as the Sayfie Review or POLITICO Florida provide consumers with daily digests of political news, while traditional newspapers such as the *Tampa Bay Times* (formerly *St. Petersburg Times*) and the *Miami Herald* provide coverage of the activities of the government.

23.2 Extant Datasets

As the second sub-national project under the CAP umbrella, the Florida Policy Agendas Project is designed to replicate many of the processes of Pennsylvania, the first sub-national project.[1] By maintaining this continuity we can pursue true apples-to-apples comparisons of sub-national units. Florida's unique Sunshine Law requires transparency of most, if not all, activities of political elites, allowing us to maximize direct comparability to the Pennsylvania Project.

23.2.1 *Bills*

The primary dataset of the Project is a set of over ten thousand bills sponsored by the Florida House of Representatives. We predominantly chose odd-numbered years as they are the first year of the two-year session and not an election year.[2] Each member of the Florida House of Representative may propose only six substantive bills a year, making their bill proposal decisions critical. Each bill must be proposed and properly drafted before the start of each session. The Speaker largely controls which bills are assigned to committees. Additionally, committee chairs can absorb individual bills into so-called "committee bills," with different topics.[3]

Our work on the Florida legislature's bill proposals lead us to examine the linkages between legislators' personal preferences and obligations to their constituents. Legislators share relationships with each other that form a network of interdependent bill proposal choices, while also balancing the many needs of the electorate. At the end of this chapter, we provide an example of using our data to explore networks of bill proposals by members of the Florida House of Representatives.

23.2.2 Biographical Data of Florida State Legislators

As part of analyzing the behaviors of members of the Florida legislature, we have collected a comprehensive biographical dataset that encompasses ascriptive characteristics and traits, historical information, political backgrounds, and potential conflicts of interest. These data allow researchers to examine the role of personal attributes in agenda-setting.

Personal attributes—including gender and race to education, ambition, offices and jobs held, and marital status—were collected from legislators' own websites as well as aggregating datasets such as Project VoteSmart. Political attributes—committee assignment, party status, vote share, and membership in the party leadership—were obtained from the Florida House of Representatives archives and the state election bureaus. These data provide the potential for identifying common networks of lawmakers, providing identification strategies for the development of new agendas, or demonstrating associations between topics and lawmakers' backgrounds.

A unique aspect of the Florida Policy Agendas Project is its focus on the financial incentives of lawmakers. Due to the state's Sunshine Law, all politicians in the state must file annual financial disclosure forms. On each form they are required to list the source of all incomes, assets, or liabilities, (complete with the name of the company and an address) and the amount of each kind of income, asset, or liability. We are in the process of coding each source of income reported on financial disclosure forms using the Florida Policy Agendas Project codes. Legislators' incomes are primarily drawn from their careers in the law, or state government, or as entrepreneurs. Intercoder reliability before reconciliation is approximately 70 to 75 percent, largely due to the opacity surrounding the precise tasks of each source of income.

23.2.3 Newspaper Data—the Sayfie Review

In Florida, there are several major metropolitan areas, each with its own unique set of media institutions and history. As a result, there is no major statewide newspaper or media organization that both elites and the public read daily or weekly. The Sayfie Review, an online news digest, collected by a well-connected Florida journalist and political insider and targeted for political elites, is our data source for media agendas coding. The Sayfie Review incorporates stories from major Florida newspapers as well as national news organizations. Additionally, the Review relies on subscribers to identify stories that the Review's staff do not initially publish, creating a quasi-crowdsourced media environment. In this way, stories read by the public are also pushed to politicians, providing the Florida Policy Agendas Project with a reliable, comprehensive source of political news.

The Sayfie Review began in 2005, limiting its historical application, but has maintained a similar theme throughout its existence. News stories are broadcast as one-sentence headlines (similar to the Huffington Post or Drudge Report) complete with an embedded link to the original article. The Project has scraped hundreds of thousands of Sayfie Review headlines and has begun coding.[4] Coding of these headlines has begun for 2011, 2013, and 2015.[5] We strive for major-topic intercoder reliability of 90 percent, despite the limits imposed by a headlines-only approach.

23.3 Codebook

The Florida Policy Agendas coding structure for topics and subtopics largely mirrors that of the various national projects, and heavily borrows from the Pennsylvania Policy Agendas Project (McLaughlin et al., 2010). While the topic and subtopic coding scheme developed by Pennsylvania is largely appropriate for Florida policy agendas, certain codes not relevant to the Florida economy, such as Code 805, "coal mining and production" were removed. Additionally, because Pennsylvania and Florida, the only two sub-national CAP projects in the United States, differ on several important dimensions (the Florida legislature is a term-limited legislature with a short, 60-day legislative session whereas the Pennsylvania legislature meets largely year-round and has no term limits), the codebook was developed to reflect attributes of the Florida legislature that drive policy agendas in ways very different from Pennsylvania.

The codebook was initially constructed in the summer of 2014. The codebook details the project history, developers, and provides detailed instructions for undergraduate coders. It also provides useful information for researchers wishing to utilize Florida Policy Agendas data.

23.4 Coder Training

Coders are primarily undergraduate university students trained to code bills, headlines, and legislator occupations according to the Comparative Agendas

Policy topic codes. Coders are generally trained for a month before being permitted to code data to be used in the analysis. Previously coded observations are used for training purposes. Coders are first trained to code observations according to CAP topic and subtopic, before proceeding to other variables (described below). Coders meet with the supervising graduate student once per week for training. Graduate supervisors check coders' intercoder reliability each week. Typically, coders begin with a 67 percent rate of agreement on main CAP codes, and 40 percent agreement on subtopics for bills and headlines. Coders are not permitted to code usable data for analysis until they reach over 90 percent agreement on main codes and 85 percent for subtopics (both bills and headlines). Students only code legislator occupations by main code; and, as with bills and headlines, are permitted to code usable data when intercoder reliability reaches 90 percent or more.

Zoho Creator, an existing coding interface, facilitates the implementation of the Comparative Agendas Coding framework. We balance and accomplish several objectives with this interface. First, we create a database of bills and newspaper articles that can be easily (and independently) coded by multiple coders and can be efficiently verified and reconciled. Second, we have built a system whereby the bills and news articles can be easily linked by date/constructed week. Third, we have developed a platform that can also be accessed by multiple coders remotely, so the coders can complete their coding assignments from their own computers and at their leisure. Finally, we are able to overcome the possible problem where coders could inadvertently delete data since Zoho Creator's dynamically updated datasets are hidden from coder view.

23.5 Data Example

The focus of the Florida Policy Agendas Project is on exploring the relationships between lawmakers, media inputs, and agendas. Florida's one-party dominance belies large areas where both Republicans and Democrats cooperate across partisan lines, and on nonpartisan issues, to address the needs of the rapidly growing state. We summarize this chapter by discussing some preliminary findings and promising avenues for future work.

Partisanship is not the primary reason why legislators work on particular agendas. Figure 23.1 shows the coalitions of Democrats (in black) and Republicans (in grey) on various agendas. Clearly, Democrats and Republicans work on issues together, rather than focusing on "Black State" or "Grey State" agendas. For example, we would expect Democrats to prioritize environmental issues and for Republicans to eschew environmental regulation, but we find Republicans eager to propose legislation on the environment.

Figure 23.1. Communities of legislators and issues, by partisanship
Source: Comparative Agendas Project—Florida

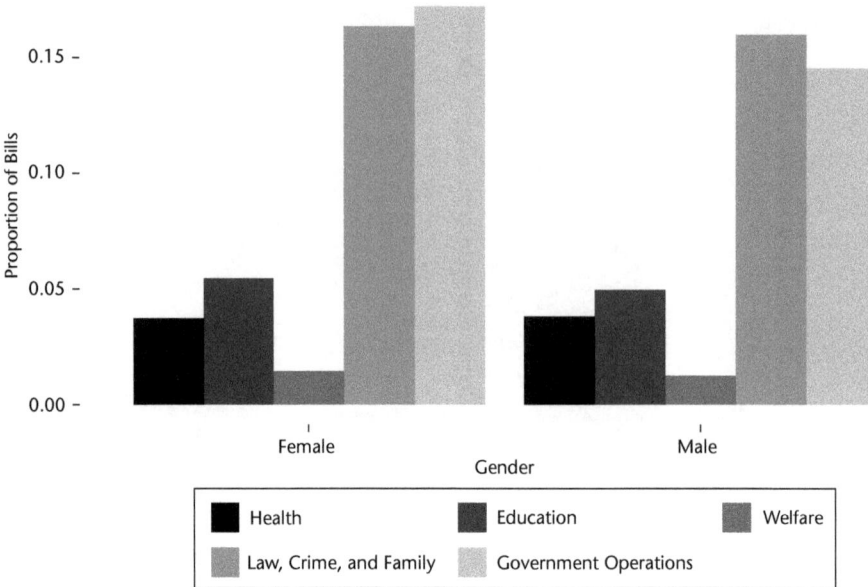

Figure 23.2. Proportion of bills introduced, for men and women, across "women's issue" topics

Source: Comparative Agendas Project—Florida

When partisanship fails to explain networks of bill proposals, we turn to other potential explanations. Gender is often used as an explanation of differing agendas, with "women's issues" and "men's issues" highlighted in the literature (Bratton and Haynie, 1999). And gender may be related to legislative effectiveness in the US Congress (Volden et al., 2013). Yet Florida's legislature does not appear to have a distinct set of "women's issues." As noted in Figure 23.2, gender does not illuminate differences between members of the Florida House of Representatives. The legislative priorities of women, and their ability to successfully implement those agendas, remains an open question in the American states.

Yet there are interesting linkages between legislators, and these can reveal how politicians work together to influence policy in the Sunshine State. In Figure 23.3 we provide visual evidence of the coalitions of lawmakers who propose legislation on similar agendas, and how those bill proposals form "topic communities" of agendas.

Colors indicate groups of lawmakers with similar policy agendas, as measured by the topics of bills they introduce. While partisanship is not a predictor of coalition membership, there do appear to be clear coalitions of lawmakers existing on various issues (and topic families). Even when ignoring predominant topics such as government operations, personal factors and not party or ideology appear important. Interestingly, despite stable Republican dominance and high

Figure 23.3. Communities of legislators and issues: "topic communities" by year

Source: Comparative Agendas Project—Florida

incumbent retention rates, the topic families themselves shift from year to year. For example, transportation and education formed a large topic family in 2013, but not in 2011 or 2015.

23.6 Conclusion

The Florida Agendas Project data have enabled collection of legislative and media outputs, consistent with the goals of the broader Comparative Agendas Project. Initial data analyses facilitated the examination of several important questions in the literature, such as the role of partisanship and gender in the development of agendas in the Florida legislature. As our project continues to accumulate data and explore other aspects of governance, we will provide data on a fascinating sub-national government with a unique set of cultures, political institutions, and economic institutions.

Notes

1. As stated in the Pennsylvania codebook, there are some policies that US sub-national governments do not attend to, including international trade. As such, the Florida Policy Agendas codes do not include those topics, while adding additional codes that US state governments prioritize. Our codes are identical to the codes Pennsylvania uses, to maximize comparison.
2. In election years, Florida legislators use bill proposals as position-taking documents to prepare for their election campaigns. When choosing when to begin collection of data, we prioritized odd-numbered years to avoid the potential of examining legislation where the lawmaker had no intention to change policies. As our project continues, we are coding even-numbered years with the objective of testing that empirical question.
3. While the original legislator cannot submit another bill proposal if one of their six bills is subsumed into a committee bill, committee bills do have the advantage of allowing the legislature to adapt to crises that arise after bills are proposed but before the legislative session ends. Without committee bills, Florida would only be able to react to emergencies in special sessions or the following calendar year.
4. The Project made a conscious decision to only code based on the headlines, rather than the underlying articles. While this introduces a source of error, the reasons to opt for a headlines-only approach are straightforward. Many Sayfie headlines from older years include broken embedded links. In recent years, newspapers have implemented paywalls as a revenue source. These combined pressures would create more nonrandom sources of error—through major selection effects—than coding based on headlines.
5. For the purposes of our research projects, we randomly sampled bills from these three years. Work on completing these years is ongoing.

References

Bratton, K. A., and Haynie, K. L. (1999). Agenda-Setting and Legislative Success in State Legislatures: The Effects of Gender and Race. *The Journal of Politics*, 61(3): 658–79.

McLaughlin, J. P., Wolfgang, P., Leckrone, J. W. et al. (2010). The Pennsylvania Policy Database Project: A Model for Comparative Analysis. *State Politics & Policy Quarterly*, 10(3): 320–36.

Volden, C., Wiseman, A. E., and Wittmer, D. E. (2013). When Are Women More Effective Lawmakers than Men? *American Journal of Political Science*, 57: 326–41.

24

Pennsylvania Policy Database Project

Jay Jennings, Stefanie Kasparek, and Joseph McLaughlin

The Pennsylvania Policy Database Project (PPDP) was built by faculty-supervised students at Temple University and five other universities with the support and cooperation of the Pennsylvania General Assembly. Also participating in the initial construction phase of the project were students and faculty members at Pennsylvania State University, Carnegie Mellon University, the University of Pittsburgh, Pennsylvania State University Harrisburg, and the University of Pennsylvania. Since 2010, the project has been exclusively maintained and updated by Temple University students. The project allows users to trace the history of public policy in the Commonwealth since 1979. It is the first sub-national project within the Comparative Agendas Project, having been started in 2006; PPDP has been releasing its data to the public since 2010 (see McLaughlin et al., 2010).

24.1 The Government and Politics of Pennsylvania

Pennsylvania's government is similar to the US federal government with separate legislative, executive, and judicial branches. The General Assembly is the legislative body and consists of a lower house—the House of Representatives, and an upper house—the Senate.

The General Assembly consists of fifty Senators and 203 members of the House of Representatives. All 203 members of the House and half of the Senate (25 members) are elected biannually. The General Assembly is a continuing body during the term for which its representatives are elected. In national assessments of state legislatures, the Pennsylvania General Assembly is regarded as a full-time and professional legislature.

The governor of Pennsylvania (PA), who is the head of the executive branch, is elected every four years and limited to two consecutive terms. Among the governor's numerous duties are: the appointment of executive officials, management of the executive branch, veto power over legislation, commander-in-chief of the Commonwealth's military force, and the power to pardon. In addition, the governor proposes the general fund budget in February and March, which has to be enacted before the beginning of the fiscal year on July 1st. Local governments in the United States are creatures of state government and possess no independent sovereignty. Many states, including Pennsylvania, grant at least some local governments "home rule," which generally means that in addition to the powers specifically delegated to them by the legislature, they can adopt legislation and exercise powers neither specifically reserved to the state government nor specifically prohibited to local governments.

Article Five of the Pennsylvania Constitution vests judicial power in a unified system that includes three courts of appeal: the Supreme Court, the Superior Court, and the Commonwealth Court. The Courts of Common Pleas are trial courts and have original jurisdiction in all matters not exclusively reserved to the appeals courts. Courts of Common Pleas are established in sixty judicial districts. In addition, there are a number of minor courts including magisterial district courts and municipal courts in Philadelphia and Pittsburgh. The Supreme Court is Pennsylvania's highest court and holds the Commonwealth's supreme judicial power. Pennsylvanian judges are generally elected through partisan elections for ten-year terms and are eligible for retention elections.

Pennsylvania is a competitive two-party state. While Republicans and Democrats have frequently shared power over the past several decades, Republicans have held a continuous majority in the Senate since 1994. Most of the state's Democratic base is concentrated in and around its cities, particularly the two largest—Philadelphia and Pittsburgh. Most of the Republican base is found in rural counties in central Pennsylvania and along the northern border with New York State. Pennsylvania's suburbs and smaller urban areas are home to the most competition between the parties.

24.2 Datasets

The PPDP provides access to more than 215,000 state and news media records on the history of public policy in the Commonwealth. The database includes an extensive array of government records, news accounts, and opinion data (see Table 24.1).

Table 24.1. The datasets of the Pennsylvania Policy Database Project

Dataset	Period cover	Available on the CAP website (Y/N)	Total Number of records available
Hearings House	1979–2016	Y	5,655
News Clips	1979–2018	Y	69,788
Bills, Resolutions, and Laws	1979–2016	Y	102,728
Governor's Budget Address	1979–2018	Y	11,018
Budget (Total Spending)	1979–2014	Y	14,414
Most Important Problem	1994–2018	Y	1,254
Executive Orders	1979–2018	Y	332
Pennsylvania Supreme Court	1979–2012	N	5,044
Governing Magazine	1988–2018	N	8,095
Legislative Service Agency Reports	1979–2018	N	986
General Fund Balance	1979–2014	N	36

Source: Comparative Agendas Project—Pennsylvania

The data have been coded in accordance with the Comparative Agendas Project (CAP) for all of its major and minor topic codes and gets updated constantly. In order to capture Pennsylvania's specific issues, the database includes additional and in part substantively different data in unique topics like coal mine subsidence and reclamation. Beyond that, the Pennsylvania database includes tools for analysis of the legislative process itself. Its consistency with CAP facilitates international, federal, and state policy comparisons at large.

In order to avoid inconsistencies in terminology and change in meaning, each individual record has been read, abstracted, and double-blind coded by two student workers. An exception is the coding of over 100,000 bills, which are the centerpiece of the database. Here, one student has been replaced by a computer using a custom-made policy-coding software. The results have been proven highly consistent with the human coders. In case of disagreements among the coders, the research manager tie breaks votes.

Overall, PPDP provides different series of data for the Comparative Agendas Project. A challenge exists for news clips, as no dominant news source covers the entire state. The Pennsylvania media data therefore lack comparability with *The New York Times* data in the US Policy Agendas Project. Instead, news clips data rely on collections of news reports from diverse newspapers and electronic media across the state produced every working day by Capitol press offices. As compared to the US Project, which reflects the policy focus of the *Times*, as a proxy for the national media, the PA project reflects the news media's policy focus *as it perceived* by government decision-makers. The project abstracts and codes under major topics a random sample of 10 percent of the news reports produced by Capitol press offices. House Hearings are complete and provide abstracts written by the House Archives staff in addition to information on committee specifics and legislative discussions.[1] The annual governor's Budget Address is seen as equivalent to the president's State-of-the-Union address and coded in quasi-sentences. A total of over eight thousand sentences or sentence fragments results in accurate policy coding over time. The comprehensive coverage of Executive Orders is an exclusive part of the Pennsylvania database. *Governing* magazine focuses on trends in state and local government, coded by major topics. The Franklin Marshall College Poll provides PPDP with the most important problem (MIP) question for Pennsylvania residents beginning in 1994. Through a unique licensing arrangement, the project includes and codes Westlaw's abstracts of Pennsylvania Supreme Court decisions.

Finally, the two budget data series (total spending all funds and general fund balance) have unique characteristics. The general fund balance dataset is drawn directly from annual reports produced by the National Governors Association and the National Association of State Budget Officers and has no counterpart in the national project or CAP. It represents Pennsylvania's fiscal condition as opposed to its policy attention, but fiscal condition profoundly affects the state's policy choices. The total spending dataset codes the Census Bureau's *State Government Finances* data into the CAP major topics. Users of the project should be aware that the PA spending codes and data are not consistent with the US Project's budget data, which use topics devised by the US government's Office of Management and Budget (OMB) and have to be crosswalked to the Policy Agendas coding scheme for comparability with other projects.

24.3 Specificities and Perspectives

Users of our data should be aware of two special characteristics associated with PPDP. The first characteristic is obvious: Pennsylvania is a sub-national state and therefore differences in scope and focus of the agenda exist. State governments in the United States are considered to have a greater degree of sovereignty than sub-governments in most of the world's two dozen or so federalist nations. US states are primarily responsible for, or play a large role, in determining education, healthcare, welfare, public safety, and many other policy issues. Viewed in this way and in their sweeping powers with respect to local governments, Pennsylvania is more similar to a unitary, or non-federalist, nation than to the US federal government. There are, however, policy areas not focused on by Pennsylvania policymakers that would be focused on by most national states. In particular, international relations, foreign trade, and defense are policy topic areas that are sparsely used in our datasets. Because our codebook was based on the US Policy Agendas and now CAP codebooks, the Pennsylvania codebook needed to add additional codes to capture areas of policymaking not relevant to the US federal government. Two prominent examples can be found in the banking, finance, and commerce topic code. The US federal government does not regulate most professional services or the sale of alcohol, so the Pennsylvania project codebook added codes for these important state policy areas. In addition, PPDP includes a major topic for the state's extensive activities relating to the establishment and regulation of local governments.

The second special characteristic of PPDP is that it was initially funded by the PA General Assembly. This is worth noting because it influenced the level of detail collected in our data, particularly within the legislation dataset. A large focus was placed on accurately assessing the legislative history of each bill introduced to the General Assembly. Because our data link directly to the General Assembly's online archives, users of our project[2] can not only graph patterns of policy attention reflected by the aggregation of bills, resolutions, and laws (called "acts" in our database) but can, by clicking on embedded links, call up the actual text of all legislation as introduced and all subsequent amendments, a summary of the legislative history of each and every bill, and for many, if not most, the online record of House and Senate debate on the measure, including roll call votes. Although most of this legislative history functionality has not been incorporated into the CAP website, users should be aware that tools for analyzing the legislative process are available for each bill on our project's website.

24.4 Data Analysis Example

Since 1859, the drilling of oil and natural gas wells, most recently through the process known as fracking, has shaped Pennsylvania's landscape significantly through extensive industrialization of the land. PA residents and advocates have raised serious concerns about environmental damage and about health and drinking water safety. The relationship between drinking water safety and fracking has long been disputed by oil and gas companies and received only limited attention by lawmakers for long stretches of time. Since the early 2000s, Pennsylvania experienced a dramatic increase in natural gas and oil production. Figure 24.1 reflects this development and displays the significantly changed awareness of state legislators towards drinking water safety and the fracking of natural gas and oil.

Figure 24.2 provides information on attention the media and the governor's Budget Address pay to the issues of drinking water safety and natural gas and oil as a source of energy. Media has generally paid more attention to the environmental aspects of fracking than to the energy one. Data on the governor's Budget Address indicates that, in line with the received legislative attention, the governor increasingly also paid more attention to the issue of natural oil and gas in his address in the past ten years.[3]

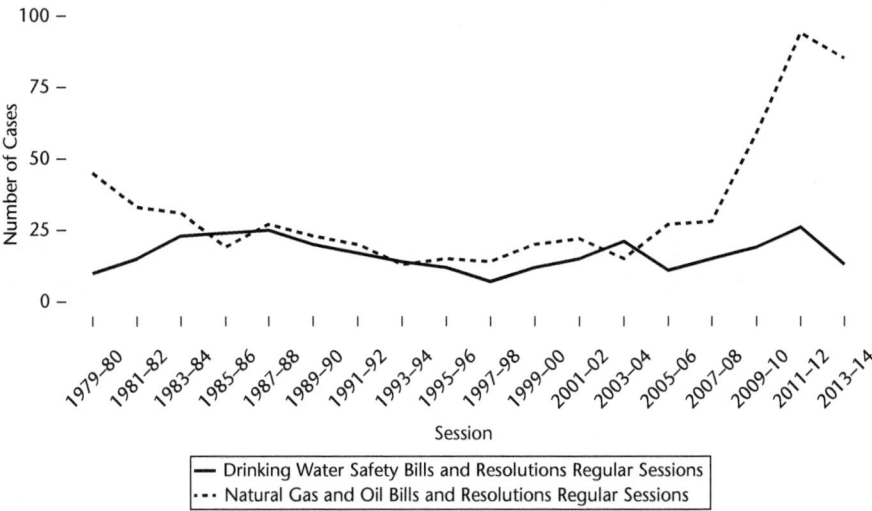

Figure 24.1. Drinking water safety bills and resolutions vs. natural gas and oil bills and resolutions

Source: Comparative Agendas Project—Pennsylvania

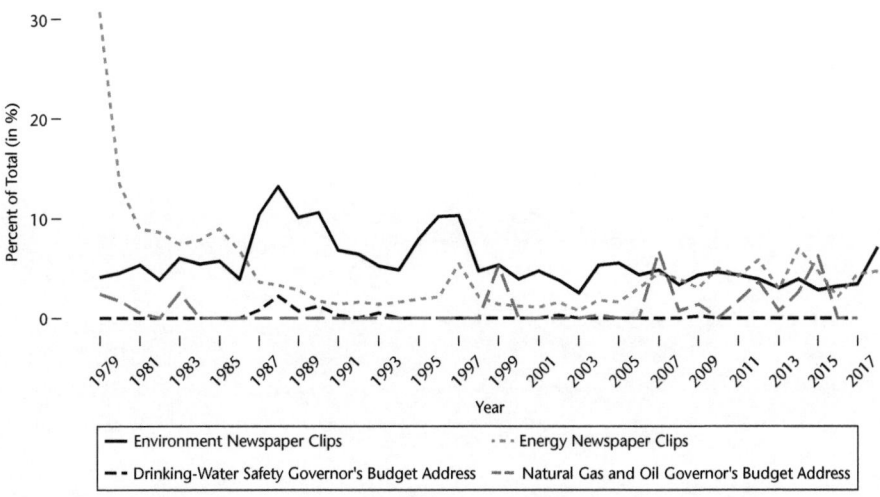

Figure 24.2. Percentage of news clips and governor's address for drinking water safety and natural gas and oil

Source: Comparative Agendas Project—Pennsylvania

Notes

1. The Senate does not consistently archive its records of hearings; hence the dataset is not comprehensive.
2. The CAP analysis tool is not able to provide this detailed information. Instead, it links to the PPDP website for a more detailed analysis tool and the original documents.
3. The data can be displayed as "percentage of total" or in raw numbers.

References

McLaughlin, J. P., Wolfgang, P., Leckrone, J. W., Gollob, J., Bossie, J., Jennings, J., and Atherton, M. J. (2010). The Pennsylvania Policy Database Project: A model for comparative analysis. *State Politics & Policy Quarterly*, 10(3), pp. 320–36.

Part III
Comparative Perspectives

25

The Public Agenda

A Comparative Perspective

Shaun Bevan and Will Jennings

25.1 The Public Agenda and Theories of Agenda-Setting

If the political agenda consists of those subjects or problems that are the focus of policymakers at a given moment in time (Kingdon, 1984), then the public agenda refers more specifically to the issues that are atop the public's mind, or the concerns and anxieties prevalent in the wider social milieu. When an issue makes it onto the public agenda, it is more likely to be put on the formal political agenda. Agenda-setting in public opinion is thus a prerequisite for achieving policy change. Such an argument was developed by Cobb and Elder (1972), who distinguished between the "systemic" and "institutional" agenda. The systemic agenda consists of "all issues that are commonly perceived by members of the political community as meriting public attention" (Cobb and Elder, 1972: 85). Even before an issue can reach the systemic agenda it must satisfy a number of criteria: the public must be aware that there is a problem, often via media coverage, there must be consensus that action needs to be taken, and government must be seen as *capable* of doing something about it. The institutional agenda, on the other hand, is "that list of items explicitly up for the active and serious consideration of authoritative decision makers" (Cobb and Elder, 1972: 86). When an issue reaches the attention of the executive, legislature, or judiciary, this is the precursor to the possibility of policy change (Jones and Baumgartner, 2004: 2). The public agenda matters, then, in reflecting the broader set of concerns within a society that are seen as needing addressing. This in turn feeds into the "problem stream" (Kingdon, 1984) of concerns preoccupying decision-makers in and around government.

As Jones (1994) observes, shifts in issue salience can occur due to a change in the underlying facts of a situation, or due to changes in the meaning of "facts." Public attentiveness to crime might rise, for example, either because of increasing levels of victimization or, instead, because media or political elites start to talk about the issue as being a problem. Studies find that the public agenda tends to closely track this "problem status" of certain issues (e.g., Hibbs, 1979; Hudson, 1994). Elites can alternatively mobilize attention to issues (e.g., Carmines and Stimson, 1989; Cohen, 1995; Lovett et al., 2015). The agenda-setting power of elites may lead the level of public concern to bear little relation to the degree to which there is a problem. Another reason why changes occur in the public agenda is that new problems or events demand attention—since the mass public have limited capacity in the number of topics that can be attended to at a given moment in time (McCombs and Zhu, 1995). Increased coverage of so-called "killer issues" (Brosius and Kepplinger, 1995) can move some issues off the agenda altogether while leaving others unaffected. Simply explaining what gains traction on the public agenda is crucial for accounts of agenda-setting.

The dynamics of change in the public agenda can be sporadic and rapid or slow and gradual. In general, issue attention tends to move more quickly than preferences (Jones, 1994). For example, bouts of disorder or the occurrence of a dangerous dog attack can induce "moral panics" and over-reactions about perceived problems or threats (Cohen, 1972; Hood and Lodge, 2002; Jennings et al., 2017). Birkland (2011: 180) defines "focusing events" as "sudden, relatively rare events that spark intense media and public attention because of their sheer magnitude or, sometimes, because of the harm they reveal." These events draw attention to dormant issues or concerns, taking the form of natural or manmade disasters, accidents, scandals, terrorist attacks, financial crises, protests, or other incidents. Events such as 9/11, or the United Kingdom's fuel protests of 2000, can result in a sudden rise in issue salience. Upsurges in attention can lead to pressure on policymakers to take action in those domains characterized by stability. The public agenda can also move slowly, as attention adjusts incrementally in response to long-term trends or cycles of social and economic change. For example, attention to the economy tends to track consumer sentiment (Wlezien, 2005) while concern about inflation and unemployment follow these indicators directly (Hibbs, 1979; Hudson, 1994). Such patterns of issue attention matter in understanding the different sorts of pressure on policymakers.

In this chapter we consider theoretical perspectives on possible causes and effects of the public agenda: specifically, (1) media agenda-setting and (2) agenda representation. We assess the benefits of comparative analysis of the public agenda, and insights this might provide on differences between political systems or policy contexts. For example, it can show how the concerns of particular national publics differ, how these reflect cross-national differences in the issues that the media attend to, and the seeming influence over the priorities of policymakers. We then consider the most important problem (MIP) survey question, and its variants, as a measure of the public agenda. We compare the public agenda in the United States, the United Kingdom, and Spain—describing similarities and differences in trends over time, both in terms of the content and patterns of change and stability in the public agenda. Our analysis then considers how media coverage and problem status are linked to public attention for selected issues (the economy and crime) and how the public agenda impacts on the policy agenda over time. This reveals that the public agenda tends to respond to the severity of policy problems—for the economy and crime—and slightly weaker evidence for the agenda-setting power of the media.

25.2 Causes and Effects of the Public Agenda

What shapes the public agenda? It has long been argued that mass media exerts substantial agenda-setting influence in determining the issues that are atop the public's mind. In their famous study, McCombs and Shaw (1972) highlighted that the content of media coverage impacted on the priorities of voters. Through funneling the attention of its audience towards certain topics, the mass media condition the issues that the public is more likely to consider important. News coverage tends to favor "episodic" frames, reporting stories about specific events or cases, above more "thematic" frames relating to policy problems or social conditions (Iyengar, 1991). This bias in news framing means the public agenda is often shaped by events as well as responses to the emergence of social problems that require attention from policymakers.

An alternative perspective of what shapes the issue content of the public agenda suggests it responds to fluctuations in severity of the *problem status* of particular issues (Wlezien, 2005; John et al., 2013: Ch. 7). This sort of public response to the discovery of emergent policy problems was implicit to Anthony Downs' (1972) seminal theory of the issue attention cycle. For example, public concern about inflation and unemployment are shown to track their actual levels (Hibbs, 1979; Hudson, 1994). Similarly, public attention to the issue of strikes tracks the scale of industrial disputes in the United Kingdom (Jennings and Wlezien, 2011). The final possibility is that the public agenda is influenced by elite mobilization. That is, policymakers use their rhetorical or institutional platform to draw public attention to specific issues. As an example, the US president is able to use the State of the Union Address to talk about particular policy areas, eliciting a response from the mass public (e.g., Cohen, 1995; Lovett et al., 2015). In parliamentary systems, legislators

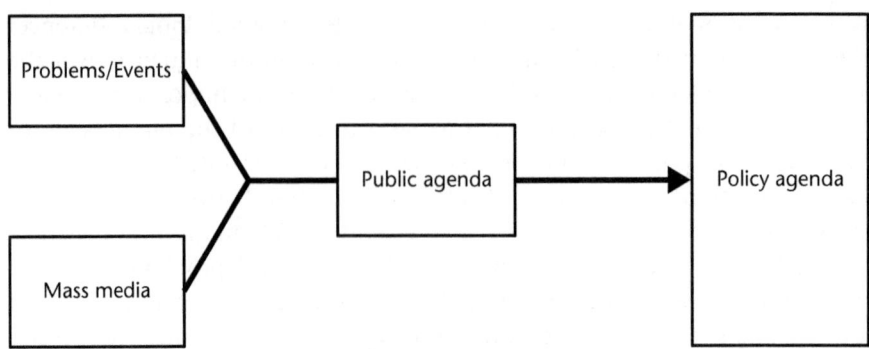

Figure 25.1. Models of the public and policy agenda
Source: Comparative Agendas Project

can highlight particular issues through asking questions in formal debates. Even here, elites rely on mass media for coverage in order that their rhetoric reaches its public audience.

How does the public agenda influence public policy? The logic is straightforward: if an issue is the subject of public attention, then it is more likely to be considered important by policymakers, and put on the formal agenda (e.g., Cobb and Elder, 1972; Kingdon, 1984; Baumgartner and Jones, 1993). If this expectation applies to attention to issues within specific domains, it follows that the policy priorities of government in the aggregate correspond to the issue priorities of the public (e.g., Jones and Baumgartner, 2004; Jones et al., 2009; Chaqués-Bonafont and Palau, 2011; Lindeboom, 2012; Alexandrova et al., 2016). Some go further and expect over-time aggregate correspondence between the public agenda and the policy agenda (e.g., Jennings and John, 2009; John et al., 2011; Bevan and Jennings, 2014). "Dynamic agenda representation" refers to the process through which the issue priorities of the public are translated into the policy priorities of government (Bevan and Jennings, 2014). While it is possible that the public and policymakers are responding simultaneously to the problem status of issues, congruence between the public and policy agenda indicates some level of democratic performance—though is not the same as responsiveness to public preferences for policy (Jennings and Wlezien, 2015). Possible relationships between problems/events, mass media, the public and policy agenda are illustrated in Figure 25.1, though are by no means exhaustive.

25.3 Comparing the Public Agenda

Most studies of the public agenda are limited to a single country (see Bevan et al., 2016 for an exception), and often a single policy domain or subset of policy domains (e.g., the economy, foreign affairs, defense). These provide insights on the factors that shape the public agenda—such as social and economic conditions or mass media—and its impact on policymakers in different contexts, but there is limited scope for generalization. Not least, studies often depend on measures that are not directly equivalent or cannot be replicated. Yet one might expect variation in the sorts of issue priorities on the public agenda across countries and political systems. This might be due to differences in the particular values of a country, or its historical set of state institutions (e.g., welfare state regimes). It might also reflect variations in the contemporary set of policy problems facing a polity (e.g., economic crises, crime rates, public health emergencies), and the signals provided to the mass public by elites (such as by political parties).

Taking a comparative perspective to analysis of the public agenda offers the promise of addressing questions that have been little explored. How do the issue priorities of citizens vary across countries? What differences are there in the stability or instability of the public agenda? How much influence does mass media have in different political systems? Does responsiveness of the policy agenda to the public agenda vary across political institutions and countries? These questions can only be properly resolved through systematic cross-national comparison based on equivalent measures of the public and policy agendas. Data collected through the Comparative Agendas Project offers such an opportunity.

25.4 Measuring the Public Agenda

To measure the public agenda, scholars have often used aggregate responses to the survey question asking about the most important problem (MIP) or most important issue (MII) facing the country (e.g., McCombs and Shaw, 1972; MacKuen and Coombs, 1981; Jones, 1994; McCombs and Zhu, 1995; Soroka, 2002; Jones and Baumgartner, 2004; Jones et al., 2009; John et al., 2013; Bevan and Jennings, 2014; Green and Jennings, 2017).[1] These responses are taken to characterize the broader public salience of issues at particular points in time and over time. Much research shows that MIP responses indicate the issues on people's minds (e.g., Jones, 1994; Soroka, 2002; Bartle and Laycock, 2012; Jennings and Wlezien, 2011). Simply, the proportion of the public naming an issue as the most important indicates its prominence on the agenda relative to other issues. If "the economy" is mentioned by 50 percent of respondents and crime is mentioned by just 10 percent, this indicates that the economy is a more prominent issue on the public agenda. Change over time in the proportion of MIP responses for an issue indicates that it has increased or decreased in its prominence on the public agenda. While an imperfect measure of the *importance* that individuals attach to a given issue, the MIP does indicate those issues at the forefront of public attention.

Survey data on the MIP (or MII) over long periods of time is in short supply. In the United States and the United Kingdom, data is available back to the 1940s, while regular data is available for Germany since the mid-1980s and Spain from the 1990s. In other countries data tends to be sparser. In Europe, the Eurobarometer series offers a measure of MII that covers up to twenty-seven countries from the early 2000s, but it includes survey responses for just seven issues (the economy, immigration, pensions, environment and energy, law and order, terrorism, and international relations), and is not based on open-ended responses. Within the CAP, then, data on the public agenda is dependent on the duration and reliability of time series of MIP responses—which are not available for every country.[2] Whereas it is typically possible to reconstruct measures of the policy agenda based on the historical record (such as from speeches, laws, or budgets), it is not possible to retrospectively collect data on mass opinion.

At the time of writing (summer, 2017), we have access to MIP data recoded according to the CAP coding system for Spain, the United Kingdom, and the United States. Data for Hungary has recently been added to the CAP data system, and data for Germany is due to be made available soon. One of the advantages of using the CAP coding system is that the issue categories used can be standardized (with topics referring to the same policy area), while information is not necessarily lost if coded at the subtopic as well (where MIP response categories exactly match CAP subtopics). The system makes comparative analysis rather more straightforward than using the original survey data—where there are often variations across countries, and over time, in the categories of "problems" that are used by survey organizations (as an example, MIP responses about health in the United States tend to refer to "healthcare" or "Medicaid," whereas in the United Kingdom the "National Health Service" is more commonly used). Each of these series is measured using aggregate annual responses to the MIP or the MII question as a percentage of all responses (including "other" responses).[3] These provide a measure of the broader public prioritization of topics at particular points in time. Our analysis here is therefore limited to these three countries, but in future it should become possible to include other national and sub-national cases as the data coverage of CAP increases. Researchers may in future need to decide whether to focus their comparative analyses on a smaller N of cases but for a longer time period, or for a larger N of cases with shorter time series.

For the purposes of this chapter, we treat the MIP and MII questions as interchangeable, since they have been shown to exhibit a high degree of common variance (Jennings and Wlezien, 2011).[4] It is important to note, however, that these are not measures of public preferences (Wlezien, 2005;

Jennings and Wlezien, 2015), and responses may vary according to egocentric and sociotropic versions of the question (Bevan et al., 2016).

25.5 Analysis

25.5.1 Comparing Public Agendas in United States, the United Kingdom, and Spain

In the analysis that follows we focus upon the period for which we have overlapping data for all three countries, between 1993 and 2012. This enables a direct comparison of the public agendas of these countries over the same period. Figure 25.2 plots a horizontal bar chart of the average proportion of MIP responses, by issue, over that period, for each of the three countries. MIP responses are shaded dark grey for the United States, medium grey for the United Kingdom, and light grey for Spain. This simple analysis provides some immediate insights into the issues that dominate the public agenda in these countries. Firstly, these reveal the dominance of macroeconomic issues (at around 30 percent to 40 percent), health (around 10 percent) and crime (over 10 percent) during this time period. That the economy is the top priority tells us quite a lot about the similarities between public agendas in the United States, the United Kingdom, and Spain—countries with distinct political systems and values. We also see similarities in the level of public attention to

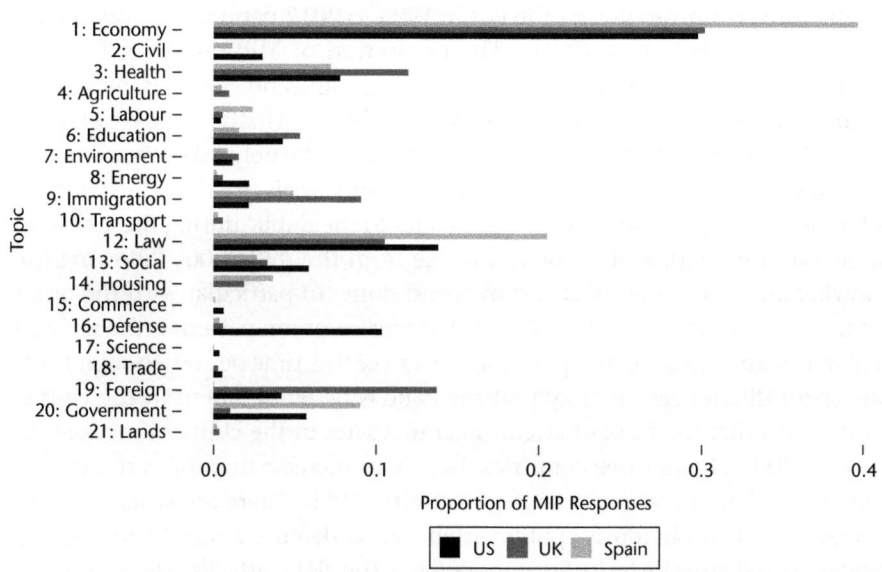

Figure 25.2. Average MIP response, by major topic, 1993–2012
Source: Comparative Agendas Project

225

education (around 5 percent in the United States and the United Kingdom, though less than half this in Spain) and the environment (but at a low level of between 1 percent and 2 percent). The differences across countries are especially interesting: immigration is a much more salient issue in the United Kingdom (at just under 10 percent of the public agenda) than in either Spain (where it is around 5 percent) or the United States (where it is just over 2 percent).

Additionally, defense attracts a substantial proportion of the attention of the US public (around 10 percent), due to the salience of security issues in the wake of September 11th. In contrast, UK public opinion is focused on international affairs—in part due to conflicts in Eastern Europe during the 1990s, but also because of how MII responses about defense and international affairs were coded by the survey organization. Finally, the running of government takes up a good part of public attention in Spain, reflecting the dissatisfaction of the Spanish public with issues such as corruption and the management of government during parts of this period. In many ways, what is striking about the pattern we observe is the degree of similarity across these three very distinct national political systems. But comparison enables us to identify importance differences too.

25.5.2 Tracking the Public Agenda over Time

In addition to considering level-differences in public attention to policy issues in the three countries during the entire 1993 to 2012 period, it is also helpful to consider variation over time. The proportion of MIP responses for each topic in the United States, the United Kingdom, and Spain is plotted in Figure 25.3. A number of observations can be made. Firstly, the overall trend in public attention to the economy, which approximately takes the form of a U-shape, is the same in all three countries. This reveals the shared experience of decline in importance of economic issues to the public during the 1990s, in a period of growth, and a rise in salience from the mid-2000s following the slowing and worsening of economic conditions (in particular with the onset of the global financial crisis in 2008). Another common pattern is the rise and fall of law and crime on the public agenda over this time period, though there are slight differences; notably that the issue is never as salient in the United States, and that the peak of attention comes later in the United Kingdom (in around 2007). In all three countries there is an increase in public attention to the issue of immigration at some point after 2000. There are striking differences too. Most obviously, public attention to defense issues in the United States spiked massively in 2001, following the 9/11 attacks. Despite major terror attacks in Spain (the Madrid bombings of 2003) and the United Kingdom (the London 7/7 bombings of 2005) there were no similar increases

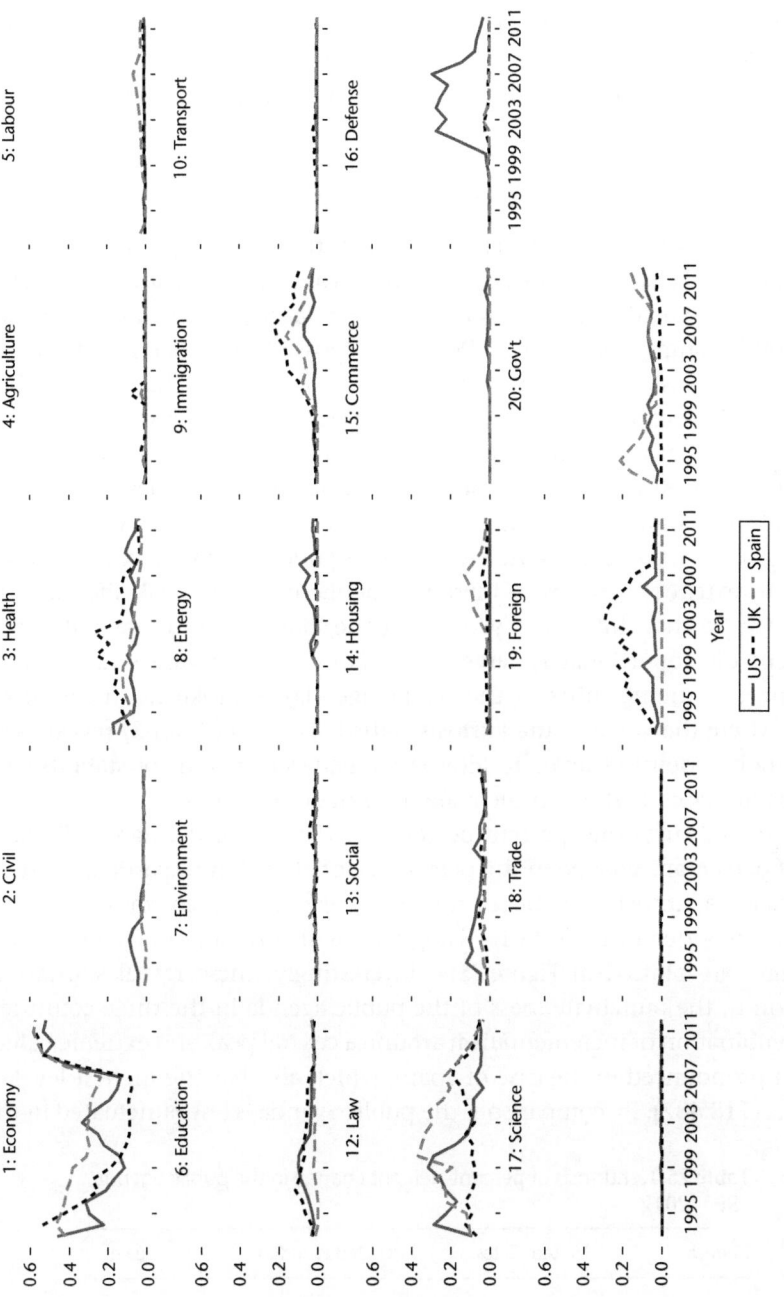

Figure 25.3. United States, United Kingdom, and Spain, 1993–2012

Source: Comparative Agendas Project

in the public agenda. Another difference across the countries relates to health, where the public agenda in the United States was fairly stable throughout the period (at least after the Clinton healthcare plan was abandoned in 1994), and steadily declined in Spain, but rose and then fell in the United Kingdom. Each reveals the distinctive cross-national dynamics of the issue of health.

25.5.3 Stability and Instability in the Public Agenda

We are also interested in the degree to which the public agenda is stable, or subject to rapid change, in the attention that is assigned to issues. Just as in the study of punctuated equilibrium in policy agendas (e.g., Jones and Baumgartner, 2005; Baumgartner et al., 2009), it is possible to discern patterns of stability and instability from aggregate distributions of change in public attention. This can be done, specifically, through plotting of the data on year-on-year changes in the content of the public agenda, and calculation of kurtosis scores. Kurtosis is a measure of the relative "peakedness" of a given distribution. Compared against a normal distribution, those with positive kurtosis (i.e., "leptokurtosis") have a large, slender central peak that corresponds to extended periods of inertia in public opinion, weak shoulders to reflect the relative infrequency of moderate changes, and "fat tails" that represent disproportionately large numbers of extreme values (i.e., corresponding to extreme shifts in the public agenda). Leptokurtic distributions (those where the value of the kurtosis statistic is greater than 3) reveal cases where public opinion tends to alternative between periods of stability and occasional dramatic shifts in the issue priorities of the public.

Our analysis uses the "percent-percent" method (considering the distribution of percentage change in the percentage of attention to particular issues) to calculate a kurtosis statistic for the public agenda in each country overall. These are reported in Table 25.1. Histograms of distributions of change, across all issues, are plotted in Figure 25.4. Interestingly, these reveal substantial variation in the punctuatedness of the public agenda in the three countries. The combination of incrementalism around a central peak and extreme values is most pronounced in the case of Spain, which also has the highest level of kurtosis (118.487). By comparison, the public agenda is less punctuated in the

Table 25.1. Kurtosis of percent-percent change in the public agenda, 1993–2012

Country	United States	United Kingdom	Spain
Kurtosis	24.315	61.573	118.487
N	276	312	238

Source: Comparative Agendas Project

228

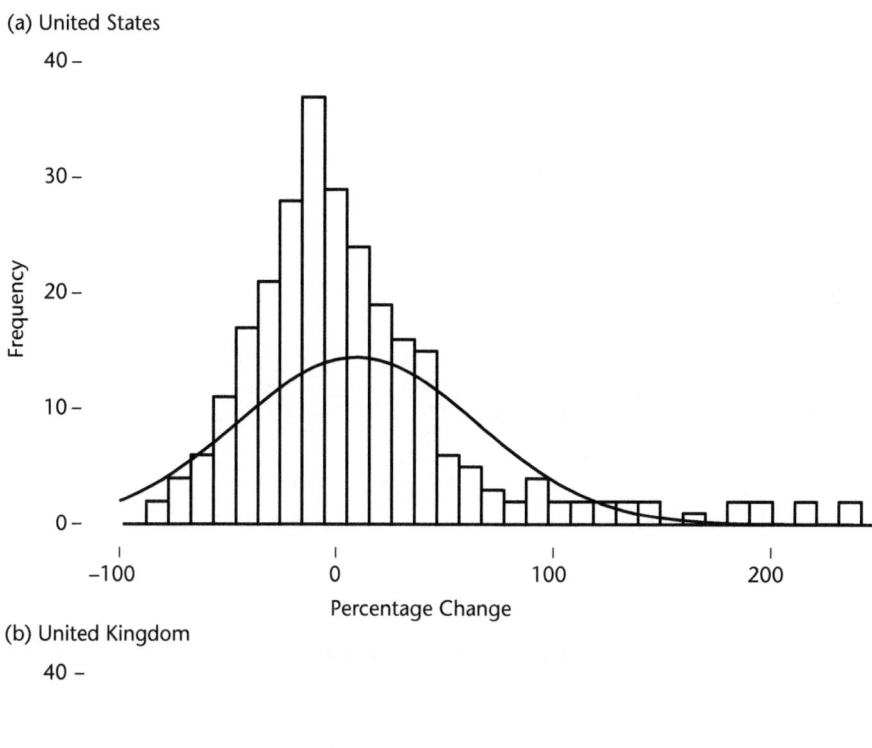

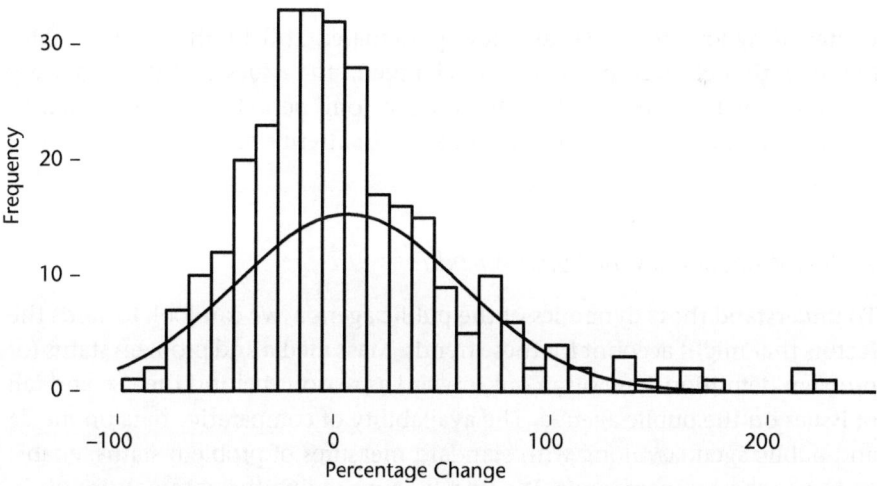

Figure 25.4. Histogram of percent-percent change in the public agenda, 1993–2012

Source: Comparative Agendas Project

(c) Spain

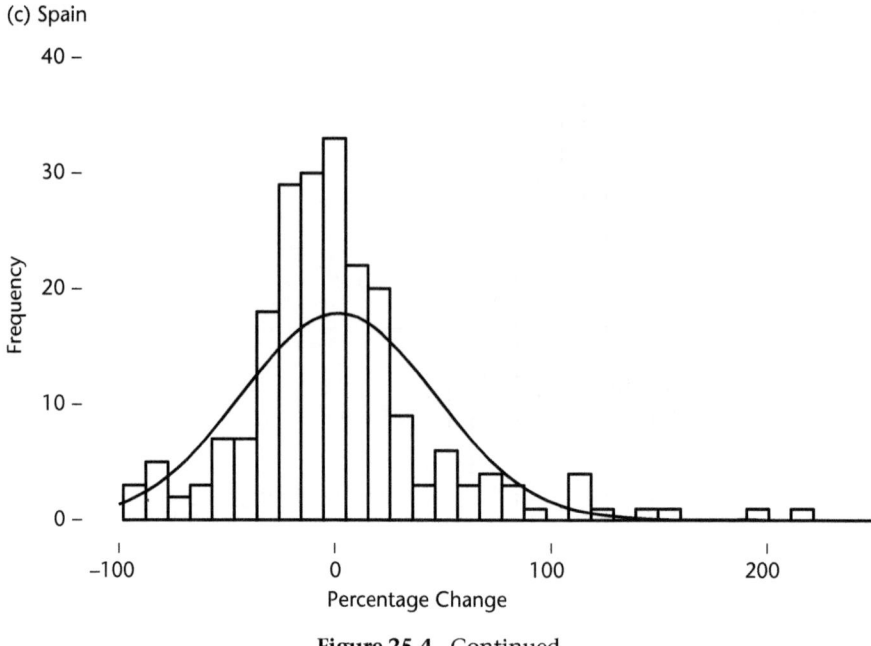

Figure 25.4. Continued

United Kingdom (61.573), and less punctuated still in the United States (24.315), though even in these cases change in the issues that the public are concerned with tends to alternate between long periods of incrementalism and infrequent but large jumps or collapses in attention.

25.5.4 What Shapes the Public Agenda?

To understand these dynamics of the public agenda, we can look towards the factors that might account for these trends. Mass media and problem status (or problem definitions) are often put forward as reasons behind the rise and fall of issues on the public agenda. The availability of comparative data on media and public agendas, along with standard measures of problem status, enable us to test these expectations. We start by considering the common trends in measures of policy problems and MIP responses, in the domains of the economy and crime. We opt for these in part because they are issues where decent objective measures of problem status can be identified (e.g., for the former, economic growth, unemployment, and inflation rates, and for the latter, crime rates), and because these are of substantial importance to citizens (as was shown in Figure 25.2).

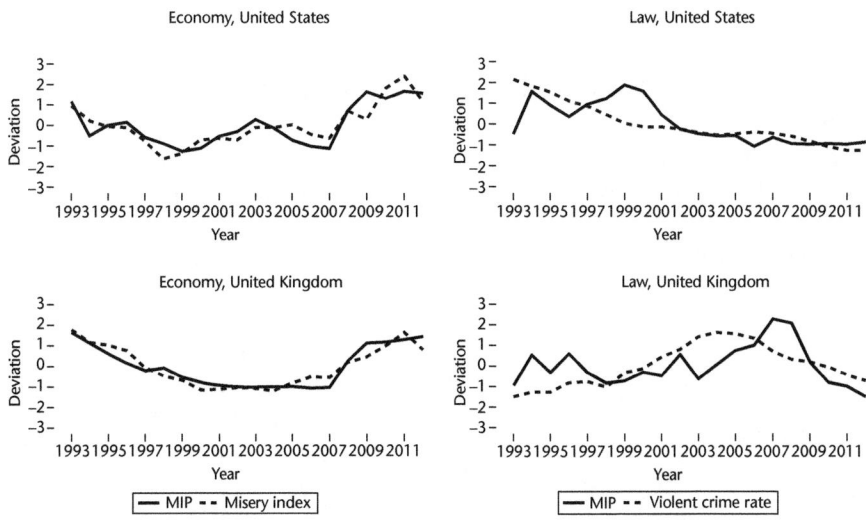

Figure 25.5. Problem status and MIP responses, 1993–2012
Source: Comparative Agendas Project

In the panels on the left-hand side of Figure 25.5 we first plot our measure of economic conditions, the combined unemployment and inflation rate (also known as "the misery index"), against the proportion of MIP responses mentioning the economy in the United States and the United Kingdom respectively. These variables are standardized to facilitate comparison.[5] Figure 25.5 reveals an impressive degree of congruence between the proportion of the public naming the economy as the MIP and the misery index in both the United States and the United Kingdom. Indeed, the trends in the two countries are notably similar—with the prominence of the economy on the public agenda declining from the early 1990s with the improvement of economic conditions, and rising sharply from 2007 with the onset of the global financial crisis. Similarly, in the panels on the right-hand side of Figure 25.5 we plot "problem status" for law and crime in the United States and the United Kingdom, as measured by the rate of violent crime, against the proportion of MIP responses on this issue. This again reveals correspondence between the public agenda and objective measures of policy problems, consistent with previous studies of public opinion on the issue of crime (Miller, 2016; Jennings et al., 2017). While the series do not move as closely together over time as for the economy, the public agenda nevertheless tends to follow changes in the rate of violent crime in the longer term; declining in the United States following the fall of crime rates from the mid-1990s, and rising in the United Kingdom until the mid-2000s after a period of rising crime and falling thereafter. On the basis of these issues there is evidence that the public agenda moves at least partly in response to changes in exogenous policy conditions.

Next, in Figures 25.6(a) and 25.6(b) we consider how news coverage of issues by the mass media moves in tandem with the public agenda over time in the United States and Spain.[6] This is another mechanism which might be expected to influence the issues of concern to the public. In the United States,

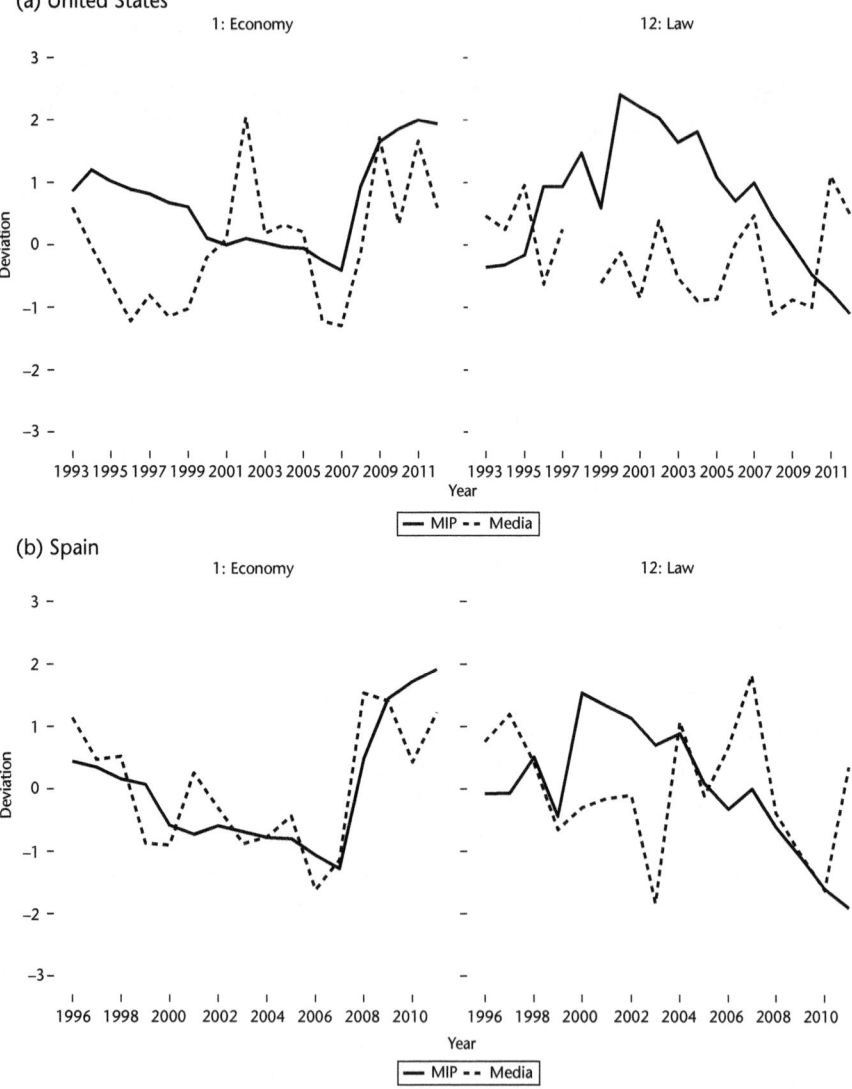

Figure 25.6. Media and MIP responses, 1993–2012

Source: Comparative Agendas Project

the media agenda is measured with a systematic random sample of the New York Times Index. In Spain, it is based on coding of all the stories published in the front pages of *El Mundo* and *El País*, the two highest circulation newspapers in Spain. We focus on the issues of the economy and law and crime, again. Here, interestingly, the correspondence between the public and media agendas in the United States is much weaker than observed previously for problem status. On the issue of the economy there is some covariation in these series around the time of the global financial crisis in 2007–8, but this is much weaker, and there is little commonality between MIP responses and media coverage on the issue of law and order. In Spain, the evidence for the media–public nexus is quite different. For the economy, the media and public agendas move remarkably closely together over time; declining in the 1990s prior to a sharp rise in 2008. While the degree of correspondence is less for the issue of law and crime it still appears that these move together for periods of time (although there are also moments of divergence). The available CAP data thus provides evidence, already, of the potential linkages between mass media and the public agenda—or at least common responses of these societal agendas to changes in the policy problems facing society.

25.5.5 Representation via the Public and Policy Agenda

It is possible to assess the degree of correspondence between the issue priorities of the public and those of policymakers. For this, we use data on the policy agenda of executive speeches. That is, the US State of the Union Address, the UK Queen's Speech (Jennings et al., 2011), and the Spanish prime minister's investiture or state-of-the nation speech (Chaqués-Bonafont et al., 2015). These annual statements by, or on behalf of, the executive have been shown to be a reliable and meaningful indicator of the policy priorities of government (Mortensen et al., 2011). In Table 25.2 we present bivariate correlations between MIP responses and the proportion of the executive speech assigned to each topic in each country. We focus on the period between 1993 and 2012 because this is the period where we have data over the entire period for all three countries (though note that one or two policy topics are missing due to the lack of availability of MIP data). If we start with the mean correlation across all issues, this offers interesting insights into the degree of agenda representation in each country. Perhaps unsurprisingly, the majoritarian Westminster model of the United Kingdom observes the lowest rate of correspondence between public and policy agendas (0.31, p = 0.00). In contrast, Spain (0.68, p = 0.00) displays the highest rate of consistency with the public agenda, which may reflect the proportional electoral system through which its governments are elected, though it is also a unitary parliamentary state. The degree of representation is higher in the United States too (0.58, p = 0.00), potentially indicating that its

Table 25.2. Correlations of the public and policy agendas (executive speeches), 1993–2012

Topic	United States		United Kingdom		Spain	
	Correlation	p	Correlation	p	Correlation	p
All topics	0.58	0.00	0.31	0.00	0.68	0.00
1: Economy	0.75	0.00	0.69	0.00	0.83	0.00
2: Civil	0.11	0.64	–	–	0.08	0.73
3: Health	0.70	0.00	0.04	0.88	0.30	0.20
4: Agriculture	–	–	–0.12	0.61	0.02	0.93
5: Labor	0.07	0.77	–0.17	0.47	0.29	0.22
6: Education	0.57	0.01	0.38	0.10	0.37	0.11
7: Environment	–0.04	0.85	–0.14	0.56	–0.17	0.51
8: Energy	0.43	0.06	0.11	0.64	–0.05	0.83
9: Immigration	0.20	0.39	0.04	0.86	0.72	0.00
10: Transport	–	–	–0.03	0.90	0.37	0.11
12: Law	0.67	0.00	0.07	0.78	0.67	0.00
13: Social	0.65	0.00	0.24	0.32	–0.30	0.20
14: Housing	–	–	–0.01	0.98	0.50	0.02
15: Commerce	0.53	0.02	–	–	0.07	0.77
16: Defence	0.45	0.05	–0.11	0.64	0.13	0.60
17: Science	–0.04	0.86	0.51	0.02	–	–
18: Trade	–0.05	0.83	0.52	0.02	–	–
19: Foreign	0.22	0.35	0.59	0.01	0.10	0.66
20: Gov't	0.12	0.62	0.01	0.96	0.33	0.15
21: Lands	–	–	0.62	0.00	–0.34	0.18

Source: Comparative Agendas Project

federal–presidential system encourages a high level of responsiveness to the issue priorities of the public (see Bevan and Jennings, 2014).

Looking across issues, a high level of correspondence between the public and policy agenda is observed for the economy, with a positive correlation ranging between 0.69 (United Kingdom) and 0.83 (Spain), significant at the 99 percent confidence level in all cases. This is arguably unsurprising given the high salience of economic issues to voters whatever the political context. The variation in the degree of representation for other issues offers some insights into the specific politics of each country during the 1993 to 2012 period. For the United States, we see substantial positive and significant correlations between the public and policy agenda for healthcare, education, law and crime, welfare, domestic commerce, and defense. The strongest correlations observed are for healthcare (0.70, p = 0.00), law and crime (0.67, p = 0.00), and social welfare (0.65, p = 0.00), all issues that were on the political agenda during the Clinton, Bush, and Obama administrations—and which were salient to the public too at different points in time. For the United Kingdom, the domains in which agenda representation is found are quite different, with positive and significant correlations for technology, foreign trade, and international affairs. The latter was an issue of importance to policymakers and to the public during this period, in view of troubles in the Balkans in the late 1990s (due to Britain's military involvement in peace-keeping operations), the 9/11 attacks, and the conflicts in Iraq and Afghanistan. In Spain, there are positive and significant correlation for immigration, law and crime, and housing. The strongest correlation is observed for immigration (0.72, p = 0.00), an issue that moved atop the political agenda in the 2000s as a result of unprecedented waves of migration and a fast-growing foreign-born population.

25.5.6 Public and Policy Agendas over Time

The final part of our comparative exploration of the public agenda considers the extent to which the public agenda moves in parallel with the policy agenda *over time*, again using data on executive speeches for our measure of the policy agenda of government. For this we focus on the economy and law and crime, issues where substantial congruence was observed in static analysis of representation (with the exception of law and crime in the United Kingdom). Using the data in this way provides insight on the dynamic relationship between the public's issue priorities and those issues that are attended to by government. If public attention to an issue increases, does the government respond? In Figure 25.7, the proportion of MIP responses on each of these topics is plotted against the proportion of the executive speech assigned to the same topic. Here we expand the time window of our analysis to the maximal amount of data available for each country. In the United States, this enables us to consider the period between 1947 and 2012. Here we see a good deal of common movement in the public and policy agendas over time for the economy and for law and crime. By simply eyeballing the data we can see that there are common peaks and troughs in the public and policy agendas. There are periods where the series drift apart, too. For example, as US public concern about the economy reached almost 80 percent of MIP responses during the late 1970s, presidential attention to the issue in the State of the Union Address did not increase to the same extent, although there was a subsequent increase in 1982. Similarly, economic downturns in the early 1990s and 2008 saw parallel increases in the public and policy agenda on economic issues, but with the MIP series appearing to move before the shift in policymaking attention.

In the United Kingdom, the public's preoccupation with the economy as an important problem facing the country undergoes much larger movements than government's attention to the issue in the Queen's Speech, reaching a similar level of MIP responses as in the United States at around the same time period—in 1981 and 1982 respectively. Large increases in public concern about the economy at times of economic crisis, in 1991 and 2008 respectively, coincide with (much smaller) increases in attention of British government to

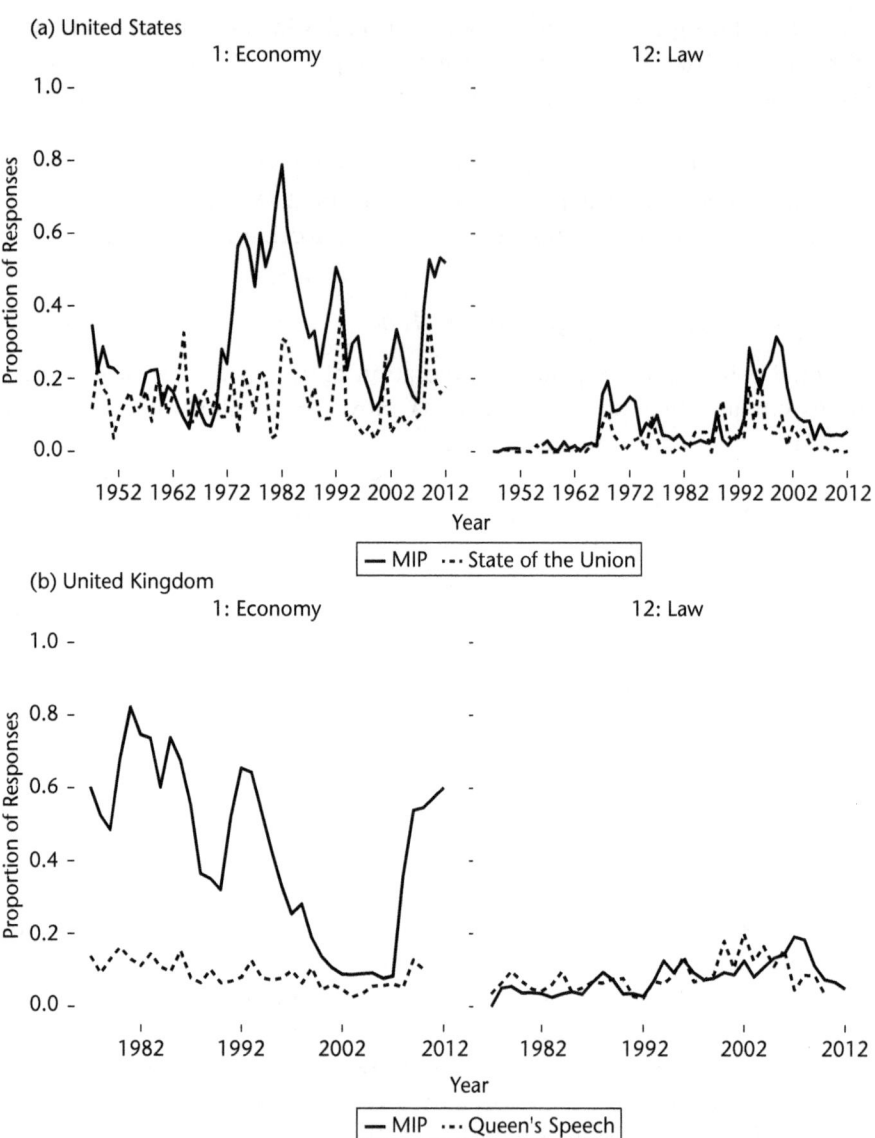

Figure 25.7. Executive speeches and the public agenda
Source: Comparative Agendas Project

the issue. On the issue of crime, the public and policy agendas move together, rising gradually from the 1970s onwards, and then falling after the mid-2000s.

In Spain, over a somewhat shorter time period, between 1993 and 2012, the parallels in the dynamics of the public and policy agenda are striking. While the proportion of MIP responses on each of these issues is higher

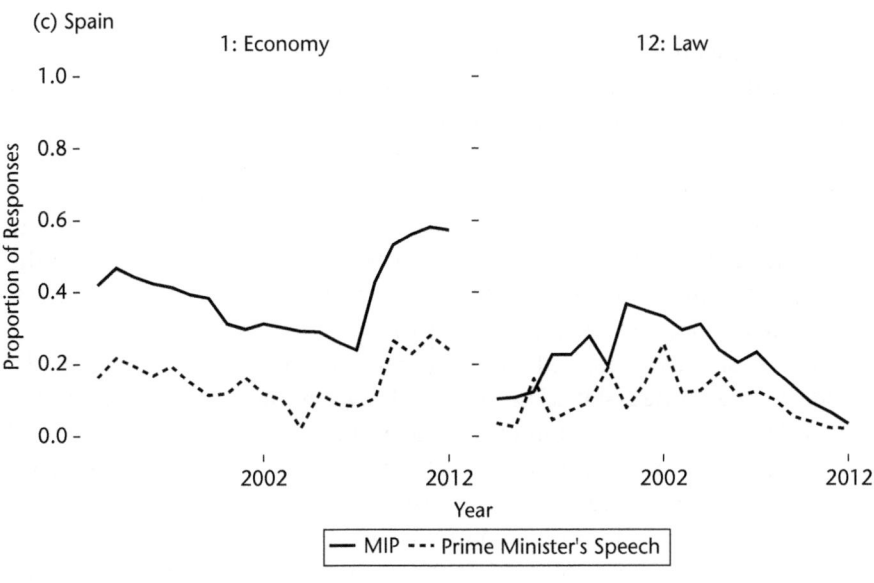

Figure 25.7. Continued

than the share of the policy agenda in the prime minister's speech, the trends are highly similar. For the economy this sees a decline in attention before 2008, and a sharp jump in the public and policy agenda thereafter. With regard to law and crime, the importance of the issue to the public rose during the 1990s, peaking around in 2000s, with the public agenda tending to lead attention of the government to it. There is evidence, then, that the policy agenda is subject to common variation as the public agenda over time, consistent with the idea of "dynamic agenda representation" (Bevan and Jennings, 2014).

25.6 Conclusion

In this chapter we have explored how a comparative perspective might offer insights into the public agenda. Much research is preoccupied with questions such as: What shapes the public agenda? How does the public agenda influence public policy? Yet most studies of the public agenda are confined to a single country, and often a single policy domain or subset of policy domains (such as the economy and foreign policy). By taking a comparative approach, it becomes possible to reflect on how and why the issues that are important to citizens vary across countries, the extent to which these issue priorities are subject to change over time, and the degree to which the public agenda is reflected in the priorities of policymakers. Systematic comparison, based upon the application of a common policy-content coding scheme, provides opportunities for inferences regarding the effects of political institutions and context. Data collected through the Comparative Agendas Project offers such an opportunity for advances in understanding of how the wider set of issues on the "systemic" agenda matter for composition of the formal decision-making agenda. Here, the survey measure on the most important problem facing the country is the most widely available measure of the public agenda (though noting the limitations of this measure too).

Our analysis has compared the issues that are prominent on the public agenda in the United States, the United Kingdom, and Spain. This reveals similarities, such as the prominence of economic issues, healthcare, law and crime, education and environment, and differences, such as the high salience of defense in the United States in contrast to the United Kingdom and Spain, and higher salience of immigration in the United Kingdom in comparison to either Spain or the United States. It also tells us quite a lot about how public attention is structured in these countries with distinct political systems and values. We further considered the correspondence between policy problems, mass media, and the public agenda. This revealed that the public agenda moves closely in parallel with exogenous measures of policy problems—at least in the salient policy domains of the economy and crime. We also showed that there is some parallelism in the agendas of mass media and the public, though the precise direction of temporal causality was not untangled here.

Further, our analysis considered possible effects of the public agenda, in particular the degree of correspondence—both static and over time—between public opinion and the policy agenda of government. Interestingly, we find the lowest level of "agenda representation" in the Westminster-system of the United Kingdom, and the highest in Spain, a unitary parliamentary system in which governments are elected through proportional representation. The degree of agenda representation is high in the United States too, under its federal–presidential system, consistent with previous work (see Bevan and Jennings, 2014). On specific issues, the highest level of correspondence between the public and policy agenda is found for the economy, unsurprisingly given the crucial importance of economic considerations to vote choice. Yet there is variety in the pattern of representation too, which reflect the particular domains in which policymakers are more representative of the concerns of citizens. For example, healthcare, law and crime, and social welfare are issues where the attention of policymakers lines up with that of citizens. In Spain, policymakers' attention to immigration tends to be higher when it is also an important issue for the public. And in the United Kingdom, this correspondence of attention is discovered for technology, foreign trade, and international affairs. When we look at the representational linkage in attention over time for selected issues, we observe similar patterns. Taking the economy and law and crime, common over-time movement is observed in the public and policy agendas. There is evidence, then, that the policy agenda is subject to common variation as the public agenda over time, consistent with the idea of "dynamic agenda representation" (Bevan and Jennings, 2014).

What we have presented here only hints at the possibilities of the CAP data for use in future analysis. Other researchers may wish to compare differences and similarities in the public agenda across more countries or more issues. Studies may focus on comparison of trends for specific policy domains (e.g., health, immigration), taking a more fine-grained approach to understanding factors that shape the series presented here and their interaction. Further research may also use methods specifically for diagnosing the dynamic interaction of the public agenda with other societal and institutional agendas. For example, vector autoregression models or Granger causality tests might be used to unpick the temporal relationship between public, media, and policy agendas at different time points. Researchers may also wish to explore the relationship between the public agenda and different "channels" or levels of policymaking (e.g., Jones et al., 2009; Bevan and Jennings, 2014). Regardless of the analytical or methodological proclivities of individual researchers, these comparative data provide the opportunity for systematic cross-national analysis of the public agenda over time, in conjunction with a wide range of other measures of policy activity.

Notes

1. Formulations of the MIP and MII questions vary slightly. In the United States, the survey question asks "What do you think is the most important problem facing this country today?" whereas in the United Kingdom, since 1959, it has been worded "Which would you say is the most urgent problem facing the country at the present time?" (before then it was closer to the US version, "What is the most important problem facing the country at the present time?").
2. Obviously other opinion surveys with other survey questions exist in CAP countries as well. However, these questions are more likely to suffer similar issues in regards to length and most importantly do not clearly match onto the CAP system of attention based coding like MIP and MII measures do.
3. The percentage of MIP responses is standardized as a share of all responses, so the total is equal to 100%.
4. Gallup discontinued polling and the MIP series in the United Kingdom in 2001; however, since 1977 Ipsos-MORI has asked a survey question about the most important issue (MII). It is possible to combine these data series to construct a

continuous measure of the public agenda (e.g., Bevan and Jennings, 2014). Here we just use the MII series for the period between 1993 and 2012.

5. Calculated as the raw value minus the mean, divided by the standard deviation.

6. Data on the media agenda in the United Kingdom was not available at the time of writing.

References

Alexandrova, P., Rasmussen, A., and Toshkov, D. (2016). Agenda Responsiveness in the European Council: Public Priorities, Policy Problems and Political Attention. *West European Politics*, 39(4): 605–27.

Bartle, J., and Laycock, S. (2012). Telling More than They Can Know? Does the Most Important Issue Really Reveal What Is Most Important to Voters? *Electoral Studies*, 31(4): 679–88.

Baumgartner, F.R., Breunig, C., Green-Pedersen, C. et al. (2009). Punctuated Equilibrium in Comparative Perspective. *American Journal of Political Science*, 53(3): 602–19.

Baumgartner, F. R., and Jones, B. D. (1993). *Agendas and Instability in American Politics*. Chicago: University of Chicago Press.

Bevan, S., and Jennings, W. (2014). Representation, Agendas and Institutions. *European Journal of Political Research*, 53(1): 37–56.

Bevan, S., Jennings, W., and Wlezien, C. (2016). An Analysis of the Public's Personal, National and EU Priorities. *Journal of European Public Policy*, 23(6): 871–87.

Birkland, T. (2011). *An Introduction to the Policy Process: Theories, Concepts and Models of Public Policy Making*. London: Routledge.

Brosius, Hans-B., and Kepplinger, M. H. (1995). Killer and Victim Issues: Issue Competition in the Agenda-Setting Process of German Television. *International Journal of Public Opinion Research*, 7(3): 211–31.

Carmines, E.G., and Stimson, J. A. (1989). *Issue Evolution: Race and the Transformation of American Politics*. Princeton: Princeton University Press.

Chaqués-Bonafont, L., and Palau, A. M. (2011). Assessing the Responsiveness of Spanish Policymakers to the Priorities of their Citizens. *West European Politics*, 34(4): 706–30.

Chaqués-Bonafont, L., Palau, A. M., and Baumgartner, F. R. (2015). *Agenda Dynamics in Spain*. Basingstoke: Palgrave Macmillan.

Cobb, R. W., and Elder, C. D. (1972). *Participation in American Politics: The Dynamics of Agenda-Building*. Boston: Allyn & Bacon.

Cohen, J. (1995). Presidential Rhetoric and the Public Agenda. *American Journal of Political Science*, 39(1): 87–107.

Cohen, S. (1972). *Folk Devils and Moral Panics*. London: Paladin.

Downs, A. (1972). Up and Down with Ecology: The Issue Attention Cycle. *Public Interest*, 28: 38–50.

Green, J., and Jennings, W. (2017). Party Reputations and Policy Priorities: How Issue Ownership Shapes Executive and Legislative Agendas. *British Journal of Political Science*, 1–24. DOI:10.1017/S0007123416000636.

Hibbs, D. A. (1979). The Mass Public and Macro-Economic Policy: The Dynamics of Public Opinion towards Unemployment and Inflation. *American Journal of Political Science*, 2(3): 705–31.

Hudson, J. (1994). Granger Causality, Rational Expectations and Aversion to Unemployment and Inflation. *Public Choice*, 80(1/2): 9–21.

Iyengar, S. (1991). *Is Anyone Responsible? How Television Frames Political Issues*. Chicago: Chicago University Press.

Jennings, W., Bevan, S., and John, P. (2011). The Agenda of British Government: The Speech from the Throne, 1911–2008. *Political Studies*, 59(1): 74–98.

Jennings, W., Farrall, S., Hay, C., and Gray, E. (2017). Moral Panics and Punctuated Equilibrium in Public Policy: An Analysis of the Criminal Justice Policy Agenda in Britain. *Policy Studies Journal*, 1–27. DOI: 10.1111/psj.12239.

Jennings, W., and John, P. (2009). The Dynamics of Political Attention: Public Opinion and the Queen's Speech in the United Kingdom. *American Journal of Political Science*, 53(4): 838–54.

Jennings, W., and Wlezien, C. (2011). Distinguishing between Most Important Problems and Issues? *Public Opinion Quarterly*, 75(3): 545–55.

Jennings, W., and Wlezien, C. (2015). "Problems, Preferences and Representation." *Political Science Research and Methods*, 3(3): 659–81.

John, P., Bertelli, A., Jennings, W., and Bevan, S. (2013). *Policy Agendas in British Politics*. Basingstoke: Palgrave Macmillan.

John, P., Bevan, S., and Jennings, W. (2011). The Policy-Opinion Link and Institutional Change: The Policy Agenda of the United Kingdom and Scottish Parliaments, 1977–2008. *Journal of European Public Policy*, 18(7): 1052–68.

Jones, B. D. (1994). *Reconceiving Decision-Making in Democratic Politics: Attention, Choice, and Public Policy*. Chicago: University of Chicago Press.

Jones, B. D., and Baumgartner, F. R. (2004). Representation and Agenda Setting. *Policy Studies Journal*, 32(1): 1–24.

Jones, B. D., and Baumgartner, F. R. (2005). *The Politics of Attention: How Government Prioritizes Problems*. Chicago: University of Chicago Press.

Jones, B. D., Larsen-Price, H., and Wilkerson, J. (2009). Representation and American Governing Institutions. *Journal of Politics*, 71: 277–90.

Kingdon, J. (1984). *Agendas, Alternatives, and Public Policies*. New York: HarperCollins.

Lindeboom, G.-J. (2012). Public Priorities in Government's Hands: Corresponding Policy Agendas in the Netherlands? *Acta Politica*, 47(4): 443–67.

Lodge, M., and Hood, C. (2002). Pavlovian Policy Responses to Media Feeding Frenzies? *Journal of Contingencies and Crisis Management*, 10(1): 1–13.

Lovett, J., Bevan, S., and Baumgartner, F. R. (2015). Popular Presidents Can Affect Congressional Attention, for a Little While. *Policy Studies Journal*, 43(1): 22–43.

McCombs, M. E., and Shaw, D. L. (1972). The Agenda-Setting Function of Mass Media. *Public Opinion Quarterly*, 36(2): 176–87.

McCombs, M., and Zhu, J.-H. (1995). Capacity, Diversity, and Volatility of the Public Agenda: Trends from 1954 to 1994. *Public Opinion Quarterly*, 59(4): 495–525.

MacKuen, M. B., and Coombs, S. L. (1981). *More Than News: Media Power in Public Affairs*. Beverly Hills: Sage Publications.

Miller, L. (2016). *The Myth of Mob Rule: Violent Crime and Democratic Politics*. Oxford: Oxford University Press.

Mortensen, P. B., Green-Pedersen, C., Breeman, G. et al. (2011). Comparing Government Agendas: Executive Speeches in the Netherlands, United Kingdom, and Denmark. *Comparative Political Studies*, 44(8): 973–1000.

Soroka, S. N. (2002). *Agenda-Setting Dynamics in Canada*. Vancouver: University of British Columbia Press.

Wlezien, C. (2005). On the Salience of Political Issues: The Problem with "Most Important Problem." *Electoral Studies*, 24(4): 555–79.

26

From Public to Publics

Assessing Group Variation in Issue Priorities in the United States and Israel

Amnon Cavari and Guy Freedman

A rich body of work examines trends in the salience of issues among people in democratic regimes. The focus of most of this work is on aggregate measures of issues and the causes and effects of its dynamics (see, for example, Bevan, Jennings, and Wlezien, 2016; Jennings and Wlezien 2015; Jones, 1994; Jones and Baumgartner, 2004; MacKuen and Coombs, 1981; McCombs, 1999; McCombs and Shaw, 1972; McCombs and Zhu, 1995; Reher, 2015; Soroka, 2002; Soroka and Wlezien, 2010). For the most part, these studies treat the public as a homogenous whole, with collective issue interests—commonly referred to as the public agenda—that move as a unit in response to new information and events. Despite the common use of this measure in existing research and the rich analysis of individual-level responses to attitudinal measures, very little attention has been given to the causes of issue priorities of individuals and groups. Why do some people prioritize one issue over the other? How do different demographic and political groups differ in their priorities? In this chapter, we address these questions by testing the effect of conventional demographic factors on issue priorities in two countries—the United States and Israel. The two countries differ in the issue that dominates their public agenda—macroeconomics in the United States and foreign affairs and defense in Israel. Yet, demographic groups in each country demonstrate varying issue priorities that are compatible with existing theories about public interest. This variation reveals the importance of turning our attention from an overall, average public agenda, to an individual and group priorities. That is, from public agenda to public agendas.

26.1 The Public Agenda and Issue Priorities

The issues that are most important to people are first and foremost affected by events, the political environment, and the way they are presented by the media and political elites. Therefore, similar to the parallel change of issue preferences among most demographic groups (Page and Shapiro, 1992), issue priorities are usually shared by most people and most groups. And yet, issue priorities are more dynamic than issue positions and are less affected by predispositions and ideological commitments (Jones, 1994). This dynamic may depend on an individual's characteristics such as income, education, and race. For example, a person with a permanent, high-paying job, may prioritize the economy during economic downturns but shift her attention to other issues such as the environment or foreign policy during more stable economic times. In contrast, a person with no permanent job is more likely to consistently prioritize economic issues. Similar contrasts can be made about other demographic differences and for other issues.

Several, relatively dated, studies examine group differences and generally point to similarities between demographic groups rather than differences (Douglass, Cleveland, and Maddox, 1974; Jones, 1994; Smith, 1980, 1985). A more recent study examined individual-level responses to the MIP question and demonstrates significant differences in focus on foreign vs. domestic issues among partisan and ideological groups (Heffington, Beomseob Park, and Williams, 2017). To what extent, however, can we identify differences between demographic groups? Do people vary in their issue priorities based on their own life experiences? And, can we identify differences between more defined issues rather than overall, rough comparisons of domestic vs. foreign issues?

There are several reasons to expect variation among people and groups. First, people have different motivations for naming what is their biggest concern and these motivations vary across demographic groups (McCombs, 1999). For instance, some people may be motivated to choose a problem out of self-interest, while for others, the motivation may be peer influence or a sense of civic duty (see McCombs, 1999 for a full analysis of these and other motivations). If motivations are different, we should expect that priorities will vary as well.

Second, demographic groups vary in their attention and response to media coverage of different issues (Berinsky and Karpowitz, 2005; Cavari, 2017). Mainly, groups with most at stake in a given issue are more sensitive than others to changes in that area. While problems do not usually affect a single sector, some sectors may be more sensitive than others to the effect of certain problems. For instance, we may expect crime to be a greater problem for people with lower income, lower levels of education, or minorities, who may be subject to greater crime rates compared to the entire population.

Third, the variation in attention and response is consistent with the notion of issue publics. According to this notion, the public is not monolithic in its interest and attention. Rather, the public is divided into issue publics—groups of individuals that have specialized interests and patterns of attentiveness (Converse, 1964; Krosnick, 1990; Popkin, 1991). While problems may affect multiple sectors and concerns may rise and fall in parallel for multiple sectors, we can expect differences in the relative concern of various groups. For example, when crime rates are high, people from most sectors may report crime as the most important problem. But, some—for instance people who live in poorer neighborhoods—may tend to report this more than others, because their exposure to the consequences of higher crime rates is greater.

In focusing on variation in the public agenda, we are therefore interested in assessing issue priorities of individuals and in identifying group variations. We examine this with two case studies—the United States and Israel. The two countries differ considerably in the main issues that are on the political agenda. In the United States, a majority of Americans focus on economics followed by defense and foreign affairs (Cavari, 2017). In Israel, a clear first among a majority of the Israeli public is defense and foreign affairs (Galnoor and Blander, 2018). Still, in each country, we should expect that the relative importance people attribute to an issue is affected by individual and group characteristics that shape public opinion and interest. Furthermore, while the overall public interest may vary between countries, we may find similarities in the relative prioritization of comparable demographic groups. That is, while Americans are overall more concerned with economics and Israelis are concerned with foreign affairs, variation in issue focus among demographic groups may present more similarities than differences. For example, people from lower economic status in both countries may focus more on economics than people from higher economic status—regardless of their respective political environment. This most-different comparison (Tarrow, 2010) is therefore used to illustrate our main argument: that researchers should turn their attention from the public agenda to public *agendas*.

26.2 MIP Data

To assess the issue priorities of Americans and Israelis, we rely on a series of surveys in each country that ask respondents what is the most important problem facing the country.[1] This question, commonly referred to as the MIP question, is one of the few attitudinal survey questions to have been asked consistently since the beginning of public opinion polling. While the scope and quality of data vary between the United States and Israel, the MIP series offer a dynamic measure of issue priorities for longitudinal studies in both countries (Soroka, 2002; Cavari, Rinker, and Freedman, 2017).

The MIP question is an open-ended question. Each respondent is asked to name the problem she thinks is most important. Following the survey, interviewers ascribed the responses to several issue categories.[2] These issue categories are usually detailed yet not consistent across surveys. For example, problems relating to high taxes may be grouped into a "taxes" category or together with "inflation" or "high cost of living." Problems with the environment are sometimes grouped into one category, but in other surveys, they are separated to several more specific environmental issues such as "water pollution," "air pollution," and "litter and garbage." Similarly, foreign events and defense priorities are grouped into regions—"South-East Asia," "Middle East," and so forth—or are categorized by the priorities that respondents mention—"war," "defense," "foreign aid." We, therefore, coded all responses into the major topics of the Comparative Agendas Project (CAP).[3]

For the US series, we collected from the Roper iPoll archive all surveys between 1947 and 2015 that ask Americans the most important problem (MIP) facing the nation question and which offer individual-level data.[4] The wording of the MIP question in all surveys is relatively similar: "In your opinion, what do you think is the most important problem facing this country today?" The dataset includes 815,680 responses to the MIP question from 580 surveys (including only samples of US national adults). Most surveys were conducted by Gallup (47 percent) and CBS/NYT (32 percent). Nearly all of the remaining 20 percent are evenly divided between ABC News (7 percent), Princeton Survey Research Associates (6 percent), and LA Times (5 percent).

Viewed together, the responses to all surveys amount to 1,739 unique responses, which we coded using the CAP codebook. The US data are relatively detailed and rich, and hence allow for coding of subcategories—especially macroeconomics. We combine defense (category 16) and international affairs (category 19) into one category—foreign affairs—because of strong similarities between them in public responses (Baumgartner and Jones, 2002).

Data on the Israeli public agenda are not as rich or readily available as in the United States. The question is not asked in most commercial surveys and most of them are not publicly available or have sufficient academic supervision. We, therefore, rely on the Israel National Election Studies (INES), administered every election cycle since 1969 and are considered the best and most extensive time series data in Israel (15 surveys, on average every 3.29 years). Each survey asks the MIP question, yet with some variation. Several surveys ask a question similar to the US one, whereas others ask respondents to mention the most important problem the *government* must take care of.[5] Finally, surveys extend to Israeli Arabs only from 1996 forward and therefore we focus on Israeli Jews only.

We code all responses according to the CAP codebook.[6] The data are less detailed making it very difficult to differentiate between categories and impossible to code for subtopics. This may be because of poor coding of the open-ended responses by the interviewers or because of the characteristically unspecific responses of the Israeli interviewee. Unlike the US data, there are clearer differences between defense and security and foreign affairs. In the interest of comparable design, we treat the two as subcategories of an overall issue on the public agenda—defense and foreign affairs.

Despite the limitations of the Israeli data, they offer the most detailed time series of the public agenda. To the best of our knowledge, this is the first analysis of the Israeli public agenda—aggregate or individual—over time.[7]

26.3 Issue Priorities in the United States

Figure 26.1 illustrates trends in the aggregated public agenda of seven major categories (rounded share of overall agenda) in the United States: macroeconomics (36 percent), defense and international affairs (25 percent), crime, law, and family (9 percent), civil rights (6 percent), government operation

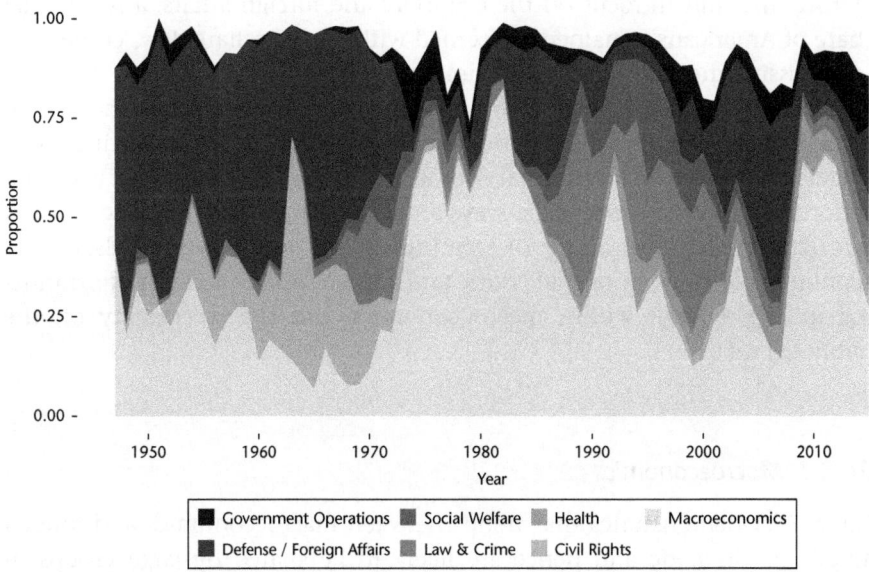

Figure 26.1. The map of American Public Agenda, 1947–2015

Source: Top line responses to the MIP item in 805 surveys, available from the Roper iPoll Archive (1947–2015, N = 1,038,783)

(6 percent), social welfare (5 percent), and health (4 percent). Together, these topics amount to more than 90 percent of the public agenda. The figure is a stacked area plot. The area each category occupies stands for the relative percent of respondents who indicated an issue that is grouped under the respective category. Plotted together, the issue map in Figure 26.1 summarizes dynamic changes in the public agenda in over sixty years of data.

During the first two decades following World War II, the majority of Americans prioritized foreign affairs, replacing their immediate post-war focus on economic and domestic issues. Civil rights issues emerged as a dominant priority during the Civil Rights movement of the 1950s and 1960s, slowly decaying by mid-1970s. Starting in the early 1970s, the deteriorating economy and the energy crisis shifted the priorities of Americans to the economy. This period of economic instability was followed by renewed public interest in foreign affairs during the Reagan presidency.

Starting from the 1980s, social welfare issues have begun to occupy an increasing share of the public agenda, and, especially in the 1990s, more Americans were concerned about problems relating to other domestic issues such as law, crime, and family, health, and, a decade later, to immigration. The 9/11 terrorist attacks and subsequent US involvement in two large-scale wars—Afghanistan and Iraq—resulted in a temporary burst of public interest in foreign policy issues. Following the economic meltdown in 2008, public attention shifted again away from foreign policy and back to the economy. During this shift in focus on the economy and foreign affairs, a substantial share of Americans remained concerned with social welfare, law, crime, and family issues, health, and immigration.

Going beyond the general "map" of public agenda, we examine individual-level data and test the effect of demographic factors on issue priorities. We, therefore, collected conventional demographic variables—sex, race, age, education, and income—from all surveys and examine the relative effect of each one of them on issue priorities of Americans. We examine two models: macroeconomic priorities among all issues, and a more specific analysis of prioritizing unemployment within macroeconomics, the largest category on the public agenda.

26.3.1 Macroeconomics

Figure 26.1 demonstrates that trends between macroeconomics and foreign affairs are dramatic and hence are likely to be shared by large groups in American society. Yet these general trends may still conceal offsetting changes among particular subgroups and individuals. To test this, we estimate individual issue priorities. Because several categories are relatively small—under

2 percent—we combine these topics into one catch-all category (7 percent of the total agenda). We include indicators for sex, race, age, levels of education, and income levels. Given the categorical nature of the dependent variable, we estimate a multinomial logistic regression. Our base outcome is the second most voluminous issue on the public agenda: foreign affairs (including defense and international affairs). Because of quality and consistency of the independent variables we limit our analyses to data from 1960 forward. To account for issue salience, we include a covariate of the share of each category in each survey. By including this covariate of overall share, our estimates account for variation from the general trend rather than overall attention to an issue. We also account for time by clustering the standard errors by survey.

In this chapter, we focus only on the effect of these factors on prioritizing macroeconomics (in comparison to the base outcome: foreign affairs). We present the results graphically (complete tables can be requested from authors). Figure 26.2 graphically summarizes the results of the main comparison. A positive coefficient indicates a positive relationship between the factor or covariate and macroeconomic priorities, compared to foreign priorities. A negative coefficient indicates a negative relationship, in this case meaning prioritizing foreign issues over macroeconomics. The horizontal lines indicate the 90 percent confidence intervals. If these cross zero, the effect is statistically zero.

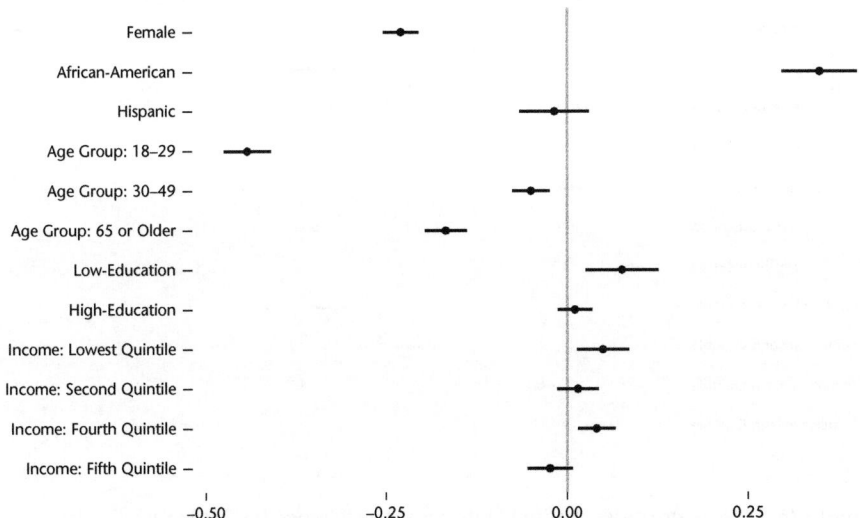

Figure 26.2. Issue priorities, United States: macroeconomics (vs. foreign affairs)

Source: Point estimates and 90 percent confidence intervals following multinomial logistic regression, MIP Surveys 1980–2015

249

The results indicate that sex, race, age, education, and income are all associated with issue priorities. Females are less likely than men (reference group) to prioritize macroeconomics over foreign issues. African Americans are more likely to prioritize macroeconomic issues than whites (reference group). Youngest and oldest are less likely to prioritize macroeconomic issues compared to people in middle age. And lowest education and income levels focus on macroeconomics more than foreign issues.

26.3.2 Macroeconomics—Minor Topics

Further to test differences between groups, we break macroeconomics into its subcategories and examine individual priorities on these issues. Our independent variables and model specifications are the same as the general model discussed above. In the interests of this chapter, we focus here only on the comparison of unemployment and budget, the two most voluminous subcategories. These subcategories also represent the most dominant tension in economic policy, pitting Keynesian and Monetarist, balanced budget policies (see, for example, Hall, 1993). The results of our main comparison are summarized in Figure 26.3.

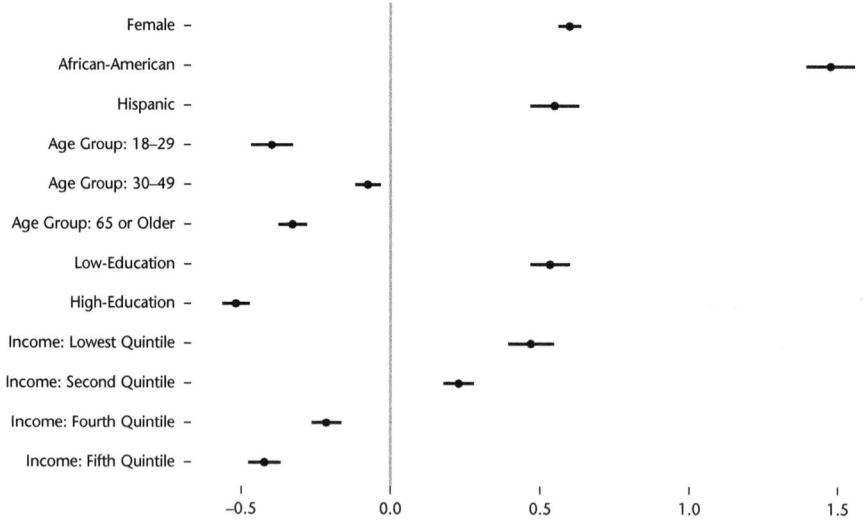

Figure 26.3. Issue priorities, United States: unemployment (vs. budget)

Source: Point estimates and 90 percent confidence intervals following multinomial logistic regression, MIP Surveys 1980–2015

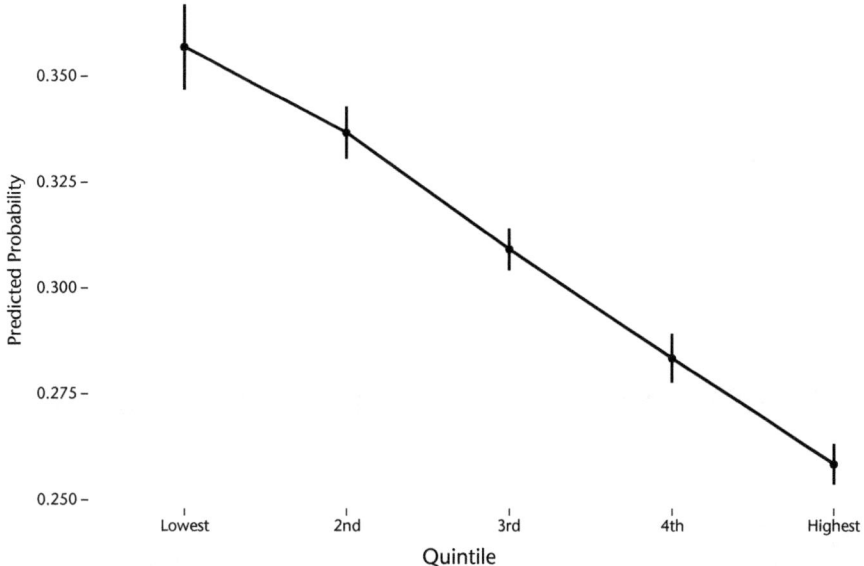

Figure 26.4. Predicted probability, unemployment (of macroeconomics)

Source: Predicted probabilities and 95 percent confidence intervals following multinomial logistic regression, holding all other variables constant at their mean, MIP Surveys, 1980–2015

The results demonstrate substantial differences among most demographic groups. Mainly, people who are disadvantaged in the labor force, tend to prioritize unemployment—females, African Americans and Hispanics, uneducated (without High School diploma) and first and second income quintiles. People who are stronger economically tend to prioritize the budget—males, whites, people with a college degree, and top income quintiles.

To illustrate the magnitude of the effect, Figure 26.4 plots the predicted probabilities of each income group. The range is from 0.36 to 0.26, that is, the predicted probability that a person earning within the lowest income quintile will prioritize unemployment as the economic issue is 0.36. The predicted probability for the highest income quintile is 0.26. Considering that this difference is after controlling for race, gender, education, and age, it is substantial.

The model accounts for time and hence reflects the average advantage over time. And yet, the differences are consistent over time. We illustrate this in Figure 26.5, which plots the coefficients of the four income groups (except middle quintile, used as reference) for each year since 1980. Throughout the thirty-five years of data, the lowest two income quintiles were more likely to prioritize unemployment. While the trends are less clear regarding the fourth quintile, the top 20 percent of earners have been almost consistently less focused on unemployment (and hence on budget, the base category).

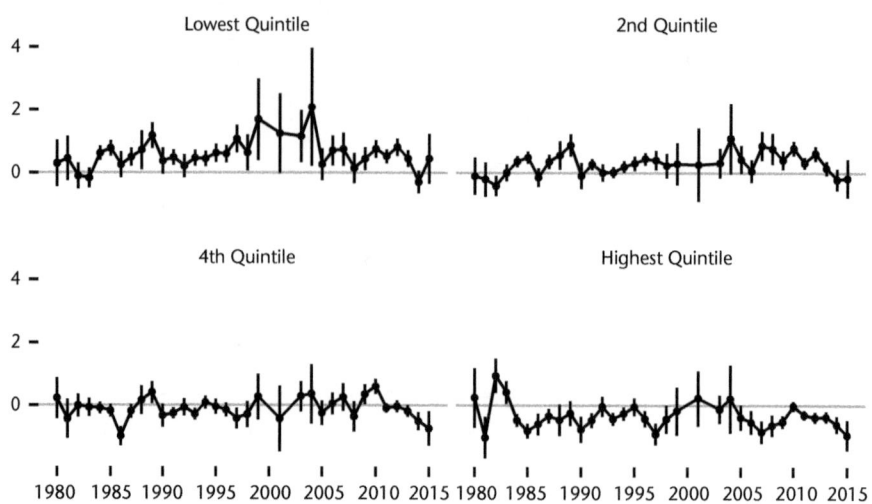

Figure 26.5. Predicted probability, unemployment (of macroeconomics)

Source: Markers represent coefficients of income group following separate year regressions, spikes represent 90 percent confidence intervals, MIP surveys, 1980–2015

The results are consistent with mounting evidence and interest in recent years about the growing inequality in the United States, its sources and its effect on the political system. A series of articles and books on this topic points to the fact that elected officials and public policy are largely unresponsive to the policy preferences of millions of low-income Americans, leaving their political interests to the ideological whims of what incumbent elites may dictate (Achen and Bartels, 2016; Bartels, 2016; Carnes, 2013; Gilens, 2012; Hacker and Pierson, 2010). We add to this debate by demonstrating that people from different social status differ in their policy agenda. Mainly, racial minorities, people with no formal education, and lowest income quintiles tend to focus on the economy and employment considerations.

26.4 Issue Priorities in Israel

Figure 26.6 illustrates the relative share of the seven most voluminous categories on the public agenda—macroeconomics, civil rights, education, immigration, welfare, foreign/defense,[8] and government. The Israeli data are based on election surveys, and therefore cannot be interpreted as a continuous measure of the public agenda. We therefore plot the data over time using a stacked bar chart instead of a stacked area plot used for the US data.

As can be expected in a country that is in a constant military conflict, the category of defense/foreign affairs occupies a substantial share of the public

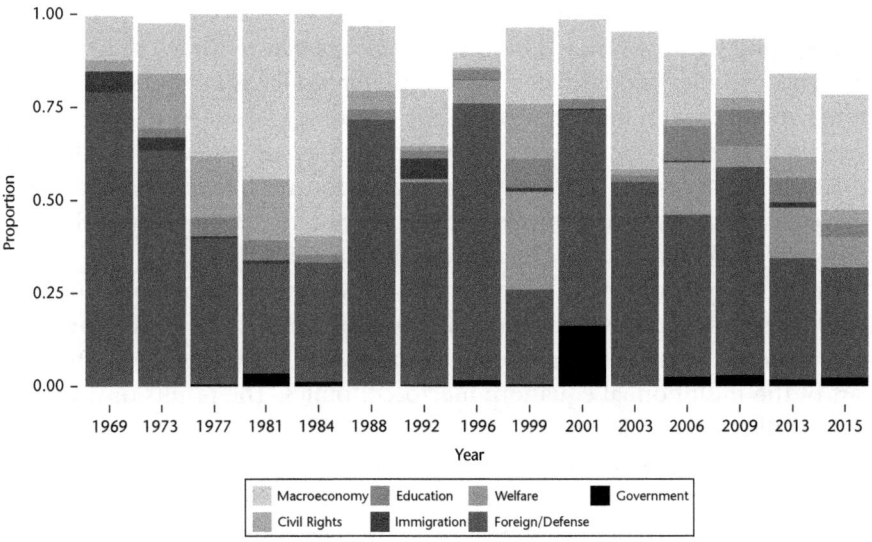

Figure 26.6. The map of Israeli Public Agenda, 1969–2015

Source: Aggregate responses to the MIP item from the Israel National Election Studies (1969–2015, N = 22,832 in 15 surveys)

agenda (48.6 percent). Macroeconomics follows with a quarter of the public agenda (26 percent). The other major issues include civil rights (8.4 percent), education (4.2 percent), immigration (1.6 percent), welfare (3.8 percent), and government operations (2.1 percent). Health and law and crime that are more dominant in the United States are replaced here by education and immigration. Israel has a public healthcare system that is paid by social security income tax and provides health services to every citizen. Law and crime has traditionally been a less prominent issue in Israel and is only recently becoming a concern. In contrast, education in Israel is centralized and massive waves of immigration challenges social order and government services.

The shifts between macroeconomics and defense/foreign affairs confirm the conventional wisdom about the public agenda in Israel. During the 1960s and early 1970s, Israelis were mostly concerned about defense and foreign issues. During that time, Israel was fighting two wars—in 1967 and 1973—and was in a military conflict between them (The War of Attrition, 1968–70). In the second half of the 1970s, Israelis responded to the struggling economy—like in other places in the world—by focusing on the economy. With the break-out of the first Intifada (in 1987), Israelis turned back to foreign and security issues.

From the late 1990s until today, the dominance of the two issues has slightly subdued by a more diversified issue attention that includes issues like welfare, civil rights, and education. This trend in public attention is aligned with the decline of the large parties and decreasing stability of governing coalitions.[9]

To assess variation in individual priorities, we collected conventional demographics and political variables used in research on Israeli public opinion. This includes sex, ethnicity (Mizrahi refers to Jewish people who come from families that immigrated from Arab countries; Sabra refers to people who were born in Israel; the reference category is Ashkenazi Jews who immigrated to Israel from Western, primarily European countries), religious sentiment, age, education, and social status (Arian and Shamir, 2008; Hirsch-Hoefler, Canetti, and Pedhazur, 2010; Shamir and Arian, 1999).[10]

Similar to our model of US issue priorities, we estimate a multinomial logistic regression to explain the likelihood of prioritizing each issue. Our base outcome is defense and foreign affairs. We examine here only the first part of the multinomial equation: macroeconomics. The results of this analysis are illustrated in Figure 26.7.

The results suggest limited differences between groups. Mainly, women, religious respondents, and older people are less likely to prioritize economic issues over foreign (defense and security). Younger respondents (aged 30–49) are more concerned about foreign affairs than the economy. Sex and age behave similarly to the US model—women and older people are more concerned with foreign affairs than with the economy. We find no significant differences between ethnic groups, education groups, and social status.

The limited findings are consistent with the conventional knowledge about Israeli politics—that the concern about security and foreign affairs is wide

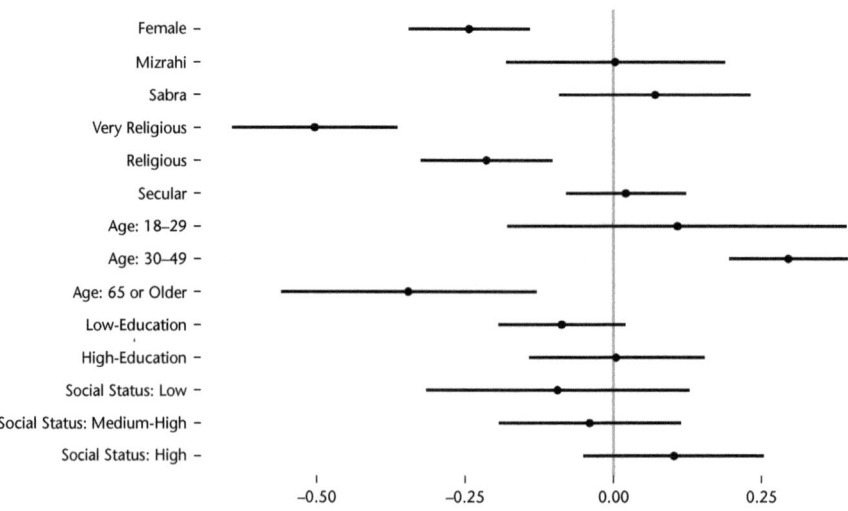

Figure 26.7. Issue priorities, Israel: macroeconomics (vs. foreign affairs)

Source: Point estimates and 90 percent confidence intervals following multinomial logistic regression, MIP surveys (1969–2015)

(nearly half of Israelis report this as their primary concern) and cuts across most demographic (and political) divisions (Galnoor and Blander, 2018).

Further to assess the public agenda and variation among demographic groups on this issue, we follow the CAP coding and recode this unified category into its two original categories: defense (16) and foreign affairs (19). Defense refers to Israel's physical security and includes responses such as defense, security, terrorism, war, as well as the IDF budget and soldier's rights (33 percent of total agenda). Given the Israeli geopolitical environment, the overwhelming majority of the foreign affairs category includes mentions of peace or the Arab–Israeli conflict (specific mentions of war/security are included in defense and security), and some mentions of relations with other countries and Israel's standing in the world (16 percent of total agenda). Focusing only on these two topics, we estimate a binary logistic regression to predict the choice between foreign affairs (primarily peace and conflict related), over mentions of defense and immediate security issues.

Results, displayed in Figure 26.8, reveal several important differences between demographic groups, differences that are consistent with the conventional wisdom about political divides in Israel. Secular people, older people, and those of high social status tend to prioritize the conflict over questions of physical security and defense. This is aligned with electoral trends demonstrating that secular, older Ashkenazi people from higher income levels tend to vote for left-leaning parties. These parties focus their campaign and party platform on the conflict and its solution rather than on the immediate security issues

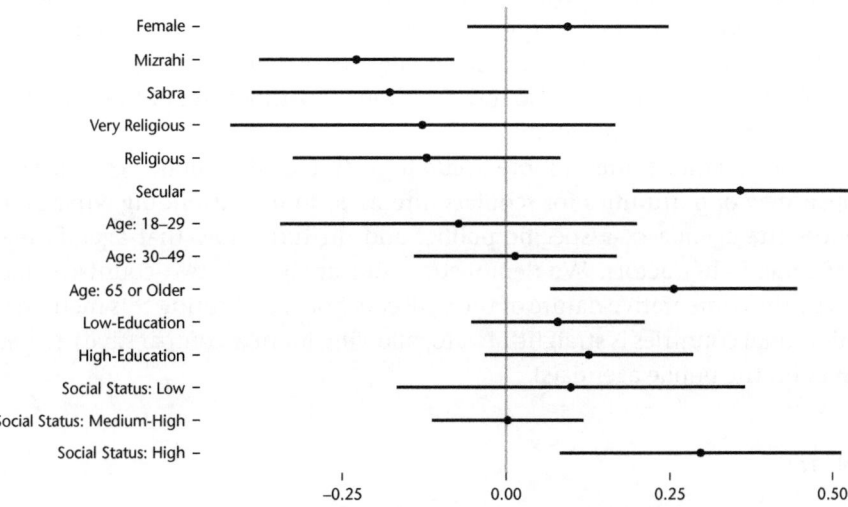

Figure 26.8. Issue priorities, Israel: peace/conflict (vs. defense)

Source: Point estimates and 90 percent confidence intervals following multinomial logistic regression, MIP surveys (1969–2015)

that the conflict produces (Arian and Shamir, 2008; Shamir, Dvir-Gvirsman, and Ventura 2017).

26.5 Conclusion

A rich body of work has established that the public agenda is affected by events and how they are presented to the public. When political elites or the media focus on an issue, citizens, and especially those who are tuned to the political process, focus on that issue, voice their concern about the issue, and as a consequence may adjust their voting preferences. And yet, overall trends conceal offsetting variations within the public. People who share similar life experiences are affected by the same events and actions but respond differently as a function of their own interests and daily experiences. In this chapter we reveal this variation in two very different countries—Israel and the United States. In both, we find significant differences between some of the most dominant demographic divides. Despite significant differences in the overall agenda focus in these countries, some of the group differences are similar in both countries, demonstrating the comparable interests people have based on their own life experiences and problems.

The findings affect our understanding of the political process. Electoral and legislative theories often focus on the problems most salient to the public, and issue ownership posits that when a problem becomes salient, a party may benefit from it electorally if it is perceived better equipped to solve it or more concerned in solving it (Egan, 2013). Therefore, understanding the variation in issue priorities raises new questions about the electoral benefits of focusing on these issues. A party may gain electorally not only if it is associated with the problem most salient, but also if the relevant constituencies of the party find the issue to be most important.

These variations offer a more accurate picture of the public agenda. They open new opportunities for scholars interested in understanding what influences the agenda of a specific public, and, in turn, how that agenda may influence other actors. We demonstrate our analysis of two countries. But, given the comparative nature of the CAP codebook, replicating this method to additional countries is straightforward, allowing for new comparative perspectives on the public agenda(s).

Notes

1. For a discussion of the differences between issues and problems see Jennings and Wlezien (2011). For a discussion of "problems" as a measure of public agenda, see Eshbaugh-Soha and Peake (2011: 99–100).

2. Because all MIPs are not recorded verbatim but into categories defined and sorted by the pollster and interviews, the data are not primary data. This, however, is a problem shared by all studies and datasets that rely on the MIP data from commercial surveys commonly used in existing research. It may also be a larger concern in earlier surveys in which pollsters tended to code responses into a small number of categories. As time progressed, coding became more detailed and includes a larger number of categories, allowing greater distinction between responses.

3. Available online at http://www.policyagendas.org/codebooks/topicindex.html. Categorization of responses results in inevitable data loss, and further analysis is limited by the definition and classification of the categories used. A significant problem is the wide definition of macroeconomics under the Policy Agendas Project, which joins together unemployment with national budget, price control, and taxation. As a result, the welfare policy category is smaller and encompasses significantly different policy issues than is generally included in a social welfare issue ownership category. Despite these limitations, categorization is important for allowing a unified content code across time and the advantage of using the Policy Agendas Project codebook is that it is publicly available and used by studies examining changes in policy agendas and sharing similar interests with the current project.

4. The MIP question is one of the few attitudinal survey questions to have been asked consistently since the beginning of public opinion polling. Thus, the MIP series offers a dynamic measure of issue priorities for longitudinal studies and is a common source of the public agenda (Soroka, 2002). It is an open-ended question, where each respondent is asked to name the problem she thinks is most important. For a discussion of "problems" as a measure of public agenda, see Eshbaugh-Soha and Peake (2011: 99–100).

5. In 1969 and 1973 interviewers recorded more than one response. We use only the first mention from these two surveys.

6. Adapted for Israel by David Levi-Faor, Ilana Shpaizman, Hila Bar-Nir, Nir Kosti, Roi ben-David, Natan Milkowski, and Hana Dar-Hershkowitz.

7. We thank Ran Rinker for his work on gathering the Israel dataset.

8. As in the United States, we combine categories 16 (defense) and 19 (international affairs). We also include in this category all issues connected to the occupied territories.

9. For a more developed discussion of the public agenda and issue diversity over time see Cavari, Rinker, and Freedman, 2017.

10. We use subjective report of social status because this question was asked consistently. Income was asked in only four surveys.

References

Achen, C. H., and Bartels, L. M. (2016). *Democracy for Realists: Why Elections Do Not Produce Responsive Government*. Princeton: Princeton University Press.

Arian, A., and Shamir, M. (2008). A Decade Later, the World Had Changed, the Cleavage Structure Remained: Israel 1996–2006. *Party Politics*, 14(6): 685–705.

Bartels, L. M. (2016). *Unequal Democracy: The Political Economy of the New Gilded Age*. Princeton: Princeton University Press.

Baumgartner, F. R., and Jones, B. D. (2002). *Policy Dynamics*. Chicago: University of Chicago Press.

Berinsky, A. J., and Karpowitz, C. F. (2005). *Turbulent Times: The Nation's Most Important Problem and the Media Agenda, 1964–1971*. http://web.mit.edu/berinsky/www/TurbulentTimes.pdf.

Bevan, S., Jennings, W., and Wlezien, C. 2016. An Analysis of the Public's Personal, National, and EU Issue Priorities. *Journal of European Public Policy*, 23(6): 871–87.

Carnes, N. (2013). *White-Collar Government: The Hidden Role of Class in Economic Policy Making*. Chicago: University of Chicago Press.

Cavari, A. (2017). *The Party Politics of Presidential Rhetoric*. New York: Cambridge University Press.

Cavari, A., Rinker, R., and Freedman, G. (2017). Public Agenda, Issue Diversity and Political Stability in Israel, 1969–2015. Paper presented at the Annual Meeting of the Comparative Agendas Project (CAP), Edinburgh, Scotland, June 15–17, 2017.

Converse, P. E. (1964). *The Nature of Belief Systems in Mass Publics: Ideology and Discontent*. London: Free Press of Glencoe.

Douglass, E. B., Cleveland, W. P., and Maddox, G. L. (1974). Political Attitudes, Age, and Aging: A Cohort Analysis of Archival Data. *Journal of Gerontology*, 29(6): 666–75.

Egan, P. J. (2013). *Partisan Priorities: How Issue Ownership Drives and Distorts American Politics*. New York: Cambridge University Press.

Eshbaugh-Soha, M., and Peake, J. (2011). *Breaking through the Noise: Presidential Leadership, Public Opinion, and the News Media*. Stanford: Stanford University Press.

Galnoor, I., and Blander, D. (2018). *The Handbook of Israel's Political System*. Cambridge: Cambridge University Press.

Gilens, M. (2012). *Affluence and Influence: Economic Inequality and Political Power in America*. Princeton: Princeton University Press.

Hacker, J. S., and Pierson, P. (2010). *Winner-Take-All Politics: How Washington Made the Rich Richer—and Turned its Back on the Middle Class*. New York: Simon and Schuster.

Hall, P. A. (1993). Policy Paradigms, Social Learning, and the State: The Case of Economic Policymaking in Britain. *Comparative Politics*, 25(3): 275–96.

Heffington, C., Park, B. B., and Williams, L. K. (2017). The "Most Important Problem" Dataset (MIPD): A New Dataset on American Issue Importance. *Conflict Management and Peace Science*. DOI: 10.1177/0738894217691463.

Hirsch-Hoefler, S., Canetti, D., and Pedahzur, A. (2010). Two of a Kind? Voting Motivations for Populist Radical Right and Religious Fundamentalist Parties. *Electoral Studies*, 29(4): 678–90.

Jennings, W., and Wlezien, C. (2011). Distinguishing between Most Important Problems and Issues? *Public Opinion Quarterly*, 75(3): 545–55.

Jennings, W., and Wlezien, C. (2015). Preferences, Problems and Representation. *Political Science Research and Methods*, 3(3): 659–81.

Jones, B. D. (1994). *Reconceiving Decision-Making in Democratic Politics: Attention, Choice, and Public Policy*. Chicago: University of Chicago Press.

Jones, B. D., and Baumgartner, F. R. (2004). Representation and Agenda Setting. *Policy Studies Journal*, 32(1): 1–24.

Krosnick, J. A. (1990). Government Policy and Citizen Passion: A Study of Issue Publics in Contemporary America. *Political Behavior*, 12(1): 59–92.

MacKuen, M. B., and Coombs, S. L. (1981). *More than News: Media Power in Public Affairs*, Vol. 12. Beverly Hills: Sage Publications.

McCombs, M. (1999). Personal Involvement with Issues on the Public Agenda. *International Journal of Public Opinion Research*, 11(2): 152–68.

McCombs, M., and Zhu, Jian-H. (1995). Capacity, Diversity, and Volatility of the Public Agenda Trends from 1954 to 1994. *Public Opinion Quarterly*, 59(4): 495–525.

Page, I. B., and Shapiro, Y. R. (1992). *The Rational Public: Fifty Years of Trends in Americans' Policy Preferences*. Chicago: University of Chicago Press.

Popkin, S. L. (1991). *The Reasoning Voter*. Chicago: University of Chicago Press.

Reher, S. (2015). Explaining Cross-National Variation in the Relationship between Priority Congruence and Satisfaction with Democracy. *European Journal of Political Research*, 54(1): 160–81.

Shamir, M., and Arian, A. (1999). Collective Identity and Electoral Competition in Israel. *American Political Science Review*, 93(2): 265–77.

Shamir, M., Dvir-Gvirsman, S., and Ventura, R. (2017). Taken Captive by the Collective Identity Cleavage: Left and Right in the 2015 Elections. In *The Elections in Israel, 2015*, ed. M. Shamir and G. Rahat. New York: Routledge, 147–72.

Smith, T. W. (1980). America's Most Important Problem—A Trend Analysis, 1946–1976. *The Public Opinion Quarterly*, 44(2): 164–80.

Smith, T. W. (1985). The Polls: America's Most Important Problem Part I: National and International. *The Public Opinion Quarterly*, 49(2): 264–74.

Soroka, S. N. (2002). *Agenda-Setting Dynamics in Canada*. Vancouver: University of British Columbia Press.

Soroka, S. N., and Wlezien, C. (2010). *Degrees of Democracy: Politics, Public Opinion, and Policy*. Cambridge: Cambridge University Press.

Tarrow, S. (2010). The Strategy of Paired Comparison: Toward a Theory and Practice. *Comparative Political Studies* 43(2): 230–59.

27

Protest and Agenda-Setting

Stefaan Walgrave and Rens Vliegenthart

The Comparative Agenda Project (CAP), originating within the domain of public policy, mainly deals with the issue attentiveness of political institutions like parliament (questions and bills) or government (laws, budgets, and speeches). The agenda approach in political science—an approach holding that political attention is scarce, that it is a pre-condition for policy-making, and that attention is consequential (Green-Pedersen and Walgrave, 2014)—has not only been used to study institutional politics, but also increasingly to examine how society is connected to and influences the political process. Indeed, the agenda-setting approach is gradually being used more to examine political representation and the responsiveness of politics to societal demands (Pitkin, 1969).

The responsiveness of political issue priorities to public issue priorities, and of political issue positions to public issue positions for that matter, is one of the most central benchmarks of democratic quality. Any notion of democracy inevitably implies that what politicians are doing and prioritizing matches to some extent what citizens want them to do and act upon (Miller and Stokes, 1963). To assess democratic quality, and more specifically the congruence between political priorities/positions and public priorities/positions, one needs data about what politics is prioritizing and doing on the one hand and what society demands politics to prioritize/do on the other. The CAP data are very useful in that respect.

There are, in particular, three *societal* agendas studied in CAP that allow us to assess the interaction between societal demands and political priorities: public opinion, news media coverage, and protest. Public opinion mostly measured by most important problem questions (Wlezien, 2005) grasps the raw issue priorities of the aggregate, mostly uninterested and unmobilized part of the population. Media coverage is not only a reflection of public opinion but also of the real world problems hitting the system, of journalistic priorities and news selection processes, and of elites that are successful in placing their priorities in the media. Protest—the number, type, and size of protest events in a country or region—forms a useful measure of the priorities of a mobilized and active part of the citizenry, the so-called issue publics (Krosnick, 1990). Famously, Schattschneider (1960) has argued that politics is driven by the mobilization of bias (the interests of some specific but active groups). Protest agenda data are one way of assessing what the public, or at least a part of it, wants politicians to do.

27.1 The Agenda Effect of Protest

What people who protest want most is first of all attention. When social movements stage protest events or when groups of citizens spontaneously come together to express their grievances they most of the time cry out for politicians to care about the issue. Mobilization around issues with the aim of keeping those issues *off* the political agenda does not exist. In the broader field of social movement studies, the question whether protest matters is probably the most important one. Researchers have struggled with this fundamental question for many years, and the answers they have given have been mixed and contradictory (Amenta, Caren, Chiarello, and Su, 2010; Uba, 2009).

The reason for the inconclusive results is that scholars have disagreed about what exactly one should understand under movement "impact" (Giugni, McAdam, and Tilly, 1999). While we acknowledge that some movements might be less driven by the desire to gain political attention than others, we think it is safe to assume that all movements do want attention for their issues and cause. In that case, one can simply study the impact of social movements by examining whether their protests lead to political attention. If attention, or an increase of attention, for an issue on the parliamentary or governmental agenda is systematically preceded by protest on the same issue, chances are that the protest has an agenda-setting effect on what parliamentarians or government ministers are addressing. Similarly, also the reversed relationship can be studied—is the protest agenda influenced by the parliamentary or government agenda?

Such an agenda perspective on the impact of protest is not new and has been apparent in a great many studies published during the last few decades. Burstein and Freudenburg (1978) were probably the first to take movement size and protest activity as the independent variable and political attention, the number of US Senate votes on the topic, as the dependent. Another example is the work by Soule, McAdam, McCarthy, and Su (1999), that, in a study of US congressional hearings and roll call votes about women's issues, found that protest incidence is a *consequence* of political attention and not a cause. In another study, King, Bentele, and Soule (2007) take protest as the independent variable when trying to model US congressional attention to a number of so-called "rights issues" while controlling for a whole range of alternative agenda-setters. The number of congressional hearings increases when the number of protests goes up, they find. By far most of these earlier protest-and-political-agenda studies are non-comparative: they use evidence from one country only, predominantly the United States, and they do not compare cross issues and, thus, across protests and social movements.

We know of two published studies that have employed an agenda perspective on protest impact and that drew on country- or issue-comparing evidence. Both these studies have relied on Comparative Agenda Project data. The work by Walgrave and Vliegenthart (2012) in Belgium found that, across all issues and movements, the frequency of protest is more important for the political agenda than the size of protest. The parliamentary agenda and the governmental agenda are both affected by protest, even the legislative agenda is influenced by preceding protest. Protest size has an effect, but it is largely mediated by media attention. Increasing the complexity of agenda power of protest further, their results suggest that these effects differ across issues. Some of the impact of protest frequency remains confined to specific issues only, more concretely the typical issues of the so-called news social movements, such as environment, peace, women's rights, and human rights.

A recent study by Vliegenthart and (many) colleagues (2016) includes comparative protest data in six Western European countries and basically asks the same question: Is protest followed by an increase in political attention for the protest issue? As in the Belgian case, they do find an effect of protest on parliamentary questioning. In their analyses, pooling the various countries in one dataset, they specify that the effect of protest is fully mediated by mass media coverage. Protests lead to increasing news coverage of the protest issue and this, in turn, affects what politicians are questioning about in the six parliaments under study. Maybe the most interesting thing is that the mediated impact of protest on parliament differs across countries. Countries under majoritarian rule do witness a stronger (mediated) protest effect than countries with proportional electoral systems. Clear government responsibilities mean that protest matters more.

So, the agenda-setting effect of protest is determined by the issue under investigation, as well as the political context in which the protest takes place. A third moderating factor that has been investigated is the political party: Do different political parties respond differently to protest? Hutter and Vliegenthart (2018) use the same CAP-coded data to demonstrate that parties are more likely to respond to protest when they are in opposition and if competing parties responded to those issues as well.

This chapter's aim is not to re-examine whether, how, and to what extent protest has an agenda effect on whom. Rather, we want to showcase the breath and relevance of the CAP protest data by providing an overview of the existing datasets as well as some more descriptive analyses to get a bit more insight into the data.

27.2 Methods

For this study, we rely on the protest dataset used in the study by Vliegenthart et al. (2016) on the agenda-setting impact of protest on parliament in six Western European countries. The following countries and periods are included in our analyses: the Netherlands (1995–2011), Spain (1996–2011), the United Kingdom (1997–2008), Switzerland (1995–2003), France (1995–2005) and Belgium (1999–2010).

Except for Belgium, data are not coded directly according to the CAP codebook, but the data are recoded from protest event data collected by Kriesi (2012) and colleagues. These data are an updated and extended version of the data used by Kriesi et al. (1995) that focused on the presence and breakthrough of new social movements in several Western European countries. When it comes to the coding of protest events, the selection of the source of information is a topic of serious debate. In this case, newspapers are used to collect information about protest events. More specifically, the following newspapers are included in the analysis: *The Guardian* (UK), *Le Monde* (France), *NRC Handelsblad* (Netherlands), *El Pais* (Spain), and *Neue Zürcher Zeitung* (Switzerland). Only the Monday editions are coded, not only for pragmatic reasons, but also because these newspapers cover the events of the weekend before. Protest events are occurring a lot more frequently on Saturday and Sunday than on weekdays. All events that were reported on, including those up to a week before and after the publication date of the newspaper, are coded.

The first source of potential bias can thus be found in the partial use of newspaper material. The second source is the use of newspaper data as such. All kind of selection processes make it more likely for certain type of events to get into the newspapers than others. A lot of research has been devoted to which events are favored by journalists. Characteristics such as event size and the occurrence of violence and issue attention cycles are important, while also cross-media differences are found (see for example, Earl, Martin, McCarthy, and Soule, 2004; Ortiz, David, Myers, Daniel, Walls, Eugene, and Diaz, 2005). Biases cannot be totally avoided but the data selection is based on the idea of making the bias "as systematic as possible" (Koopmans, 1995: 271).

The selected newspapers are comparable. They are all quality newspapers, with a nation-wide reach and none of them has a very strong political leaning.

While the cross-national and longitudinal stability in the patterns of selection bias is still a contested topic, recent studies show that the sampling strategy used here does not deviate largely from encompassing strategies of data collection (Giugni, 2004; Hutter and Swen, 2014; McCarthy, Titarenko, McPhail, Rafail, and Augustyn, 2008). Most important, the results show that over-time dynamics in protest mobilization on particular issues is traced accurately with the chosen approach. Since those dynamics are key for agenda scholars, these data offer a valuable source.

The obtained dataset includes 4,925 protest events in five countries, involving around 49 million participants. One of the characteristics that was included in the coding was the "goal" of the protest. An extensive list of 103 goals was used. These goals were recoded by the authors to fit the CAP major issue categories. The recoded goals fall into only seventeen different CAP categories (16 for Spain and the United Kingdom where immigration is not a major category). The analyses we present in this chapter are based on those seventeen categories. As commonly done also for other agendas, our media-protest coverage measures gauge the relative share of protest events covered in the media that are devoted to an issue in a given country during a given month.

Note that for Belgium a separate protest dataset was collected. In this case, data come directly from police records and are coded directly according to the major CAP categories. Thus, these data were thus collected fully independently from media coverage. We use the same seventeen categories we use for the other countries for Belgium.

27.3 Results

In this chapter, we present three different exploratory analyses. First, we look at the overall descriptives and compare protest issues across countries (see Table 27.1). Second, we look at the extent to which issue attention is correlated (both cross-sectionally as well as over time) and to what extent we can speak of a transnational protest agenda, which would fit the argument in the social movement literature on the transnationalization of protest (della Porta and Tarrow, 2005). Third, we single out two issues: defense and civil rights and liberties that might have become more salient on the protest agenda due to the 9/11 attacks and the subsequent political developments.

While the total N, the number of protests in the recorded periods, in the different countries, does not deviate tremendously—protest is ubiquitous and has become a normal way of doing politics—there clearly are similarities and differences in the six countries we study here. The number one topic overall is civil right and liberties. In four countries, the share of protest on this macro issue exceeds 10 percent and the average share is 19 percent; one fifth of all

Table 27.1. Descriptive statistics: Share (proportion) of attention for each issue per country across all recorded protest events per country

Issue	NL	ES	UK	CH	FR	BE
Macroeconomics	0.017	0.033	0.013	0.040	0.042	0.012
Civil rights and liberties	0.159	0.084	0.222	0.259	0.131	0.090
Health	0.025	0.030	0.055	0.031	0.041	0.035
Agriculture and fishery	0.024	0.003	0.008	0.027	0.033	0.020
Labor and employment	0.048	0.050	0.027	0.026	0.045	0.099
Education	0.039	0.031	0.009	0.006	0.060	0.040
Environment	0.070	0.020	0.100	0.043	0.028	0.058
Energy	0.013	0.001	0.014	0.014	0.017	0.007
Immigration and integration	0.068	0.028	0.085	0.055	0.102	0.130
Transportation	0.029	0.003	0.031	0.102	0.025	0.019
Law, crime, and family	0.015	0.004	0.006	0.025	0.031	0.085
Social welfare	0.020	0.003	0.005	0.004	0.061	0.022
Comm. develop., planning, and housing	0.019	0.021	0.108	0.001	0.021	0.012
Defense	0.035	0.002	0.012	0.044	0.021	0.027
Foreign trade	0.006	0.014	0.059	0.058	0.013	0.004
International affairs and foreign aid	0.086	0.454	0.021	0.158	0.041	0.055
Government operations	0.021	0.033	0.013	0.056	0.118	0.043
N	3,258	2,960	2,240	1,836	2,159	2,040

Note: Scores do not add up to 1 (or 100 percent) as some issues are left out because they are not part of the recoded protest agenda. Furthermore, the protest agenda has months when no events are staged or questions are asked, lowering overall means.

Source: Comparative Agendas Project

protests deal with this topic. The topic that is least affected by protest is, a little remarkably, social welfare. In three of the countries less that 1 percent of protest is devoted to the topic, the average is 2 percent. All other topics are situated between these two extremes. Interestingly, there is a remarkable spread of protest over issues with most issues getting a fair deal of protest "attention."

There are some differences across countries with protest on issues soaring in one country and being almost entirely absent in another. A case in point here is the issue of international affairs. In Spain, during the research period, almost half (45 percent) of the protests was about this issue. In the United Kingdom, the issue received scant attention and only one in every fiftieth (2 percent) protest event was about this issue. Another example is community development, planning, and housing. It is a particularly sensitive issue in the United Kingdom with more than one in ten protests (11 percent) dealing with it. Yet, in Switzerland, if there is any conflict regarding this issue, it is not fought out using a protest strategy at all: hardly any protests were recorded (0.1 percent).

The data allow us to make other observations that maybe go against what we expect when we think about protest. While we may think of the education sector, with plenty of highly schooled and politically skilled teachers, to be particularly contentious, this is not clearly the case in the six countries we look at here; in none of the countries does the share of educational protests exceed 10 percent. The topic of immigration is now widely divisive, and it

Table 27.2. Correlation between protest agendas (cross-sectional, aggregated over the entire research period)

	NL	ES	UK	CH	FR	BE
NL	1.000	0.448	0.746	0.840	0.591	0.599
ES		1.000	0.023	0.512	0.083	0.175
UK			1.000	0.634	0.438	0.356
CH				1.000	0.497	0.322
FR					1.000	0.569
BE						1.000

Note: $N = 17$, Pearson correlation.
Source: Comparative Agendas Project

plays an important role in the recent electoral successes of populist parties and candidates. Yet, it is not an issue that attracted particularly frequent protest until a few years ago. It testifies again that right-wing anti-immigrant populism—the countries under study like Belgium, the Netherlands, Switzerland, and France have about the strongest right-wing populist parties around—is not a phenomenon of demonstrations and protest but rather one of electoral discontent.

How do the countries compare? Are some countries' protest agendas more similar than other countries? Table 27.2 presents Pearson correlations of the full protest agendas between countries, aggregating the data into the seventeen issue categories. All correlations are positive, so there is a unified, underlying distribution of protest attention over issues. This matches the idea that attention to issues is similarly distributed in different countries, indicating that protesters in different countries care similarly about issues. Agenda scholars have used the concept of "issue intrusion" to refer to these strong similarities in allocating attention over issues (Green-Pedersen and Wilkerson, 2006).

Still, some of the cross-country correlations are very small while others are extremely high. When it comes to protest issues, the United Kingdom and Spain are the two most different countries $(r = 0.023)$. Although both are majoritarian political systems, protest-wise they have almost nothing in common. The two most similar countries are the United Kingdom and Switzerland. What happens on the streets in these two countries is very much the same; people protest for almost exactly the same issues $(r = 0.840)$. The United Kingdom and the Netherlands are very similar as well $(r = 0.746)$, while France and, again, Spain are very different $(r = 0.083)$. Overall, the Spanish protest agenda seems to be the most different while the United Kingdom's protests are most similar to what happens in the other countries.

Table 27.3 presents similar data but now aggregated at a monthly level, while controlling for systematic differences in issue attention by including dummies for all issues (fixed effects). This analysis thus focuses solely on over-time variation: Does attention for specific issues go up and down in a similar

Table 27.3. Correlation between protest agendas across time (cross-sectional, aggregated across (overlapping) months)

	NL	ES	UK	CH	FR	BE
NL	1.000	−0.002	−0.016	−0.041	0.027	0.004
ES		1.000	0.027	0.046	0.058	0.009
UK			1.000	0.058	−0.013	−0.008
CH				1.000	0.071	−0.073
FR					1.000	0.022
BE						1.000

Note: N = 1, 500–4, 255, Pearson correlation controlled for issue differences (fixed effects).
Source: Comparative Agendas Project

way in different countries? The picture looks very different compared to the cross-issue analysis. It is not at all the case that countries are witnessing similar protest events at roughly the same point in time. In fact, none of the correlation comes close to being substantial; the largest correlation is $r = 0.071$ between the protest agendas in Switzerland and France. What these data tell us is that, while the *overall* agenda seems to be similar and the same issues impose themselves on different nations' streets, *when* precisely those issues receive attention varies heavily across countries. Thus, protest is still largely determined by local events, the national policy cycle, and the timing of local political decisions. For example, all countries may have witnessed increasing protest on bread-and-butter issues against the backdrop of austerity measures taken by European governments after the financial crisis; but they took different measures at different points in time and it is hard to speak of a common, transnational protest cycle challenging these austerity measures.

Agenda work has showed that real world events sometime forcefully hit a political system and that these events disrupt the existing agenda. The terrorist attacks on the United States on September 11, 2001 are such an event. They led to several wars, to stricter liberty laws, and to widespread security measures in many countries. Most of us will also remember the widespread protest against the War on Iraq with even the biggest worldwide protest event ever recorded in human history in February 2003 (Walgrave and Rucht, 2010). Has 9/11 and its violent aftermath left its traces on the protest agenda in European states? We look at protest of the issues regarding defense and civil rights and liberties before and after 9/11. Table 27.4 presents a comparison of means.

In four of the six countries under study, we see that, after 9/11, the number of protest events dealing with the defense issue is significantly higher. This shows that external events can impose themselves forcefully on the agenda and that even protest is following real world events. For the second topic, we only see a significant effect in one country: Belgium. This might actually reflect protests directed at the European Union, since many of those protests

Table 27.4. Mean comparisons between monthly protest attention for defense and civil rights and liberties before and after 9/11 (Twin Tower attacks in the United States)

	Defense			Civil rights and liberties		
	pre 9/11	post 9/11	Sign.	pre 9/11	post 9/11	Sign.
NL	0.050 (84)	0.024 (109)		0.157 (84)	0.160 (84)	
ES	0.003 (76)	0.034 (109)	*	0.081 (76)	0.086 (109)	
UK	0.033 (64)	0.172 (76)	***	0.233 (64)	0.212 (76)	
CH	0.032 (92)	0.112 (16)	*	0.274 (92)	0.171 (16)	
FR	0.021 (87)	0.020 (40)		0.124 (87)	0.147 (40)	
BE	0.014 (44)	0.035 (76)	**	0.057 (44)	0.110 (76)	*

Note: Number of observations in brackets. * $p < 0.05$, ** $p < 0.01$, *** $p < 0.001$.
Source: Comparative Agendas Project

taking place in Brussels are targeting the European Union and its institutions that have been very involved in discussions on privacy issues.

27.4 Conclusion

This chapter was devoted to the protest agenda. Via protest, citizens try to draw attention to issues and, in many instances, protesters explicitly aim to set the agenda. We reviewed the literature that shows that protest can be successful: under specific circumstances protest can exert agenda power and push elites to increase their attention to the underlying issue. The number of studies that uses an explicit agenda approach to the effect of protest remains rather limited though. We still do not know much about the exact mechanism that translates protest issues into political attention. Protest was measured in a rather simplistic way, only the frequency of protest events on issues was taken into account. Following accounts that state that the number of participants, who the protesters are, and how they behave may affect the (agenda) power they can exert (Tilly, 2006) we would expect the agenda impact of events that are populated by numerous, worthy, unified, and committed protesters to be bigger than of protests that do not exhibit these features (Wouters and Walgrave, 2017).

Additionally, we have discussed protest here mainly as an input agenda to politics. Protest has other functions and political meanings, of course. In fact, much of what drives protesters is not an instrumental motivation to change or affect policy or to reach an external goal, but rather the wish to express oneself and to show that one disagrees (Van Stekelenburg, 2006). Following this idea, the protest agenda in CAP might be used to measure a kind of "mood" in public opinion (Stimson, 1991). Yet, what happens on the streets and which issues people protest about, is also determined by civil society that yield a supply of events on the protest market and by the strength of the respective social movement sectors in a country. It is this versatility of the protest agenda that makes this data series particularly attractive but at the same time tricky and sometimes hard to interpret.

References

Amenta, E., Caren, N., Chiarello, E., and Su, Y. (2010). The Political Consequences of Social Movements. *Annual Review of Sociology*, 36(1): 287–307.

Burstein, P., and Freudenburg, W. (1978). Changing Public Policy: The Impact of Public Opinion, Antiwar Demonstrations, and War Costs on Senate Voting on Vietnam War Motions. *American Journal of Sociology*, 84(1): 99–122.

della Porta, D., and Tarrow, S. (2005). *Transnational Protest and Global Activism*. Lanham: Rowman and Littlefield.

Earl, J., Martin, A., McCarthy, J. D. and Soule, S. A. (2004). The Use of Newspaper Data in the Study of Collective Action. *Annual Review of Sociology*, 30: 65–80.

Giugni, M. (2004). *Social Protest and Policy Change: Ecology, Antinuclear, and Peace Movements in Comparative Perspective*. Lanham: Rowman and Littlefield.

Giugni, M., McAdam, D., and Tilly, C. (1999). *How Social Movements Matter*. Minneapolis: University of Minnesota Press.

Green-Pedersen, C., and Wilkerson, J. (2006). How Agenda-Setting Attributes Shape Politics: Basic Dilemmas, Problem Attention and Health Politics Developments in Denmark and the US. *Journal for European Public Policy*, 13(7): 1039–52.

Green-Pedersen, C., and Walgrave, S. (2014). *Agenda Setting, Policies, and Political Systems*. Chicago: University of Chicago Press.

Hutter, S. (2014). Protest Event Analysis and its Offspring. In *Methodological Practices in Social Movement Research*, ed. D. della Porta. Oxford: Oxford University Press, 335–67.

Hutter, S., and Vliegenthart, R. (2018). Who Responds to Protest? Protest Politics and Party Responsiveness in Western Europe. *Party Politics*. https://doi.org/10.1177/1354068816657375.

King, B. G., Bentele, K. G., and Soule, S. A. (2007). Protest and Policymaking: Explaining Fluctuation in Congressional Attention to Rights Issues, 1960–1986. *Social Forces*, 86(1): 137–63.

Koopmans, R. (1995). Appendix: The Newspaper Data. In *New Social Movements in Western Europe: A Comparative Analysis*, ed. H. Kriesi. Minneapolis: University of Minnesota Press, 253–73.

Kriesi, H. (ed.) (2012). *Political Conflict in Western Europe*. Cambridge: Cambridge University Press.

Kriesi, H., Koopmans, R., Duyvendak, J. W., and Giugni, M. G. (1995). *New Social Movements in Western Europe: A Comparative Analysis*. Minneapolis: University of Minnesota Press.

Krosnick, J. A. (1990). Government Policy and Citizen Passion: A Study of Issue Publics in Contemporary America. *Political Behavior*, 12(1): 59–92.

McCarthy, J., Titarenko, L., McPhail, C. et al. (2008). Assessing Stability in the Patterns of Selection Bias in Newspaper Coverage of Protest during the Transition from Communism in Belarus. *Mobilization: An International Quarterly*, 13(2): 127–46.

Miller, W. E., and Stokes, D. (1963). Constituency Influence in Congress. *American Political Science Review*, 57: 165–77.

Ortiz, D., Myers, D., Walls, E., and Diaz, Maria-E. (2005). Where Do We Stand with Newspaper Data? *Mobilization*, 10: 397–419.

Pitkin, H. F. (1969). *The Concept of Representation*. Berkeley: University of California Press.

Schattschneider, E. E. (1960). *The Semi-Sovereign People*. New York: Holt.

Soule, S. A., McAdam, D., McCarthy, J., and Su, Y. (1999). Protest Events: Causes or Consequence of the US Women's Movement and Federal Congressional Activities. *Mobilization*, 4(2): 239–56.

Stimson, J. A. (1991). *Public Opinion in America: Moods, Cycles, and Swings*. Boulder: Westview Press.

Tilly, C. (2006). WUNC. In *Crowds*, ed. J. t. Schnapp and M. Tiews. Stanford: Stanford University Press, 289–306.

Uba, K. (2009). The Contextual Dependence of Movement Outcomes: A Simplified Meta-Analysis. *Mobilization*, 14(4): 433–48.

Van Stekelenburg, J. (2006). Promoting or Preventing Social Change: Instrumentality, Identity, Ideology and Group-Based Anger as Motives of Protest Participation. PhD dissertation, Department of Social Psychology, VU-University.

Vliegenthart, R., Walgrave, S., Wouters, R. et al. (2016). The Media as a Dual Mediator of the Political Agenda–Setting Effect of Protest: A Longitudinal Study in Six Western European Countries. *Social Forces*, 95(2): 837–59.

Walgrave, S., and Rucht, D. (2010). *The World Says No to War: Demonstrations against the War on Iraq*. Minneapolis: Minnesota University Press.

Walgrave, S., and Vliegenthart, R. (2012). The Complex Agenda-Setting Power of Protest: Demonstrations, Media, Parliament, Government, and Legislation in Belgium (1993–2000). *Mobilization*, 17(2): 129–56.

Wlezien, C. (2005). On The Salience of Political Issues: The Problem with "Most Important Problem." *Electoral Studies*, 24: 555–79.

Wouters, R., and Walgrave, S. (2017). Demonstrating Power: How Protest Persuades Political Representatives. *American Sociological Review*, 82(2): 361–83.

28

The Media Agenda

Rens Vliegenthart and Stefaan Walgrave

28.1 Introduction

The media agenda has a prominent place in the Comparative Agendas Project (CAP). The number of countries that include some kind of media coverage as an agenda to investigate is substantial—in most instances (national) newspaper coverage, but also, for example, radio news (in Denmark) has been coded. Interestingly enough, the media agenda as a separate entity has received little attention in the published work that comes from the data collection efforts (as, for example, the government agenda). In most instances, it is discussed in connection to the political agenda, and the notion of political agenda-setting *by* the media is central in many of those publications. In the second instance, this might not be so surprising, since the fact that agenda-setting—as a theory that relates to the effect media attention has on public and political attention—is already known and has been widely applied in the field of (political) communication since the early 1970s (see McCombs and Shaw, 1972). Additionally, comparative studies that look at cross-national similarities and differences in media coverage—both issue attention, as well as more detailed characteristics such as frames and valence (tone)—are widely available (e.g., Strömbäck and Van Aelst, 2010), which makes the study of the media agenda in isolation in many instances not very innovative.

In this chapter, we discuss the few studies that focus on the structure and properties of the media agenda, with a particular interest in the dynamics that might be at play across different outlets (so-called intermedia agenda-setting), and we also discuss the findings from the various political agenda-setting studies that focus on the impact of media on politics. The empirical part of this chapter will discuss the media agendas in a variety of countries, and looks into similarities and differences between them.

28.2 The Media Agenda: One of a Kind?

Media arguably play an important role in modern societies: they form the most important resource for most citizens to be informed about politics, current affairs, and a wide variety of specific issues. The media agenda can be argued to be the most responsive to external signals compared to other policy agendas such as the parliamentary one. Journalists can decide on a day-to-day basis (or even much quicker) to change their topical focus when (unexpected) external events warrant this. We can see that this reflected in the (statistical) properties of the media agenda. Walgrave and Vliegenthart (2010) demonstrate that the media agenda is—more than for example the parliamentary agenda—strongly affected by a cascading process. Cascading refers to the imitation by one actor of other actors, which—in the case of large numbers of actors—results in explosive adjustments. On the one hand, mass-media outlets are autonomous actors that do not formally depend on each other and outlets can decide independently whether or not they pay attention to a specific issue or event. On the other hand, those outlets do not act in a vacuum—they compete heavily with other outlets for the same readers and viewers in a market that is inherently bounded. Furthermore, sanctions are immediate. Viewer rates and readership are monitored at short intervals. Because of the highly visible nature of media, they are by definition communicating actors. Finally, the news media game is relatively low cost, at least compared to many other institutions. Newspapers are published daily, television stations broadcast several newscasts per day, and online news is constantly updated. All those characteristics do not hinder media from undergoing strong cascading processes. And indeed, Walgrave and Vliegenthart's study on Belgian policy agendas shows that this is reflected in the statistical properties of the media agenda: its skewed distribution is more driven by cascading processes than is the distribution of the parliamentary agenda.

Also Boydstun and colleagues (2014) make the observation that the media agenda is a volatile one: media can go into "storm" mode from one moment to the other and devote large proportions of attention to the same event. Imitation plays an important role in the occurrence of a media storm. These storms are not without consequences: the impact of the media agenda on the political agenda is larger when media go into storm mode (Walgrave et al., 2017).

The strong mimicking behavior of separate media outlets also becomes apparent in the intermedia agenda-setting study by Vliegenthart and Walgrave (2008). Again using Belgian data, they demonstrate that intermedia agenda-setting is a highly contingent process, depending on issue, outlet, and time characteristics. Overall, however, the general influence of various outlets on each other is considerable and larger than, for example, the influence of political parties on each other in the parliamentary realm (Vliegenthart et al., 2011).

Overall, the studies on the characteristics of the media agenda demonstrate that, compared to other agendas, the media agenda is characterized by high levels of responsiveness and volatility and that various outlets that jointly constitute the agenda strongly influence each other. The next question is then how this media agenda might influence other agendas, and this is what most media work in the CAP is devoted to: the political agenda-setting power of the media.

28.3 Political Agenda-Setting by the media

The interaction between politicians and journalists is one that intrigues many scholars in the fields of both political science and communication science. In general, two types of approaches are used to study this relationship. First, surveys among both politicians and (political) journalists have been conducted, asking, for example, questions about their subjective assessment of media power in the political realm. These studies show that throughout Western Europe, politicians attribute a lot of influence to the media, while journalists are more reluctant to assign to themselves a determining influence (Van Dalen and Van Aelst, 2014). The second approach looks at actual political behavioral "content," such as parliamentary debates and questions and legislation on the one hand, and media coverage on the other hand. Here, at least in the European context, an agenda-setting perspective is dominant and many of the recent studies rely on CAP data. The main question that is addressed is to what extent the media are able to influence the political agenda. In other words, the influence of the media on politics is most often investigated, while the reversed relationship is a lot less often considered. The basic concept that is focused upon is thus issue *attention* or *salience*. The idea of political agenda-setting can be considered as an extension of public agenda-setting that focuses on the impact of media attention on public attention (McCombs and Shaw, 1972) and demonstrates that media can to a considerable extent determine what people think about.

In political agenda-setting research, often quantitative content analysis of both media outlets and political documents is used to assess attention to a certain issue, or to a whole range of issues. Per item researchers determine what the main issue is and in most instances data are aggregated to weekly or monthly levels and absolute or relative issue attention measures are constructed for both realms. In the final analyses, time-series techniques are applied to investigate to what extent changes in attention for issues in the political realm are preceded by changes in attention for the same issues in media coverage.

Following the widely cited article by Stefaan Walgrave and Peter Van Aelst (2006), recent years have seen a plethora of studies that discuss possible "contingent" factors that determine the presence and/or strength of the political agenda-setting power of the media. A wide range of moderators is considered, ranging from institutional factors such as the type of government (Vliegenthart et al., 2016), time (for example mediatization, see Vliegenthart and Walgrave, 2011a), media and content characteristics (such as tone, Thesen, 2013; or frames, Sevenans and Vliegenthart, 2016).

The results found in political agenda-setting research are not univocal: while most studies find some effect of media on politics, not all of them do (see e.g., Vliegenthart and Mena Montes, 2014). Furthermore, there also turn out to be significant differences in the size of the impact. In their overview article, Walgrave and Van Aelst (2006) discuss the then available empirical studies and provide a set of seven "contingent" factors: characteristics that might moderate the agenda-setting impact of the media on politics. Since then, multiple studies have increased our insight and knowledge about those contingent factors, many of them using CAP data, or data that are comparable.

First, they consider variation in the operationalization of the independent variable: the issue type under consideration, as well as which media are considered. Regarding the first, different issues might witness different levels of agenda-setting impact. As Soroka (2002) shows for Canada, unobtrusive issues—those issues that are not directly experienced by politicians or citizens are most susceptible to media effects. Different outlets might also have different consequences. When asking parliamentary questions, Van Aelst and Vliegenthart (2014) show that Dutch parliamentarians rely heavily on printed media, and especially on the most widely read popular newspaper *De Telegraaf*. Recently, content characteristics other than attention are considered as possible moderators. For the Danish context, Thesen (2013) shows that especially negative news has an impact on issue priorities of political (opposition) parties. Sevenans and Vliegenthart (2016) show that conflict framing moderates agenda-setting effects: if an issue is more often discussed in terms of conflict, politicians are more likely to respond. Finally, Van der Pas (2014) shows that a political party basically only responds to coverage that is framed in line with its own preferences.

Second, temporal characteristics are of importance. Walgrave and Van Aelst discuss the distinction between election times and normal times. In the first instance, the impact of media is more limited, since media act less as autonomous and their coverage needs to be more balanced, because the fairness and balance of the coverage is more clearly monitored by politicians and voters.

An additional temporal effect is mediatization: this theory suggests an increasing dominance of the media on politics. In line with this, Vliegenthart and Walgrave (2011a) find that during the period 1990–2000 the media's agenda-setting impact on Belgian MPs increases.

Third, institutional rules are argued to moderate agenda-setting effects. For example, the mere fact that in Switzerland parliament only meets four times a year, the direct effect of media on politics will be relatively limited (Tresch et al., 2013).

Fourth, the internal functioning of political actors is a possible moderating factor. If, for example, political parties or the government includes multiple individuals that have to agree on a response to media coverage, it might well delay such a response.

Fifth, and maybe most importantly, the political configuration matters. One of the most obvious examples is the distinction between governing parties and opposition parties. Several studies have shown that opposition parties report more strongly to media coverage, since they do not face any constraints to use media content in their attempts to challenge the government (Vliegenthart and Walgrave, 2011a; 2011b; Green-Pedersen and Stubager, 2010). In a cross-national perspective the electoral and political system might also matter. Vliegenthart et al. (2016) show that in countries with a single-party government, the effect of the media on opposition parties is larger than in countries with a multiparty government. In the latter instance, opposition parties might feel more constrained in using media content, since co-operation with government parties is likely in the future. For government parties, they find the reverse effect: in single-party situations these parties have the luxury to ignore media content. Using media content as input for parliamentary questions in that context means inherently addressing their own party, while in a multi-party system, other coalition parties can be addressed or even attacked as well.

Finally, the operationalization of the dependent variable matters. Walgrave and Van Aelst (2006) distinguish between what they label "symbolic" political agendas and "substantial" political agendas. Symbolic political agendas often have little impact on actual policy, but are also more responsive. The most often used example is parliamentary questions, which can either be submitted continuously (written) or weekly (oral). They offer good opportunities for politicians and parties to signal their responsiveness and issue priorities, but are very often without "real" consequences. Researchers do find that particular symbolic agendas are responsive to media coverage, while more substantial ones (legislation for example) are less so. Substantial agendas are usually slow—it takes a long time to draft a bill—and are, as a consequence, more path-dependent and less prone to surges in media attention for issues. This is not to say that the media cannot, for example, have an impact on legislation, but that it is less likely to happen (Van Aelst et al., 2015), or may be less easy to establish.

Overall, CAP studies have been influential in identifying the circumstances under which the media agenda affects the political agenda. Efforts to compare cross-nationally have been especially fruitful in increasing our understanding of the interaction between the media and politics.

28.4 Empirical Example

28.4.1 *Data*

For this study, we rely on the dataset that has been used in the study by Vliegenthart et al. (2016) on the agenda-setting impact of the media on parliament in six Western European countries. The following countries and periods are included in our analyses below: the Netherlands (1995–2011), Spain (1996–2011), the United Kingdom (1997–2008), Switzerland (1995–2003), France (1995–2005) and Belgium (1999–2010). Here, we pose the question to what extent media agendas are similar across the various Western European countries and whether we can identify any intermedia agenda-setting effects that transcend national borders.

The data encompass country-level codings of front-page coverage of one or two newspapers, and in the case of Denmark, national radio broadcasts—also following the methodology of CAP. All newspapers included in the analyses are widely read quality broadsheets. For the United Kingdom *The Times* was coded (only the Wednesday front page), for Spain *El Pais* and *El Mundo*, for Belgium *De Standaard*, for the Netherlands *NRC Handelsblad* and *De Volkskrant* (13 percent sample stratified by year), for Switzerland *Neue Zürcher Zeitung*, and for France *Le Monde*. A total number of 63,482 articles are coded for this analysis, relying on the CAP codings, in which nineteen major categories are included. For more descriptive information on each of the topics, Table 28.1 provides information. We only use the years that are available and limit our analysis to the period 1999–2003.

The main variable is the monthly share of newspaper coverage for an issue from the total newspaper coverage that month. First of all, we look at the correlation in attention between the various countries to test the overlap between the various national media agendas. Second, we test for each country's media agenda the effect of other countries' agendas. We do so in a country-level pooled time-series model, using ordinary least squares regressions with panel-corrected standard errors and a lagged dependent variable. Additionally, we lag the values for the independent agendas, in order to guarantee correct causal ordering.

Table 28.1. Presence of major topics (shares) per country

Topic	NL	BE	ES	UK	CH	FR
Macroeconomics	0.035	0.044	0.030	0.025	0.077	0.067
Civil rights and liberties	0.014	0.027	0.066	0.015	0.070	0.072
Health	0.042	0.044	0.039	0.045	0.028	0.039
Agriculture and fishery	0.017	0.023	0.011	0.018	0.018	0.012
Labor and employment	0.021	0.034	0.017	0.048	0.026	0.046
Education	0.020	0.027	0.025	0.030	0.030	0.020
Environment	0.007	0.013	0.013	0.011	0.012	0.017
Energy	0.006	0.010	0.016	0.007	0.017	0.004
Transportation	0.038	0.027	0.027	0.046	0.062	0.011
Law, crime, and family issues	0.119	0.097	0.162	0.100	0.035	0.070
Social welfare	0.004	0.010	0.009	0.009	0.012	0.006
Community development, planning, and housing	0.006	0.007	0.008	0.012	0.011	0.010
Banking, finance, and domestic commerce	0.070	0.082	0.039	0.031	0.039	0.055
Defense	0.032	0.072	0.084	0.130	0.121	0.074
Space, science, technology, and communications Foreign trade	0.019	0.018	0.038	0.037	0.019	0.025
International affairs and foreign aid	0.000	0.010	0.006	0.002	0.013	0.020
Foreign trade	0.146	0.079	0.058	0.049	0.157	0.091
Government operations	0.138	0.170	0.169	0.045	0.209	0.140
Public lands and water management	0.000	0.004	0.002	0.026	0.002	0.001

Source: Comparative Agendas Project

28.4.2 Results

We first look at the distribution over the various categories. There is considerable overlap in the "large" categories across countries. Law, crime, and family issues is such a large category, receiving considerable attention in each of the six countries. The same goes for government operations, with the exception of the United Kingdom, which seems to be slightly distinct from the other countries in several other respects as well. The United Kingdom, for example, scores substantially higher on "defense."

Table 28.2 reports the overall correlations between the various countries. Indeed we can see that these correlations are substantial—with an average r of 0.717. All countries have similar agendas, again with the exception of the United Kingdom, which only correlates moderately (in most instances between 0.4 and 0.5) with the other countries.

A very similar picture arises when we look at the correlations that use monthly-level scores instead of scores aggregated over the whole period (see Table 28.3). The overall correlation is slightly lower ($r = 0.553$), but still substantial. Again, we find the United Kingdom to be deviating most from other countries, while the highest correlation is between the neighboring, same-language countries Belgium and the Netherlands.

Table 28.2. Correlation between countries (aggregated agendas)

	BE	ES	UK	CH	FR
NL	0.882	0.784	0.475	0.751	0.800
BE		0.884	0.540	0.815	0.902
ES			0.631	0.680	0.821
UK				0.429	0.480
CH					0.884

Note: N = 19.
Source Comparative Agendas Project

Table 28.3. Correlation between countries (monthly-level data)

	BE	ES	UK	CH	FR
NL	0.737	0.638	0.259	0.610	0.645
BE		0.714	0.332	0.652	0.706
ES			0.447	0.592	0.670
UK				0.267	0.349
CH					0.682

Note: N = 1,140 (19 major topics x 60 months).
Source: Comparative Agendas Project

Table 28.4. Explaining issue attention

	NL	BE	ES	UK	CH	FR
NL_{t-1}	0.794***	0.146***	0.037	−0.037	0.074	0.046
BE_{t-1}	0.279	0.472***	0.072*	−0.040	0.051	0.037
ES_{t-1}	0.032	0.126**	0.800***	0.252***	0.041	0.103**
UK_{t-1}	−0.001	−0.002	0.009	0.393***	−0.013	0.013
CH_{t-1}	0.028	0.080**	0.029	0.050	0.687***	0.124***
FR_{t-1}	0.058+	0.074+	0.014	0.025	0.134**	0.532***
Constant	0.002+	0.004**	0.002+	0.011***	0.004**	0.005***
R-squared	0.800	0.685	0.821	0.316	0.707	0.685

Note: Results from an OLS regression with panel corrected standard errors. Unstandardized coefficients are reported. + p < 0.10; ** p < 0.01; *** p < 0.001.
Source: Comparative Agendas Project

Table 28.4 focuses on the question of whether any causal relationships exist between the various national media agendas. The table summarizes the results from regression models with each of the countries' agendas being the dependent variable once. The results demonstrate that in various instances, other national agendas have an intermedia agenda-setting impact—though to a limited extent. For all countries, we find that attention for an issue predicts the current attention for that issue, though to varying degrees: regression coefficients range from 0.800 (Spain) to 0.393 (United Kingdom). In some countries, we find that international media have little influence on the media agenda, most notably in the Netherlands, where we see that only the Swiss media agenda marginally affects the media agenda. In other countries, for example in France and Belgium, we see considerable effects from various other countries. Overall, the results are mixed, but results point to especially large influences from neighboring countries (Netherlands for Belgium, France for Switzerland, Spain and Switzerland for France).

28.5 Conclusion

The media agenda has become a central one in the study of policy agendas and CAP. In the past, it has been especially used in the study of the media's influence on politics. This research field that focuses on political agenda-setting is strongly empirically driven and has expanded rapidly in the last decade. This is not surprising for several reasons. First of all, while research into the media effects on public opinion and behavior has received ample attention since the early 1970s (and before), the focus on how media also impact the behavior of politicians has remained until recently less often investigated, while the conviction that this impact might be considerable has grown. This is, for example, reflected in the rise of the *mediatization* literature (Strömbäck, 2008) that focuses on the fundamental changes politics has undergone due to the increased dominance of the media in society. But while mediatization scholars have been strong in theorizing, empirical research has remained relatively scarce in this research tradition. For political agenda-setting, the reversed seems to be the case: the proposed mechanism is straightforward (issue attention in one realm affects issue attention in the other realm) and empirically relatively easy to investigate and the CAP framework offers an excellent starting point to do so. Thus, researchers willing to capture at least some of this type of media effects empirically are likely to turn to an analysis of political agenda-setting. Second, the increased digital availability and accessibility of both parliamentary records and media content for longer periods of time have made it possible to track the relationship between media content and parliamentary content in a longitudinal perspective, making it possible to systematically compare periods with, for example, different political constellations. Third, also the tools with which the available data can be analyzed have developed quickly. Computer-assisted topic-classification software makes the coding task—so far done by human coders—less laborious and expensive. The application of time-series analysis tools, now easily accessible in standard statistical packages, allows for a robust estimation of effects.

As the overview presented in this chapter shows, there is cumulating evidence suggesting that a multitude of factors have an impact on the size of the impact of the media on politics. The empirical example given shows that with a sole focus on media agendas, interesting insights can be obtained as well. The considerable overlap in media agendas across various Western European countries reflects the importance of the international context in the construction of news. Results from the effect analyses, though preliminary, hint at existing patterns of influence, where the media do follow issue attention in foreign outlets. These findings are relevant in the larger context of international news-flow research (Wu, 2000) that explicitly addresses when news from other countries is reported, and when it is not.

References

Boydstun, A. E., Hardy, A., and Walgrave, S. (2014). Two Faces of Media Attention: Media Storm versus Non-Storm Coverage. *Political Communication*, 31(4): 509–31.

Green-Pedersen, C., and Stubager, R. (2010). The Political Conditionality of Mass Media Influence: When Do Parties Follow Mass Media Attention? *British Journal of Political Science*, 40(3): 663–77.

McCombs, M. E., and Shaw, D. L. (1972). The Agenda-Setting Function of Mass Media. *Public Opinion Quarterly*, 36(2): 176–87.

Sevenans, J., and Vliegenthart, R. (2016). Political Agenda-Setting in Belgium and the Netherlands: The Moderating Role of Conflict Framing. *Journalism and Mass Communication Quarterly*, 93(1): 187–203.

Soroka, S. N. (2002). Issue Attributes and Agenda-Setting by Media, the Public, and Policymakers in Canada. *International Journal of Public Opinion Research*, 14(3): 264–85.

Strömbäck, J. (2008). Four Phases of Mediatization: An Analysis of the Mediatization of Politics. *The International Journal of Press/Politics*, 13(3): 228–46.

Strömbäck, J., and Van Aelst, P. (2010). Exploring Some Antecedents of the Media's Framing of Election News: A Comparison of Swedish and Belgian Election News. *The International Journal of Press/Politics*, 15(1): 41–59.

Thesen, G. (2013). When Good News Is Scarce and Bad News Is Good: Government Responsibilities and Opposition Possibilities in Political Agenda-Setting. *European Journal of Political Research*, 52(3): 364–89.

Tresch, A., Sciarini, P., and Varone, F. (2013). The Relationship between Media and Political Agendas: Variations across Decision-Making Phases. *West European Politics*, 36(5): 897–918.

Van Aelst, P., Melenhorst, L., van Holsteyn, J., and Veen, J. (2015). Lawmaking and News Making: Different Worlds after All? A Study on News Coverage of Legislative Processes in the Netherlands. *The Journal of Legislative Studies*, 21(4): 534–52.

Van Aelst, P., and Vliegenthart, R. (2014). Studying the Tango: An Analysis of Parliamentary Questions and Press Coverage in the Netherlands. *Journalism Studies*, 15(4): 392–410.

Van Dalen, A., and Van Aelst, P. (2014). The Media as Political Agenda-Setters: Journalists' Perceptions of Media Power in Eight West European Countries. *West European Politics*, 37(1): 42–64.

Van der Pas, D. (2014). Making Hay While the Sun Shines Do Parties Only Respond to Media Attention When the Framing Is Right? *The International Journal of Press/Politics*, 19(1): 42–65.

Vliegenthart, R., and Montes, N. M. (2014). How Political and Media System Characteristics Moderate Interactions between Newspapers and Parliaments Economic Crisis Attention in Spain and the Netherlands. *The International Journal of Press/Politics*, 19(3): 318–39.

Vliegenthart, R., and Walgrave, S. (2008). The Contingency of Intermedia Agenda Setting: A Longitudinal Study in Belgium. *Journalism and Mass Communication Quarterly*, 85(4): 860–77.

Vliegenthart, R., and Walgrave, S. (2011a). When the Media Matter for Politics: Partisan Moderators of the Mass Media's Agenda-Setting Influence on Parliament in Belgium. *Party Politics*, 17(3), 321–42.

Vliegenthart, R., and Walgrave, S. (2011b). Content Matters: The Dynamics of Parliamentary Questioning in Belgium and Denmark. *Comparative Political Studies*, 44(8): 1031–59.

Vliegenthart, R., Walgrave, S., Baumgartner, F. R. et al. (2016). Do the Media Set the Parliamentary Agenda? A Comparative Study in Seven Countries. *European Journal of Political Research*, 55(2): 283–301.

Vliegenthart, R., Walgrave, S., and Meppelink, C. (2011). Inter-party Agenda-Setting in the Belgian Parliament: The Role of Party Characteristics and Competition. *Political Studies*, 59(2): 368–88.

Walgrave, S., Boydstun, A. E., Vliegenthart, R. and Hardy, A. (2017). The Nonlinear Effect of Information on Political Attention: Media Storms and US Congressional Hearings. *Political Communication*.

Walgrave, S., and Van Aelst, P. (2006). The Contingency of the Mass Media's Political Agenda-Setting Power: Toward a Preliminary Theory. *Journal of Communication*, 56(1): 88–109.

Walgrave, S. and Vliegenthart, R. (2010). Why are Policy Agendas Punctuated? Friction and Cascading in Parliament and Mass Media in Belgium. *Journal of European Public Policy*, 17(8): 1147–70.

Wu, H. D. (2000). Systemic Determinants of International News Coverage: A Comparison of 38 Countries. *Journal of Communication*, 50(2): 110–30.

29

Parliamentary Questions

Enrico Borghetto and Laura Chaqués-Bonafont

The goal of this chapter is to explain how policymakers prioritize issues across time and countries, focusing on one specific type of parliamentary activity: oral questions in plenary sessions. According to existing research about the policy process and the dynamics of policy change (Baumgartner and Jones, 1993, 2015), one should expect important regularities in the way policymakers pay attention to issues in the parliamentary arena in Western democracies. As Jones and Baumgartner (2005) emphasize for the United States, issue attention most of the time is highly concentrated on a few topics, and shifts in attention rarely occur following gradual adaptations to the growing importance of some new issues, but rather as a result of alarming and urgent adjustments to new social, political and/or economic conditions. Policymakers' responses to new issues is almost nil until the severity of problems force them to take action, which generally results in sudden increases in issue attention. These punctuations in issue attention reflect policymakers' reactions to the signals from their environment and only occur when issues reach a threshold, at which time they are impossible to ignore. When signals are strong enough, policy issues can no longer be neglected, capturing a disproportional amount of attention in the political agenda (Jones and Baumgartner, 2005).

Concentration of issue attention and dramatic responses to growing problems (or punctuations) occur in a context of cognitive and institutional constraints. Individuals do not have the cognitive capacity to process and interpret information about any issue simultaneously, and even if they could do so, the rules governing the political system impose important limits to the number of issues policymakers can process at a given point of time (Baumgartner and Jones, 1993; Jones and Baumgartner, 2005). Many issues are worthy of policymakers' attention, but not all of them can get onto the political agenda at the same time (Jones and Baumgartner, 2005; Kingdon,

1984). As a result, any correspondence between the dynamics of problem severity and policymakers issue attention tends to be low across time.

Following this line of research we test the general applicability of the punctuated equilibrium theory, and also explain some of the main characteristics of parliamentary activities in advanced democracies in recent decades (Copeland and Patterson, 1994; Wiberg, 1995; Döring, 1995; Green-Pedersen, 2010). Is over-time change in issue attention during question time incremental or rather stable and occasionally interrupted with radical changes? To what extent does economic recession generate an increasing concentration of issue attention to a set of issues? Do policymakers increasingly engage in non-legislative parliamentary activities as a mechanism of party competition? These questions have generated an intense debate in agenda-setting and legislative studies in recent decades. Our goal is to explore these trends by focusing on a specific type of non-legislative activity: oral questions. The analysis relies on the data available in eight countries of the Comparative Agendas Project webpage—Belgium, Denmark, France, Germany, Italy, the Netherlands, Portugal, Spain, The United Kingdom, and Switzerland.[1] Time coverage differs across countries but the shortest span is a decade, so as to allow longitudinal studies. The final aggregated dataset, summarized in Table 29.1, contains almost 45,000 coded questions, making it the most complete dataset on non-legislative activities ever examined (to date). For each oral question, each team provided information about the date the oral question was submitted, the issue the oral question deals with (classified using one of the 21 topics and 230 subtopics of the CAP codebook), and, when available, the political party asking the question.

The chapter is structured as follows. Section 29.1 describes some of the features of oral questions and provides basic information about the merged CAP databases. The following sections go on to analyze available data. Section 29.2 analyzes to what extent oral questions are increasing over time

Table 29.1. Codification of oral questions by CAP

Country	Start	End	No. of elections	No. of cabinets	No. of questions	% Opposition
Belgium	1988	2010	6	10	8223	58.5
Denmark	1997	2012	6	7	1945	100.0
France	1995	2005	3	7	1176	68.5
Italy	1997	2014	5	12	4298	55.3
Netherlands	1984	2008	8	10	1394	79.3
Portugal	2003	2014	4	5	1940	77.8
Spain	1983	2015	9	9	16,342	73.0
United Kingdom	1998	2008	3	4	8617	61.5

Source: Comparative Agendas Project

across countries. These findings are taken up in Section 29.3, which asks whether these trends occur in parallel to a growing fragmentation of the oral questions agenda and whether this trend is affected by economic recession. Section 29.4 explores hypotheses drawn from the literature on punctuated equilibrium, more specifically on the impact of institutional friction on issue attention change, asking whether the latter follows a leptokurtic distributional form and what can account for cross-country variation. In Section 29.5 we summarize our findings.

29.1 Oral Questions as Attention-Seeking Devices

In most Western non-presidential democracies, parliamentary rules define oral questions as one of the most important instruments available to individual deputies or/and parliamentary groups to monitor and publicly challenge governmental activities. Yet, empirical research demonstrates oral questions are also issue attention-seeking devices that individual MPs and/or parliamentary groups use to fulfill different political purposes. On some occasions, MPs ask questions as a way to raise attention about issues important to their constituencies, on other occasions they may simply show their concern and their thinking about highly politicized issues and/or events, while at other times, they are mainly oriented to highlight the flaws and weaknesses of governmental performance (Wiberg, 1995; Green-Pedersen, 2010; Green-Pedersen and Mortensen, 2010; Seeberg, 2013; Bevan and John, 2016; Chaqués-Bonafont et al., 2015; Borghetto and Russo, 2018; Salmond, 2014).

Oral questions constitute a crucial element of the symbolic political agenda. However, as Figure 29.1 and Table 29.1 illustrate, their use varies greatly across the eight advanced democracies under analysis. In the two majoritarian parliamentary systems—in the United Kingdom and in Spain—the mean number of oral questions is significantly above the average. British and Spanish members of the executive receive a median number of 755 and 483 questions per year. In contrast, in those countries in which there is a larger number of parties with parliamentary representation the mean number of questions is significantly lower: France (106 questions a year), Denmark (122 oral questions a year), Portugal (168), and the Netherlands (171), with the only exception being Belgium (357 oral questions a year).

Formal rules partly explain how political parties use oral questions. In most countries parliamentary rules define the functions and procedures of oral questions, their timing, frequency, and duration, which vary considerably from country to country. In contrast to other parliamentary activities, the institutional friction—defined as the cost to reaching an agreement—associated with oral questions is quite low (Baumgartner et al., 2009;

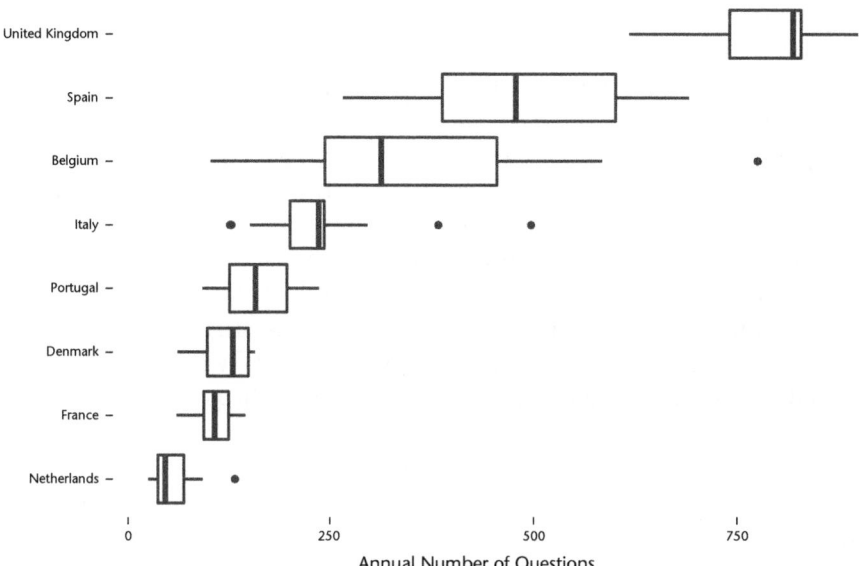

Figure 29.1. Distribution of annual number of oral questions across countries (box-plots)
Source: Comparative Agendas Project

Baumgartner and Jones, 2015). To introduce an oral question there is no need to engage in any voting procedure. MPs can introduce oral questions about any issue they consider important provided that the issue is publicly relevant, falls directly under the responsibility of the executive, and does not deal with personal or private matters of its members.

In general, formal rules establish that all members of parliament (MPs) can participate during question time on a regular basis, usually every week during parliamentary sessions. Differences exist regarding whether oral questions are asked by deputies as individual members like in Denmark or the Netherlands, or as a part of a parliamentary group. In those political systems with strong party discipline, the capacity of individual MPs to highlight some issues during question time is limited by party leaders, who become key veto players, able to impose important limits on who asks questions about which issues and when (Rozerberg and Martin, 2011; Martin, 2011; Russo, 2011). Formal rules also define the maximum number of questions that can be scheduled per session and the pattern of distribution of oral questions across individual representatives and/or parliamentary groups. In Italy, all groups have the same allotment of questions regardless of the number of seats (Russo and Cavalieri, 2016), while in Spain, the allotment of oral questions per session for each parliamentary group varies across legislatures depending on the number of seats of each group (Chaqués-Bonafont et al., 2015). As a result, question time in Spain has a larger scope—questions per session in Spain range from twenty-four to twenty-eight depending on the legislature, double that of Italy. In contrast, in the United Kingdom, parliamentary rules do not establish formal restrictions about the number of questions that can be scheduled during question time (Bevan and John, 2016).[2]

Opposition parties are more active than governing parties during question time in all countries. As described in Table 29.1, in Denmark, the parties in government do not participate in question time, while in the case of Belgium, Italy, or Spain the party in government asks on average more than 40 percent of the oral questions per session. In the case of Belgium and Italy, it originates from the presence of large internally fragmented majority coalitions (Russo and Cavalieri, 2016; Vliegenthart and Walgrave, 2011), while in the case of Spain the explanation is more related to formal rules (Chaqués-Bonafont et al., 2015). In the case of governing parties, question time represents a venue where MPs can address "friendly" questions to the cabinet, namely questions that aim to highlight and give publicity to policy achievements and governmental success. In contrast, opposition parties' questions are employed to force the government to talk about highly controversial issues, emphasizing policy failures and social discontent. In doing so, as several scholars in the CAP community have already demonstrated (Green-Pedersen, 2010; Chaqués-Bonafont and Baumgartner, 2013; Baumgartner and Chaqués-Bonafont, 2015; Vlingehart et al., 2016) opposition parties follow media attention. In a context of agenda scarcity (e.g., number of questions per session), deputies and parliamentary groups tend to concentrate their attention on those issues that have gained media attention (e.g., newspaper front pages) especially those that emphasize the flaws and mismanagement of the governing party and/or that increase the visibility of those issues that are more rewarding in electoral terms (Baumgartner and Chaqués-Bonafont, 2015).

In short, oral questions are not simply instruments available to MPs to oversee governmental activities, but important attention-seeking devices that political parties use to fulfill their goals, mainly to maximize their chances of re-election. Most of the time, opposition parties ask oral questions to signal attention about issues that are not necessarily linked to governmental activities (John and Jennings, 2011; Chaqués-Bonafont et al., 2015; Chaqués-Bonafont and Palau, 2011). On the contrary oral questions of majority MPs are mostly about governmental success and policy achievements and leave aside highly controversial issues that may erode governmental support in the next elections (John et al., 2013; Chaqués-Bonafont et al., 2015). What is more, we argue, formal rules contribute to explaining some cross-national difference in the number of questions, especially in terms of agenda capacity—here the mean number of oral questions in a particular period of time. Section 29.2 goes deeper into the analysis of oral questions as attention-seeking devices focusing on the evolution of oral questions across time.

29.2 Party Competition and the Increase in Parliamentary Questioning

Agenda-setting scholars highlight that non-legislative activities are gaining importance as instruments for party competition in most advanced democracies (Döring, 1995; Döring and Hallerberg, 2004; Franklin and Norton, 1993). For some authors (Wiberg, 1995) this increment is linked to the expansion of the public sector and the growing complexity of society. As the scope of governmental activities increase, MPs have to devote an increasing share of their time and resources to monitoring the cabinet and public administration activities. Other authors (Döring, 1995) suggest the increment of non-legislative parliamentary activities is linked to the increasing professionalization of parliaments. Informational and human resources at MPs' disposal have grown exponentially in recent decades, especially after the consolidation of information communication technologies, and this enables MPs to develop their activities in a more efficient and productive way. Other authors argue that the growing importance of non-legislative activities is not necessarily linked to the scope of public affairs, or increasing parliament's professionalization, but to party competition (Green-Pedersen, 2010). Oversight activities have progressively become an arena where political parties compete, by emphasizing those issues that are the most beneficial to their cause (Mair, 1997). According to this view, oral questioning is an instrument political parties use to reinforce issue ownership. Political parties emphasize those issues for which they have a reputational advantage—either because most citizens perceive the party as especially capable of handling a specific issue, or simply as a result of a spontaneous identification between the party and an issue—in order to maximize political rewards (Budge and Farlie, 1983; Petrocik, 1996; Erikson et al., 2002).

In any case, according to the party competition approach, political parties will increasingly engage in non-legislative activities as a means to highlight the issues that maximize their chances of re-election. In order to test this argument, we ran a simple OLS regression model, in which the dependent variable is the number of oral questions per year in each country, and the independent variable is time, measured by year since the start of the series (positive coefficients indicate increase across time). To check for the autoregressive nature of the time series, the model includes the number of oral questions asked in the previous year as a control variable.

Overall, results do not lend support to the party competition hypothesis (see Figure 29.2). Non-parliamentary activities are increasing in Belgium, Denmark, Italy, and Portugal—coefficients are positive but not significant in the case of Portugal—but not in France, Spain, the Netherlands, and the United Kingdom. Actually, in the case of France and Spain coefficients are

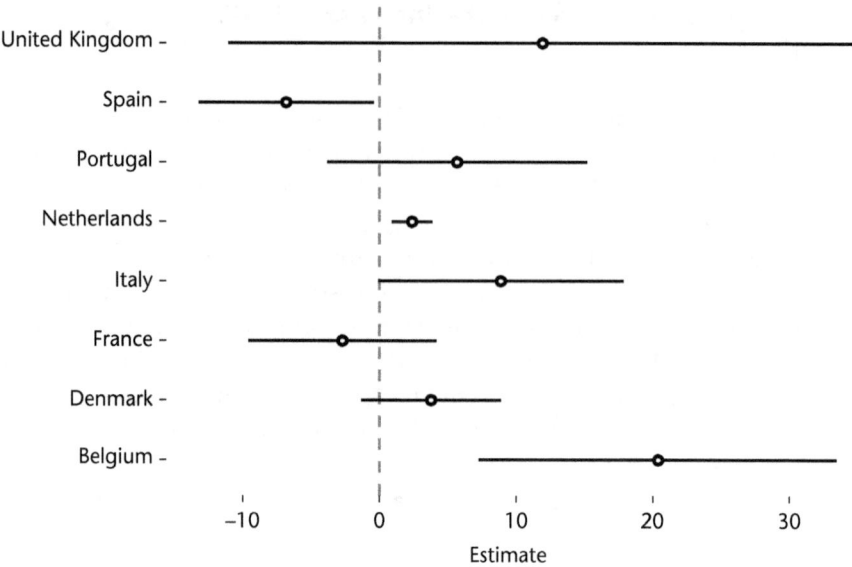

Figure 29.2. Estimated effect of the passing of time on the number of oral questions
Source: Comparative Agendas Project

negative, indicating a decline in the number of oral questions across time. In the case of Spain, this decline is linked to both changing parliamentary rules in 2008 and economic recession (see Chaqués-Bonafont et al., 2015 for a discussion). Both factors radically transformed the functioning of non-legislative activities in Spain from one of issue competition, in which the party in government and the main opposition party asked the same number of questions, to a new scenario in which the incentives for the governing party to actively participate in the question period were reduced to the minimum.

These trends are clearly illustrated in Figure 29.3, which describes the number of questions asked by governing and opposition parties across time. In the case of Spain, the average number of questions declined dramatically after 2008, and this holds especially in the case of the governing party: the annual number of questions dropped from an average of 155 before 2008 to sixty-four questions a year, less than three per session. In contrast, in the case of the United Kingdom, the number of questions of both governing and opposition parties follows a stable pattern without much variation over time.

In short, these findings question previous research about the increase of non-parliamentary activities as a party competition strategy. Contrary to previous findings non-legislative activities have increased in some advanced democracies but not in others and this is related to institutional factors and changing economic conditions. The next question is whether non-legislative

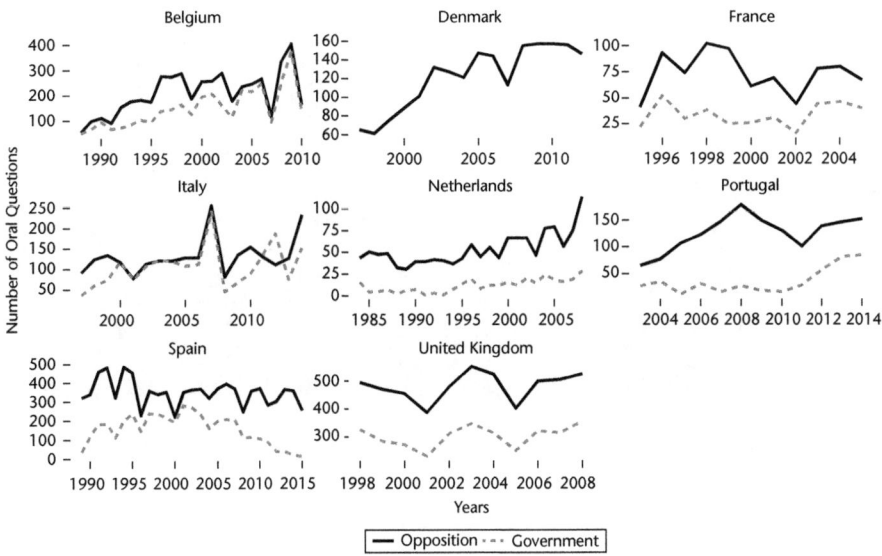

Figure 29.3. Number of oral questions over time
Source: Comparative Agendas Project

activities are increasingly more diverse across issues and whether this is linked to agenda capacity.

29.3 Fragmentation of Issue Attention

Agenda-setting studies highlight that in a context of cognitive and institutional constraints policymakers tend to focus their attention on a few issues. They do so because individuals do not have the cognitive capacity to process and interpret information about all issues at the same time—bounded rationality—and even if they could do so, institutional factors impose important constraints on how policymakers prioritize issues across time (Baumgartner and Jones, 2015, 1993). Cognitive and institutional factors oblige policymakers to select which issues to prioritize by taking into account either pressing events like the collapse of a nuclear-power plant, the issues their constituents identify as most important—like unemployment, or the mass influx of refugees from Syria—or the issues that occupy most of the attention in the media or in the parliamentary arena. In any case, following Jones and Baumgartner (2005) one should expect issue attention to tend to concentrate on a few issues.

There are several methods to analyze agenda diversity (see Jones and Baumgartner, 2005, for a discussion). First, we describe agenda diversity taking as the unit of analysis the percentage of oral questions dealing with an issue

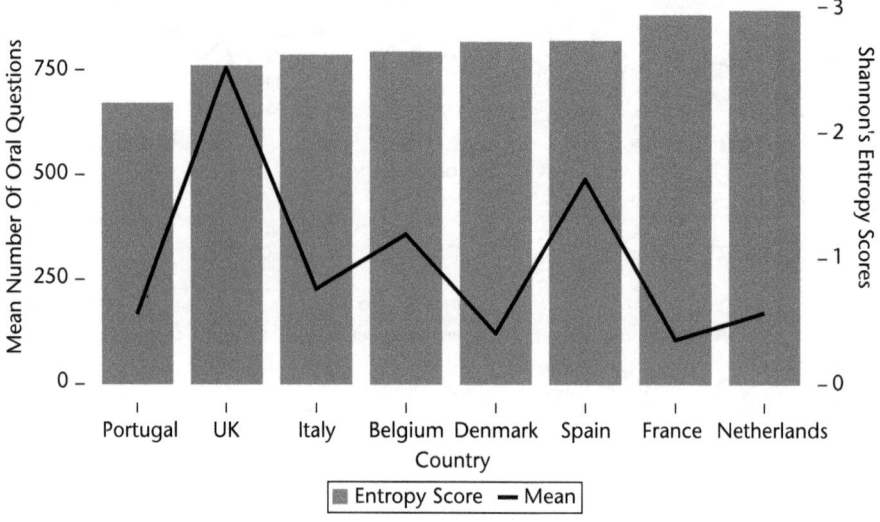

Figure 29.4. Agenda fragmentation
Source: Comparative Agendas Project

across time (years) in each country using Shannon's entropy scores. This measure provides an indicator of the relative concentration or dispersion of issue attention for each country (Boydstun et al., 2014). The score ranges from 0 to the natural log of 21 (note that the CAP methodologies classifies the political agenda across 21 issues). The higher the score, the less concentrated is the policy agenda.[3] As Figure 29.4 illustrates issue attention is highly diversified across issues during question time in all countries, but there still exists some significant cross-national variation. In the Netherlands and France agenda diversity is high, especially when compared with other countries like Portugal. Also, Figure 29.4 shows that agenda diversity—distribution of attention across issues—is not linked to agenda capacity, that is, the number of questions.

Next, we test whether agenda diversity changes across time. According to existing research, one should expect agenda concentration to increase as a consequence of dramatic events and especially during periods of deep economic crisis. In particular, after 2008, most of the Eurozone was plunged into a deep financial and economic crisis, degenerating in some countries into a public debt and bank defaults. The collapse of major financial institutions and the ensuing liquidity crisis called for urgent and, sometimes, dramatic responses by policymakers, mainly in the form of large-scale rescue packages for the banking sector, industrial bailouts, labor market reforms, and, in some cases, cuts in public service provision (Pisani-Ferry, 2014; Laeven and Valencia, 2008). The magnitude of the global financial crisis left little room for political parties to select which issues to prioritize. Bad economic news is difficult to ignore and thus gets priority over anything else, pushing off the agenda anything not directly linked with economic conditions (Jennings et al., 2011). Signals about non-crisis-related issues are not completely neglected, but they do not receive as proportional a response as they would in normal times (Chaqués-Bonafont et al., 2015; Borguetto and Russo, forthcoming).

To describe whether issue attention is affected by changing economic conditions we compute for each country a regression model where the number of subtopics is the dependent variable and the independent variable is time elapsed from the start of the series (measured by year) and the annual unemployment rate (data retrieved from Eurostat). Note that here we use a different method to describe agenda fragmentation by focusing on the number of issues political parties are paying attention to while introducing oral questions. Results are quite similar to those studies using entropy scores as a dependent variable (see Chaqués-Bonafont et al., 2015 for a detailed discussion).

Results are summarized in the coefficient plot in Figure 29.5.[4] As expected the number of issues is increasing in all countries (positive point estimates of "Time"), although just the Netherlands and Denmark reach the 95 percent confidence interval. Only Spain shows a decrease. Vice versa, an increase in the unemployment rate, *ceteris paribus*, is normally associated with a narrower agenda. Spain, Portugal, and Italy, among the countries hit most hard by the

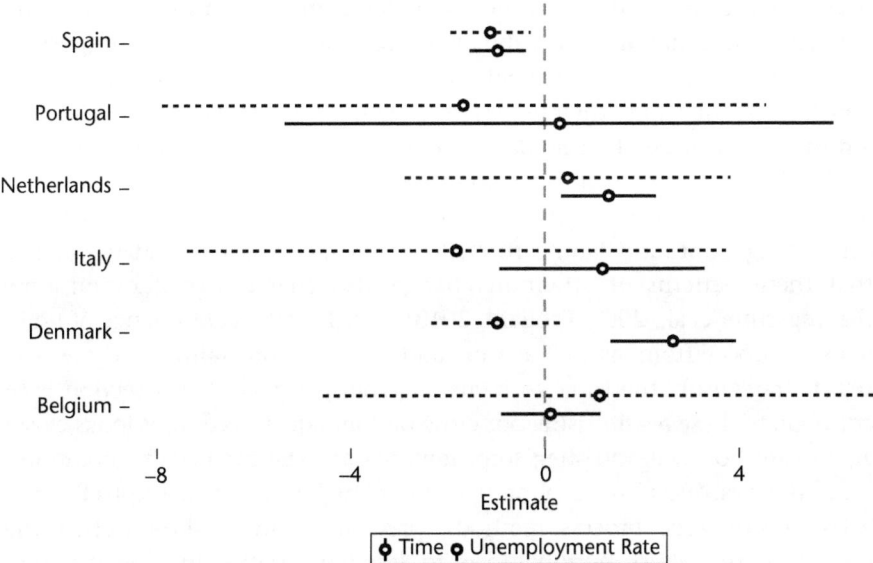

Figure 29.5. Estimated effect of the passing of time and the unemployment rate on the number of topics
Source: Comparative Agendas Project

economic crisis (but also Denmark), all report a negative coefficient, although only in the Spanish case it is statistically significant. As Chaqués-Bonafont et al. emphasize (2015) high unemployment led to increased attention to economy-related issues in Spain, while other issues—rights, education, environment, transportation, crime, and scientific research—were simply pushed off the agenda. Governments' disproportionate attention to the state of the economy came at the cost of disregarding other issues.

Other effects of the economic crisis are, on the one hand, a diminished possibility for MPs of governing parties to engage in oversight activities as a way to highlight governmental successes and to give visibility to policy decisions that may be electorally rewarding. On the other hand, under bad economic conditions, opposition parties have greater incentives to ask oral questions emphasizing the problems associated with economic recession and highlighting policy failures as a way of eroding confidence in the governing party and maximizing electoral rewards (Chaqués-Bonafont et al., 2015; Borghetto and Russo, 2018).

29.4 Parliamentary Questions and Institutional Friction

How do policymakers select the topic of their parliamentary questions? Do they tend to react proportionally to the intensity of demands for their attention or do they respond only when the signals coming from society are strong enough? Understanding the dynamics of policy reactions is important because it unveils how policymakers detect, prioritize, and solve problems, namely how they fulfill their representative function. One of the most important insights provided by agenda studies over the last decade is that, because of the limits of human information processing and institutional resistance to change, policy issue attention is mostly stable with occasional bursts of activity (e.g., Jones and Baumgartner, 2005). Previous works provided evidence that these patterns of attention change also characterize question time (Baumgartner et al., 2009; Brouard, 2013). Faced with an abundance of problems to choose from, as well as time and resource constraints, party leaders select strategically the topic to focus on. The first goal of this section is to corroborate these results using our cross-national data. Second, it looks closer at one case, Portugal, and offers some tentative answers for how the procedures regulating oral questions account for its record high levels of attention changes.

Using stochastic process methods, previous analyses showed that the most appropriate distributional form to describe variation in issue attention change is a leptokurtic curve. Unlike normal distributions, leptokurtic distributions are characterized by a high peak (representing a great number of small or no changes) and fat tails (indicating the presence of a remarkable number of large changes). Two main factors account for this dynamic: cognitive/organizational friction and institutional friction. Both are at play when signals from society about relevant problems compete to capture the attention of policymakers. They act as retarding forces, slowing the reaction of the system to new information. Yet, when the amount of pressure reaches a threshold that is impossible to ignore, these issues capture a disproportionate amount of attention.

We hypothesize that these same dynamics are also at play during question time. Most of the time MPs are expected to follow some sort of lead from their party when choosing the content of questions, with ideology and issueownership concerns weighing heavily on their decisions. Without pretensions to describe an actual scenario, one can picture left-wing MPs giving priority to employment concerns (among other things) and right-wing MPs making a case for the interests of the business world. In such a world, question time would be rather monotonous and predictable. This is clearly a scenario that any spectator of, for instance, the Prime Minister's Question Time at Westminster can easily dismiss. Especially after the introduction of television coverage, Question Time has become a stage where parties compete by publicly reacting to the big issues of the day. A stage where opposition parties jump on the news that can embarrass the government or push forward new issues that the governing parties have refused to address until then but that have ended up on the media's radar. What is more, the low costs associated with oral questioning—especially when interventions must be quick and requires little party coordination—encourage this sort of activity.

We argue that the interaction of both scenarios, one where ideology and issueownership considerationsmatter alongside incentives to ride thewave of public opinion and the media, should produce the stick–slip dynamics expected by punctuated equilibriumtheory. To check whether this is the case we calculated the yearly percentage-percentage change for each of the eight countries and twenty-one issues included in our aggregated dataset (see Figure 29.6).

Attention changes range from a minimum of –1 (an issue that received attention at time t_0 disappears at time t_1) to a maximum of 22 (2220 percent increase in attention from the previous year). The mean change is 0.18, representing an average attention shift of 18 percent. Figure 29.6 shows frequency distributions of all issue attention changes across countries. Each of the plots reports also the L-kurtosis, a measure of the level of peakedness in a distribution that is—in comparison with the normal kurtosis—less sensible to extremes. As a rule, when distributions exhibit a L-kurtosis higher than 0.123, the average level in a normal distribution, they can be classified as leptokurtic.[5]

All country data reveal some level of leptokurtosis. The mean cross-country L-k is 0.29, with a standard deviation of 0.05. The lowest and highest

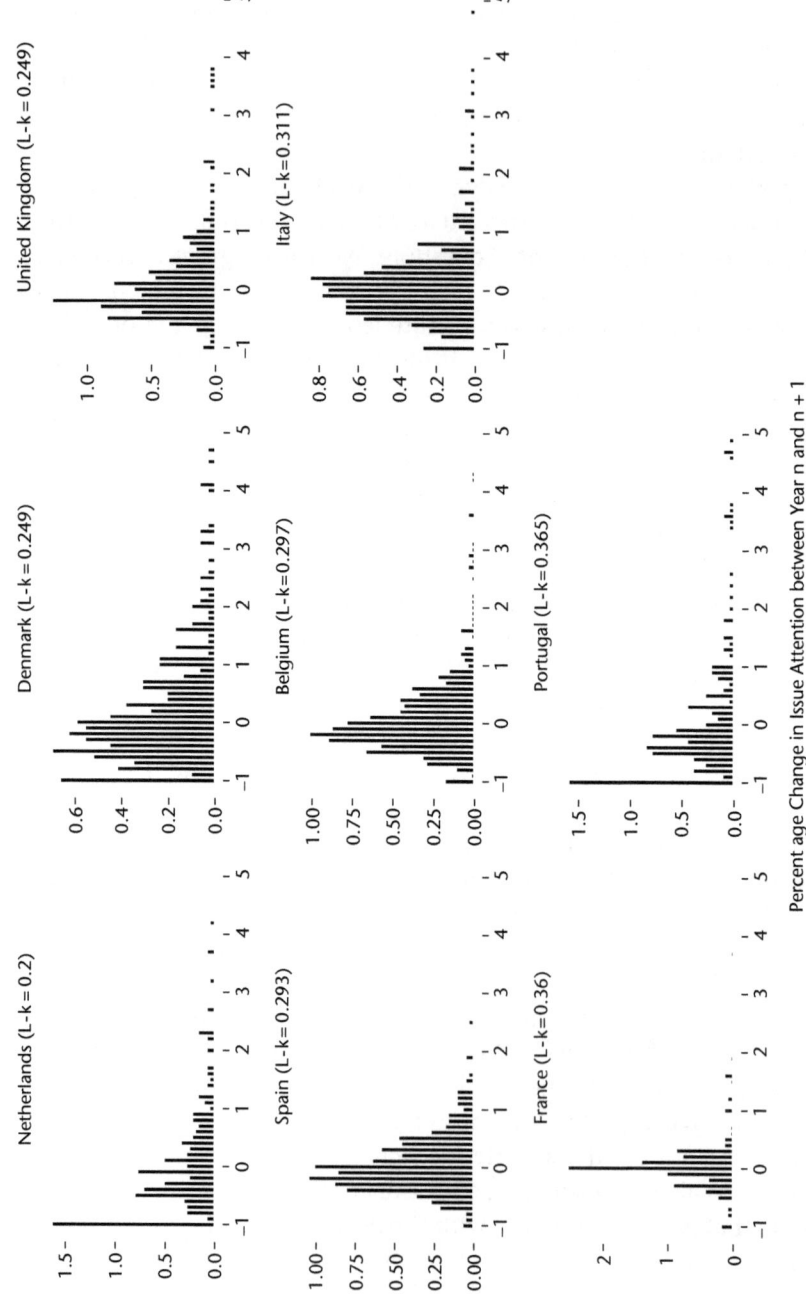

Figure 29.6. Distribution of attention change across countries
Source: Comparative Agendas Project

values are reached respectively by the Netherlands (L-k = 0.2) and Portugal (L-k = 0.365). As expected, values are somewhat lower in comparison with other institutions affected by higher levels of institutional friction, such as the budget (Jones et al., 2009), but they are perfectly in line with previous findings on parliamentary oral questions and interpellations in Belgium and Denmark (Baumgartner et al., 2009) as well as France (Brouard, 2013). Oral questioning confirms itself an intermediate activity in the decision-making chain, so it is reasonable to expect milder levels of leptokurtosis.

On the other hand, our data still reveal some level of unexplained variation in our pool of eight countries. For instance, the level of issue volatility is remarkably different in the Netherlands and Portugal. In the latter case, it is more likely to witness dramatic changes in attention for a specific issue from year to year. In line with the literature on punctuated equilibrium (e.g., Baumgartner et al., 2009; Jones et al., 2003, 2009) and its more recent elaborations (Breunig and Koski, 2012; Epp, 2015; John and Bevan, 2012), one can argue that both institutional and political factors account for this variation. Space constraints do not permit carrying out a full comparative analysis here. For this reason, the rest of this section will limit itself to exploring the possible factors explaining the comparatively higher level of punctuatedness in Portugal, the case featuring the highest level of L-kurtosis.

Among the plausible determinants, the first worthy of mentioning is the level of party-elite control over the content of oral questions. Portuguese question time is organized as a structured debate between the prime minister and parliamentary group frontbenchers. Only rarely are backbenchers allowed to take the floor during these debates. This implies that the content of questions is strictly agreed beforehand by the parliamentary group directorate. On the other hand, backbenchers are allowed to pursue their personal agenda through other outlets, for instance by asking written questions. We argue that the requirement of party coordination in the preparation of question time should impose a filter over the selection of topics. It should take longer for the party leadership to shift attention to a new topic, but when an agreement is reached on the party strategy, they should devote a disproportionate amount of attention to it. Vice versa, when backbenchers are allowed to participate and are left relatively free rein in the choice of questioning, collectively they should tend to focus on a higher variety of issues, reacting more promptly to signals coming from society, especially from their constituencies. Institutional friction should be higher in the former case with respect to the latter. Arguably, another procedural characteristic of question time in Portugal weighs substantially on issue volatility. Since the 2007 reform of the Rules of Procedures in the Portuguese assembly, every other question time session, the PM has had the power to set the agenda of the day. On those days, the debate kicks off with a PM's statement on a preferred issue, followed by questions from the floor that are required to be germane to the topic (although this rule is not strictly implemented). These rules impose strict constraints on the scope and evolution of the overall agenda. More specifically, they attribute effective agenda-setting power to the government. When the cabinet has interest in drawing attention to a topic, it can use both PM-led debates and, in "ordinary" question time debates, "friendly" questions submitted by its supporting MPs. This is a procedure that clearly injects a high level of institutional friction in the system and helps explain the high record of punctuation in Portugal.

29.5 Conclusion

In this chapter, we compare non-parliamentary activities across seven countries for the last decades, using a comprehensive database of more than 45,000 oral questions. Our findings question previous research about the increase of non-parliamentary activities as a party competition strategy. Contrary to previous findings non-legislative activities have increased in some advanced democracies but not others and this is related to institutional factors and changing economic conditions. Also, the chapter illustrates that parliamentary agendas are increasingly fragmented across issues, and this trend is unrelated to agenda capacity. Actually, countries with a larger number of oral questions—mainly the United Kingdom and Spain—have a less fragmented agenda than countries like the Netherlands or Denmark, with a low number of oral questions per session. Again, Spain is the only country that exhibits a decrease in agenda diversity and this is significantly connected with economic recession. After 2008, a large set of issues, especially those related with health, education, and the environment were simply pushed off the agenda. Finally, results also corroborate the punctuated-equilibrium hypothesis. Issue attention evolves following radical changes or punctuations.

Notes

1. Some of these databases are already available on the CAP website. Note that Germany, Greece, and Switzerland are also in the process of releasing their data.
2. For a broad overview about formal rules regulating parliamentary questioning see Wiberg (1995) and Russo and Wiberg (2010), the country reports in the present book, and the websites of national projects' national parliaments.
3. Shannon's H Entropy $= - \Sigma \, p(x_i) * \ln p(x_i)$ where xi represents a dimension, $p(x_i)$ is the proportion of total attention the dimension receives, $\ln p(x_i)$ is the log of the

proportion of attention the dimension receives, using the total number of possible dimensions as the base of the log (Boydstun et al., 2014). For a discussion about the advantages of entropy compared to other indicators of agenda diversity see Jennings et al., (2011) or Boydstun (2014).

4. Results are mostly similar using as a dependent variable the Shannon's entropy score.
5. The "percentage-percentage" method calculates change as the difference between the percentage of the total agenda devoted to a single issue in one year (t_1) and its percentage value in the preceding year (t_0), divided by its percentage value in the preceding year (t_0). Compare with the "percentage" method (which relies on counts) this measure assumes a fixed total level of governmental capacity to attend to issues over time.

References

Baumgartner, F. R., and Chaqués-Bonafont, L., 2015. All News Is Bad News: Newspaper Coverage of Political Parties in Spain. *Political Communication*, 32(2): 268–91.

Baumgartner, F. R., and Jones, B. D. (1993). *Agendas and Instability in American Politics*. Chicago: University of Chicago Press.

Baumgartner, F. R., and Jones, B. D. (2015). *Politics of Information*. Chicago: Chicago University Press.

Baumgartner, F. R., Breunig, C., Green-Pedersen, C. et al. (2009). Punctuated Equilibrium in Comparative Perspective. *American Journal of Political Science*, 53(3): 603–20.

Bevan, S., and John, P. (2016). Policy Representation by Party Leaders and Followers: What Drives UK Prime Minister's Questions? *Government and Opposition*, 51(1): 59–83.

Borghetto, E., and Russo, F. (forthcoming). The Determinants of Party Issue Attention in Times of Crisis: From Agenda Setters to Agenda Takers? *Party Politics*, 24(1): 65–77.

Boydstun, A. E., Bevan, S., and Herschel, T. F. (2014). The Importance of Attention Diversity and How to Measure it. *Journal of Public Policy*, 42(2): 173–96.

Breunig, C., and Koski, C. (2012). The Tortoise or the Hare? Incrementalism, Punctuations, and their Consequences. *Policy Studies Journal*, 40(1): 45–68.

Brouard, S. (2013). Issue Attention in Parliament: Evidence of a Stick–Slip Process of Attention Allocation in the French National Assembly. *The Journal of Legislative Studies*, 19(2): 246–60.

Budge, I., and Farlie, D. (1983). Party Competition—Selective Emphasis or Direct Confrontation? An Alternative View with Data. In *West European Party Systems: Continuity and Change*, ed. H. Daalder and P. Mair. London: Sage, 267–305.

Chaqués-Bonafont, L. C., and Palau, A. M. (2011). Assessing the Responsiveness of Spanish Policymakers to the Priorities of their Citizens. *West European Politics* 34(4): 706–30.

Chaqués-Bonafont, L., and Baumgartner, F. R. (2013). Newspaper Attention and Policy Activities in Spain. *Journal of Public Policy*, 33(1): 65–88.

Chaqués-Bonafont, L., Palau, A. M., and Baumgartner, F. R. (2015). *Agenda Dynamics in Spain*. London: Palgrave.

Copeland, G. W., and Patterson, S. C. (eds) (1994). *Parliaments in the Modern World: Changing Institutions*. Ann Arbor: Michigan University Press.

Döring, H. (ed.) (1995). *Parliaments and Majority Rule in Western Europe*. New York: St Martin's Press.

Döring, H., and Hallerberg, M. (2004). *Patterns of Parliamentary Behavior: Passage of Legislation across Western Europe*. Aldershot: Ashgate Publishing.

Epp, D. A. (2015). Punctuated Equilibria in the Private Sector and the Stability of Market Systems. *Policy Studies Journal*, 43(4): 417–36.

Erikson, R. S., MacKuen, M., and Stimson, J. A. (2002). *The Macro Polity*. Cambridge: Cambridge University Press.

Franklin, M. N., and Norton, P. (1993). *Parliamentary Questions: For the Study of Parliament Group*. New York: Oxford University Press.

Green-Pedersen, C. (2010). Bringing Parties into Parliament: The Development of Parliamentary Activities in Western Europe. *Party Politics*, 16(3): 347–69.

Green-Pedersen, C., and Mortensen, P. B. (2010). Who Sets the Agenda and Who Responds to it in the Danish Parliament? A New Model of Issue Competition and Agenda-Setting. *European Journal of Political Research*, 49(2): 257–81.

Jennings, W., Bevan, S., Timmermans, A. et al. (2011). Effects of the Core Functions of Government on the Diversity of Executive Agendas. *Comparative Political Studies*, 44(8): 1001–30.

John, P., Bertelli, A., Jennings, W., and Bevan, S. (2013). *Policy Agendas in British Politics*. London: Palgrave.

John, P., and Bevan, S. (2012). What Are Policy Punctuations? Large Changes in the Legislative Agenda of the UK Government, 1911–2008. *Policy Studies Journal*, 40(1): 89–108.

John, P., Bevan, S., and Jennings, W. (2011). The Policy–Opinion Link and Institutional Change: The Legislative Agenda of the UK and Scottish Parliaments. *Journal of European Public Policy*, 18: 1052–68.

Jones, B. D., and Baumgartner, F. R. (2005). *The Politics of Attention: How Government Prioritizes Problems*. Chicago: University of Chicago Press.

Jones, B. D., Sulkin, T., and Larsen, H. A. (2003). Policy Punctuations in American Political Institutions. *American Political Science Review*, 97(1): 151–69.

Jones, B. D., Baumgartner, F. R., Breunig, C. et al. (2009). A General Empirical Law of Public Budgets: A Comparative Analysis. *American Journal of Political Science*, 53(4): 855–73.

Kingdon, J. W. (1984). *Agendas, Alternatives, and Public Policies*. Boston: Little, Brown.

Laeven, L., and Valencia, F. (2008). Systemic Banking Crisis: A New Database, IMF Working Papers, 08/224, IMF, Washington, DC.

Mair, Peter (1997). *Party System Change: Approaches and Interpretations*. Oxford: Oxford University Press.

Martin, S. (2011). Parliamentary Questions, the Behaviour of Legislators, and the Function of Legislatures: An Introduction. *The Journal of Legislative Studies*, 17(3): 259–70.

Petrocik, J. R. (1996). Issue Ownership in Presidential Elections, with a 1980 Case Study. *American Journal of Political Science*, 40(3): 825–50.

Pisani-Ferry, J. (2014). *The Euro Crisis and its Aftermath*. Oxford: Oxford University Press.

Rozenberg, O., and Martin, S. (2011). Questioning Parliamentary Questions. *The Journal of Legislative Studies*, 17(3): 394–404.

Russo, F. (2011). The Constituency as a Focus of Representation: Studying the Italian Case through the Analysis of Parliamentary Questions. *The Journal of Legislative Studies*, 17(3): 290–301.

Russo, F., and Cavalieri, A. (2016). The Policy Content of the Italian Question Time: A New Dataset to Study Party Competition. *Rivista Italiana di Politiche Pubbliche*, 11(2): 197–222.

Russo, F., and Wiberg, M. (2010). Parliamentary Questioning in 17 European Parliaments: Some Steps towards Comparison. *The Journal of Legislative Studies*, 16(2): 215.

Salmond, R. (2014). Parliamentary Question Times: How Legislative Accountability Mechanisms Affect Mass Political Engagement. *The Journal of Legislative Studies*, 20(3): 321–41.

Seeberg, H. B. (2013). The Opposition's Policy Influence through Issue Politicisation. *Journal of Public Policy*, 33(1): 89–107.

Vliegenthart, R., and Walgrave, S. (2011). Content Matters the Dynamics of Parliamentary Questioning in Belgium and Denmark. *Comparative Political Studies*, 44(8): 1031–59.

Wiberg, M. (1995). Parliamentary Questioning: Control by Communication? In *Parliaments and Majority Rule in Western Europe*, ed. H. Döring. New York: St Martin's Press, 179–222.

30

Connecting Government Announcements and Public Policy

Christian Breunig, Emiliano Grossman, and Tinette Schnatterer

Governments regularly make announcements; important public speeches punctuate political life. The American State of the Union or the British Queen's Speech are moments that draw wide political attention as they outline the policy programs for months and, sometimes, years to come. In most advanced democracies, these speeches set policy goals and fix priorities on the government agenda. A close link between government announcements and legislative capacity of governments is often assumed (Breeman et al., 2009; John and Jennings, 2010; Mortensen et al., 2011) and a few studies have already looked into this link for individual countries (Chaqués-Bonafont, Palau, and Baumgartner, 2015; Lovett, Bevan, and Baumgartner, 2015). A comprehensive cross-national study on the way policy announcements are translated into policy output is, however, still missing.

The present chapter provides a systematic study on the link between governments' announcements in speeches and their actual legislative behavior. Drawing on a growing literature on the link between electoral pledges, made by parties in their election programs, and actual policy outcome, we extend the debate on the "program to policy link" to "the announcement to policy link." In this chapter we consider speeches as work programs presented by governments and investigate how these work programs are transformed into political action. The focus of this study therefore is pledge fulfillment of governing parties in-between elections.

We also examine a number of alternative mechanisms for law production based on the literature on institutional effects on legislative activity (Carey, 2008; Martin and Vanberg, 2011). We consider governments' majority status, the disproportionality of the electoral system, and the proximity to the next election. Based on the recent experience in many European countries that shows that an unfavorable economic context can depress the influence of other variables, we pay special attention to the potential influence of the economic context on the legislative output. Testing systematically for the influence of other, institutional, political, and economic factors that could possibly influence the legislative capacity of parliaments, the present chapter contributes to a better understanding of law-making activities and connects works on legislative politics with studies of public policy. Adopting a longitudinal and cross-national research design, we are able to identify if common or diverging patterns across countries exist. The chapter brings together data on legislative outputs and government speeches coded thematically according to the Comparative Agendas Project for eight countries over the last twenty years. This dataset enables us to study government's policy commitments by analyzing how much they prioritize particular policy fields.

The rest of this chapter is structured as follows: Section 30.1 broadens the literature on pledge fulfillment by including government speeches. Section 30.2 puts forward a series of alternative explanations to account for legislative capacity. Section 30.3 describe the data and highlights differences—in terms of productivity and prioritization—in legislative capacity across the eight countries. The results of a series of preliminary multivariate analyses show that introducing a political topic during a government speech substantively impacts the number of laws voted in this policy domain. We close by offering venues for future research that highlight the close link between literatures on pledge fulfillment, legislative politics, and public policy.

30.1 Expanding the "Program to Policy Link"

Electoral pledges made by parties in their election programs can be linked to actual policy outcomes or effective outputs (Klingemann, Hofferbert, and Budge, 1994; Mansergh and Thomson, 2007; Mortensen et al., 2011; Naurin, 2011; Royed, 1996; Thomson et al., 2012). Hofferbert and Budge (1992) show for instance that party platforms are correlated with spending priorities, irrespective of diverging political structures, even in countries with supposedly weak parties such as the United States. Different studies for individual countries come to similar conclusions. Analyzing eighteen articles on election promise fulfillment in North America and European countries Francois Pétry and Benoît Collette come up with an average fulfillment rate of electoral pledges of 63 percent. These findings suggest that the "program to policy link" (Thomson, 2001) works, and that examining actual policy output is important. At the same time, this proposition contradicts other studies showing that policy responsibility based on government power is much more important for governments' issue agendas than their partisan composition (Mortensen et al., 2011).

As the general assumption underlying most democratic theory is that voters will give a mandate to their representatives to implement a given policy program, studying the extent to which these pledges are congruent with subsequent government policy is intrinsically important. When it comes to predicting legislative capacity, however we argue that political intentions, as expressed in party manifestos, may not necessarily be the appropriate outlet for making pledges. Changes in the economic situation, social movements, or interest-group activity are all factors that can have an impact on the capacity of governments to fulfill their promises while others, such as external events and intra-party competition can create new incentives to change priorities in between elections. Naurin (2011) considers therefore that the apparent discrepancy between the high degree of pledge fulfillment observed in many studies and the widespread image of unreliable politicians can be explained by the absence of studies on non-electoral promises. Based on this observation, some studies have recently extended research on pledge fulfillment on the way coalition agreements in Belgium, the Netherlands, and Italy are translated into policies (Calvo, 2014; Timmermans, 2006) as well as on the factors that determine whether legislative pledges made by Polish governments actually become laws (Zubek and Klüver, 2015). While the latter approach has the advantage of covering the whole legislative period, what these studies have in common is that they focus exclusively on coalition governments.

We argue that government speeches are an appropriate tool for assessing what governments plan to actually do because they signal the government's initial intention and incorporate necessary adjustment of promises once they are in power. Government speeches are obviously exercises in political communication. Voters are likely to hold the executive accountable for their work program. As a regular—typically yearly—exercise, speeches have to achieve the difficult exercise of tackling problems, as they emerge, and convincing the electorate that they are in line with the wider government program (Mortensen et al., 2011). That means that speeches can potentially reflect the political color of the government, but in speeches government may also anticipate or respond to voters' demands or may simply respond to problems as they emerge. Given the flexibility of adjustment, speech-making is thus an exercise in reconciling electoral pledges (situated further back in the chain of events and occuring only once in every election cycle) with a changing political and economic reality.

Most Western democracies feature some kind of yearly general policy speech by the head of government. These speeches usually outline the policy goals for the upcoming year or parliamentary session. They therefore are considered to be highly visible and important signals of government priorities, an "annual snapshot of executive priorities" and are supposed to reflect the "commitment to specific legislative proposals" (Jennings, Bevan, and John, 2011). Systematic research on these executive policy agendas however remains "surprisingly limited" (Mortensen et al., 2011: 973) and very few studies on government speeches have taken a comparative perspective (Hobolt and Klemmensen, 2008).

We contend that emphasis on particular policy domains in government declarations is translated into a higher legislative capacity in this policy domain. Because of the limited amount of legislative time available, governments have to prioritize their agenda for the forthcoming session of parliament (John and Jennings, 2010). Via government speeches the governments communicate their general priorities and the specific measures that the executive intends to address in the coming year. Hence our policy announcement hypothesis states that more emphasis in speeches leads to more legislative activity in the mentioned policy domain.

30.2 Institutional Features and the "Program to Policy Link"

Government's capacity to keep its announcements does not depend on its goodwill only. Rather, the implementation of the stated promises depends on a number of facilitating or hindering factors that influence law production in particular policy domains. In order to determine which type of explanation is most convincing, we take a mainly exploratory approach to those questions. The first alternative explanation concerns the government status. Among the different types of government, the following order can be derived from the literature (Müller and Strom, 2003; Strom, 1990) that explores coalition politics and assignment of government responsibility. Generally speaking, we expect a single-party majority government to have the strongest capacity and incentive to implement its goals. Single-party governments face no or little opposition to legislate their preferences. Moreover, blame-shifting is more difficult under these circumstances, as the power is more concentrated in the hands of the head of government (Lijphart, 1999; Powell and Whitten, 1993). This also means that politicians should anticipate a stronger electoral sanction if they do not make good on promises (Soroka and Wlezien, 2010), which, in turn, should create a strong incentive in favor of sticking to the content of yearly announcements. For other types of governments, the danger of intra-coalitional struggles should on average lead to less legislative capacity in particular domains.

Minimum-winning coalitions, where the main party has enough leverage to impose major agreements, have to find compromise within the governing coalition in order to pass legislation. We accept that in most cases these compromises have been made before governments promotes their agenda in a speech. Single-party minority governments, under certain circumstances, are relatively efficient, as seminal work by Strøm (1990) shows. Surplus governments are more complicated. The legislative success of surplus governments is conditional on how a coalition comes together, the potential antagonism between coalition members, and the pivotal character of the party holding the post of prime minister. Taken together, we have the following expectation: single-party majority governments should have the greatest incentive and capacity to legislate in particular policy domains.

There is a large body of literature suggesting that the more fragmented a political system is, the less effective the government is likely to be (Calvo, 2014; Soroka and Wlezien, 2010; Tsebelis, 2002). Electoral systems are assumed to have a strong influence on the capacity of governments to produce working majorities in the legislature (Lizzeri and Persico, 2001; Reynolds et al., 2005). Since Duverger's work, it is generally assumed that proportional electoral systems lead to more fragmented party systems and therefore less effective government (Duverger, 1954). In line with this literature, we expect majoritarian electoral systems to result in a lower number of parties. This low level of fragmentation leads to a higher capacity to legislate in particular policy domains. In short, the more majoritarian an electoral system, the higher the capacity to legislate in particular policy domains.

Along with these institutional factors, the electoral calendar might affect the capacity to legislate in particular policy domains. Politicians seek to manipulate government activities in order to increase their chances of re-election (Blais and Nadeau, 1992). While existing studies mainly focus on the impact of the electoral cycle on the manipulation of the business cycles (Franzese, 2002; Nordhaus, 1975; Rogoff and Sibert, 1988), we assume that as elections come closer, the incentive to legislate increases as well. The benefits (and costs) of (not) making good on promises significantly increase as elections approach. Governing parties therefore strengthen their effort to carry out their program under these circumstances but also try to tackle ongoing legislative initiatives before the end of the legislation. Therefore we expect that, compared to the rest of the legislative period, incentives to legislate in particular policy domains increase in the pre-electoral periods.

30.3 Data and Methodology

Several measures of government attention, legislative outputs, and institutional features need to be assembled in order to examine how government speeches and political institutions shape policy agendas. For key measures, we rely on the large database of the Comparative Agendas Project (CAP).

In particular, we were able to assemble two series of policy agendas—government speeches and legislation—from eight countries—Canada, Denmark, France, Germany, the Netherlands, Spain, the United Kingdom, and the United States—for the period between 1983 and 2004. All agendas data were coded according to the CAP project Master Codebook. We achieved a cross-country and cross-topic amalgamation of the data by generating a new major topic called "national unity," by placing all immigration-related codes into the major topic civil rights and liberties, and by pooling all major topic areas into seven macro topic areas (see also Bertelli and John, 2013). These seven topic areas are summarized in Table 30.1. All categories are mutually exclusive and complete.

We constructed the policy agendas variables in the following way. For speeches, we computed the proportion of all quasi-sentences for each macro area per quarter. We carried these proportions over to the following quarters until a new speech is delivered. For laws, we counted all passed legislation per macro topic for each quarter. The quarterly legislative output per topic is our measure of legislative capacity. In order to grasp this measure better, we present two visual aids. Figure 30.1a displays how many laws were passed in each macro topic area for each country. Between 1983 and 2004, nearly

Table 30.1. Generating the policy agendas macro categories

Macro category[a]	Policy Agendas categories
Economy	Banking and commerce Labor and employment Macroeconomy
Infrastructure	Energy Public lands Science and technology Transportation
Welfare	Culture Education Healthcare Housing Social welfare
Foreign policy	Defense Foreign trade International relations
Law	Civil rights and liberties Law, crime, and family issues
Environment	Agriculture Environment
Government	Government operations National unity State and local issues

Note: [a] Issues on the left are comprised of the issues on the right.
Source: Comparative Agendas Project codebook

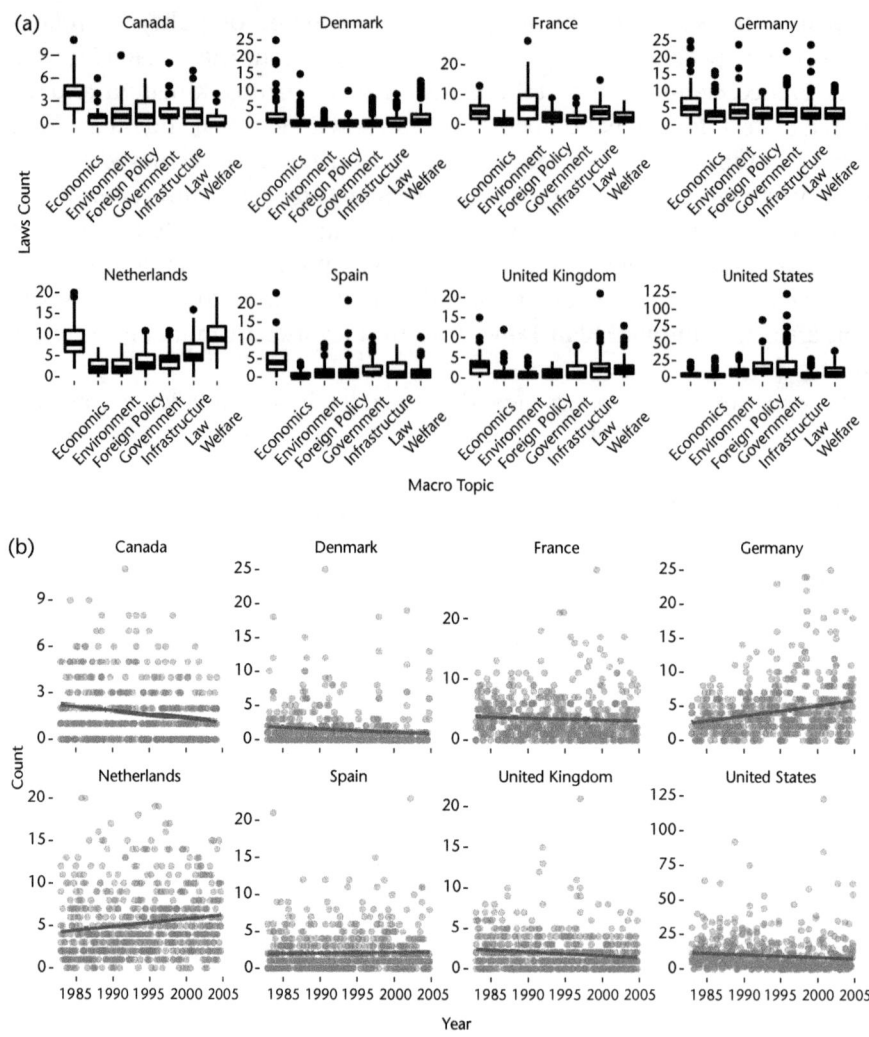

Figure 30.1. Legislative activities across countries

Notes: The boxplot (30.1a) displays the number of laws per topic in each country and quarter. The scatterplot (30.1b) displays the number of laws per quarter on each issue. The black line is the trend as a polynomial regression fit.

Source: Comparative Agendas Project

18,000 laws were passed in the eight countries. This ranged from 792 in Denmark to 5,974 in the United States with Spain and France being closest to the average. Among the countries studied here, 1,298 laws were passed in the topic area "environment," while the most prominent area was "economics" with 3,380 laws. Figure 30.1 nicely illustrates that there is some variation in the different topic areas per country. For example, the areas "government" and "infrastructure" are more heavily legislated in the United States then in most other countries. Likewise, France is quite active in foreign policy and Canada on economic issues. In fact, a χ^2-test on the underlying contingency table indicates that statistically significant differences among topic counts exist across countries.

For comparison, Figure 30.1b plots the legislative activity for each country per quarter. The dots represent the number of laws passed for each macro topic area per quarter and the black line is the polynominal regression fit. The line suggests that legislative activity slightly increased over time in the Netherlands and Germany and slightly decreased in Canada and the United States. With the exception of the United States, lawmakers pass on average less than five laws in a particular topic area per quarter. The large dispersion of the data points for some countries, such as the United States, the United Kingdom, and Spain also shows that some countries are more prone to punctuation than others. For example, we can't easily find some positive outliers in quarterly topic counts in the Netherlands. Taken together, both plots suggest that quarterly topic-count data displays substantial variation across topics, countries, and time, confirming earlier observations made by Brouard et al. (2009).

We rely on a variety of secondary sources for our remaining covariates. We concentrate on two measures of institutions. First, at the electoral level, we used Gallagher's disproportionality index (Gallagher, 1991). Second, we capture government type using a fivefold classification: (1) single-party majority government, (2) minimal winning coalition, (3) surplus coalition, (4) single-party minority government, and (5) multiparty minority government. Note that the US presidential system is classified as single-party majority. We constructed a binary measure for campaign periods using an indicator for the quarter preceding the election. Arguments based on distinct spending patterns of governments (Blais, Blake, and Dion, 1993; Cameron, 1978) connect constituency preferences and electoral promises with government spending based on ideology. It is more difficult to develop an argument about why partisanship relates to legislative capacity. One line of reasoning would be that Leftists parties are more prone to rely on government for addressing market failures and other societal needs. We measure government ideology on a –100 to 100 scale and calculated as the weighted average of the number of seats of each party and their CMP-based left–right dimension score. The data and method are from Cusack and Engelhardt (2002). Finally, the misery index combines information on inflation and the unemployment rate (from the OECD). Based on the recent experience in many European countries we expect an unfavorable economic context to depress the influence of other variables. Put differently, in a context of economic recession, the economy will draw a lot more attention and put an end to "politics as normal." The basic descriptive statistics are listed in Table 30.2. We removed thirty legislative

Table 30.2. Descriptive statistics, N = 4718

Statistic	Mean	St. Dev.	Min	Max
Laws	3.79	5.98	0	123
Government speech	0.13	0.12	0.00	1.00
Government ideology	6.37	16.67	−28.44	35.84
Government type	2.16	1.39	1	5
Campaign	0.22	0.42	0	1
Disproportionality	7.91	7.18	0.37	24.61
Misery	11.64	4.96	5.10	32.00

Source: Comparative Agendas Project

quarters because of legislative inactivity during that time. The resulting sample is a balanced panel with 4,718 observations and no missing values.

Our estimation strategy has to account for two important issues. First, the dependent variable is count data with a large amount of zero values. Second, the data structure is nested. The dependent variable measures the number of laws passed for a particular macro topic in a given country and quarter. Likewise, some of the covariates are hierarchically structured. In order to account for both issues,[1] we rely on a zero-inflated negative binomial estimation (Agresti, 2013; Zuur, 2009). A Vuong test indicated that a zero-inflated negative binomial is superior to other modeling alternatives.

The estimation contains a two-part mixture model that accounts for the zeros from the point mass as well as from the count component. For our models, both parts contain all covariates. While we test several model specifications below, the full model can be described as: $y = Xb + Zg + e$ where y are the quarterly count of passed laws in a topic area, X is the matrix of the following covariates—speeches, government ideology, campaign, disproportionality, government type, misery, and Z is the design matrix for the fixed effects for topic, country.

30.4 Results and Discussion

We estimated a zero-inflated negative binomial model predicting quarterly count of laws per topic from the introduced covariates. Table 30.3 presents the results from three models in order to ascertain the robustness of our findings. The table illustrates that the estimated effects are stable across model specifications. Given this stability, our interpretation concentrates on the full model (Model 3) and within that model on the component that estimates the counts of legislative activity.

The core theoretical expectation of this chapter is that policy proposals introduced by governments in their annual speeches are translated into

Table 30.3. Regression results from a zero-inflated negative binomial

Count component	Model		
	(1)	(2)	(3)
Government speech	6.99***	0.31*	0.30*
	(.16)	(0.17)	(0.16)
Government ideology			0.01***
			(0.001)
Single-party majority government			0.03
			(0.13)
Minimal winning coalition			−0.05
			(0.22)
Surplus coalition			0.08
			(0.20)
Single-party minority government			0.22
			(0.15)
Multiparty minority government			0.11
			(0.21)
Campaign			0.54***
			(0.04)
Disproportionality			0.03***
			(0.01)
Misery			0.02***
			(0.01)
Economy		0.85***	
		(0.07)	
Environment		0.17**	1.04***
		(0.07)	(0.06)
Foreign policy		0.39***	−0.46***
		(0.09)	(0.06)
Government		0.41***	−0.43***
		(0.07)	(0.06)
Infrastructure		0.53***	−0.33***
		(0.07)	(0.06)
Law		0.46***	−0.39***
		(0.07)	(0.06)
Welfare		0.49***	−0.36***
		(0.07)	(0.05)
DE		0.94***	1.39***
		(0.07)	(0.20)
DK		0.31***	0.49**
		(0.09)	(0.20)
ES		0.22***	0.24**
		(0.07)	(0.11)
FR		0.74***	0.75***
		(0.07)	(0.13)
NL		1.14***	1.74***
		(0.07)	(0.21)
UK		0.20***	0.09
		(0.07)	(0.08)
US		1.81***	1.91***
		(0.07)	(0.10)
N	4,718	4,718	4,718
Log likelihood	−12,724.84	−10,509.97	−10,352.12

(*continued*)

Table 30.3. Continued

Zero component	Model		
	(1)	(2)	(3)
Government speech	−1,328.47***	−0.55	−0.20
	(413.61)	(2.46)	(2.43)
Government ideology			−0.001
			(0.01)
Single-party majority government			−13.99
Minimal winning coalition			−9.68
			(1,146.26)
Surplus coalition			−9.50
			(996.87)
Single-party minority government			−10.23
Multiparty minority government			−11.11
			(1,146.26)
Campaign			−0.53
			(0.35)
Disproportionality			0.07
			(0.16)
Misery			−0.11
			(0.07)
Economy		−9.49**	
		(4.80)	
Environment		−6.10*	7.93
		(3.37)	
Foreign policy		−3.38	10.65
		(3.58)	
Government		−5.84*	8.16
		(3.43)	
Infrastructure		−5.73*	8.30
		(3.35)	
Law		−6.16*	7.79
		(3.39)	
Welfare		−6.71*	7.19
		(3.46)	
DE		−8.26	−12.40
		(51.47)	(1,149.57)
DK		5.67*	3.74
		(3.33)	(1,147.01)
ES		0.39	−0.20
		(3.63)	(2.13)
FR		−8.62	−16.20
		(65.38)	(915.66)
NL		−9.56	−18.49
		(109.97)	(2,243.11)
UK		2.47	2.52
		(3.26)	(4.13)
US		−5.87	−8.44
		(34.77)	(114.83)
N	4,718	4,718	4,718
Log likelihood	−12,724.84	−10,509.97	−10,352.12

Note: * p < 0.1; ** p < 0.05; *** p < 0.01.

Source: Comparative Agendas Project

legislative action. Our estimation suggests that we can't reject the policy announcement hypothesis, i.e., the estimated effect is statistically different from zero *ceteris paribus*. The estimates indicate that as the proportion of a particular topic in a government speech increases, legislative activity on that topic increases too. The estimated effect on the log count of laws is about 0.30. Given this finding, we are able to offer some empirical evidence that directly links governments' annual promises with their action. A simple representational linkage therefore seems intact.

In order to gauge the predicted size of these effects, Figure 30.2 plots the range of speech shares on a topic with the predicted number of laws on a topic using the estimates from model 3. In order to make this prediction we hold all continuous variables at their mean and use economic issues in Germany by a minimum winning coalition government as typical values for the three nominal variables. The figure suggests that even when government does not discuss a topic during a speech, it is likely that, on average, seven laws on that topic are passed. One the other hand, if an executive leader just speaks on one topic (i.e., speech share = 1.0), the model predicts that over nine laws are passed on that topic. Our estimates indicate that substantive differences exist, especially when we recall that lawmakers pass on average about five laws per topic in a quarter in our sample. The substantive impact of executive speeches is even more remarkable if we compare it to the estimated effect of economic downturns. Our estimates indicate that even in the worst economic situations lawmakers just pass eighteen laws on a topic.

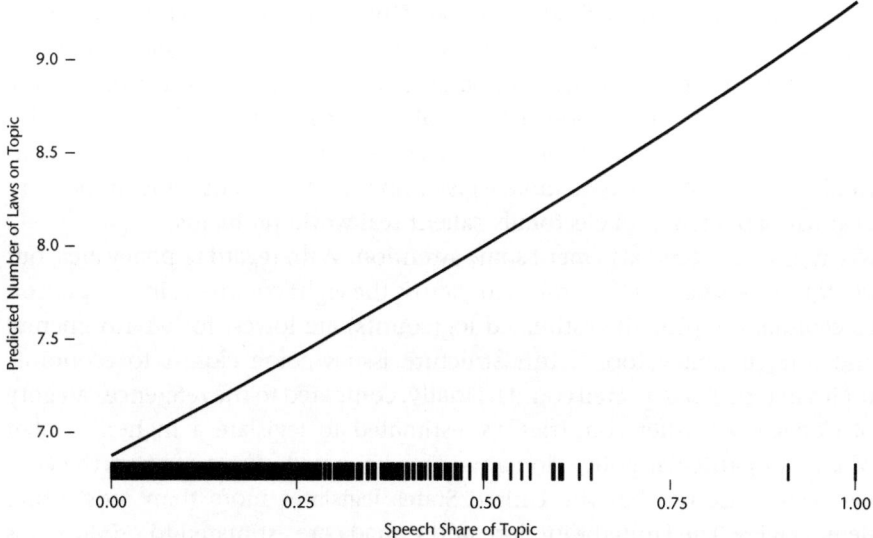

Figure 30.2. Predicted number of laws on a topic (full-count model)
Source: Comparative Agendas Project

In addition to government speeches, the theoretical section put forward that two sets of institutions—government type and the electoral disproportionality—influence the content of policy agendas. We proposed that more centralized power would lead to more legislative activity. In particular, out of the institutionalist literature emerged the notion that single-party governments should pass more legislation than minority and/or coalition governments. However, our estimation suggests that government type has no statistically significant relationship with law counts once we include country and topic fixed effects. We also considered the influence of the electoral system and argued that electoral systems that lead to more fragmented governing stymies legislative activity. Our estimates are inconclusive here. In both models, the estimates are statistically significant, but the sign of the coefficient changes once we include country and topic fixed effects. In Model 3, the expected change in the log(count) for a one-unit increase in disproportionality is 0.03. This estimation suggests that more disproportional electoral systems produce more laws, which runs counter to our proposed hypothesis.

For the remaining hypotheses, the following results stand out. First, conservative governments are more active in passing laws then left governments. This estimate is statistically significant but relatively small in size. Again, this estimate is contrary to our expectation. It remains challenging to develop an argument why the ideological composition of government per se should affect legislative activity. Second, the electoral cycle hypothesis cannot be rejected. Governments pass more legislation in pre-election times. In the last three months before an election the expected log(count) is 0.54 higher than at other moments of the legislative period. This might be the case because they want to push through remaining issues on their legislative agenda or showcase their ability to govern when campaign season starts. Third, for the misery index—i.e., the combination of unemployment rate and inflation—we also find a positive and statistically significant effect. When the economy is in trouble, government passes more legislation across different topics in order to deal with apparent and electorally salient real world problems.

The "fixed effects" also merit some attention. With regard to policy area, our descriptive assessment is confirmed. Across the eight countries, in comparison to economic topics, the estimated log(counts) are lowest for environmental and foreign policy topics. Infrastructure issues come closest to economic topics in terms of expected counts. Finally, compared to the reference category of Canada, all other countries are estimated to legislate a higher number of laws in particular policy domains. The estimated effects confirm the conventional wisdom that the United States legislates more than most other democracies. The United Kingdom and Canada are estimated to produce less topic-specific legislation. These estimates go well with the arguments put forward in Baumgartner et al. (2009), which suggest that some countries are more likely to engage with policy problems more incrementally then others. Overall, the statistically significant effects of the topic and country dummies suggest that legislative production depends to a substantial part on issue area and national peculiarities that are not captured in our model so far echoing the work of Matt Grossmann (2013) on issue-area differences in policymaking in the United States.

Finally, we offer some sense of how substantive the estimates effects for each covariate is vis-à-vis each other. Figure 30.3 displays the changes in predicted counts based on Model 3. For continuous variables, we use the minimum and maximum value for predictions and for nominal variables, we display the factor with the smallest and largest prediction. For speeches, the first difference is close to five; when there is no speech on a topic, on average, eight laws are passed, but when a speech is on a single topic nearly thirteen laws are passed on that issue. The change in the number of predicted laws on a topic increases from about seven for an extreme left to an predicted number of eleven laws for an extreme right government. The figure also shows that government passed more laws in times of economic turmoil (circa 15 vs 8 in the best times). Similar predicted counts are obtained for disproportionality. Government type did not produce statistically different estimates and the substantive difference between the least and most active government type is also fairly small. Finally, topic and country effects are huge, highlighting again that legislative activity varies substantively by issues area and institutional differences, beyond government type and electoral system.

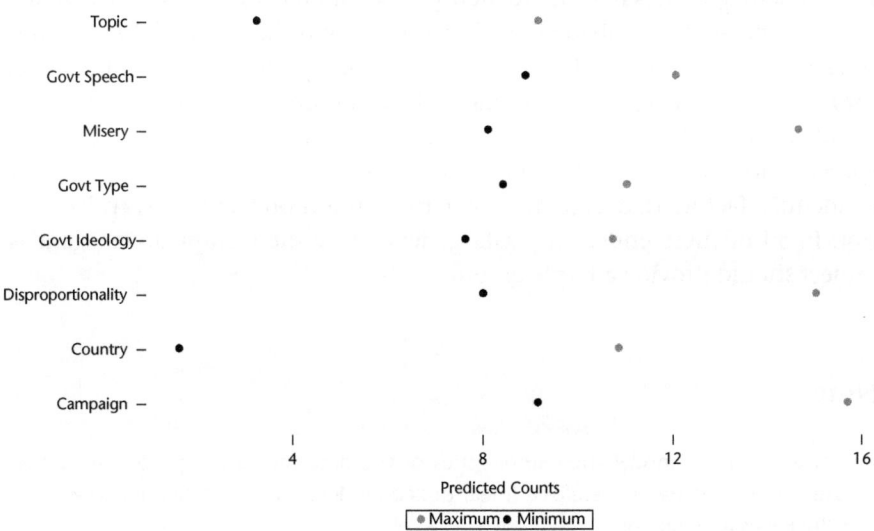

Figure 30.3. Predicted number of laws on a topic (mean values)
Source: Comparative Agendas Project

30.5 Conclusion

The exploratory analysis in this chapter delivered some important insights and opened new perspectives for the research on the pledge–policy outcome link. We extended previous work in comparative politics on the linkage between party programs and government action. In contrast to previous work, we argued that government speeches provide a tighter and more appropriate link between government promises and their legislative capacities because government speeches occur in short time periods and thereby enable government to readjust their work program given the multiple of political, social, and economic changes. Our regression results highlight that introducing a political topic during a government speech substantively impacts the number of laws voted in this policy domain. Government announcements on economic issues even turned out to have a stronger influence on the number of economic laws than the effect of the actual economic situation of the country. Our longitudinal and cross-national approach thereby clearly illustrated that government speeches are a useful precursor for legislative capacity. As the work of the executive is not limited to law-making activities, further research should extend these analyses to other types of government activities such as the conclusion of treaties, decrees, troop deployment, budgetary measures, and so on.

The chapter raises additional questions for future research. In particular, it would be interesting to compare party manifestos of governing parties and government speeches in order to identify the differences and overlaps. While the identification of individual pledges was beyond the scope of this chapter, tracking pledges through the policy process could provide important insights into the dynamics of pledge fulfillment. Another promising research direction could consist in looking into the interaction of the announcement effect of speeches and political, institutional, and economic control variables in order to identify factors that determine whether an announcement is realized or not. In all of these endeavors, data generated by the Comparative Agendas Project should provide a fertile ground.

Note

1. Another way to model the complexities of the data-generating process would be using a zero-inflated generalized linear mixed model for count data (ZIGLMMs) or a fully Bayesian strategy.

References

Agresti, A. (2013). *Categorical Data Analysis*. 3rd ed. Hoboken: Wiley & Sons.

Baumgartner, F. R. et al. (2009). Punctuated Equilibrium in Comparative Perspective. *American Journal of Political Science*, 53(3): 603–20.

Bertelli, A. M., and John, P. (2013). Public Policy Investment: Risk and Return in British Politics. *British Journal of Political Science*, 43(4): 741–73.

Blais, A., Blake, D., and Dion, S. 1993. Do Parties Make a Difference? Parties and the Size of Government in Liberal Democracies. *American Journal of Political Science*, 37(1): 40–62.

Blais, A., and Nadeau, R. (1992). The Electoral Budget Cycle. *Public Choice*, 74(4): 389–403.

Breeman, G. et al. (2009). Political Attention in a Coalition System: Analyzing Queen's Speeches in the Netherlands 1945–2007. *Acta Politica*, 44(1): 1–27.

Brouard, S. et al. (2009). Comparer les productions législatives : enjeux et méthodes. *Revue internationale de politique comparée*, 16(3): 381–404.

Calvo, E. (2014). *Legislator Success in Fragmented Congresses in Argentina: Plurality Cartels, Minority Presidents, and Lawmaking*. Cambridge: Cambridge University Press.

Cameron, D. R. (1978). The Expansion of the Public Economy: A Comparative Analysis. *American Political Science Review*, 72(04): 1243–61.

Carey, J. M. (2008). *Legislative Voting and Accountability*. Cambridge: Cambridge University Press.

Chaqués-Bonafont, L., Palau, A. M., and Baumgartner, F. R. (2015). *Agenda Dynamics in Spain*. Basingstoke: Palgrave Macmillan.

Cusack, T. R., and Engelhardt, L. (2002). The PGL File Collection: File Structures and Procedures. *Wissenschaftszentrum Berlin für Sozialforschung*. Working paper. https://www.wzb.eu/www2000/bal/usi/leute/cusack/pdf/pgl_structures_and_procederes_ce.pdf.

Duverger, M. (1954). *Political Parties: Their Organization and Activity in the Modern State*. London: Methuen.

Franzese, R. (2002). Electoral and Partisan Cycles in Economic Policies and Outcomes. *Annual Review of Political Science*, 5: 369–421.

Gallagher, M. (1991). Proportionality, Disproportionality and Electoral Systems. *Electoral Studies*, 10(1): 33–51.

Grossmann, M. 2013. The Variable Politics of the Policy Process: Issue-Area Differences and Comparative Networks. *The Journal of Politics*, 75(1): 65–79.

Hobolt, S. B., and Klemmensen, R. (2008). Government Responsiveness and Political Competition in Comparative Perspective. *Comparative Political Studies*, 41(3): 309–37.

Hofferbert, R. I., and Budge, I. (1992). The Party Mandate and the Westminster Model: Election Programmes and Government Spending in Britain, 1948–85. *British Journal of Political Science*, 22(2): 151–82.

Jennings, W., Bevan, S., and John, P. (2011). The Agenda of British Government: The Speech from the Throne, 1911–2008. *Political Studies*, 59: 74–98.

John, P., and Jennings, W. (2010). Punctuations and Turning Points in British Politics? The Policy Agenda of the Queen's Speech, 1940–2005. *British Journal of Political Science*, 40(3): 561–86.

Klingemann, H.-D. et al. (1994). *Parties, Policy and Democracy*. Boulder: Westview Press.

Lijphart, A. (1999). *Patterns of Democracy: Government Forms and Performance in Thirty-Six Countries*. New Haven: Yale University Press.

Lizzeri, A., and Persico, N. (2001). Provision of Public Projects under Alternative Electoral Incentives. *American Economic Review*, 91: 225–39.

Lovett, J., Bevan, S., and Baumgartner, F. R. (2015). Popular Presidents Can Affect Congressional Attention, for a Little While. *Policy Studies Journal*, 43(1): 22–43.

Mansergh, L., and Thomson, R. (2007). Election Pledges, Party Competition and Policymaking. *Comparative Politics*, 39(3): 311–29.

Martin, L., and Vanberg, G. (2011). *Parliaments and Coalitions: The Role of Legislative Institutions in Multiparty Governance*. Oxford: Oxford University Press.

Mortensen, P. B. et al. (2011). Comparing Government Agendas Executive Speeches in the Netherlands, United Kingdom, and Denmark. *Comparative Political Studies*, 44(8): 973–1000.

Müller, W. C., and Strom, K. (2003). *Coalition Governments in Western Europe*. Oxford: Oxford University Press.

Naurin, E. (2011). *Election Promises, Party Behaviour and Voter Perceptions*. Basingstoke: Palgrave Macmillan.

Nordhaus, W. D. (1975). The Political Business Cycle. *Review of Economic Studies*, 42(2): 169–90.

Powell, Jr., Bingham, G., and Whitten, G. D. (1993). A Cross-National Analysis of Economic Voting: Taking Account of the Political Context. *American Journal of Political Science*, 37(2): 391–414.

Reynolds, A., Reilly, B., and Andrew, E. (2005). *Electoral System Design: The New International IDEA Handbook*. Stockholm: International IDEA.

Rogoff, K., and Sibert, A. (1988). Elections and Macroeconomic Policy Cycles. *The Review of Economic Studies*, 55(1): 1–16.

Royed, T. (1996). Testing the Mandate Model in Britain and the United States: Evidence from the Reagan and Thatcher Eras. *British Journal of Political Science*, 26: 45–80.

Soroka, S., and Wlezien, C. (2010). *Degrees of Democracy : Politics, Public Opinion, and Policy*. New York: Cambridge University Press.

Strom, K. (1990). *Minority Government and Majority Rule*. Cambridge: Cambridge University Press.

Thomson, R. (2001). The Programme-to-Policy Linkage: The Fulfilment of Election Pledges on Socio-Economic Policy in the Netherlands, 1986–1998. *European Journal of Political Research*, 40(2): 171–97.

Thomson, R., Royed, T., Naurin, E. et al. (2012). The Program-to-Policy-Linkage: A Comparative Study of Election Pledges and Government Policies in Ten Countries.

Timmermans, A. (2006). Standing Apart and Sitting Together: Enforcing Coalition Agreements in Multiparty Systems. *European Journal of Political Research*, 45: 263–83.

Tsebelis, G. (2002). *Veto Players: How Political Institutions Work*. Princeton: Princeton University Press.

Zubek, R., and Klüver, H. (2015). Legislative Pledges and Coalition Government. *Party Politics*, 21: 603–14.

Zuur, A. F. (2009). *Mixed Effects Models and Extensions in Ecology with R*. New York: Springer.

31

The Europeanization of Parliamentary Attention in and out of the European Union

France, Spain, the Netherlands, and Switzerland Compared

Pascal Sciarini, Frédéric Varone, Roy Gava, Sylvain Brouard,
Julien Navarro, Anna M. Palau, and Rens Vliegenthart

31.1 Introduction

This chapter highlights the usefulness of Comparative Agenda Project data to study the Europeanization of parliamentary attention. Initially, the literature in the field has focused on the institutional and organizational responses to the challenges raised by European integration for national parliaments (Maurer and Wessels, 2005; Raunio and Hix, 2000; Raunio, 2009, 2005; Saafeld, 2005; Goetz and Meyer-Sahling, 2008; Auel et al., 2015b, 2015a; Finke and Herbel, 2015). More recently, scholars have started to look at the attitudinal and behavioral dimension, i.e., at what national members of parliaments (MPs) actually do in EU affairs. We join this literature and examine how and to what extent Europe is politicized in national parliaments. To answer this question, we rely on a longitudinal and comparative analysis of the Europeanization of parliamentary questions (PQs).

Our contribution is twofold. First, our chapter puts the findings of recent country studies on the Europeanization of PQs (Gava et al., 2017; Navarro and Brouard, 2014; Palau, 2012; Senninger, 2017) to a comparative test across four countries: Three EU member states (France, Spain, and the Netherlands) and a country that is not member of the EU but strongly influenced by it (Switzerland). In addition, the selection of countries includes cases with and without strong Eurosceptic parties, which are said to contribute to the politicization of EU affairs in domestic politics. Second, we adopt a policy agenda perspective and analyze the distribution of MPs' attention on Europeanized policy issues, in comparison with domestic issues. We share the view that the amount of attention that political actors can devote to various policy issues is not unlimited. While this arguably holds especially so on EU-related issues, information about the policy issues that are addressed by national parliaments in their control activities about the European Union is still surprisingly scarce.

Section 31.2 presents the broader context of the study, which pertains to the Europeanization of parliamentary activities, and Section 31.3 the data and the coding. Based on that we then study variations in the Europeanization of PQs over time, across countries, and across issues. We formulate expectations and we test them with descriptive statistics on a rich collection of data covering two to three decades depending on the country, and including thousands of PQs. The concluding section summarizes the main findings and highlights their broader implications.

31.2 The Europeanization of Parliamentary Activities

In most Western democracies, there has been a shift in the balance of power between the government and the parliament with respect to legislation (Baldwin, 2004). The government initiates most laws (Strom et al., 2003) and dominates the legislative process more generally. As a result, the role of parliament has changed, and its control function, scrutinizing government actions, has become a crucial aspect of parliamentary activities (Green-Pedersen, 2010; Vliegenthart and Walgrave, 2011). These changes hold even more true in Europeanized decision-making processes that are said to strengthen the government (Moravcsik, 1994) and to lead to "de-parliamentarization" (Goetz and Meyer-Sahling, 2008). However, parliaments have "fought back" and several institutional reforms have been implemented to achieve a better balance between the executive and legislative branches (Auel and Christiansen, 2015; Raunio, 2009; Winzen, 2013). National parliaments have obtained new opportunities for participation in EU-related affairs, new information rights, and extended oversight powers, in particular through their European Affairs Committees (EAC).

Accordingly, most authors have focused on these institutional innovations. For instance, Auel et al. (2015a, 2015b) have developed an index that captures the institutional strength of national parliaments in EU affairs. Their so-called OPAL score combines eleven indicators organized

318

along three dimensions: access to relevant and timely information about Europeanized policymaking processes, parliamentary infrastructure such as the role of EACs, and MPs oversight and influence rights. According to the OPAL score, among the three EU member states included in our study, the Netherlands has a strong national parliament in EU affairs, Spain has a weak parliament and France falls somewhere in-between (Auel and Christiansen, 2015). This international comparison is based on formal rules enabling MPs to scrutinize Europeanized policymaking processes, but not on the effective MPs scrutiny activities per se.

Furthermore, while EU scrutiny in EACs is an important part of democratic accountability in EU affairs, it nevertheless comes with some severe constraints (Senninger, 2017): Access to the EACs is limited to small groups of MPs, and the agenda of EACs is limited by the European Union's legislative agenda, which prevents MPs from adding issues to the agenda. In sum, we argue that formal scrutiny rules, parliamentary infrastructures and EACs activities do not reflect the whole spectrum of MPs strategies to exert their control on EU affairs led by the government, and to bring new Europeanized issues on the political agenda.

Indeed, MPs can also resort to the more classical toolkit of agenda-setting and scrutiny instruments to address EU-related policy issues. Asking questions to specific ministers or the cabinet as a whole is "the main instance of parliamentary control" (Vliegenthart and Walgrave, 2011). Further to their control function, PQs also serve as information gathering and communication channels towards political parties, the media, and the public (Bailer, 2011). MPs may use PQs to voice the preferences of their electoral constituencies or interest groups, to draw attention to specific topics and to develop a competence reputation on these topics. Finally, it is worth noting that individual PQs, unlike EAC activities, have no limitations in terms of issue agenda. MPs can ask questions on whatever EU-related issues they wish to address. This, in turn, allows for the analysis of which EU-related issues MPs do actually address in their day-to-day scrutiny work, and for comparing the allocation of attention to policy issues in domestic versus Europeanized PQs.

In sum, we claim that PQs that MPs introduce to put EU-related issues on the parliamentary agenda help to assess the degree of Europeanization of parliamentary attention. Section 31.3 presents the empirical setting and how we have applied the classification scheme developed in the Comparative Agendas Project to code PQs in the four countries under study. We then investigate how the share of Europeanized PQs has evolved over time in the four countries, whether the EU integration process and Eurosceptic parties have contributed to the Europeanization of parliamentary attention and, finally, whether PQs on Europeanized issues cover a small or a broad range of policy domains. This will eventually help us to assess whether some sort of "re-parliamentarization" is at work with respect to parliamentary scrutiny.

31.3 Coding of Parliamentary Questions (PQs)

Our dataset comprises PQs asked by MPs in France, the Netherlands, Spain, and Switzerland and covers two to three decades. We coded different types of PQs that can all serve as control activities with which the parliament monitors what the government is doing or not doing, or as information devices that MPs can use to communicate with their constituencies and the broader public. Research periods and types of questions differ somewhat across countries, depending on national institutional rules and data availability: For France our dataset includes oral questions to the government from 1988 to 2007; for Spain oral questions from 1986 to 2013; for the Netherlands written questions from 1995 to 2011; and for Switzerland written questions and interpellations from 1983 to 2013. Although the research periods are not identical, this should have limited effects on the results, given the simple descriptive statistics on which we rely. Similarly, procedures to ask PQs differ across countries, but in all four countries there is some kind of limitation to the number of questions that MPs can ask. The total number of questions varies from about 11,000 in France to 36,000 in the Netherlands (see Table 31.A.1 in the Appendix).

To identify whether a PQ is Europeanized or remains purely domestic, we relied on a computer-based keywords search in the question's full text. The list of EU-related keywords comes from the cross-national "Delors' Myth project" (Brouard et al., 2012b) and the terms include: European Union, European Community, European Economic Community, Common Market, Single Market, European Market, European Coal and Steel Community, European Atomic Energy Community, European Monetary Union and European Monetary System, European Directive, Community law, European law, and its acronyms.

To code the issue topic we have applied the coding scheme developed in the Comparative Agendas Project,[1] whereby we focus here on the twenty main issue topics. In France and Spain, the issue topic was coded for all domestic and Europeanized PQs, based on manual coding (Spain) or on a mix of manual and semi-automatic coding (France). In the Netherlands and Switzerland, a different approach was used: The issue topic was coded by hand for all Europeanized PQs, and for a subset of domestic PQs (all PQs for the years 1995–2003 in Switzerland, and a random sample of 500 questions per parliamentary year, i.e., roughly 30 percent of the total number of questions, in the Netherlands).

31.4 The Scope and Triggers of Europeanized Questions

31.4.1 *Evolution over Time and across Countries*

We first look at the evolution of Europeanization over time. The conventional wisdom is that each new step in the process of European integration increases the attention dedicated by national MPs to EU affairs. Two factors jointly contribute to this dynamic. First, the successive reforms of EU treaties (Single European Act in 1986, Maastricht in 1992, Amsterdam in 1997, Nice in 2001, and Lisbon in 2007) have redefined the overall architecture, balance of power, and policymaking competencies of EU institutions. National ratification processes of EU treaties reforms and, even more so, the resulting deepening of the European Union (expansion of authority to new policy areas and increased importance of EU political decision-making compared to domestic politics, (Börzel, 2005; Pollack, 1994)) have presumably fostered parliamentary attention to Europeanized issues. We may expect that the Europeanization of PQs has increased over time.

This expectation also applies to Switzerland, which has reached a situation of "customized quasi-membership" in the European Union (Kriesi and Trechsel, 2008). During the 1990s and 2000s, Switzerland and the European Union have concluded more than fifteen bilateral agreements in various fields (Afonso and Maggetti, 2007; Dupont and Sciarini, 2001; Dupont and Sciarini, 2007). In addition, Switzerland has unilaterally adapted to EU rules (Fischer and Sciarini, 2014; Gava et al., 2014; Sciarini et al., 2004; Sciarini, 2014). This said, the scope of EU influence remains (far) lower in Switzerland than in EU member states. Therefore, the share of Europeanized questions is likely to be lower in that country.

As a first step, we calculate the overall share of Europeanized PQs in the four countries during the 1995–2007 period. The degree of Europeanization of PQs ranges between 7.3 percent in France, 7.6 percent in Spain, 8.3 percent in the Netherlands and 8.5 percent in Switzerland. The overall share of EU-related PQs is thus similar across countries, and it is rather low. In any case, it is lower than the degree of Europeanization of legislative acts: In their comparative study of eight countries, Brouard and colleagues (2012b; König and Mäder, 2012) found that between 1988 and 2007 the average degree of Europeanization of legislation amounted to 14 percent in France (Brouard et al., 2012a), to 12 percent in the Netherlands (Breeman and Timmermans, 2012), and up to 35 percent in Spain (Palau and Chaqués, 2012). The corresponding figure was comparatively far lower in Switzerland (6 percent) (Gava and Varone, 2012). The weak share of EU-related questions in national parliaments is compatible with Auel et al.'s (2015b: 286) statement that "parliaments that spend long hours scrutinizing EU affairs in the EAC are not systematically as active when it comes to debating EU issues in the plenary."

Figure 31.1 shows the evolution of the share of Europeanized PQs over time in the four countries. Unlike expected, one does not see any increase in Europeanization. In the three EU member-states, the share of questions dealing with EU affairs fluctuates from one year to the next, but the overall picture is that of stagnation. In Switzerland, there was a sudden increase in attention to EU matters at the beginning of the 1990s, but the share of Europeanized PQs has since then stabilized on a moderate level. In fact, European integration remained a non-issue in the Swiss parliament until the late 1980s, i.e., up until the 1992 Single Market project (Sciarini, 1991).

Thus, the deepening of the European integration process has not resulted in an increase of parliamentary attention for EU-related issues over time. Alternatively, we may assume that MPs' attention to EU-related issues varies as a function of the stops-and-go of the integration process and/or as a function of the electoral cycle on the EU level (Chaqués-Bonafont et al., 2015; Boomgarden et al., 2010; Guinaudeau and Palau, 2016). If this holds, then one should witness an upsurge of Europeanized questions in years with a treaty reform, when European elections are looming, or when a member state holds the Council presidency.

Figure 31.1 provides some support for this view, and more especially for the important role played by treaty reforms and EU presidencies. In France, the first (and major) peak in attention took place in 1992 with the Maastricht

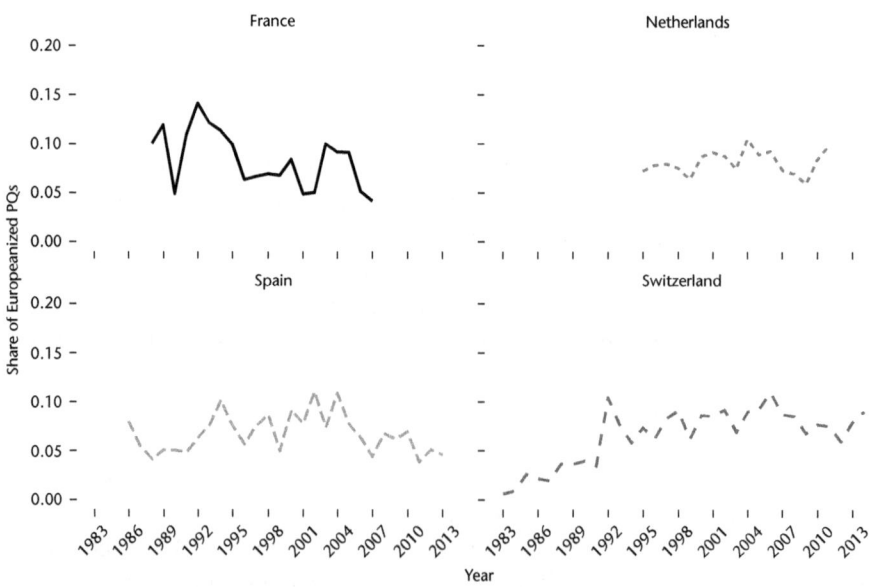

Figure 31.1. Share of Europeanized parliamentary questions
Source: Comparative Agendas Project

Treaty and related ratification referendum, a second—less marked—peak occurred in 2000 with the French presidency and the Nice summit, and a third in 2003–5 with the negotiation and ratification of the European Constitution (see also Navarro and Brouard, 2012: 102–3). While fluctuations in attention have been of a lower magnitude in Spain, we nevertheless see some peaks of attention in relation to the occurrence of relevant EU events, such as the Spanish Council presidency in 1995 and 2002 (which was also the year of the introduction of the euro currency), and the negotiation of the European Constitution in 2004—see also Chaqués-Bonafont et al., (2015). In the Netherlands, the share of Europeanized questions also reached a high at the time of negotiation and ratification of the European Constitution. Finally, in Switzerland, parliamentary attention first peaked in 1992, the year when the agreement on the European Economic Area was signed and submitted to popular ratification, and again in 2005–6, in the context of three direct democratic votes on bilateral agreements concluded with the European Union.[2]

Coming back to the differences across countries, contrary to expectations the Europeanization of PQs is not lower in Switzerland than in EU member states. This surprising result suggests that EU membership is not a decisive factor in accounting for the degree of Europeanization of MPs attention. Both the low level of Europeanization of PQs in the four countries and the comparatively higher level of Europeanization of PQs in Switzerland are compatible with the salience of EU-related issues in the media coverage of election campaigns in six European countries (Kriesi, 2007). According to this study, in the 1990s issues relating to European integration made up less than 7 percent of all issue-related statements in electoral campaigns, in these six countries. In addition, the increase of salience of EU-related issues between the 1970s and 1990s has been most substantial in the two most Eurosceptic countries included in Kriesi's (2007) study, namely Switzerland and the United Kingdom.

Turning to partisan politics, studies seeking to explain the salience of European integration in the electoral arena emphasize the proactive role of Eurosceptic parties (de Vries, 2007). Similarly, according to Kriesi and colleagues (2006, 2008) European integration is a crucial component of the new globalization cleavage introduced and/or articulated by radical right parties. Accordingly, it has been argued that MPs from Eurosceptic parties are more prone to Europeanize the parliamentary agenda. So doing, they are able to demarcate themselves from other (governmental or opposition) parties and to follow a promising vote-seeking strategy. This argument resonates with the argument of the issue ownership literature (Petrocik, 1996) that parties emphasize those issues on which they are seen as more active and competent than their rivals in their electoral manifestos and/or in their parliamentary interventions.

Scholars looking more specifically at the parliamentary scrutiny of EU issues have also stressed the role of political contestation over European integration, in particular from Eurosceptic parties, for the intensity of parliamentary control in EU affairs (e.g., Holzacker, 2002, 2005; Senninger, 2017). Therefore, we may expect that MPs from Eurosceptic parties introduce a higher share of Europeanized questions than MPs from other parties. The main Eurosceptic parties under consideration are the National Front in France, the Freedom Party in the Netherlands and the People's Party in Switzerland—there was no true anti-EU party with parliamentary representation in Spain during the period under study (Rodríguez-Aguilera de Prat, 2013).[3]

The results (not reported here) are mixed. In France and Switzerland, the share of Europeanized questions has, as expected, been higher among Eurosceptic parties than among non-Eurosceptic parties since the early 2000s. However, the opposite pattern prevails in the Netherlands, where the share of EU-related questions is smaller among anti-EU parties than among mainstream parties. The latter result suggests that Eurosceptic parties are prone to politicize European integration, but not everywhere.

31.4.2 *Issue Attention*

We now turn to the analysis of the Europeanization of PQs from a policy agenda perspective (Jones and Baumgartner, 2005). In order to better understand how parliaments work, we need to delve into the policy issues MPs deal with in their daily activities (Vliegenthart and Walgrave, 2011). The amount of attention that MPs can devote to various policy problems (e.g., macroeconomy, defense, public health, environment, etc.) is not unlimited. Their resources are scarce (i.e., limited expertise) and the parliamentary agenda is not expandable (i.e., fixed question time). MPs have to set priorities and their questions can only address a few policy issues. This holds true for both Europeanized and non-Europeanized policymaking processes. However, whereas domestic policies may potentially concern all issues, the formal EU competencies and related legislations do not cover the full range of policy domains (e.g., there is no EU policy on pensions). In addition, lots of EU directives fall under the regulatory responsibility of the executive and are thus transposed in domestic law through secondary legislation, such as governmental decrees (Grossman and Sauger, 2007; Gava and Varone, 2014). Similarly, and as already mentioned, EACs may play an important role as institutional gatekeeper of the parliamentary agenda on EU-related issues and control for the range of policy issues discussed in plenary sessions. Therefore, we expect that issue concentration of PQs is higher on EU-related (or "Europeanized") issues than on non-EU related domestic policies. Turning to the temporal perspective, with the deepening of European integration, new issue topics are put on the EU agenda of national parliaments. Accordingly, the issue dispersion of Europeanized questions has presumably increased over time.

To assess the degree of issue dispersion on Europeanized issues and on domestic issues we calculate Shannon's H, a measure of information entropy (Jennings et al., 2011). As our study is based on twenty policy topics codes, entropy scores may range from 0 to the natural log of 20 (2.997). Lower entropy scores indicate that attention is concentrated on a few policy issues and higher scores that attention is more equally distributed across issues. We calculate the entropy score for the six sub-periods mentioned above. Figure 31.2 supports the intuition that issue concentration is higher for PQs dealing with EU affairs than for PQs on domestic issues. In all countries and for all available data periods the entropy score is higher for questions on non-Europeanized issues than for questions on Europeanized issues. In other words, issue attention is more evenly balanced between the twenty issue categories in the former case than in the latter Except in France, the difference in issue concentration is fairly substantial. The fact that European integration does not cover the full range of policy issues arguably explains this relatively high concentration of MPs' attention on EU-related matters. Note that issue concentration of Europeanized PQs is lower in Switzerland than in Spain and France, and not higher in Switzerland than in the Netherlands. To account for this result, one may point to the far-reaching scope of both Switzerland–EU bilateral agreements and Switzerland's unilateral adaptation

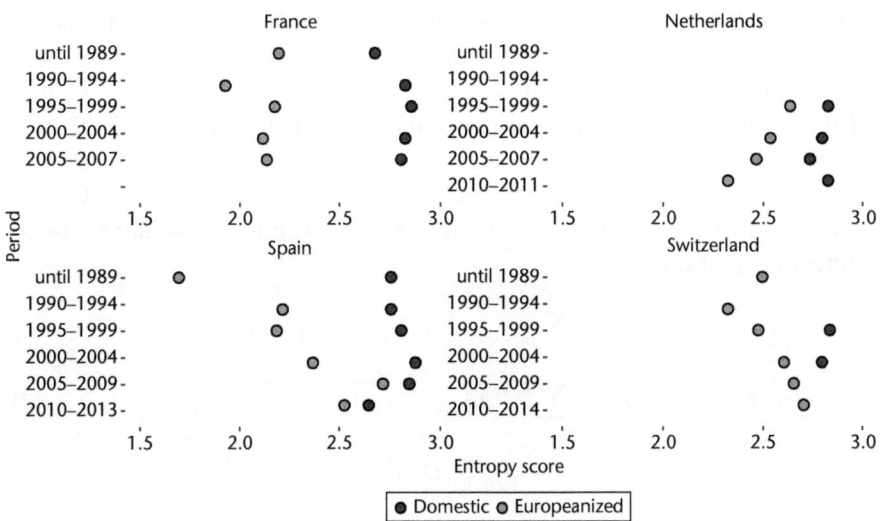

Figure 31.2. Issue concentration across countries and over time (entropy scores, Shannon's H)

Source: Comparative Agendas Project

to EU rules, and to the strong politicization of European integration in Swiss politics (Kriesi, 2007, Gava et al., 2014, Sciarini et al., 2015).

By contrast, Figure 31.2 does not support the expectation that issue concentration of PQs on Europeanized issues has reduced over time. A slight downward trend shows up only in Spain and, to some extent, in Switzerland. Pearson's correlation between the distribution of attention across policy domains on Europeanized questions between a given period and the subsequent period confirms this view: Correlations are overall high, which means that Europeanized issues that receive high (low) attention in a given period also receive high (low) attention in the subsequent period.[4] In other words, the agenda of Europeanized questions does not display any major punctuation, i.e., no surge of attention to new issue topics.[5] In spite of the successive extensions of EU authority to new policy areas over the last three decades, national MPs still tend to concentrate on the same policy issues.

Interestingly enough, Pearson's correlations between the Europeanized agendas of each pair of countries and for each of the three periods with available data (1995–9, 2000–4 and 2005–9) are high (Pearson's R from 0.51 to 0.84), which suggests that the distribution of issue attention is fairly similar across countries. The analysis of issue convergence between the countries' agendas, for the same three periods, tells a similar story (Table 31.1). The measure of issue convergence was first put forward by Sigelman and Buell (2004) in the US two–parties context, and adapted by Green-Pedersen and Mortensen (2009) to a multiparty system. We use it by analogy to assess the degree of convergence between the distributions of MPs' attention to Europeanized PQs in the four countries under study. For each country, we first calculate the average distribution of attention existing in the other three countries—for a given time period (see equation 1). Then, for each country we sum the numeric distance to the agenda of the three other countries (equation 2). Based on that, we finally calculate the issue overlap between countries (equation 3).

$$AA_{cj} = \sum_{i=1}^{n}(A_{c1\_i} + A_{c2\_i} + A_{c3\_i})/3 \qquad (1)$$

$$D_{cj} = \sum_{i=1}^{n}|AA_{cj\_i} - A_{cj\_i}| \qquad (2)$$

$$C_{j\_o} = 1 - \left(\sum_{i=1}^{n}D_{cj\_i}\right)/2 \qquad (3)$$

where n is the number of issue categories (n = 20); AA_{cj} denotes the average agenda for country j, calculated as the means of the agendas in the other three countries c_1, c_2 and c_3; D_{cj} is the difference between the agenda of country j and the average agenda in the other three countries; and C_{j_o} represents the

Table 31.1. Convergence in the distribution of issue attention on Europeanized PQs across countries

	1995–9	2000–4	2005–7
France	0.72	0.70	0.69
Spain	0.73	0.70	0.73
Netherlands	0.66	0.69	0.72
Switzerland	0.75	0.72	0.72

Source: Comparative Agendas Project

degree of issue overlap between country *j*'s agenda and that of the other three countries. So defined, convergence ranges from 0 (convergence is nil) and 100 (convergence is maximal). Table 31.1 presents the results.

Convergence amounts to about 70 percent, which is a fairly high degree, and it is also very stable across time. A closer look at the data shows that two issues tend to dominate PQs on Europeanized issues: International affairs and, to a lesser extent, agriculture. Attention devoted to international affairs (i.e., to issues relating to European integration policy in general) ranges from 21 percent of total MPs' attention in Spain and Switzerland, on average for the available years, to 26 percent in the Netherlands and up to 35 percent in France. Agriculture has attracted only 6 percent of parliamentary attention in the Netherlands and 10 percent in Switzerland, but up to 21 percent in France and 28 percent in Spain.

On the one hand, the strong concentration on international affairs suggests that MPs address EU matters mainly from the perspective of EU integration policy in general, rather than from the perspective of specific public policy issues, i.e., from the perspective of "about EU" policies rather than of "through the EU" policies (Hertner, 2015). This framing of PQs in general "EU policy" terms is arguably due to the strong power and information asymmetry that still exists in EU affairs between the executive and the legislative, and to the importance of secondary legislation to translate the (highly technical) EU regulations into domestic law.

On the other hand, the high overlap between the Europeanized parliamentary agendas across countries is presumably a sign of the importance of vertical Europeanization (Bulmer, 2007), and more specifically of the top-down influence of the European integration process on the distribution of MPs' attention on the national level. In that sense, the policy agenda addressed in PQs is very much influenced by the scope of EU authority, i.e., by the range of policy areas to which EU law applies, with agriculture being a case in point in that respect. Finally, it should be noted that the share of Europeanized questions on immigration-related issues has increased over time in both the Netherland and Switzerland, the two countries with the strongest Eurosceptic and anti-immigrant parties in the national parliament. No comparable trend is observable in France or Spain.

31.5 Conclusion

Relying on a rich collection of data we have analyzed whether and to what extent MPs in three EU member states and neighboring Switzerland use PQs to gather information on, to scrutinize government activities concerning, or to communicate to the public about EU affairs. Contrary to expectations, our data does not show an increase in the share of Europeanized PQs over time. In spite of the growing scope and extent of EU authority, national MPs do not address EU-related issues in their PQs in the 2000s more frequently than they did in the 1980s or 1990s. Similarly, we do not see the expected decrease in issue concentration over time on EU-related PQs. Finally, our results provide only partial support for the view that Eurosceptic parties proactively address EU-related issues as part of their vote-seeking strategy and, therefore, contribute to the politicization of EU integration. This holds to some extent in France and Switzerland, but not in the Netherlands.

Both the low share of Europeanized PQs and the high level of issue concentration of those questions tend to underscore the durable apathy and/or structural weakness of national MPs on EU matters. National MPs seem to be still mostly interested in domestic politics, and the "re-parliamentarization" trend observed in European policymaking does not seem to have spilled over to the specific instrument of PQs. Moreover, if they address EU affairs in their PQs, national MPs mainly ask questions about European policy in general, or they strongly focus on some specific issues such as agriculture, thus conforming to a top-down logic.

All in all, our results are thus not really good news with respect to the contribution of national parliaments to the democratic quality of the European integration process. In contrast to recent work arguing that national parliaments actually use the new procedural rules and organizational resources at their disposal to scrutinize European affairs (Auel et al., 2015b, 2015a; Finke and Herbel, 2015), we find that national MPs do not resort intensively to PQs to scrutinize government activities or to communicate with the public in EU-related affairs. This would of course be a necessary—but not sufficient—condition to improve their involvement in the European integration process and, therefore, to counter the so-called "democratic deficit."

That said, we wish to underline the illustrative and preliminary character of our results, which are based on four countries only. In future work we might attempt to extend the empirical scope of our study and to include additional EU member states. This would allow for a more robust test of cross-country differences in the degree of Europeanization across issues. The empirical data generated by the national partners of the Comparative Agendas Project offer a very rich basis to expand this line of comparative research, across policy issues, across political systems, and over time.

Appendix

Table 31.A.1. Country data

	Type of questions	Time period	No. of questions	No. of Europeanized questions	Coding of issue topic
F	Questions to the government	1988–2007	10,555	850	All domestic and Europeanized questions
NL	Written questions	1995–2011	38,068	3,040	All Europeanized questions and subset of domestic questions (sample 30 percent; N = 9,240)
SP	Oral questions	1986–2013	14,318	982	All domestic and Europeanized questions
CH	Written questions and interpellations	1983–2014	25,074	1,776	All Europeanized questions and subset of domestic questions (1999–2003; N = 7,182)

Source: Comparative Agendas Project

Notes

1. See http://www.comparativeagendas.net.
2. Switzerland's participation in the Schengen-Dublin agreement was submitted to voters' ratification in June 2005 (55 percent of yes votes), the extension of the agreement on the free movement of persons to the ten new EU member states in September 2005 (56 percent of yes votes), and Switzerland's financial contribution to the EU's Cohesion Fund in November 2006 (53 percent of yes vote).
3. To identify the Eurosceptic parties, we rely on the Chapel Hill expert survey. We code as Eurosceptic all parties that receive an average score of less than 4 on a scale ranging from 1 (strongly opposed to European integration) to 7 (strongly in favor), with 4 being the "neutral" category. Given that Switzerland has been included only very recently in the Chapel Hill expert survey we rely on our own assessment of the EU profile of Swiss political parties. While Swiss parties have all become less supportive of Switzerland's European integration in recent years, only a few parties have explicitly taken an anti-EU stance: the Greens did so at the beginning of the 1990s, the Swiss People's Party from the early 1990s on, and the small radical right parties (Swiss Democrats, Freedom Party, Lega dei Ticinesi) all along.
4. Pearson's coefficient (N = 20) ranges from 0.71 to 0.92 in Switzerland, from 0.83 to 0.96 in France, from 0.91 and 0.96 in the Netherlands and, if one excludes the most recent period, from 0.86 to 0.96 in Spain.

5. The only exception is Spain, where there was a surge of attention to macroeconomic and labor/social policy issues during the most recent period, in the context of the financial and economic crisis (see also Chaqués-Bonafont et al., 2015: 181).

References

Afonso, A., and Maggetti, M. (2007). Bilaterals II: Reaching the Limits of the Swiss Third Way? In *Switzerland and the European Union: A Close, Contradictory and Misunderstood Relationship*, ed. C. Church. London: Routledge, 215–33.

Auel, K., and Christiansen, T. (2015). After Lisbon: National Parliaments in the European Union. *West European Politics*, 38: 261–81.

Auel, K., Rozenberg, O., and Tacea, A. (2015a). Fighting back? And If Yes, How? Measuring Parliamentary Strength and Activitiy in EU Affairs. In *The Palgrave Handbook of National Parliaments and the European Union*, ed. C. Heffter, C. Neuhold, O. O. Rozenberg, and A. Tacea. Basingstoke: Palgrave Macmillan, 60–93.

Auel, K., Rozenberg, O., and Tacea, A. (2015b). To Scrutinise or Not to Scrutinise? Explaining Variation in EU-Related Activities in National Parliaments. *West European Politics*, 38: 282–304.

Bailer, S. (2011). People's Voice or Information Pool? The Role of, and Reasons for, Parliamentary Questions in the Swiss Parliament. *Journal of Legislative Studies*, 17: 302–14.

Baldwin, N. D. J. (2004). Concluding Observations: Legislative Weakness, Scrutinizing Strength? *Journal of Legislative Studies*, 10: 295–302.

Boomgarden, H., Vliegenthart, R., De Vreese, C. H., and Schuck, A. R. T. (2010). News on the Move: Exogenous Events and News Coverage of the European Union. *Journal of European Public Policy*, 17: 506–26.

Börzel, T. A. (2005). Mind the Gap! European Integration between Level and Scope. *Journal of Public Policy*, 18: 53–74.

Breeman, G., and Timmermans, A. (2012). Myths and Milestones: The Europeanization of the Legislative Agenda in the Netherlands. In *The Europeanization of Domestic Legislatures: The Empirical Implications of the Delors' Myth in Nine Countries*, ed. S. Brouard, O. Costa, and T. König. London: Springer, 151–72.

Brouard, S., Costa, O., and Kerrouche, E. (2012a). Are French Laws Written in Brussels? The Limited Europeanization of Law-Making in France and its Implications. In *The Europeanization of Domestic Legislatures: The Empirical Implications of the Delors' Myth in Nine Countries*, ed. S. Brouard, O. Costa, and T. König. London: Springer, 75–94.

Brouard, S., Costa, O., and König, T. (2012b). Delors' Myth: The Scope and Impact of the Europeanization of Law Production. In *The Europeanization of Domestic Legislatures: The Empirical Implications of the Delors' Myth in Nine Countries*, ed. S. Brouard, O. Costa, and T. König. London: Springer, 1–20.

Bulmer, S. (2007). Theorizing Europeanization. In *Europeanization: New Research Agendas*, ed. P. Graziano and M. P. Vink. London: Palgrave Macmillan, 46–58.

Chaqués-Bonafont, L., Palau, A. M., and Baumgartner, F. R. eds. (2015). *Agenda Dynamics in Spain*. Basingstoke: Palgrave Macmillan.

De Vries, C. (2007). Sleeping Giant: Fact or Fairytale? How European Integration Affects National Elections. *European Union Politics*, 8: 363–85.

Dupont, C., and Sciarini, P. (2001). Switzerland and the European Integration Process: Engagement without Marriage. *West European Politics*, 24: 211–32.

Dupont, C., and Sciarini, P. (2007). Back to the Future: The First Round of Bilateral Talks with the EU. In *Switzerland and the European Union: A Close, Contradictory and Misunderstood Relationship*, ed. C. Church. London: Routledge, 202–14.

Finke, D., and Herbel, A. (2015). Beyond Rules and Resources: Parliamentary Scrutiny of EU Policy Proposals. *European Union Politics*, 16: 490–513.

Fischer, M., and Sciarini, P. (2014). The Europeanization of Swiss Decision-Making Processes. *Swiss Political Science Review*, 20: 239–45.

Gava, R., Sciarini, P., and Varone, F. (2014). Twenty Years after the EEA Vote: The Europeanization of Swiss Policy-Making. *Swiss Political Science Review*, 20: 197–207.

Gava, R., Sciarini, P., and Varone, F. (2017). Who Europeanises Parliamentary Attention, on Which Issues and How? A Policy Agenda Perspective. *Journal of Legislative Studies*, 23: 566–93.

Gava, R., and Varone, F. (2012). So Close, Yet So Far? The EU's Footprint in Swiss Legislative Production. In *The Europeanization of Domestic Legislatures: The Empirical Implications of the Delors' Myth in Nine Countries*, ed. S. Brouard, O. Costa, and T. König. London: Springer, 197–222.

Gava, R., and Varone, F. (2014). The EU's Footprint in Swiss Policy Change: A Quantitative Assessment of Primary and Secondary Legislation (1999–2012). *Swiss Political Science Review*, 20: 216–22.

Goetz, K. H., and Meyer-Sahling, J.-H. (2008). The Europeanisation of National Political Systems: Parliaments and Executives. *Living Reviews in European Governance*, 3: 1–30.

Green-Pedersen, C. (2010). Bringing Parties into Parliament: The Development of Parliamentary Activities in Western Europe. *Party Politics*, 16: 347–69.

Green-Pedersen, C., and Mortensen, P. B. (2009). Issue Competition and Election Campaigns: Avoidance and Engagement, (unpublished paper), Aarhus University, Aarhus.

Grossman, E., and Sauger, N. (2007). Political Institutions under Stress? Assessing the Impact of European Integration on French Political Institutions. *Journal of European Public Policy*, 14: 1117–34.

Guinaudeau, I., and Palau, A. M. (2016). A Matter of Conflict: How Events and Parties Shape the News Coverage of EU Affairs. *European Union Politics*, 17: 593–615.

Hertner, I. (2015). Is It Always up to the Leadership? European Policy-Making in the Labour Party, Parti Socialiste (PS) and Sozialdemokratische Partei Deutschlands (SPD). *Party Politics*, 21: 470–80.

Holzacker, R. (2002). National Parliamentary Scrutiny over EU Issues: Comparing the Goals and Methods of Governing and Opposition Parties. *European Union Politics*, 3: 459–79.

Holzacker, R. (2005). The Power of Opposition Parliamentary Party Groups on European Scrutiny. *Journal of Legislative Studies*, 11: 428–45.

Jennings, W., Bevan, S., Timmermans, A. et al. (2011). Effects of the Core Functions of Government on the Diversity of Executive Agendas. *Comparative Political Studies*, 44: 1001–30.

Jones, B. D., and Baumgartner, F. R. (2005). *The Politics of Attention: How Government Prioritizes Problems*. Chicago: University of Chicago Press.

König, T., and Mäder, L. (2012). Going Beyond: Causes of Europeanization. In *The Europeanization of Domestic Legislatures: The Empirical Implications of the Delors' Myth in Nine Countries*, ed. S. Brouard, O. Costa, and T. König. London: Springer, 95–108.

Kriesi, H. (2007). The Role of European Integration in National Elections Campaigns. *European Union Politics*, 8: 83–108.

Kriesi, H., Grande, E., Lachat, R. et al. (2006). Globalization and the Transformation of the National Political Space: Six European Countries Compared. *European Journal of Political Research*, 45: 921–57.

Kriesi, H., Grande, E., Lachat, R. et al. (2008). *West European Politics in the Age Of Globalization*. Cambridge: Cambridge University Press.

Kriesi, H., and Trechsel, A. H. (2008). *The Politics of Switzerland: Continuity and Change in a Consensus Democracy*. Cambridge: Cambridge University Press.

Maurer, A., and Wessels, W. (2005). *National Parliaments on their Ways to Europe: Losers or Latecomers?* Baden-Baden: Nomos.

Moravcsik, A. (1994). Why the European Community Strengthens the State: Domestic Politics and International Cooperation. Working Paper No. 52, Center for European Studies, Harvard.

Navarro, J., and Brouard, S. (2014). Who Cares about the EU? French MPs and the Europeanisation of Parliamentary Questions. *Journal of Legislative Studies*, 20: 93–108.

Palau, A. M. (2012). Does Europe Matter? An Analysis of the Salience of EU Affairs in the Spanish Parliament (1986–2011). Annual Conference of the Comparative Agendas Project, 2012 Antwerp, June 27–29.

Palau, A. M., and Chaqués, L. (2012). The Europeanization of Law-Making in Spain. In *The Europeanization of Domestic Legislatures: The Empirical Implications of the Delors' Myth in Nine Countries*, ed. S. Brouard, O. Costa, and T. König. London: Springer, 173–96.

Petrocik, J. R. (1996). Issue Ownership in Presidential Elections, with a 1980 Case Study. *American Journal of Political Science*, 40: 825–50.

Pollack, M. A. (1994). Creeping Competence: The Expanding Agenda of the European Community. *Journal of European Public Policy*, 14: 95–145.

Raunio, T. (2005). Holding Governments Accountable in European Affairs: Explaining Cross-National Variation. *The Journal of Legislative Studies*, 11: 319–42.

Raunio, T. (2009). National Parliaments and European Integration: What We Know and Agenda for Future Research. *The Journal of Legislative Studies*, 15: 317–34.

Raunio, T., and Hix, S. (2000). Backenbechers Lear to Fight: European Integration and Parliamentary Government. *West European Politics*, 23: 142–68.

Rodríguez-Aguilera De Prat, C. (2013). *Euroscepticism, Europhobia and Eurocriticism. The Radical Parties of the Right and Left vis-à-vis the European Union*. Bruxelles: PIE-Peter Lang.

Saafeld, T. (2005). Deliberate Delegation or Abdication? Government Backbenchers, Ministers and European Union Legislation. *The Journal of Legislative Studies*, 11: 343–71.

Sciarini, P. (1991). Le role et la position de l'Assemblée fédérale dans les relations avec la Communauté européenne depuis 1972. In *Das Parlament—'Oberste Gewalt des Bundes'?* ed. Parlamentienste. Berne: Haupt, 403–23.

Sciarini, P. (2014). Eppure si muove: The Changing Nature of the Swiss Consensus Democracy. *Journal of European Public Policy*, 21: 116–32.

Sciarini, P., Fischer, A., and Nicolet, S. (2004). How Europe Hits Home: Evidence from the Swiss Case. *Journal of European Public Policy*, 11: 353–78.

Sciarini, P., Fischer, M., and Traber, D. eds. (2015). *Political Decision-Making in Switzerland: The Consensus Model under Pressure*. Basingstoke: Palgrave Macmillan.

Senninger, R. (2017). Issue Expansion and Selective Scrutiny—How Opposition Parties Used Parliamentary Questions about the European Union in the National Arena from 1973 to 2013. *European Union Politics*, 18: 283–306.

Sigelman, L., and Buell, E. H., Jr. (2004). Avoidance or Engagement? Issue Convergence in US Presidential Campaigns, 1960–2000. *American Journal of Political Science*, 48: 650–61.

Strom, K., Müller, W. C., and Bergman, T. eds. (2003). *Delegation and Accountability in Parliamentary Democracies*. Oxford: Oxford University Press.

Vliegenthart, R., and Walgrave, S. (2011). Content Matters: The Dynamics of Parliamentary Questioning in Belgium and Denmark. *Comparative Political Studies*, 44: 1031–59.

Winzen, T. (2013). European Integration and National Parliamentary Oversight Institutions. *European Union Politics*. 14: 297–323.

32

Horizontal and Vertical Attention Dynamics

Environmental Problems on Executive Policy Agendas in EU Member States

Gerard Breeman and Arco Timmermans

32.1 The Conditional Attention to Environmental Problems

In December 2015, the United Nations Climate Conference in Paris was organized to create a stronger commitment from countries to address the global warming problem. Political attention and policies were seen to lag behind the urgency of the problem. Almost twenty years earlier, in 1997, increasing awareness of the global warming problem made countries sign the international Kyoto Protocol, which came into force some eight years later and led former US-vice president Al Gore to produce the dramatic documentary *An Inconvenient Truth*. The venue change from executive office to cinema helped disseminate a sense of urgency towards the climate change problem. But despite the film's success and broad verbal support of its message, attention waned when the international economic crisis broke out in 2008. Against continuing warnings from international experts such as Nicolas Stern and organizations for environmental policy advice (Scruggs and Benegal, 2012), public and political attention to the economy overshadowed the climate change problem on the national and international agendas.

Similar attention waves for the environment occurred in earlier decades, as in 1972 when the Club of Rome warned with its "The Limits to Growth," and in 1987 when the Brundtland Report "Our Common Future" confronted publics and governments with new warnings about the economic–environmental trade-off (Beder, 2002). Governments in the late 1980s took up the environmental theme, to degrade it again to a lower priority some years later. Public and political attention to environmental problems is always conditional: it depends on what else becomes a matter of concern.

The environment is not unique in showing this pattern of rise and fall in attention and the expanding or narrowing problem definitions connected to it. Attention to other policy problems, such as unemployment, terrorism, and immigration, also rises and spreads, but then drops again to become the business of small communities of specialists and those with ongoing strong beliefs or interests in them (Schattschneider, 1960; Downs, 1972; Cobb and Elder, 1983; Baumgartner and Jones, 1993). Environmental attention has thus gone up and down for the past fifty years in most democracies. While in recent years environmental issues have come to be linked to energy questions to set a new and mobilizing policy agenda, in earlier times we saw attention cycles in which environmental problems were connected to agriculture, water, soil and air quality, and to industry and welfare. For some, environmental protection is a moral matter; for others, it is a luxury good that is related disproportionately to income.

Problems may have attributes that we consider "objective" (even in an era of alternative facts and allegations of fake news), but the sense of urgency around such problem characteristics and even their very recognition is constructed by actors in venues of public and political agenda-setting. Environmental experts everywhere can testify how scientific evidence may quickly become politicized (Weingart, 1999). Shifts in executive office show the pervasive impact of opportunistic problem construction on the top priorities of government. In venues of agenda-setting, attention to a particular problem is always relative to other topics that may attract more electoral support and enable government performance. Issues to be addressed by policymakers are in constant competition.

The idea that issues compete for space and priority on the political agenda has informed studies of agenda-setting. In the past ten years, this phenomenon of issue competition has become a central focus of the Comparative Agendas Project. Analysis of cycles of issue attention on public and political agendas has moved on from studies of national executives, legislatures, media, and so on, to supranational (European Union, see Princen, 2009; Daviter, 2011; Alexandrova et al., 2012) and international organizations (UN etc., see for example Lundgren et al., 2017), and also to subnational levels of governance (states, see Weissert and Uttermark, 2017); provinces (see Foucault and Montpetit, 2014); and municipalities (see Breeman et al., 2014; Mortensen, forthcoming). In all these institutional settings, issues compete with one another and the agenda may evolve from a limited to a broad scope that sets the space for new issues to enter, and then narrows again leading to some problems being sacrificed.

Less is known about the way attention for an issue or major topic travels up and down vertically, from one level of government to another. Such vertical traveling of attention may involve prioritization at different levels of government at similar points in time. Princen (2009), for example, has shown that for a time, attention to the environment in the institutions of the European Union (EU) ran parallel to how member state governments were addressing this theme. But it also may be that, instead of spilling over, attention enters one level of governance and leaves the other level. In such instances, multi-level agenda-setting may involve a substitution effect in the attention to issues. As political institutions at a level of governance develop and expand their policymaking jurisdictions, problem attention may flow with it. When policy-influencing actors monitor jurisdictional development, they may travel along with it and in this way further strengthen the shift in attention locus. If attention across topics is contingent, it also may be contingent between different levels of government.

Such forces of complimentary or substitutive attention in multilevel agenda-setting may not work equally across political systems, as countries differ in their domestic institutional and political structures and agenda-setting dynamics. The federal or unitary structure of a political system may provide a relevant difference, as may separation of powers between branches of government, the relevant number of political parties, the strength of parliamentarism, and the institutional setup of organized interest that may lead to an acceleration or slowing down of attention and policy change (Green-Pedersen and Wolfe, 2009; Timmermans, 2001). When in 2010, Belgium experienced the longest-ever government formation process worldwide (541 days), European Council president and former Belgian prime minister Herman van Rompuy said that "this episode of prolonged interim government with a minimal policy agenda in my home country is no obstacle to economic and monetary crisis management, as the institutions of the European Union are well placed to take care of it" (*Le Soir*, December 23, 2010). This was a rather optimistic estimate about the capacity of the European Union to reach consensus on economic and monetary policy, but it may illustrate the idea of contingency of agenda-setting and policymaking in multilevel governance, such as in the European Union and its member states.

In this contribution, we analyze multilevel agenda-setting on the environment in the European Union and four of its member states: Denmark, the Netherlands, Spain, and the United Kingdom.[1] We consider how within each of these countries attention to the environment has evolved since the early 1980s and how sensitive this topic has been to the nature of issue competition within the domestic policy agenda. We move from what we call horizontal attention dynamics to analyzing the vertical dimension of multilevel agenda-setting: whether attention to the environment on the national agenda has run parallel or was asynchronous to the pattern of attention to the environment in the European Union.

In this multilevel attention dynamic, three patterns may occur: the environment may have been up and down on the domestic and EU agenda in parallel; the national agenda may display earlier attention rises compared to the European Union; or the European Union may have been the forerunner in addressing environmental problems, with member states following. This analysis has an exploratory purpose to indicate directions of studying attention politics in a multilevel context.

The theory and empirical analysis presented here build on earlier work on attention dynamics and on environmental agenda-setting by Sheingate (2000, 2006), Baumgartner (2006), Knill and Liefferink (2007), Princen (2009), Green-Pedersen and Wolfe (2009), and Keskitalo et al. (2012). Our central question is: In what way has multilevel governance, with its similar or overlapping policy jurisdictions at different layers of government, had an effect on the rise and decline in attention to the environment? In focusing on the environment as a major topic, we also consider the more specific subtopics—issues—that may enter or leave the agenda over time. Further, as attention and problem definition are fundamentally constructed in the real world of political pushing and pulling, we include linkages of environmental issues to subjects that may formally belong to a different policy domain (energy, agriculture, etc.—see Appendix 32.1.A). We also consider how attention to the environment is in competition with another major topic, the economy. We do this because policy entrepreneurs in countries and in the European Union couple or decouple issues in order to mobilize attention towards or away from environmental matters. Our empirical data come from the country teams within the Comparative Agendas Project and the group analyzing policy agendas in the European Union, in particular the European Council, which is the supreme agenda-setting institution of the European Union (Foret and Rittelmeyer, 2013).[2]

In the next section we present our theoretical perspective on attention dynamics of issue competition and multilevel agenda-setting. Then we discuss our measurement and data, followed by the analysis of patterns since 1982 in the executive agendas of Denmark, the Netherlands, Spain, and the United Kingdom in relation to attention cycles on environmental issues on the agenda of the European Council. We end this contribution with our main conclusions, the possibilities and limits of generalization, and indicate how theoretical and empirical work on multilevel attention dynamics may be developed further.

32.2 Horizontal and Vertical Attention Dynamics

32.2.1 *Horizontal Attention Dynamics: Issue Competition*

In his early and often-cited theoretical model of (environmental) issue attention, Downs (1972) posited that attention patterns are cyclical. Writing in the early 1970s, he predicted that the rising prominence of ecology in public and political debates in the United States would be temporal and be followed by a decline. In Downs' issue attention cycle, a "pre-problem stage" is followed by a phase of discovery and political actors claiming they are able to solve the problem, and then a stage of fading enthusiasm as problems appear to be more intractable than expected and portrayed, and a public that becomes more concerned with other problems. Later in time, attention to the same problem then may recycle. While the bird's eye view of environmental attention in fifty years given in the introduction of this chapter may indeed exhibit such cycles, work done after Downs also led to a qualifier of his model: Public and political interest evolves in rises and falls, but environmental policy built up since some starting point produces a legacy—attention does not drop to as low as it was whenever it began (Guber, 2001). Also in other policy domains dealing with entirely different issues, political attention does not disappear and a degree of stability in policy production occurs after the initial build-up of institutions endowed with this task, for which Baumgartner and Jones introduced the concept of policy monopoly (Baumgartner and Jones, 1993; Baumgartner, Green-Pedersen, and Jones, 2006). Downs overstated the effects of opportunistic behavior by politicians in response to the public mood, and understated the significance of institutionalization of a policy domain and the constant generation of attention to problems within it.

The most ambitious and comprehensive approach to studying the process and content of agenda-setting following this early work is the theory of punctuated equilibrium, and the extensive empirical analysis on policy agendas developed by Jones and Baumgartner (2005). Typically, this work does not focus on single issues but considers the whole range of problems that governments face, and analyzes how different agendas constructed in the spheres of politics, the media, and the public are related. Agendas may expand and contract over time as issues are scheduled for attention or intrude unexpectedly. While initially this approach to policy agendas was limited to the United States, an international Comparative Agendas Project was launched in order to facilitate large-scale empirical analysis of political attention to problems over a long period of time (Baumgartner, Green-Pedersen, and Jones 2006). A central notion in this emerging work was (and still is) that issues are in constant competition for space on the agenda, and certainly for a top priority position. We call this phenomenon of issue competition horizontal attention dynamics, in which "horizontal" refers to the way in which agenda-setting at certain moments in time involves trading off between issues. The most drastic way this may happen is that one issue is neglected and the other receives full attention. Agenda capacity limits may enhance such competitive processes. At different points in time, cross sections of the same policy agenda will thus show varying levels of attention to issues, some of which may reach prominence, and others may be kept low or even left out.

Thus far, issue competition has been considered mostly for the entire policy agenda in political systems, with no focus on any specific issue placed in its competitive context within the agenda-setting venue. Jennings et al. (2011), for example, employ an entropy measure to analyze the diversity of the domestic policy agenda in European countries, and find that three core functions of government (measured at the main topic level) condition the space for other issues: running the economy, securing international relations, and maintaining or reforming government and administration. Likewise, Alexandrova et al. (2012) analyze the evolution of the political agenda of the European Council, the most prominent agenda-setting institution in the European Union. In these analyses, it appears that the varying distributions of attention to issues involves both a narrowing and a widening of the scope of the agenda.

Given the core functions of governments and the competitive nature of attention, attention to environmental issues is conditioned, and thus not only depends on the nature of environmental problems themselves, but also on the overall structure of political concerns of governments. This kind of horizontal, or cross-sectional, attention dynamic, may vary not only between types of policy agendas and venues within countries, but also between similar venues and policy agendas produced in them in different countries.

Venues have institutional properties conducive to the replication and aggregation of particular problem frames and they also have their own institutional properties that lead to more or less agenda capacity, inducing problem expansion and dramatization or narrowing the circle of participants and facilitating depoliticization. The media have different dynamics of attention and problem portrayal from legislative committees, and regulatory agencies with specific professional target groups differ in the way they address issues when presenting their policy priorities to the general public.

These differences in venues, and thus also in the policy agendas produced in them, have been studied systematically in the Comparative Agendas Project. Work produced in the last decade has shown that changes in agendas and in policies over time can indeed be better understood when venues and policy agendas are compared. Input agendas overall appear to involve lower levels of friction to change than output agendas, such as laws or budgets, which are costly to overhaul (Baumgartner et al., 2009).

32.2.2 *Vertical Attention Dynamics: Multilevel Agenda-Setting*

A comparative perspective thus can help our understanding of the working of venues and the dynamics of policy agendas between countries, for the agenda at large or for specific topics. But the dynamics of attention within a country may result not only from domestic issue competition or domestic venue change. It also may be influenced by venues and policy agendas outside the country, in particular at a level of governance that is linked institutionally (and legally) to it, such as the European Union in relation to its member states. This is the vertical dimension, which may involve formal hierarchy, but even if enforcement of attention "down" from above is not strict or weak, it may influence domestic attention. This is multilevel agenda-setting, which becomes more important as agenda-setting happens at different levels of governance with similar or overlapping jurisdictions for the same issue or topic.

Multilevel governance is described as "a system of continuous negotiation among nested governments at several territorial tiers—supranational, national, regional, and local" (Hooghe and Marks 2003: 234). This means that the boundaries between different levels of policymaking are blurred and different patterns of interaction and power games are played. It also means that member states lose part of their sovereignty and in this process lose some (or even much) of their capacity to set the policy agenda—they are no longer able to monopolize the domestic agenda on issues in the relevant policy domain (Braun and Santarius, 2008; Marks et al., 1996).

While in theory, multilevel governance is seen to influence agenda-setting dynamics at both the national and the EU level, empirical analysis of the interplay between levels of governance in the European Union is still scarce. Does the expansion of a policy jurisdiction at the EU level go with rises in attention at the national level (Princen, 2009; Princen and Rhinard, 2006)? Or is there evidence that, as Rhodes (1994) argues, multilevel and vertical governance hollows out the national state, and domestic actors with stakes in a topic move their venue shopping to the higher level, such as to the institutions of the European Union? If this shift occurs, it may imply a decline in attention for a policy topic within national-level institutions. Agenda-setting at one, higher level then substitutes rather than drives or reinforces agenda-setting at the other, lower level.

In short, the vertical dynamics of multilevel agenda-setting may involve similar or dissimilar directions of issue attention at the relevant levels of governance. Member states in the European Union are not simply mechanically connected to the EU institutions, but have their own institutional setting that may be more or less conductive, and likewise, (party) political conditions may favor the domestic tracking of the EU policy agenda or they may push attention flows towards very different issues. The institutionalization of attention to a topic in a political system for example may vary with the extent to which a leading political party (or a majority coalition of parties) promotes such institutionalization (Green-Pedersen and Wolfe, 2009).

Domestic political parties are important actors in setting the national policy agenda, making constant trade-offs for attention to issues, and this is also where in multilevel agenda-setting the horizontal dynamics of issue competition may come into play. While the literature on EU policymaking considers institutional, political, and cultural reasons for member states to stay close to or deviate from the European policy agenda (and its implementation), domestic issue competition has not received much space in theory and empirical analysis thus far.

In this contribution, we focus on the way in which vertical attention dynamics of multilevel governance may, at the domestic level, be influenced by the horizontal dimension, the competition between policy topics for national agenda priority. We consider one specific type of policy agenda, the executive agenda of the European Union and the executive agenda in different EU member states. The central topic in our analysis is environmental policy, a field of shared competences of the European Union and its member states, and on which the European Union has developed a strong policy legacy. Environmental problems are typically seen as matters addressed in a multilevel governance system (Pollack, 2000; Hooghe and Marks, 2001; Marks, Hooghe, and Blank, 1996). Studies of environmental policy also indicate that the European Union has become a global leader in setting the environmental policy agenda (Keleman and Vogel, 2010). Further, a characteristic of the environment as a domain of regulatory policy in the European Union is that costs of policy and implementation are carried to a significant extent by the member states (Fairbrass and Jordan, 2004).

Based on the possibilities for environmental attention dynamics to develop, we present two hypotheses. The first hypothesis follows the argument in the agenda-setting literature that attention in one venue triggers and increases attention in another venue. This cascading effect has been found for media and political venues (S. Pralle, 2006; S. B. Pralle, 2006; Walgrave and Vliegenthart, 2010). Also from a multilevel perspective, attention at one level of governance may spark attention at the other level (Collinson, 1999). In studying environmental policy, Princen (2009) observes a parallel development in attention within EU institutions and member states. We expect that environmental issues discussed at the EU level will be followed by an increase of attention at the member states level. Thus our first hypothesis is:

Hypothesis 1 on vertical, multilevel dynamics:

If attention to the environment rises or declines on the EU agenda, then attention in member states rises or declines as well.

The horizontal attention dynamics we incorporate by looking at—according to the literature—a strongly competitive topic to the environment: the economy. Some scholars even argue that the environment is a luxury good to which attention rises only at times when the economy is high and incomes develop positively. Conversely, in this line of argument, when economic problems rise, domestic attention to the environment declines.

Hypothesis 2 on horizontal, issue competition dynamics:

If attention to the economy rises, then attention to the environment declines, and if attention to the economy declines, then attention to the environment rises.

The question is how these dynamics relate to each other. Do EU member states show both dynamics at the same time? Or do some member states show a stronger pattern for the horizontal dynamic while other member states for the vertical dynamic? Within EU member states, the trading off of the environment for economy on the agenda may be reinforced by the institutionalization of environmental policymaking in EU institutions, which is among the most developed of all policy domains in the European Union (Princen, 2009). The expectation then may be that the multilevel dynamic will be more dominant than the issue competition dynamic. However, an alternative argument is that small countries with an open economy are more likely to show a horizontal dynamic rather than a vertical pattern, which means that attention to the environment is more dependent on the levels of attention to the economy.

The empirical analysis that follows includes four countries. For these countries, executive agendas have been content coded. Similarly, the policy agenda was coded for the European Council. In our hypotheses, we do not include different expectations for the four countries. The aim of the present analysis is to explore how attention dynamics may work for one venue type and one topic in a multilevel governance context. We thus take an open empirical view on the two types of agenda-setting dynamics in the four countries, and consider the extent to which patterns between them are similar or different, and what this may mean for our understanding of the evolution of attention to a major policy topic.

32.3 Data and Method of Analysis

A key feature of policy agendas research is the use of a similar codebook containing nineteen main topic categories such as macroeconomy, international affairs, and health, and nearly 250 subtopic categories for more specific subjects, such as income tax, international human rights, and the regulation of medicines (Baumgartner and Jones 2002; Jones and Baumgartner, 2005; John and Margetts, 2003). In this chapter, we focus on the political attention given to environmental issues. This includes topics as different as solid waste recycling, climate change, water pollution, or asbestos. We extended the original set of subtopics on environment in the coding system to energy issues and some other subtopics from different topic categories that also relate to the environment. Appendix 32.A.1 gives a detailed list of the (sub)topics included in this research.

The data for this analysis were collected in different national policy agendas projects, mapping attention to problems across all policy fields in different venues over varying periods (John and Jennings, 2012). The coding protocol has been comparable in all countries. All entries are double coded until an intercoding reliability was reached of 85 percent on the main topics and 80 percent on the subtopics. We included two small (Denmark and the Netherlands) and two larger EU member states (the United Kingdom and Spain) in our analysis. Besides having data available on these countries, these member states also represent the entire spectrum of forerunners in environmental policymaking (Denmark and the Netherlands), a middle of the road country (the United Kingdom), and a latecomer (Spain) (Liefferink and Andersen, 1998). Appendix 32.B.1 provides an overview of the major trends and topics about the environment in the four member states studied.

We use executive speeches as an indicator of government attention on the national level and the European Council Conclusions as an indicator of attention to problems at the Union level. The executive speeches are given at the opening of the parliamentary year. In these speeches, governments communicate their plans for the coming year. Previous research found that speeches are a valid indicator of executive attention (Breeman et al., 2009; Jennings, Bevan, and John, 2011; Mortensen et al., 2011). The European Council Conclusions contain the main statements produced in European summits, which are organized four to six times per year. All heads of state or government of the European Union take part in these summits and they discuss general policy concerns, intentions, and outlooks on future topics of interest to the European Union. Council Conclusions are comparable to executive speeches—a formal agenda at a high political level, displaying the most important policy plans for the coming period. We aggregated the data on the European Council Conclusions to be able to make year-to-year comparisons with the executive speeches. Table 32.1 summarizes the data used.

The annual executive speeches are coded per sentence or quasi-sentence.[3] Dutch Speeches of the Throne are read by the Monarch at the 3rd Tuesday in September when the annual budget is presented, but they are written entirely by the government (Breeman et al., 2009). The British Queen reads the speech in October or November at the opening of the parliamentary year, except after an election (Jennings et al., 2011). This speech is also written by the government. The Danish executive speech is read by the prime minister on the first Tuesday in October during the opening ceremony of the parliament (Mortensen et al., 2011). Finally, the Spanish speech is presented by the prime minister who has more discretion in setting the moment compared to the other countries (Mortensen et al., 2011).

Table 32.1. Data sources of executive speeches

	Period	Statements in total	Statements about environment (absolute value)	Statements about environment (proportion)
United Kingdom	1982–2012	2,293	66	2.9%
Denmark	1982–2012	9,964	310	3.1%
The Netherlands	1982–2012	5,484	244	4.4%
Spain	1982–2012	10,424	101	1.0%
European Council conclusions	1982–2012	42,436	1,901	4.5%

Source: Comparative Agendas Project—United Kingdom, Spain, the Netherlands, and Denmark

32.4 Empirical Patterns in Four Member States and the European Union

To understand the relationship between attention to the environment at EU level and at member state level, we compare the trends of attention at both levels and also analyze the specific contents of these trends. Typical of the punctuated equilibrium pattern in political attention and policy changes is the alternation between periods of stability and small changes interrupted by more drastic shifts. Figure 32.1 shows the development in attention to environmental problems over time in the different executive speeches relative to the pattern in the European Council. A look at these four figures shows considerable variation between domestic attention distributions over time.

The United Kingdom has clear spikes of attention in 1989, 2001, and 2009. Spain shows, as expected, late-starting attention to the environment but with spikes upward in 2001 and 2009. The Netherlands displays one clear spike of attention in 1989 and two waves of attention between 1987 and 1992 and between 1995 and 1999, and some rise also in 2009–10. Denmark shows a number of separate spikes of attention, in 1988, 1994, 1997, 2010, and 2012. The European Council Conclusions show attention spikes around 1990, 2002, 2007, and 2009.

32.4.1 *Vertical Attention Dynamics: Multilevel Agenda-Setting*

Comparing the trends of the member states and the European Union, we observe that, after 2000, the average level of attention to the environment in the European Union was systematically higher than in the four member states. This shows institutionalization at the EU level, where environmental policy is a strong domain of supranational competence and where, since the Lisbon Treaty of 2009, increased jurisdiction in energy policy provided issue connection possibilities. As a venue of high politics in which member states

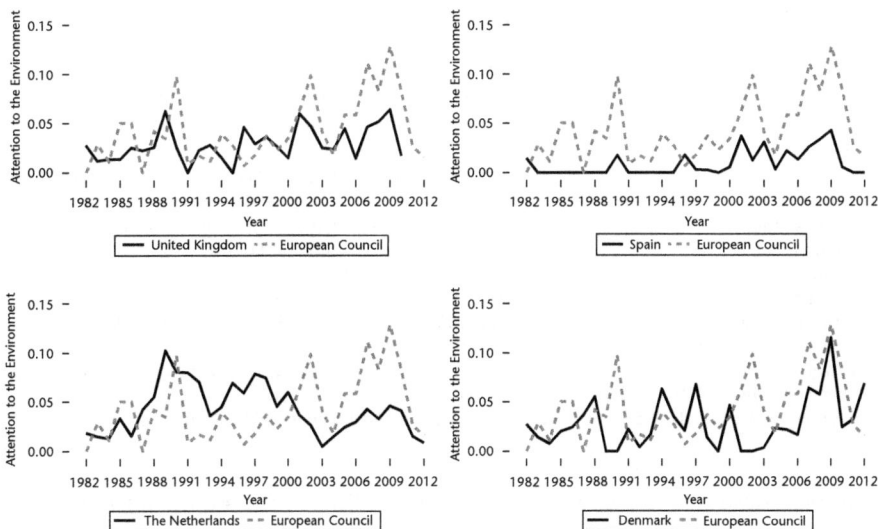

Figure 32.1. Attention to the environment at national and EU level
Source: Comparative Agendas Project

are directly represented, the European Council agenda not only followed national attention patterns but has also taken a leading agenda-setting role in the timing of attention to environmental problems.

When comparing the trends in the United Kingdom and Spain on the one hand and in the Netherlands and Denmark on the other hand we observe that the speeches of the United Kingdom and, to some extent, also in Spain follow the same pattern of attention as observed at the European level. The trends in Denmark and the Netherlands rather suggest that national attention to environmental matters follow a different pattern. If we correlate the attention of all the four countries with the attention at the EU level, we also find support for these observations (see Table 32.2).

Correlations in the United Kingdom and Spain are higher and significant compared to those of the Netherlands and Denmark. The regression analysis (linear) between attention to the environment of the two governance levels further confirms that the United Kingdom and Spain are more strongly related to the EU attention dynamic than the Netherlands and Denmark are. We found this pattern in both directions, whether the European Union was taken as dependent or independent variable. Thus, for the United Kingdom and Spain, we find evidence for Hypothesis 1: the rise and decline in attention at the national level to environmental issues follows the pattern of attention in the European Council. Note, however, that we cannot draw conclusions about the direction of this relation. From our analysis one cannot conclude

Table 32.2. Vertical mechanism: Multilevel effect

	UK 1982–2012 N = 31	SP 1982–2012 N = 31	NL 1982–2012 N = 31	DK 1982–2012 N = 31
Correlation	R = 0.46380566	R = 0.644978	R = 0.002848	R = 0.270876
p-value	p = 0.008587***	p = 8.97E-05***	p = 0.98787	p = 0.140505

EC taken as the
   independent
   variable
	Regression coeff.=
	0.241127316
		Regression coeff.=
		0.246759334
			Regression coeff.=
			0.002116018
				Regression coeff.=
				0.216041

EC taken as dependent variable	Regression coeff.= 0.892125	Regression coeff.= 1.685837	Regression coeff.= 0.003832	Regression coeff.= 0.33963

Note: Regression between the relative attention per year for the environment in the executive speeches of four member states and the minutes of the European Council meetings.

Source: Comparative Agendas Project—United Kingdom, Spain, the Netherlands, and Denmark

whether these two member states are responding to the European Union or that the European Union is responding to the member states.

Why are the Netherlands and Denmark following their own pattern and the United Kingdom and Spain are not? First of all, because Denmark and the Netherlands were early agenda-setters on environmental issues. Paradoxically, from a qualitative analysis summarized in Appendix 32.B.1, we learn that, in dealing with environmental issues, Denmark and the Netherlands were referring to the European Union earlier than the British and Spanish governments. During the first peak of attention, both Denmark and the Netherlands emphasized the importance of the role of the European Union in environmental policymaking, particularly for those issues that cross domestic borders. This speaks to the analysis of EU environmental policy development by Keleman and Vogel (2010), who argue that EU institutions provided crucial venues of support and institutionalization for those member states where domestic environmental standards were already quite strict—and who thus would benefit from environmental policy diffusion driven by the European Union "down" to the other member states. At the same time, both countries were building institutions to deal with environmental issues. In Denmark, the environment was being linked to socio-economic welfare policies, while in the Netherlands monitoring systems for specific sectoral environmental policies were being developed.

Compared to Denmark and the Netherlands, governments in the United Kingdom and particularly in Spain referred much less to environmental policies in their executive agendas. When the United Kingdom was referring to the environment at all, it was mainly related to the creation of its national institutions without much reference to the EU level. The focus was on setting up river boards and environmental agencies for England, Wales, and Scotland. Spain had a different starting position compared to the other countries as it became a member state in 1986 after its national democratization process had come on track. This country started to build environmental institutions in the 1990s, and made increasing reference to the European Union at the turn of the century and in following years.

The forerunner position of Denmark and the Netherlands pushed their attention to the environment to higher levels compared with the United Kingdom and Spain. It also explains why they followed their own agenda dynamic, different from that of the European Union. The United Kingdom and Spain only caught up when, and if, the European Union was discussing environmental issues.

The second reason why Denmark and the Netherlands do not line up with the EU attention dynamic comes forth when we consider the question of why the executive agendas in Denmark and particularly in the Netherlands show no continued rise but rather conditional attention to the environment after 2000.

In the Netherlands, this may be because of the ever-closer regulatory regime set at the EU level. Talking about the environment usually implies referring to EU rules. And with declining voters' appreciation of the European Union, politicians have become anxious to mention EU policies at all. In the last decade, it has even become a political risk to talk about EU policies. Green-Pedersen and Wolfe (2009) found that, in Denmark, the institutionalization of environmental attention came despite the transfer of important decision-making authority in this domain to the European Union, and the pattern in our findings indicate a recent catching-up with EU policy in this country (see the rise in from 2006 to 2008).

The increasing executive attention in the United Kingdom and Spain following the rise of the EU environmental policy agenda remained at a lower level compared to the early attention waves in Denmark and in the Netherlands. This may signify that executive attention in the United Kingdom and Spain increased to a level just sufficient for the European Union-mandated domestic policy development. Another driving condition for this rising attention in the late-coming countries United Kingdom and Spain may be that, when their national executives were catching up with EU policy initiatives, the environment was expanding into a broader global theme—more pressing on the domestic executive agenda as other international and global themes or focus events also have such an agenda effect (Birkland, 1997).

32.4.2 *Horizontal Attention Dynamics: Issue Competition*

A third reason for the different patterns between the United Kingdom and Spain compared with Denmark and the Netherlands brings us to our second hypothesis. It is a classic pattern in agenda-setting that attention to one policy topic is contingent on the amount of attention other policies get. This is why in the theory section above we started with issue competition. In multilevel agenda-setting, issue competition (or, as we called it, horizontal attention dynamics) has remained under-considered. Here, we focus on economic issues relative to environmental issues. Downs (1972) already indicated that the environment is negatively associated with the economy. Breeman and Timmermans (2008) also showed this relation to be true for the Netherlands. Hence, we analyze how much domestic attention to the environment and the increasing role of the European Union have been pushed up or down by the salience of economic issues on the domestic agenda.

Figure 32.2 shows the cycles of attention to the environment and to macro-economic issues. The general pattern that may be observed in the attention given to macroeconomic topics is a declining trend (except for Spain) with attention increasing from 2009 onwards (except for Denmark). The declining line in the United Kingdom is more erratic than in the Netherlands and Denmark. For the entire period all four countries exhibit higher levels of attention for the economy; the economy is simply considered more important on the executive agenda than the environment, and even when facing no major economic trouble, attention to environmental issues is still conditioned by the amount of space on the agenda.

When we relate the trends between the economy and the environment and compare the four countries, different patterns emerge. Both the United Kingdom and Spain are rather erratic and there seems to be no meaningful pattern

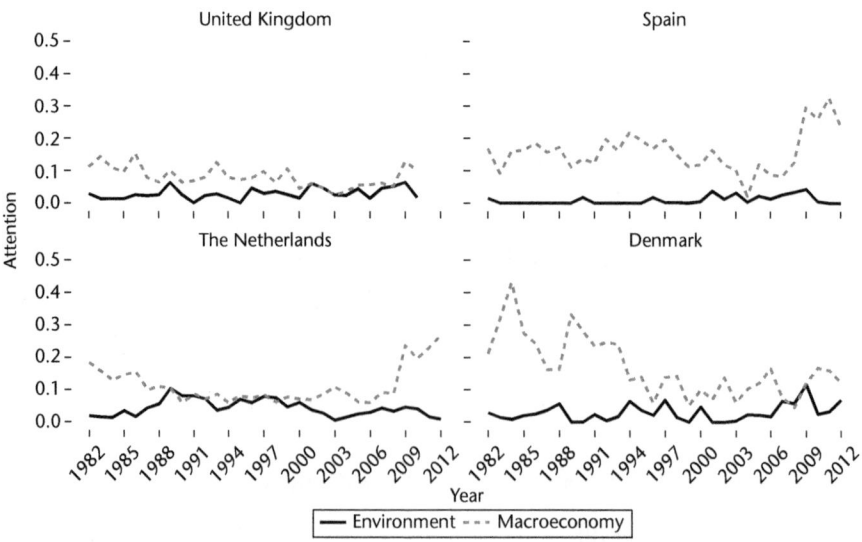

Figure 32.2. Attention to the environment and macroeconomy at national level
Source: Comparative Agendas Project

Table 32.3. Horizontal mechanism: Issue competition

	UK 1982–2012 N = 31	SP 1982–2012 N = 31	NL 1982–2012 N = 31	DK 1982–2012 N = 31
Correlation	R = 0.079911	R = –0.050425	R = –0.446266	R = –0.336558
p-value	p = 0.669141	p = 0.787632	p = 0.011855**	p = 0.064128#
Economy (topic 1) taken as independent variable	Regression coeff.= 0.041493	Regression coeff.= –0.01031	Regression coeff. = –0.19569	Regression coeff. = –0.0981
Economy (topic 1) taken as dependent variable	Regression coeff.= 0.1539	Regression coeff.= –0.24668	Regression coeff.= –1.01772	Regression coeff.= –1.15469

Note: Regression between relative attention per year to macroeconomic topics and the environment *within* four EU member states.

Source: Comparative Agendas Project codebook, the Netherlands—United Kingdom, Spain, the Netherlands, and Denmark

in the graph presented in Table 32.3. For the Netherlands and Denmark, however, we see almost a mirror image between the two topics, especially in the Netherlands. Consider the years 1986, 1993, 2003, and 2012. In all these years, attention to the economy went up and attention to the environment went down.

Statistical analysis supports this observation. The Netherlands and Denmark show a stronger negative correlation compared with the United Kingdom and Spain. The regression between the two topics further confirms that both topics are more strongly related in the Netherlands and Denmark than in the United Kingdom and Spain. Thus, we found a pattern opposite to that in the multilevel dynamics of attention. For the Netherlands and Denmark, we find support for Hypothesis 2: the rise in attention to the economy comes together with a decline in attention to the environment. We cannot, however, draw conclusions about the direction of the relationship.

Competition between the two main topic categories did not play much part in the United Kingdom and Spain, but it did in Denmark and particularly in the Netherlands. As we saw in the United Kingdom and Spain the multilevel dynamic occurred much more strongly between the domestic agenda for environmental issues and that of the European Union. Our findings thus suggest that in Denmark and the Netherlands attention given to environmental problems was sacrificed to that of the economy and that, conversely, the environment acquired more agenda space when the economy did not call for attention in these countries.

In Spain and the United Kingdom, such trading off did not happen to any significant degree. Though not statistically significant, in the United Kingdom a weak positive relationship existed between the attention to economic and environmental issues. Apparently, over time, in Spain and the United Kingdom attention to the environment developed in a way that was less dependent on the space on the agenda relative to economic issues, and can be seen more as catching up with the expanding European policymaking activities on environmental issues. These countries follow the attention rhythm of the European Union more than Denmark and the Netherlands.

These findings inform us about the different ways in which multilevel agenda-setting may happen for one and the same major policy topic, and within countries that all are EU member states. While attention to the environment exists in the European Union and member states, at the same time, the trends differ between the countries. This means that existing conclusions about agenda-setting on environmental issues in European countries need a qualifier: countries appear not equally sensitive in time to EU initiatives nor are they all taking frontrunner positions in agenda-setting on environmental issues. Further, domestic issue competition for attention also varies in the impact on the level of attention to environmental issues.

32.5 Conclusion

Issues that spill over across territorial and political borders also impact agenda-setting on all sides of these borders. While attention to problems within countries has become a major subject of study in the past decade, also in comparative work the multilevel dynamics of problem attention is still relatively understudied. This contribution builds on literature on multilevel governance and aims to connect such work more explicitly to agenda-setting over a long period of time. Its empirical focus is on environmental problems, a major topic that receives attention in all countries and at all levels of governance, but typically does so in quite different proportions over time.

In the European Union, the multilevel governance of environmental issues has become strongly institutionalized. We consider how this growing institutionalization and the build up of a policy legacy at the EU level relates to domestic agenda-setting. Do member states of the European Union track attention levels in the European institutions, do they seek "uploading" of their own environmental issues to the EU level, or do they shift towards other major policy topics instead? Competition between issues may reinforce the substitution of attention.

We presented two hypotheses to explore how multilevel agenda-setting on environmental issues may happen over a period of thirty years in different countries, namely Denmark, the Netherlands, Spain, and the United Kingdom, and all compared to the European Union. Our first hypothesis was that attention for the environment between the levels over time is corresponding, which speaks to the idea that the European Union and its member states must constantly connect on their policy agendas. In our second hypothesis, we moved on to horizontal attention dynamics, and stated that the environment must compete with the economy for space on the policy agenda. This in turn influences the openness of a national agenda to attention in multilevel agenda-setting on the relevant topic.

We used data on the executive agendas of the governments in these countries and the European Council. Our quantitative analysis of executive agendas has shown that in Spain and the United Kingdom attention to environmental issues mostly went up when the attention level within the European Council was also rising. In Spain, this happened increasingly over time, which indicates institution building in this policy domain after the country became a EU member in 1986. The United Kingdom shows this attention-following pattern over the entire period of thirty years. These findings support our first hypothesis on complimentary attention dynamics between the two levels of agenda-setting. In contrast, environmental agenda-setting in Denmark and the Netherlands follows a more domestic pattern and at several points in the thirty-year period even traveled in an opposite direction to that of the European Union. For these two countries, we found empirical evidence of competition for attention on the national executive agenda between the environment and the economy. At times of salience of economic issues (that is, economic hardship), the space on the executive agenda for environmental policy was reduced, and at times the topic almost entirely disappeared from the agenda. Issue competition thus may drive attention to the environment down when this topic is also addressed extensively at the EU level.

These latter findings differ from those of Green-Pedersen and Wolfe (2009) and Princen (2009), who found that there is no substitution effect, and that, particularly in Denmark, attention to the environment increased in parallel to the European Union. We can account for this by the difference in policy venues analyzed. Green-Pedersen and Wolfe analyzed attention to the environment in Denmark in parliamentary debates, not the executive agenda. This may mean that, in multilevel dynamics, different venues and policy agendas can have varying roles in promoting or downplaying attention to issues. There can be increasing levels of attention in parliament—with multiple parties—for political reasons, and for the same reasons executives may choose to keep a topic lower key. The imprint of the European Union on environmental policy may be a disincentive for the executive to pay much attention to it in the face of a public that is sceptical towards the European Union. This reason may also have played a part in the Netherlands, where since the early 2000s EU policy has become more controversial. In the Eurosceptik UK, rises in attention often followed broader international agenda-setting, in which the European Union is only one of the drivers of this attention. On the executive agenda of the United Kingdom, attention to the environment moved more in parallel to this topic becoming a major concern of global governance.

For a time, both Denmark and the Netherlands were forerunners in environmental policy (Liefferink and Andersen, 1998). We see this in our findings for the 1980s and 1990s (the 1970s are outside the period analyzed, but also show sharp attention rises for environmental problems, see Liefferink and Andersen, 1998: 159). Conversely, Spain came from an entirely different starting position on this issue in the early 1980s. Spain was building up its own institutional capacity on the environment and was catching up when the attention at EU level started to rise. Hence when the attention to the environment started to rise, it also did at the national level.

Thus, multilevel agenda-setting on environmental problems has a different meaning in countries depending on the institutional and political relationships of these countries with the level above. To fully understand multilevel governance, comparative multi-venue analysis must also be involved. The forces of complimentary or substitutive attention in multilevel agenda-setting may work differently across countries, with their variation in institutional and political structures, numbers of relevant parties, and other policy entrepreneurs seeking venue access. Such institutional and (party) political factors can add to our understanding of attention dynamics when systematically compared, with a special focus on the way they condition multilevel agenda-setting.

Our final point of discussion in this contribution is how generalizable our findings and the possible driving factors of attention dynamics may be outside the domain of environmental policy. At the outset we gave a broad view of attention dynamics in order to identify and analyze different possible routes of attention in multilevel governance. Horizontal and vertical attention dynamics may work simultaneously or interact in different ways across countries as EU member states. Our findings indicate there is not one single and simple mechanism that leads national governments to allocate attention to a major topic in the same way over time. Also, our findings indicate that in some countries, particularly those of a smaller size and open to international economic or political developments, the competitive nature of issue attention impacts on the space for problems. Not only environmental issues but also other matters may receive lower levels of domestic attention if the core functions of government are at stake (Jennings et al., 2011). The environment is unlikely to be the only theme addressed conditionally according to the space for diversity on the agenda. This possibility may be investigated by studies focusing on other domains, such as social policy, education and culture, immigration, and law, order, and crime issues, and relating them to the other core functions of government, that is, foreign relations and the structure and organization of government and administration. Analyzing the more or less competitive relationship between topics and these core functions can inform us about the thresholds for issues to get on to the policy agenda.

Acknowledgements

We thank the policy agendas country teams from Denmark: Christoffer Green-Pedersen, Peter Mortensen; the United Kingdom: Will Jennings, Shaun Bevan; and Spain: Laura Chaqués, Anna Palau for providing us with datasets and feedback. Thanks to Leticia Elias for translating the Spanish speeches. Thanks also to Edella Schlager for her comments on an earlier version of this paper presented at the Annual Conference of the Comparative Agendas Project in Edinburgh, June 15–17, 2017.

Appendix 32.A.1: Subtopics included in the data

Table 32.A.1. Subtopics included in the data

700:	General (includes combinations of multiple subtopics)
701:	Drinking water safety
703:	Waste disposal
704:	Hazardous waste and toxic chemical Regulation, treatment, and disposal
705:	Air pollution, global warming, climate change, and noise pollution
707:	Recycling
708:	Indoor environmental hazards
709:	Species and forest protection
710:	Pollution and conservation in coastal and other navigable waterways
711:	Land and water conservation (this includes code 407 from NL, DK, and EC: Environmental problems caused by agricultural activities. SP and UK did not split up this code)
798:	Research and development
799:	Other
806:	Alternative and renewable energy
807:	Energy conservation
1614:	Environmental problems caused by military activity
1902:	International resources exploitation and resources agreements and global environmental problems
2103:	Use of public natural resources such as lands and forests

Source: Comparative Agendas Project—United Kingdom, Spain, the Netherlands, and Denmark

Appendix 32.B.1: Summary of attention to environment in four countries

Table 32.B.1. Summary of attention to environment in four countries

	1970s–1988	Peak attention 1988/9	1990-4	Peak attention 1994/5	1995–2012
Denmark	National focus on specific issues: –Spatial planning –Water issues –Recycling	National focus but related to other policy domains: –Environment defined as welfare problem –Jobs creation through environmental policies –Win-win situation businesses and environment	Focus on (with EU references): –CO2 emissions –Greenhouse gasses –Air quality in general	Integrated policy focus (EU and national): –Using environment to create new jobs –Integrate environment into other policy domains	National and EU/international focus on: –Water quality in rivers and streams (national) –CO2 and climate change (international)
The Netherlands	National focus on specific issues: –Water quality (due to manure surpluses) –Soil quality –Air quality –Waddenzee	International focus: –UN climate change conference National focus: –New environmental monitor tool: national environmental policy plan –Broad environmental programs	Focus on (with EU reference): –Water and soil quality –CO2 emissions –Traffic and car emissions –Waste reduction	National and EU focus –Environmental balance sheet –CO2 emissions –Sustainable production –Air quality	National and EU/international focus on: –Climate change conferences (international) Monitoring environmental regulations (national) –Sustainable energy –Pollution by cars/traffic
United Kingdom	National focus on specific issues: –(Sea) water quality –Oil drillings –Country and wildlife policies –Coastline	National focus: –Establishing National Rivers Authority –Wildlife –Countryside	National focus on: –Landscape policies –Pollution and waste policies –Building national institutional capacity: –Environment planning agency –Environmental agencies in England, Wales, and Scotland	No peak attention, national focus on –continue same topics of previous period	National and International focus: –Hunting with dogs (national) –Kyoto Protocol –Climate change/CO2 –Long-term energy supply –Linking environment to poverty –Cooperating with G8/G20

| Spain | — | National focus:
–Relation between consumers and environment | — | National focus:
Building institutional capacity:
–Ministry of the Environment
–Zoning policy | National and EU/International focus on:
–Environmental liability act (national)
–Forest and mountain policy
–*Prestige* oil tanker disaster
–Kyoto
–CO2
–Climate change
–Marine policy (national)
–Rural development
–Pollution by industries and transport |

Source: Comparative Agendas Project—United Kingdom, Spain, the Netherlands, and Denmark

Notes

1. Spain became an EU member state in 1986, and the period analyzed ends before Brexit politics started.
2. All datasets are available at: http://www.comparativeagendas.net/.
3. A quasi-sentence is identified when two full sentences are linked together with for instance the word "and" or with a semi-colon and different topics are addressed in these separate quasi-sentences. Enumerations in a sentence that show equal stress on each topic also are split up into separate entries and coded as such.

References

Alexandrova, P., Carammia, M., and Timmermans, A. (2012). Policy Punctuations and Issue Diversity on the European Council Agenda. *Policy Studies Journal*, 40(1): 69–88.

Baumgartner, F. (2006). Punctuated Equilibrium Theory and Environmental Policy. In *Punctuated Equilibrium and the Dynamics of US Environmental Policy*, ed. R. Repetto. New Haven: Yale University Press, 24–46.

Baumgartner, F., Breunig, C., Green-Pedersen, C. et al. (2009). Punctuated Equilibrium in Comparative Perspective. *American Journal of Political Science*, 53(3): 603–20.

Baumgartner, F., Green-Pedersen, C., and Jones, B. (2006). Comparative Studies of Policy Agendas. *Journal of European Public Policy*, 13(7): 959–74.

Baumgartner, F., and Jones, B. (1993). *Agendas and Instability in American Politics*. 2nd ed. Chicago: Chicago University Press.

Baumgartner, F., and Jones, B. (eds) (2002). *Policy Dynamics*. Chicago: Chicago University Press.

Beder, S. (2002). Agenda Setting for Environmental Protection Policies. In *Green Governance: From Periphery to Power*, ed. S. Kerr, T. Buhrs, and C. Dann. Christchurch: Lincoln University Press, 22–5.

Birkland, T. (1997). *After Disaster: Agenda Setting, Public Policy, and Focusing Events*. Washington, DC: Georgetown University Press.

Braun, M., and Santarius, T. (2008). *Climate Politics in the Multi-Level Governance System: Emissions Trading and Institutional Changes in Environmental Policy-Making*. Wuppertal: Wuppertal Institute for Climate, Environment and Energy.

Breeman, G., Lowery, D., Poppelaars, C. et al. (2009). Political Attention in a Coalition System: Analysing Queen's Speeches in the Netherlands 1945–2007. *Acta Politica*, 44(1): 1–1.

Breeman, G., Scholten, P., and Timmermans, A. (2015). Analysing Local Policy Agendas: How Dutch Municipal Executive Coalitions Allocate Attention. *Local Government Studies*, 41(1): 20–43.

Breeman, G., and Timmermans, A. (2008). *Politiek van de aandacht voor milieubeleid; een onderzoek naar maatschappelijke dynamiek, politieke agendavorming en prioriteiten in het Nederlandse milieubeleid*. Wageningen.

Cobb, R., and Elder, C. (1983). *Participation in American Politics: The Dynamics of Agenda-Building*. Baltimore: Johns Hopkins University Press.

Collinson, S. (1999). "Issue-Systems", "Multi-Level Games" and the Analysis of the EU's External Commercial and Associated Policies: A Research Agenda. *Journal of European Public Policy*, 6(2): 206–24.

Daviter, F. (2011). *Policy Framing in the European Union*. Basingstoke: Palgrave.

Downs, A. (1972). Up and Down with Ecology: The Issue-Attention Cycle. *Public Interest*, 28(Summer): 38.

Fairbrass, J., and A. Jordan (2004). Multi-Level Governance and Environmental Policy. In *Multilevel Governance*, ed. I. Bache and M. Flinders. Oxford: Oxford University Press, 147–64.

Foret, F., and Rittelmeyer, Y.-S. (eds) (2013). *The European Council and European Governance: The Commanding Heights of the EU*. London: Routledge.

Foucault, M., and Montpetit, E. (2014). Diffusion of Policy Attention in Canada: Evidence from Speeches from the Throne, 1960–2008. In *Agenda-Setting from a Policy Theory to a Theory of Politics*, ed. C. Green-Pedersen and S. Walgrave. Chicago: Chicago University Press, 201–19.

Green-Pedersen, C., and Wolfe, M. (2009). The Institutionalization of Environmental Attention in the United States and Denmark: Multiple- versus Single-Venue Systems, *Governance* 22(4): 625–44.

Guber, D. L. (2001). Voting Preferences and the Environment in the American Electorate. *Society and Natural Resources*, 14(6): 455–69.

Hooghe, L., and Marks, G. (2001). *Multi-Level Governance and European Integration*. Oxford: Rowman and Littlefield.

Hooghe, L., and Marks, G. (2003). Unraveling the Central State, but How? Types of Multi-Level Governance. *The American Political Science Review*, 97(2): 233–43.

Jennings, W., Bevan, S., and John, P. (2011). The Agenda of British Government: The Speech from the Throne, 1911–2008. *Political Studies*, 59(1): 74–98.

John, P., and Jennings, W. (2012). Legislative Policy Agendas in the United Kingdom, 1910–2010. UK Data Archive, Colchester.

John, P., and Margetts, H. (2003). Policy Punctuations in the UK: Fluctuations and Equilibria in Central Government Expenditure since 1951. *Public Administration*, 81(3): 411–31.

Jones, B., and Baumgartner, F. (2005). *The Politics of Attention: How Government Prioritizes Problems*. Chicago: Chicago University Press.

Kelemen, R. D., and Vogel, D. (2010). Trading Places: The Role of the United States and the European Union in International Environmental Politics. *Comparative Political Studies*, 43(4): 427–56.

Keskitalo, E. C., Westerhoff, L., and Juhola, S. (2012). Agenda-Setting on the Environment: The Development of Adaptation to Climate Change as an Issue in European States. *Environmental Policy and Governance* 22: 381–94.

Knill, C., and Liefferink, D. (2007). *Environmental Politics in the European Union*. Manchester: Manchester University Press.

Liefferink, D., and Andersen, M. S. (1998). Strategies of the "Green" Member States in EU Environmental Policy-Making. *Journal of European Public Policy*, 5(2): 254–70.

Lundgren, M., Squatrito, T., and Tallberg, J. (2017). Stability and Change in International Policy-Making: A Punctuated Equilibrium Approach. Paper presented at the Annual Conference of the Comparative Agendas Project, June 15–17, 2017, Edinburgh.

Marks, G., Hooghe, L., and Blank, K. (1996). European Integration from the 1980s: State-Centric v. Multi-level Governance. *Journal of Common Market Studies*, 34(3): 341–78.

Mortensen, P. B., Green-Pedersen, C., Breeman, G. et al. (2011). Comparing Government Agendas. *Comparative Political Studies*, 44(8): 973–1000.

Pollack, M. A. (2000). The End of Creeping Competence? EU Policy-Making since Maastricht. *Journal of Common Market Studies*, 38(3): 519–38.

Pralle, S. (2006). The "Mouse That Roared": Agenda Setting in Canadian Pesticides Politics. *Policy Studies Journal*, 34(2): 171–94.

Pralle, S. B. (2006). Timing and Sequence in Agenda-Setting and Policy Change: A Comparative Study of Lawn Care Pesticide Politics in Canada and the US. *Journal of European Public Policy*, 13(7): 987–1005.

Princen, S. (2009). *Agenda-Setting in the European Union*. Basingstoke: Palgrave.

Princen, S., and Rhinard, M. (2006). Crashing and Creeping: Agenda-Setting Dynamics in the European Union. *Journal of European Public Policy*, 13(7): 1119–31.

Rhodes, R. A. W. (1994). The Hollowing out of the State: The Changing Nature of the Public Service in Britain. *The Political Quarterly*, 65(2): 138–51.

Schattschneider, E. (1960). *The Semisovereign People: A Realist's View of Democracy in America*. New York: Holt, Rinehart, and Winston.

Scruggs, L., and Benegal, S. (2012). Declining Public Concern about Climate Change: Can We Blame the Great Recession? *Global Environmental Change*, 22(2): 505–15.

Sheingate, A. D. (2000). Agricultural Retrenchment Revisited: Issue Definition and Venue Change in the United States and European Union. *Governance*, 13(3): 335–63.

Timmermans, A. (2001). Arenas as Institutional Sites for Policymaking: Patterns and Effects in Comparative Perspective. *Journal of Comparative Policy Analysis*, 3(3): 311–37.

Walgrave, S., and Vliegenthart, R. (2010). Why Are Policy Agendas Punctuated? Friction and Cascading in Parliament and Mass Media in Belgium. *Journal of European Public Policy*, 17(8): 1147–70.

Weingart, P. (1999). Scientific Expertise and Political Accountability: Paradoxes of Science in Politics. *Science and Public Policy*, 26(3): 151–61.

Weissert, C., and Uttermark, M. (2017). Glass Half Full: Decentralization in Health Policy. *State and Local Government Review*, 49(3): 199–214.

33

Using CAP Data for Qualitative Policy Research

Ilana Shpaizman

33.1 Introduction

The Comparative Agendas Project (CAP) is a measurement and a retrieval system (Jones, 2015). As such, it can be leveraged not only for quantitative but also for qualitative within-case analysis as it provides the researcher with access to rich and diverse material that enables the gathering and triangulating of empirical evidence for an in-depth case study. In addition, the coding procedures ensure that the content of the material under each subtopic is relevant and exhaustive. This can be especially time saving since case-study research involves going through a large volume of materials. Furthermore, due to its breadth, CAP is also useful for selecting the relevant population of policy cases when the population is less visible (Shpaizman, 2017). Although many policy scholars use CAP in qualitative within-case analysis, almost no formalization of CAP's advantages for such analysis has been done.

This chapter aims to demonstrate CAP's usefulness for case-oriented research, starting from case selection, going through familiarization with the case of interest, and ending with a collection of the needed evidence. After explaining each phase in case-oriented research and the role CAP can play, each use is demonstrated using CAP data from Spain and the United States. Specifically, case selection when the population is unknown is demonstrated using the outcome of policy drift—change in the policy impact without significant policy change (Hacker, 2004). This policy outcome was chosen because cases of drift are hard to identify without in-depth acquaintance with each case, due to drift's less visible character. Familiarization with a case and gathering relevant evidence is demonstrated using the example of child-care policy in Spain and the United States correspondingly. These countries were chosen because, as opposed to other Western countries, they lag behind in developing a comprehensive publicly financed childcare policy.

The chapter proceeds as follows. First, CAP's usefulness as a tool for identifying the relevant population of cases when the population is less visible is presented along with its limitations. Second, the way the trends tool can be used to assist the researcher to familiarize him/herself with the case in question and formulate the research questions is discussed. Third, CAP's appropriateness for evidence collection is explained. This part concludes by pointing to some of CAP's limitations to which researchers should pay attention when applying CAP in a within-case analysis.

33.2 CAP as a Tool for Identifying Relevant Population of Cases

One of the first phases of case-oriented research is identifying the relevant population of cases—all the cases that are analytically useful for the research from which the specific cases for analysis are drawn. It can also be termed the sampling frame. This population includes both positive cases where the outcome of interest took place and negative cases where it did not, although it could have. This stage is important because it has implications for the analytic findings, inferences, and generalizations made (Goertz, 2006).

The best practice for identifying the relevant population in qualitative research is first selecting positive cases based on their value on the dependent variable and then to distinguish the negative cases from irrelevant cases based on the possibility principle, according to which cases are relevant if there is at least one or a small number of independent variables predicting the outcome of interest (Goertz and Hewitt, 2006: 213).

Yet in many instances in politics and specifically in public policy and administration we cannot use this scheme because the independent variable is less visible, for example, in research on paradigmatic change, implementation gaps, or gradual policy change. In such cases, researchers find themselves looking for a needle in a haystack when trying to identify the positive and then the negative cases.

One way to overcome this challenge is to use a different case selection procedure. First, identify the entire relevant population based on the value of the independent variables and only then distinguish between positive and negative cases (Shpaizman, 2017). The relevant population may be identified by applying the possibility principle (Goertz and Hewitt, 2006). This principle can be useful because in some cases causes can be more easily traced than outcomes.

Applying the possibility principle requires a large dataset of the entire universe of cases (e.g., all the countries in the world) from which relevant cases can be drawn. In policy research, we can use CAP because it represents a broad population of policy cases. CAP data can be "cased" (Ragin and Becker, 1992) in different ways. For example, each subtopic in each project can be seen as one case (elementary education in Germany, in France, and so on). Moreover, given the data's long time span, each subtopic in each project can be divided into several cases based on the time frame (elementary education in Germany from 1950 to 1970). Some subtopics can act as more than one case. For example, the subtopic "childcare" includes information on policies regarding childcare and parental leave, and so can be divided into two cases in each project. Alternatively, several subtopics can be combined into one case; for example, air and water pollution. Consequently, CAP data can be sorted into hundreds of cases.

In addition, each observation includes not only information on the policy topic and subtopic but also contextual institutional and political information, which can be used to identify the presence or absence of various independent variables.

The usefulness of CAP for identifying the relevant population of cases can be illustrated using the outcome of policy drift. Drift is a change in the policy outcome (its operation on the ground) without significant change in the policy itself. It takes place when there is a gap between the existing policy and reality due to changes in the policy environment (e.g., demographic or technological changes), and lack of policy adjustment to these changes. As a result, while the policy remains stable, its outcome, such as its distributional effect, changes (Hacker, 2004; Hacker et al., 2015). For example, despite changes in the labor market, Congress did not adjust the US healthcare policy for many years. Consequently, existing policies did not address the new needs and the number of uninsured Americans increased (Hacker, 2004).

Positive cases of drift are extremely hard to identify without ex ante familiarization with the policy dynamics of each case over a long period. This is because drift occurs through non-decision and inaction and so we cannot observe it directly (Rocco and Thurston, 2014). As a result, to the best of my knowledge, there is no comparative research examining drift across fields and countries, and most works focus on a single national setting or policy field (Clegg, 2007; Hacker, 2004).

In order to identify relevant cases of drift using the possibility principle, we must have a theory of the independent variables leading to drift. Existing research has found that drift is more likely when the environment in which the policy is embedded is changed. In addition, the rules underlining the policy are precise or rigid, making it difficult to adjust the policy internally. Lastly, drift can result from failure to adjust the policy to reality due to veto players' success in preventing enactment (Hacker et al., 2015).

CAP cannot identify changes in the environment or rule rigidity. The only independent variable it can identify is when efforts to update the policy are blocked. Using CAP, we can recognize attempts to update the policy as indicated by the number of proposed bills on a specific subject, as well as the result of a successful blocking of policy update as indicated by the percentage of bills that fail to become law. In order to identify the relevant population of cases, the success rates of bills becoming law in all CAP subtopics in a specific project should be examined. Relevant cases of drift may be those in which the success rates of bills are the lowest compared to each country's/state's/unit's average success rate. Positive cases of drift will be those where a change in policy impact took place (Shpaizman, 2017).

The suggested method can be applied between and within all CAP projects. However, for the purpose of this chapter, it has been applied to the United States and Spain. This is first and foremost because these two projects have data series on bills and laws. In addition, most research on drift has examined US policy (Barnes, 2008; Béland, 2007; Hacker, 2004); therefore, using the US data enables us to validate the suggested method against findings from the existing research. Lastly, Spain was chosen as an example of a parliamentary democracy, since drift has been found to be prominent in parliamentary systems as well (Clegg, 2007; Gildiner, 2007).

33.2.1 Drift in the United States

To identify relevant cases of drift in the United States, the bill success rates on each subtopic from 1970, when drift became prominent (Hacker 2004), was examined. The US average success rate of bills becoming law is 15 percent (Krutz, 2005). A low success rate has been determined as less than 1 percent. The identified possible cases of drift can be seen in Table 33.1.

Table 33.1. Relevant cases of drift identified using the US CAP

The policy case	Laws/Bills success rate
Drug coverage and costs	0.56%
Long term care	0.8%
Childcare	0.49%
Taxation	0.93%
Labor unions	0.65%
White-collar crime	0.43%
Elderly assistance (including social security)	0.7%
Minority discrimination	0.7%
Rural housing	0.74%
Low-income housing assistance	0.91%
Elderly and handicapped housing	0.28%
Interest rates	0.3%

Source: Comparative Agendas Project—United States

Reviewing the existing literature reveals that some of the cases identified using CAP are also categorized as drift in the literature. For example, CAP has identified prescription drug coverage (0.56 percent success rate) and long-term care (0.8 percent) as two possible cases of drift. Hacker (2004) supports this classification. In his study of US social policy, he demonstrates that the failure to add prescription drug coverage to Medicare and include long-term care in the program resulted in policy drift that shifted the risk of healthcare costs from the government to individuals. CAP has identified employee relations and labor unions (0.65 percent) and taxation (0.93 percent) as additional cases of drift. Similarly, Hacker and Pierson (2010) discuss how attempts to update labor union policy due to changes in the labor market were blocked by employers and conservative Congress members. As a result, there was a significant decrease in union membership. In addition, they also found that the Republicans blocked any attempt to update the taxation policy, and thus contributed to growing inequality.

33.2.2 Drift in Spain

To identify relevant cases of drift in Spain, the ratio between the bills (suggested by the legislators and by the cabinet) and the laws (organic and ordinary laws) between 1982 and 2011 (the period of available data) was examined in each subtopic. The number of veto points in Spain is lower than in the United States. Consequently, the average success rate as seen in the CAP data is 53 percent. A low success rate was established as less than 20 percent. The identified possible cases of drift in Spain are seen in Table 33.2.

Reviewing the existing literature reveals that some of the identified relevant cases of drift were also identified as such in previous research. CAP identified childcare as a possible case of policy drift with 13 percent success rate. Research on childcare policy in Spain found that despite the increase in

Table 33.2. Relevant cases of drift identified using the Spain CAP

The policy case	Laws/Bills success rate
Gender discrimination	15%
Right to privacy	19%
Drinking water	15%
Low-income assistance	0%
Assistance to elderly	7%
Childcare	13%
Urban development	0%
Government appointments	19%

Source: Comparative Agendas Project—Spain

women's participation in the labor market, Spain's childcare policy lags behind other EU countries. This, among other things, is a result of issue preferences of the political parties, labor unions, and conservative civil society organizations that block policymaking (Bianculli and Jordana, 2013; León, 2007; Valiente, 2003). CAP has also identified assistance to elderly and social security as a possible case of drift (7 percent). This corresponds to studies finding that the financial situation of the Spanish social security system is worsening and that policymakers face high barriers when trying to reform existing policy. In fact, only in 2013, after many failed attempts, was the Spanish government able to pass pension reform (Boldrin, Jiménez-Martín, and Peracchi, 1999; Gruber and Wise, 2000). Lastly, CAP identified gender discrimination (15 percent) as a possible case of drift. Research has found that the gender wage gap has increased, especially for highly educated women, that there are few women serving on boards of directors, and that there are significant barriers to gender equality due to conservative policy legacies (de Cabo, Gimeno, and Escot, 2011; Pena-Boquete, 2009; Rica et al. 2008).

As seen in Tables 33.1 and 33.2, the number of possible cases of drift in the United States is higher than in Spain. This is not surprising given the US institutional system and its multiple veto points (Tsebelis, 1995). In addition, it seems that the actors which cause the policy to drift are different in the two countries. In the United States the minority party is usually the one favoring drift (Hacker and Pierson, 2010). In Spain, however, it seems that the minority party is the one trying to update the policy, and the majority party is the one causing it to drift (as evident from the many parliamentary bills that fail to become laws). This opens a new direction for further research on the nature of policy drift in different political settings. Lastly, assistance to the elderly and childcare were found in both countries as possible cases of drift. Although the outcome in both countries is the same (drift), the conditions are most likely different due to the difference in the political and institutional settings. An in-depth analysis of these two cases in the context of policy drift can shed more light on the conditions for drift's evolution and maintenance.

33.2.3 *Limitations*

Although CAP is a comprehensive and exhaustive system, it cannot identify all relevant cases, first, because it cannot identify all independent variables. Yet one should remember that some independent variables are more important than others, and therefore identifying certain independent variables may be more productive in identifying relevant cases. Second, its coding procedure may miss some significant cases. The coding scheme is based on already known topics. As a result, if a new issue rises on the agenda, it takes time before it is identified as such, and until then, it is coded under already known categories (Jones, 2015). Moreover, when new issues cannot be coded under any existing subtopic, and when there are not enough observations to justify creating a new subtopic, they will be coded under the subtopic "other," which is included in every major topic. Similarly, due to the mutual-exclusiveness characteristic, when a specific observation equally addresses two subtopic categories, it will be coded under the category "general," also available under each major topic. Some of these general observations are thus not coded according to their substantive content. Although there are not that many observations in the "general" or "other" categories, these can turn out to be significant.

33.3 CAP as a Tool for Familiarization with the Case of Interest

After identifying the relevant population and distinguishing between the positive and the negative cases, the researcher selects the specific cases of interest, usually the more important ones (George and Bennett, 2005; Goertz and Mahoney, 2012). Next, the researcher must obtain the contextual information on the case and familiarize herself with it so that she can formulate the general questions, the data requirements, and the expectations from the future gathered evidence. The familiarization is often based on previous research or interviews (George and Bennett, 2005). Relying on existing research can be insufficient when the topic of interest is understudied. Interviews can also be unsatisfactory when the researcher is not familiar with the issue in question and thus, finds it hard to ask the questions that will provide her with the relevant information.

CAP's trend analysis tool can help the researcher familiarizing herself with the case of interest and provide guidelines for future interviews. The trends tool can assist the researcher to narrow the time span based on the researcher's interests. For instance, there may be a period when more/less attention was given to a specific issue, or when there was a venue shift from one policy arena to another (e.g., from the legislator to the court), or when policymakers moved from declarations and proposals as seen, for example, in executive speeches and bills, to action, as seen in laws or budget changes. Furthermore, it can also help the researcher to formulate the research questions by narrowing the possible explanations and highlighting the puzzles.

33.3.1 *Childcare Policy in Spain*

For instance, let us assume that a researcher would like to examine the mechanisms that prevent Western countries from adopting a comprehensive childcare policy (a publicly financed universal childcare system for children

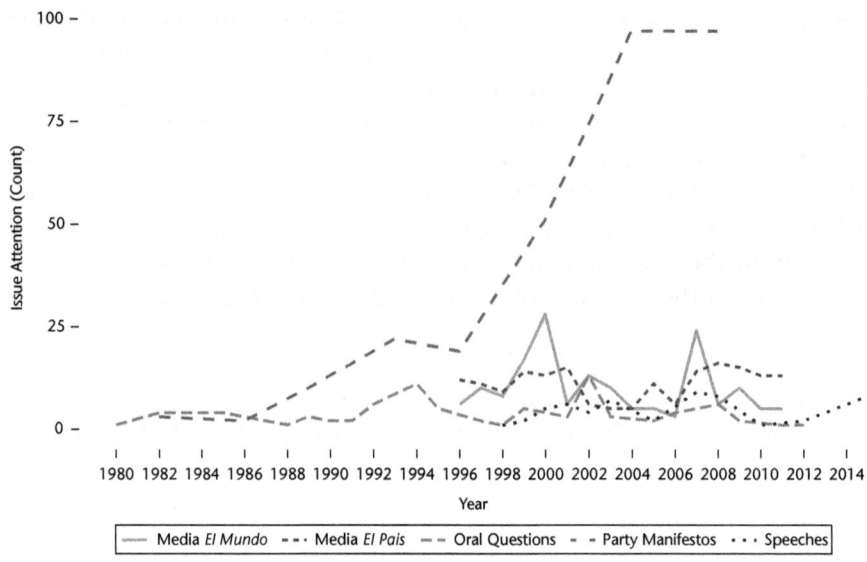

Figure 33.1. Issue attention for childcare policy in Spain (count)

Source: Comparative Agendas Project—Spain

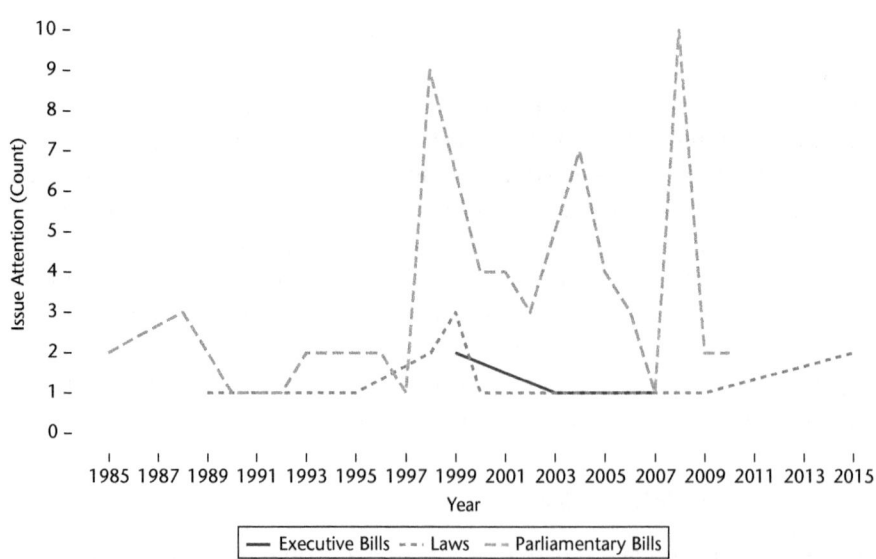

Figure 33.2. Issue attention for childcare policy in Spain in legislation (count)

Source: Comparative Agendas Project—Spain

under the age of six). One country found to lag behind in childcare policy is Spain (León, 2007). Using the trend analysis tool as seen in Figure 33.1, we find that the issue of childcare appeared on the agenda at the end of the 1990s and it has remained at a relatively high level since. This is evident from media attention, the number of bills proposed, party manifestos, and parliamentary questions. Therefore, the researcher will most likely focus on that period. In addition, the researcher could also infer that the existing childcare policy is not a result of a low level of attention. However, when comparing the different data series, we find that the increase in issue attention has not been evident throughout the series. Most of the proposed bills were parliamentary (forty-one) and not raised in the cabinet (four), and there has been relatively little legislation (nine laws) (see Figure 33.2). Consequently, the researcher can focus on the barriers that prevented the issue attention from being translated into policymaking.

33.4 CAP as a Tool for Gathering Evidence

Following familiarization with the case of interest, the researcher turns to the actual analysis. A within-case analysis is conducted as detective work, in which the researcher gathers evidence (empirical fingerprints left on a case) to increase her confidence in the presence of the suggested cause/ mechanisms for the outcome of interest (Beach and Pedersen, 2013; George and Bennett, 2005). Four types of evidence can be gathered: (1) trace evidence—evidence in which mere existence provides proof that something exists; (2) sequence evidence—evidence that demonstrates the chronology of events; (3) pattern evidence—evidence that demonstrates some statistical pattern in the evidence; and (4) account evidence—evidence based on the content of the material (Beach and Pedersen, 2013). Evidence is gathered after predictions are made regarding the empirical fingerprints the activities/ entities will leave in a case (George and Bennett, 2005).

CAP contains a rich body of empirical material, making it possible to gather all four types of evidence. Other than pattern evidence that is used in many CAP quantitative works, scholars can use the content of the source material and the long time span to identify account, trace, and sequence evidence.

Gathering evidence is insufficient for a within-case analysis, because the researcher has to evaluate whether the collected material is sufficient and reliable enough for the causal inference (Beach and Pedersen, 2013, 2014; George and Bennett, 2005). CAP is especially well suited for this purpose because it enables a triangulation of evidence from various sources and types. In order to illustrate the type of evidence that can be gathered using CAP, I will use the case of childcare policy in the United States.

33.4.1 *Lock-in Effect in Childcare Policy in the United States*

The United States does not have a federally funded comprehensive childcare policy. Its policy is composed of two major policy tools: first, various tax exemptions, and second, subsidized childcare for low-income families (Solomon-Cohen, 2001). Based on my familiarization with the case, I would argue that the lack of a comprehensive policy in the United States is a result (among other reasons) of a lock-in effect according to which, regardless of partisan identity, policymakers almost exclusively consider only those policy tools already in action (assistance to low-income families and tax exemptions), and ignore other policy solutions. In order to demonstrate the lock-in effect, I should find evidence demonstrating that (1) policymakers consider only or mostly the existing solutions, (2) in the past there were other proposed solutions that were removed from the agenda, and (3) partisan affiliation does not affect the proposed solutions.

The evidence presented here is taken from three CAP series in order to enable triangulation: bills, State of the Union addresses, and party platforms from 1974 until the present.[1] The types of evidence gathered were: account evidence based on the content of the texts, sequence evidence, which examined the evolution of the suggested policy solutions over time, and pattern evidence examining the frequency of the proposed solutions.

Congressional bills: The content of all Congressional bills from 1974 under the subtopic childcare was examined (excluding bills on parental leave) (N = 500). Based on the policy tools suggested in the bills they were distinguished into four types: tax exemption bills (N = 236), assistance to low-income families (N = 178), federally financed comprehensive childcare programs (N = 11), other (mostly concrete regulations on the quality of childcare) (N = 75). Based on the frequency of each of the types we can see that tax exemptions and assistance to low-income families were almost the exclusive solutions proposed. In addition, the analysis reveals that policymakers were familiar with other solutions as seen in the bills on federally funded comprehensive childcare services or suggestions to encourage public–private partnerships. Both parties saw the two policy tools as plausible; 43 percent of Democrats' bills included tax exemptions (compared to 54 percent of the Republican bills), and 34 percent of the Republicans bills included assistance to low-income families (compared to 37 percent of the Democratic bills).

State of the Union Address: The policy tools suggested in the addresses from 1983 (the year childcare was first mentioned in the address) were examined. The analysis found that since the end of the 1980s regardless of the party in power, tax exemptions are the main policy tool suggested. For instance, President H.W. Bush stated in 1989:

I believe we should help working families cope with the burden of childcare. I support a new childcare tax credit that will aim our efforts at exactly those families without discriminating against mothers who choose to stay at home.

(Bush, 1989)

Sixteen years later President Barak Obama suggested the same type of solution:

In today's economy, when having both parents in the workforce is an economic necessity for many families, we need affordable, high-quality childcare more than ever...And that's why my plan will make quality childcare more available and more affordable for every middle-class and low-income family with young children in America—by creating more slots and a new tax cut of up to $3,000 per child, per year. (Obama, 2015)

Party platforms: An analysis of the content of party platforms of both the Republican and the Democratic parties revealed that while during 1970s to the 1980s the Democrats suggested federally funded comprehensive childcare and this idea was removed from the agenda in the mid-1980s. Since then the only proposed solution has been tax-credit expansions. As for the Republicans, in the 1970s to the 1980s they proposed providing financial incentives for private community providers to expand childcare services. From the 1990s however, the main solution has been expanding existing tax exemptions or suggesting new ones.

A comparison between the findings in all three series reveals the same pattern. During the 1970s to the1980s there were different solutions for the problem of lack of childcare. From the mid-1980s regardless of party affiliation all policy-makers have suggested the same policy tools, mostly tax exemptions.

33.4.2 *Limitations*

CAP provides data on issue attention. As such, it does not address the policy tools, policy targets, issue definitions, and other dimensions examined in policy research (Jones, 2015). This should be taken into account when using CAP for familiarization with the case of interest. For instance, the number of laws does not imply their importance since some laws are more significant than others. Therefore, the use of CAP's trends tool for gaining acquaintance with the case of interest should be used with care and re-evaluated against other data/research. In addition, in some series, the information is coded based on the observation's heading or abbreviation. However, in some cases two observations with the same heading (e.g., bills) can address different policy targets or tools, and the same policy tools will operate differently in different countries. Therefore, when gathering and evaluating evidence, the researcher should examine the source material, paying specific attention to the context of the policy in each country.

33.5 Conclusion

This chapter has aimed to encourage more qualitative scholars to use CAP in their research by suggesting several ways in which CAP can be useful for qualitative case-oriented research. It has suggested looking at CAP as a pool of possible policy cases and as an archival system that provides the rich material needed for the analysis. In addition, it has also demonstrated that CAP trends tool could assist the researcher to familiarize herself with the case and help her to formulate the specific research questions.

The chapter demonstrated more generic ways in which CAP can be used in a within-case analysis. In practice, scholars use CAP in more concrete situations, for instance, when illustrating shadow cases or when looking for the presence of specific evidence such as laws, bills, or hearings. However, the rich and high-quality CAP data provides many opportunities for scholars to be creative not only when looking for the empirical fingerprints in a specific case, but also when trying to overcome more general challenges that exist in policy research, as in identifying a less visible population of cases. Qualitative policy scholars should further examine CAP as a methodological tool and suggest ways for overcoming other policy research challenges, for instance, identifying latent processes such as keeping issues off the agenda. Broadening the use of CAP data beyond quantitative research can not only contribute to a better understanding of causal mechanisms in the policy process but also increase the methodological pluralism in the discipline.

Note

1. The evidence presented is only that retrieved using CAP and does not represent all the evidence gathered to demonstrate the presence of the lock-in effect.

References

Barnes, J. (2008). Courts and the Puzzle of Institutional Stability and Change. *Political Research Quarterly*, 61(4): 636–48.

Beach, D., and Pedersen, R. B. (2013). *Process-Tracing Methods: Foundations and Guidelines*. Michigan: University of Michigan Press.

Beach, D., and Pedersen, R. B. (2014). "Let the Evidence Speak..."—A Two-Stage Evidence Assessment Framework for Making Transparent the Process of Translating Empirical Material into Evidence. http://papers.ssrn.com/sol3/Delivery.cfm?abstractid=2451899

Béland, D. (2007). Ideas and Institutional Change in Social Security: Conversion, Layering, and Policy Drift. *Social Science Quarterly*, 88(1): 20–38.

Bianculli, A., and Jordana, J. (2013). The Unattainable Politics of Child Benefits Policy in Spain. *Journal of European Social Policy*, 23(5): 504–20.

Boldrin, M., Jiménez-Martín, S., and Peracchi, F. (1999). Social Security and Retirement in Spain. In *Social Security Programs and Retirement around the World*, ed. David A. Wise. Chicago: University of Chicago Press, 305–53.

Bush, H. W. (1989). 1989 State of the Union address. February 9. http://www.presidency.ucsb.edu/ws/index.php?pid=29643

Clegg, D. (2007). Continental Drift: On Unemployment Policy Change in Bismarckian Welfare States. *Social Policy Administration*, 41(6): 597–617.

de Cabo, R. M., Gimeno, R., and Escot, L. (2011). Disentangling Discrimination on Spanish Boards of Directors. *Corporate Governance An International Review*, 19(1): 77–95.

George, A. L., and Bennett, A. (2005). Case Studies and Theory Development in the Social Sciences. Cambridge, MA: MIT Press.

Gildiner, A. (2007). The Organization of Decision-Making and the Dynamics of Policy Drift: A Canadian Health Sector Example. *Social Policy Administration*, 41(5): 505–24.

Goertz, G. (ed.) (2006). *Social Science Concepts: A User's Guide*. Princeton: Princeton University Press.

Goertz, G., and Hewitt, J. J. (2006). Concepts and Choosing Populations. In *Social Science Concepts: A User's Guide*, ed. G. Goertz. Princeton: Princeton University Press, 211–34.

Goertz, G., and Mahoney, J. (2012). *A Tale of Two Cultures: Qualitative and Quantitative Research in the Social Sciences*. Princeton: Princeton University Press.

Gruber, J., and Wise, D. (2000). Social Security Programs and Retirement around the World. In *Research in Labor Economics*, Vol. 18, ed. Bingley: Emerald Group Publishing, 1–40.

Hacker, J. S. (2004). Privatizing Risk without Privatizing the Welfare State: The Hidden Politics of Social Policy Retrenchment in the United States. *American Political Science Review*, 98(2): 243–60.

Hacker, J. S., and Pierson, P. (2010). Winner-Take-All Politics: Public Policy, Political Organization, and the Precipitous Rise of Top Incomes in the United States. *Politics & Society*, 38(2): 152–204.

Hacker, J. S., Pierson, P., and Thelen, K. A. (2015). Drift and Conversion: The Hidden Faces of Institutional Change. In *Advances in Comparative-Historical Analysis*, ed. J. Mahoney and K. A. Thelen. New York: Cambridge University Press, 180–208.

Jones, B. D. (2015). The Comparative Policy Agendas Projects as Measurement Systems: Response to Dowding, Hindmoor, and Martin. *Journal of Public Policy*, 36(1): 31–46.

Krutz, G. S. (2005). Issues and Institutions: "Winnowing" in the US Congress. *American Journal of Political Science*, 49(2): 313–26.

León, M. (2007). Speeding up or Holding back? Institutional Factors in the Development of Childcare Provision in Spain. *European Societies*, 9(3): 315–37.

Obama, B. H. (2015). Barack Obama: Address before a Joint Session of the Congress on the State of the Union. January 20. http://www.presidency.ucsb.edu/ws/index.php?pid=108031

Pena-Boquete, Y. (2009). A Comparative Analysis of the Evolution of Gender Wage Discrimination: Spain vs. Galicia. *Papers in Regional Science*, 88(1): 161–80.

Ragin, C. C., and Becker, H. S. (1992). *What Is a Case? Exploring the Foundations of Social Inquiry*. New York: Cambridge University Press.

Rica, S. de la, Dolado, J. J., and Llorens, V. (2008). Ceilings or Floors? Gender Wage Gaps by Education in Spain. *Journal of Population Economics*, 21(3): 751–76.

Rocco, P., and Thurston, C. (2014). From Metaphors to Measures: Observable Indicators of Gradual Institutional Change. *Journal of Public Policy*, 34(1): 35–62.

Shpaizman, I. (2016). Identifying Relevant Cases of Conversion and Drift Using the Comparative Agendas Project. *Policy Studies Journal*, 45(3): 490–509.

Solomon-Cohen, S. (2001). *Championing Child Care*. New York: Columbia University Press.

Tsebelis, G. (1995). Decision Making in Political Systems: Veto Players in Presidentialism, Parliamentarism, Multicameralism and Multipartyism. *British Journal of Political Science,* 25(3): 289–325.

Valiente, C. (2003). Central State Child Care Policies in Postauthoritarian Spain: Implications for Gender and Carework Arrangements. *Gender & Society*, 2003, 17(2): 287–92.

34

Issue Attention in West European Party Politics

CAP and CMP Coding Compared

Christoffer Green-Pedersen

34.1 Introduction

The CMP dataset has long been the central data source for the study of West European party politics. The discussions around the CMP dataset have been extensive and have covered many aspects of the dataset (cf. Gemenis, 2013). This includes the use of party manifestos as a data source (Helbling and Tresch, 2011), the use of quasi-sentences as a coding unit (Däubler et al., 2012), and, not least, how to estimate party positions from the data (Lowe et al., 2011; Budge and Meyer, 2013; Dinas and Gemenis, 2010). What has received much less attention are the consequences of the coding scheme on which the CMP dataset is based (though see Horn et al., 2017; Zulianello, 2014). However, the coding scheme applied is one of the most fundamental aspects of any dataset. Once the data has been coded in a certain way, this structures the use of the dataset profoundly. No matter how the data is transformed or re-scaled afterwards, one cannot make up for a category not found in a coding scheme, just as one cannot compensate for a survey question that was not asked.

The challenge with regard to the CMP coding scheme, however, is that it has been difficult to explore its consequences without having to recode the data. However, the growth of the CAP datasets offers new possibilities because, for a number of countries, the CAP datasets also include coding of party manifestos (e.g., Froio et al., 2017; Brouard et al., 2012). This opens up the possibility of comparing the coding of identical documents using different coding schemes. This chapter thus compares attention to a number of different policy issues identified in the CMP and in the CAP coding systems based on the coding of party manifestos for seven countries (Germany, France, the United Kingdom, the Netherlands, Belgium, Sweden, and Denmark) from

1980 onwards. Put together, the manifestos in these seven countries provide a strong basis for comparing the patterns across the two coding systems.

It is important to remember that the CMP dataset was not developed with the purpose of measuring party attention to specific policy issues. The purpose of the dataset was primarily to measure political parties' ideological positions on a left–right scale. Nevertheless, the CMP dataset has increasingly been used to measure party attention to specific policy issues (see Section 34.2). Further, the creation of the left–right (rile) scale is also based on a saliency perspective (Budge and Meyer, 2013). A better understanding of the policy content of the CMP categories is therefore also important for evaluating the left–right scale.

The general finding of this chapter is that even though the CMP scheme was not originally developed to measure attention to policy issues, it is feasible to use it for that purpose; but with caution. The level of attention to various policy issues identified based on the CMP and CAP coding schemes is relatively similar, but with a number of important exceptions. A similar pattern emerges when looking at the correlations between the two measures on similar issues. The explanation for these exceptions can be found in the differences in the coding systems that again reflect their different theoretical purposes: The CAP coding scheme measures attention to policy issues whereas the CMP scheme was developed to measure ideological policy positions. This has two important implications. One is that the CMP coding focuses on the ideological goals of certain policy measures, whereas the CAP coding focuses on the policy instruments. Thus, if a party declares that it wants to improve primary schools to reduce inequality, the CMP coding would focus on the goal of reducing inequality whereas the CAP coding would focus on the attention to primary schools. The other implication is that the CMP dataset does not aim to cover the entire policy agenda. For instance, there is no specific category for healthcare; it is included in the categories relating to the welfare state. From the policy perspective of the CAP coding, this is an important drawback, but in terms of measuring ideological positions, this is not a problem as the ideological goals of different policies relating to the welfare state are often very similar. From a broader perspective, this chapter thus points to the importance of the theoretical perspectives behind different coding schemes. Classification and categorization need a theoretical foundation that must not be forgotten when datasets are later used for different purposes.

34.2 The CMP and CAP Datasets and the Discussions around them

The CMP dataset goes back to the establishment of the Manifesto Group in 1979. The debate around the dataset took off after its publication in 2001 (Budge et al., 2001). The dataset became the major source for studying party politics in the Western world and, at the same time, a vivid debate around many aspects of the dataset has emerged (cf. Gemenis, 2013; Volkens et al., 2013). This relates to the use of party manifestos as a data source (Helbling and Tresch, 2011), the use of quasi-sentences as a coding unit (Däubler et al., 2012), the reliability of the CMP coding (Mikhaylov et al., 2012), and, not least, how to estimate party positions from the data (Lowe et al., 2011; Budge and Meyer, 2013; Dinas and Gemenis, 2010). What has received more limited attention is the CMP coding scheme (though see Horn et al., 2017; Zulianello, 2014). The scheme consists of fifty-six categories organized into seven broader domains.[1] To discuss this coding scheme, awareness of the theoretical foundation is necessary.

As stated by Volkens (2001: 96–8), the CMP coding scheme is a further development of the coding scheme that Robertson (1976: 74–5) developed to capture British party positions. The driving logic is not policy issues, but ideological 'symbols' like democracy, freedom, social justice, etc. The underlying idea is that parties' mentions of such symbols are a way to measure their ideology, or more precisely, their policy preferences. Pro and con categories on some policy items were added later as a supplement to the pure saliency approach that Robertson (1976) had originally developed. Thus, the CMP dataset has—deliberately—(cf. Robertson, 1976: 72–3) not been based on the idea of policy issues, but is an attempt to capture the broader ideological preferences of political parties. The main focus of the coding is the ideological goals that parties express, not the policy means or instruments they suggest.

The CAP system was originally developed by Baumgartner and Jones (see Chapters 1 and 2) based on policy agenda-setting theory (see Baumgartner et al., 2002). It is an explicit attempt to cover the entire policy agenda and to provide a coding system that can travel across time and countries. The primary focus is on the policy content or policy instruments that receive attention. The coding scheme has been used to code very different political activities, such as executive speeches, media news, parliamentary activities (hearings, bills, laws, parliamentary questions, etc.), and local council agendas, as well as party platforms or manifestos. The CAP coding scheme is further based on the differences between main topics (or issues) such as the economy, transportation, and education, and subtopics within each major topic, such as inflation, monetary policy, and unemployment as subtopics within the economy, and railways, air transportation, or sea transportation within transportation. The latest version of the coding system has twenty-one major topics and 213 subtopics. As each unit is coded into a subtopic, these can be aggregated in whatever way suits a particular research purpose.

The CMP and CAP dataset thus start from quite different theoretical concepts—ideological goals or symbols vs. policy instruments or policy issues. Still, sometimes ideological symbols and policy issues are difficult to distinguish.

Education, culture, and European integration feature in the CMP dataset, which in reality thus also includes a number of policy issues. At the same time, the CMP dataset is based on a saliency approach, where the salience of the different items in the coding is used to calculate party positions. Thus, despite the focus on party positions, the CMP coding system is similar to the CAP coding system in the sense that the data measures the saliency of different ideological symbols, which are often in fact policy instruments or issues.

One difference between the coding schemes lies in the fact that the CMP dataset also tries to capture positions by coding both positive and negative references to a number of issues (e.g., European integration and education). However, there are also a number of items, such as the environment, where the CMP does not distinguish between positive and negative mentions. Instead, positions on the environment are constructed by subtracting other categories from the categories measuring attention to the environment (per416 and per501). Lowe et al. (2011) and Abou-Chadi (2016) both subtract productivity (per410), whereas Meguid (2008: 89) subtracts positive mentions of free enterprise (per401), support for agriculture (per703), and negative mentions of internationalism (per109). Further, the left–right (rile) scale developed from the CMP data—probably the most widely used measure derived from the data—is based precisely on subtracting attention to different items (e.g., economic incentives (per402)—economic planning (per404)). Thus, despite the differences in the coding systems, they in fact both attempt to measure the saliency of different policy instruments or issues.

Therefore, it is not surprising that the CMP coding system has increasingly been used to study attention to different policy issues. This is the case, for instance, with regard to the welfare state (Jensen and Seeberg, 2015), education (Jakobi, 2011; Busemeyer et al., 2013), the environment (Abou-Chadi, 2016; Spoon et al., 2014), corruption (Curini and Martelli, 2015), decentralization (Toubeau and Wagner, 2016), and immigration (Abou-Chadi, 2016; Green-Pedersen and Krogstrup, 2008; Breunig and Luedtke, 2008).

In sum, both with regard to the 'core use' of the CMP dataset for deriving a left–right scale and the broader use of the dataset to measure attention to particular policy issues, a detailed understanding of the consequences of the CMP coding scheme is important. However, there has hitherto been little debate about the CMP coding scheme and how it deals with different policy issues. Horn et al. (2017) is a rare attempt to dig into the coding system. There are three aspects into which one can dig even more deeply.

The first one has to do with the delimitation of the policy issues, i.e., what are the definitional boundaries between issues. This is of course a central question for any coding scheme, but it becomes even more pressing for a coding system that is only partly based on policy issues. With education, for instance, one issue of delimitation is what distinguishes education from labor market policy, i.e., training, active labor market policy, etc. However, the CMP does not have a category for labor market policy. It has categories per701 and per702 for positive and negative mentions of labor groups, but not labor market policy. Further, technical training is supposed to be coded with 411.[2] As a coder, one looks for the best available category for coding a given sentence,[3] so the fact that no direct category for labor market policy exists may affect the number of sentences in the education category. The lack of a labor market policy category may make education the most appropriate category, which might not be the case if a category for labor market policy existed. Thus the fact that only some policy issues have a specific code in the CMP scheme, i.e., the exhaustiveness of the scheme, might also affect the coding of the policy issues that do have their own category.

The second issue relates to the interpretation of some of the categories as policy issues. Thus, the categories per601 and per602 (national way of life positive and negative) and per607 and per608 (multiculturalism positive and negative) have frequently been used to study the issue of immigration (e.g., Abou-Chadi, 2016; Green-Pedersen and Krogstrup, 2008; Alonso and Fonseca, 2012; Breunig and Luedtke, 2008). The concern about this use of the categories is that they appear to have broader coverage than just immigration.[4] Thus, the categories may sometimes include attention to issues other than immigration. This raises questions about their validity as measures of attention to immigration. Further, additional categories like 705 (underprivileged minority groups) (Green-Pedersen and Krogstrup, 2008) or even law and order (Alonso and Fonseca, 2012) are sometimes also added.

The third issue relates to the use of the CMP dataset to provide a general overview of the development of attention to policy issues. Given that only some policy issues have distinct categories, such overviews will necessarily have to focus on very broad categories such as material vs. non-material or left/right-oriented attention (e.g., Ward et al., 2015; Tavits and Potter, 2015; Albright, 2010; Green-Pedersen, 2007). The coding system also has two broad categories for positive and negative mentions of the welfare state (per504 and per505), which include diverse policy issues such as healthcare, pensions, and social housing. The CMP coding scheme thus makes difficult a general investigation of which issues rise and decline over time. Important issue developments may be hidden in the broad categories.

If one instead looks at the CAP coding system, its strengths are its inbuilt policy logic and its detailed coverage of the entire policy agenda. However, it is important to stress that the CAP scheme should not be considered a 'gold standard' to which the CMP dataset should be compared. As stated above, the main purpose of the CMP coding scheme has never been to measure attention to policy issues. This was a way of using the data that emerged after the design of the coding scheme. The CAP coding scheme also comes with limitations. Not every relevant policy topic has its own subtopic code. For instance, the CAP coding scheme does not offer a specific subtopic for climate change, but the subtopic 705 covers air pollution, global warming, and noise pollution (Carter et al., 2017). Further, from a party perspective, the major limitation of the CAP coding system is clearly that it does not provide any measure of direction that makes it possible to measure party positions directly. Still, the theoretical starting purpose of the CAP coding scheme has never been to study particular actors such as political parties, but to track attention to policy issues.[5]

To summarize, the CMP and CAP coding systems have quite different origins. The CMP coding system was set up to capture party ideology by coding policy goals. The CAP coding system was designed to measure attention to policy issues by focusing on policy instruments. However, in practice both systems are used to study party attention to different policy issues, though the CMP dataset is by far the most used scheme because the data has been available for a large number of countries for a longer period of time.

34.3 CMP and CAP Compared

Since the CMP dataset has clearly been the most widely used scheme for studying party attention, the following comparison of issue attention based on the two coding schemes is structured around the three questions raised concerning this use of the CMP dataset. Thus, the first part compares issue attention to education, crime and justice, European integration, and the environment, where categories in the CMP coding scheme exist that, at least judging by their names, appear comparable to the policy issues in the CAP scheme. The next part then looks at attention to immigration, an issue where the CMP dataset has no direct category, but where other categories are used. Finally, the analysis looks at attention to healthcare to discuss the implications of the CMP coding scheme not having a category for this policy issue. Taken together, looking at these different questions allows us to evaluate the delimitation and exhaustiveness of the CMP coding scheme.

Before comparing attention to the different policy issues across the two coding systems, a few other questions concerning the comparability of the data are necessary. The comparison below is based on seven countries from 1980 onwards where CAP coding of party manifestos exist. These are Denmark, Sweden, the United Kingdom, France, Germany, the Netherlands, and Belgium. Together, they offer an extensive empirical basis for comparing the issue attention of political parties. The CMP dataset is based on quasi-sentences. This is also the case for most CAP manifesto datasets (the United Kingdom, Sweden, Belgium, and France), but Denmark and Germany use natural sentences as coding unit (dot to dot). As shown by Däubler et al. (2012), this makes only a limited practical difference. The Dutch data is coded based on paragraphs, which must be taken into consideration when comparing with the CMP data.[6]

In terms of the parties covered, there are some differences across the two datasets. The most important differences are that the British CAP data only includes the three major parties (the Labour party, the Conservatives and the Liberal Democrats), unlike the CMP dataset, which also includes other parties represented in parliament. On the other hand, the coverage of minor Dutch parties is more extensive in the CAP dataset. Finally, concerning the French right, common programs of the parties are used for the CAP coding when they exist, and the same is the case for joint programs of the Swedish right (Alliancen) and left (Left-Alliance) in recent elections. In the analysis, only parties included in both datasets are compared.[7]

The purpose of the analysis in the following is to provide an overview of similarities and differences in both the level of attention to different policy issues identified by the two different coding schemes, and the correlation between the two measures. Further, potential explanations for differences will be discussed by looking at the coding schemes and including some examples of specific party manifestos where large differences were identified.[8]

Starting with education, the results presented in Table 34.1 indicate a significant difference across the two coding systems.[9] In all countries, the CAP coding scheme identified higher average levels of attention to education than did the CMP dataset. The difference is both statistically and substantially significant for five out of seven countries. The following discussion examines why this is the case.

Table 34.1. Comparison of CAP and CMP party attention to education (paired t-test and correlations)

Country	CAP mean	CMP mean	Difference	SE	Correlation (Pearson r)	N (no. of manifestos/countries)
Belgium	5.0	4.7	0.3	0.32	0.54	85
Denmark	7.7	5.4	2.3***	0.46	0.77	94
France	5.5	4.8	0.7	0.66	0.41	34
Germany	5.5	3.4	2.1***	0.26	0.88	46
Netherlands	7.1	5.0	2.1***	0.29	0.52	84
UK	9.2	5.6	3.6***	0.55	0.68	21
Sweden	6.2	4.5	1.7***	0.32	0.81	48
Average (across country)	6.6	4.8			0.66	7

Note: * p < 0.1, ** p < 0.05, *** p < 0.01.

Sources: CAP data, see Green-Pedersen (2018); CMP data from https://manifesto-project.wzb.eu/May 2016.

The fact that the pattern is quite consistent across all countries would indicate that the explanation should be found in the codebook itself and not particular interpretations of it in a given country.[10] In the CAP coding scheme, the major topic of education covers all policy questions related to primary education, secondary education, universities (including students), tertiary education, and vocational education. In the CMP system, education is covered by the categories per506 and per507, referring to education expansion and limitations. However, the CMP coding scheme also contains a number of other categories that may be potentially relevant with regard to education. For instance, per706 covers non-economic demographic groups like university students. The CMP coding scheme also contains categories like per503, which relates to equality and the removal of barriers for underprivileged groups. Statements about education are likely to be framed in exactly such a way and may therefore be coded here (see also Horn et al., 2017).

Thus, whereas the CAP coding scheme basically captures any policy question related to education, the CMP coding system approaches it from an ideological perspective where not all statements related to educational policy may relate to its expansion or limitation, but relate to questions about equality or certain social groups like students. Thus, the CMP categories for education would seem to only partially cover education as seen from a policy perspective. Table 34.1 also reports the correlation between the two codings. This is mostly relatively high, but with some cross-national variation. Thus, the two datasets identify relatively similar dynamics in party attention, though less so in France, the Netherlands, and Belgium.

In the same way, Table 34.2 compares the CAP and CMP mean level of attention with regard to crime and justice or law and order. The table shows that attention to crime and justice is higher according to CAP, and statistically significantly so, in five of the seven countries. The differences are somewhat

Table 34.2. Comparison of CAP and CMP party attention to crime and justice (paired t-test and correlations)

Country	CAP mean	CMP mean	Difference	SE	Correlation (Pearson r)	N (no. of manifestos/countries)
Belgium	6.2	4.4	1.8***	0.48	0.53	85
Denmark	3.6	3.7	−0.1	0.35	0.77	94
France	4.7	3.8	0.9*	0.55	0.70	34
Germany	4.3	2.5	1.8***	0.30	0.68	46
Netherlands	6.7	6.2	0.5**	0.25	0.77	84
UK	6.8	5.7	1.1***	0.27	0.88	21
Sweden	3.0	3.0	0.0	0.25	0.85	48
Average (across countries)	5.0	4.2			0.74	7

Note: * p < 0.1, ** p < 0.05, *** p < 0.01.

Sources: CAP data, see Green-Pedersen (2018); CMP data from https://manifesto-project.wzb.eu/May 2016.

smaller than what was found with regard to education. Based on the coding scheme, one should also not expect large differences.[11]

The CMP coding scheme has one category, per605, that covers questions about law and order such as enforcement of laws, support for the police, and importance of internal security. The CAP coding scheme also has a major topic called law and crime with subtopics for white-collar crime and organized crime (1202), criminal and civil code (1210), and police and other general domestic security responses to terrorism (1227). However, the CAP coding scheme also includes subtopics covering the broader judicial systems, i.e., court administration (1204), prisons (1205), and agencies dealing with law and crime (1201). Thus the most likely explanation for the higher levels of attention in the CAP coding is that such broader aspects of the judicial system are picked up by the CAP system. Further, the observations based on the two coding schemes correlate quite well, and with relatively limited cross-national variation.

Table 34.3 looks at European integration. The CMP has two categories, per108 and per110, that cover positive and negative mentions of European integration. The latter includes "opposition to specific European Union policies." The CAP scheme covers European integration in two ways. First, it is captured partly through subtopic 1910, which covers "institutional" or polity-related questions regarding the European Union—enlargement, the role of Commissions, national referendums, etc.[12] Second, statements related to the policies of the European Union are covered under the relevant policy areas. Thus, environmental policy or banking policies will be coded under the relevant policy topics. For these reasons, one would expect the level of attention found in the CMP dataset to be higher.

This is indeed what is found in Table 34.3, where the higher values for the CMP measure is statistically significant for six out of the seven countries.[13]

Table 34.3. Comparison of CAP and CMP party attention to European integration (paired t-test and correlations)

Country	CAP mean	CMP mean	Difference	SE	Correlation (Pearson r)	N (no. of manifestos/countries)
Belgium	2.1	3.0	−0.9***	0.32	0.44	85
Denmark	3.3	3.2	0.1	0.46	0.84	94
France	3.0	4.2	−1.2**	0.61	0.38	34
Germany	2.1	2.9	−0.8**	0.32	0.31	46
Netherlands	2.5	3.0	−0.5***	0.20	0.65	84
UK	2.6	3.4	−0.8***	0.29	0.76	21
Sweden	2.6	3.5	−0.9***	0.27	0.84	48
Average (across countries)	2.6	3.3			0.60	7

Note: * p < 0.1, ** p < 0.05, *** p < 0.01.
Source: CAP data, see Green-Pedersen (2018); CMP data from https://manifesto-project.wzb.eu/May 2016.

However, in substantial terms, the differences are rather small, especially when compared to education, but also to crime and justice. Thus, the differences with regard to the coding system do not seem to make a large substantial difference. This is most likely because policies emerging from the European Union are not often discussed in manifestos. Rather, statements here are focused on the polity aspects of European integration. Policies emerging from the European Union are more likely taken up in parliamentary activities such as questions to the minister (Senninger, 2017). In terms of correlation, the coefficients exhibit more cross-national variation than for the two other issues and relatively low figures for Germany, France, and Belgium. The average correlation is also lower than for education and especially crime and justice.

Attention to the environment is captured in the CMP coding scheme by the categories per416 (anti-growth economy) and per501 (environmental protection). The CAP coding system covers the environment through the major topic of environmental policy with sub-categories for a large number of aspects of environmental protection, e.g., drinking water and water pollution (701), waste disposal (702), and air pollution, global warming, and noise pollution (705). The CAP coding scheme also has a number of subtopics related to the environment such as international resources exploitation and resources agreements (1902) and natural resources, public lands, and forest management (2103), which are also included in the attention measure reported in Table 34.4.[14]

It is furthermore important to note that the two coding schemes differ in terms of the categories offered for related issues. The CAP coding scheme has a major topic for energy policy, with subtopics for nuclear power (801), coal (805), and alternative and renewable energy (806). The CMP coding scheme does not have a specific category for energy policy-related quasi-sentences. Both coding schemes have topic codes related to agriculture. The CAP coding scheme also has a major topic for agriculture-related policy, which, among others, includes a subtopic for animal and crop disease, animal welfare, and pest control (405).[15] The CMP coding scheme has a category (per703) for support for farmers and agriculture, which is thus much narrower than the CAP major issue code for agriculture.

Table 34.4 shows party attention to the environment. The general tendency is for the CMP coding system to generate higher values. The difference between the CMP and the CAP measure is thus statistically significant for five of the seven countries.[16] Substantially, this is most clearly the case for Sweden and the Netherlands, and to a more limited extent for Germany and France. The most likely explanation for this difference is the difference in related categories. This can be seen by looking at the Dutch Party for Animal Rights (PvdD). According to the CMP data, this party mainly pays attention to

Table 34.4. Comparison of CAP and CMP party attention to environment (paired t-test and correlations)

Country	CAP mean	CMP mean	Difference	SE	Correlation (Pearson r)	N (no. of manifestos/countries)
Belgium	5.7	6.2	−0.5	0.60	0.40	85
Denmark	6.3	6.7	−0.4	0.51	0.67	94
France	4.3	5.7	−1.4**	0.62	0.83	34
Germany	6.4	8.6	−2.2***	0.55	0.72	46
Netherlands	7.2	11.2	−4.0***	1.00	0.78	84
UK	4.8	5.2	−0.4**	0.26	0.92	21
Sweden	7.9	13.0	−5.1***	0.94	0.89	48
Average (across countries)	6.1	8.1			0.74	7

Note: * p < 0.1, ** p < 0.05, *** p < 0.01.

Source: CAP data, see Green-Pedersen (2018); CMP data from https://manifesto-project.wzb.eu/May 2016.

the environment: 73.8 percent of its manifesto was devoted to this issue in 2006, 74.7 percent in 2010, and 61.6 percent in 2012. According to the CAP data, the comparable figures are 24.1, 19.8, and 19.7. However, whereas the CMP coding scheme records less than 1 percent of the PvdD manifestos under attention to agriculture, the CAP coding scheme reports 38.8 percent, 38.8 percent, and 28.8 percent. Thus, a likely explanation is that various demands for protection of animal rights and regulation of agriculture made by the party are coded as related to agriculture by the CAP coding and coded as related to the environment by the CMP coding scheme, simply because no broad category for agriculture exists in the CMP coding scheme.

Another example would be the manifestos of the Swedish Green Party in 1994: Where the CMP coding scheme records 34.8 percent attention to the environment, the CAP scheme only records 15.2 percent. The CAP coding scheme then reports 5.1 percent for energy policy and 4 percent for agriculture, whereas the CMP scheme reports nothing for agriculture. Thus, it seems that the environmental categories in the CMP scheme capture statements that in the CAP scheme would be coded under energy—for instance, reduction of the use of coal to reduce CO_2 emissions. It is also worth noting that countries such as Sweden and Germany that have seen intensive political debates around nuclear power (Müller and Thurner, 2017) exhibit substantially higher values for the CMP coding, which includes nuclear power. Thus, the findings on the environment clearly underline that the use of one category within either of the two coding schemes cannot be viewed in isolation from the rest of the coding scheme. In terms of correlation, these are, with the exception of Belgium, high in comparison with the other issues. Only crime and justice has the same high cross-national average correlation. This indicates that quite similar party competition dynamics are captured by the two coding schemes.

As discussed above, the CMP coding scheme has also been used relatively widely to study attention to immigration, even though no category referring directly to this in the CMP coding scheme exists. Existing studies thus use the categories referring to positive and negative mentions of national way of life (per601 and per602) and the categories referring to positive and negative mentions of multiculturalism (per607 and per608). These categories are often combined with other categories, typically per705, favorable mentions of underprivileged minority groups like immigrants, homosexuals, and the disabled (Meguid, 2008: 90; Alonso and Fonseca, 2012; Green-Pedersen and Krogstrup, 2008). The CAP coding scheme has one category related to general immigration and refugee issues. In terms of neighboring issues, both coding schemes have a category for crime and justice, as discussed earlier.

Table 34.5 shows the results from a comparison of two different measures of immigration from the CMP data. CMP1 contains per601, per602, per607 and per608, which seem mostly closely related to immigration. CMP2 then added per705. In all cases except France, CMP1 identifies less average attention to immigration than the CAP measure,[17] but the differences are smaller than those found on issues such as education and the environment and not significant for France, the Netherlands and the United Kingdom. This finding would speak in favor of including more categories to capture attention when using the CMP scheme, as is typically done. However, the question then is whether this also measures attention that is not related to immigration.

Table 34.5 would indicate that this could indeed be the case for some countries. For all countries other than Sweden and Denmark, the CMP2 measure produces values that are higher, and statistically significantly so, than the CAP measure.[18] The results would thus indicate that by including per705, one also captures attention to underprivileged minority groups other

Table 34.5. Comparison of CAP and CMP party attention to immigration (paired t-test and correlations)

Country	CAP mean	CMP1 mean	Difference	SE	Correlation (Pearson r) (CAP/CMP1)	CMP2 mean	Correlation (Pearson r) (CAP/CMP2)	N (no. of manifestos/ countries)
Belgium	3.0	2.2	0.8***	0.34	0.30	4.1***	0.32	85
Denmark	6.0	5.1	0.9*	0.62	0.74	6.2	0.79	94
France	2.7	3.3	−0.6	0.62	0.54	5.5***	0.44	34
Germany	3.1	1.7	1.4***	0.27	0.47	3.7***	0.71	46
Netherlands	3.6	3.3	0.3	0.48	0.37	6.0***	0.36	84
UK	1.9	1.3	0.6	0.58	−0.1	2.7*	0.12	21
Sweden	2.0	1.0	1.0**	0.41	0.38	1.8	0.38	48
Average (per country)	3.2	2.6			0.39	4.3	0.45	7

Note: * p < 0.1, ** p < 0.05, *** p < 0.01.

Sources: CAP data, see Green-Pedersen (2018); CMP data from https://manifesto-project.wzb.eu/May 2016.

than immigrants, i.e., the disabled or homosexuals. Compared to the other issues, the correlations between the CAP and CMP measures are generally much weaker than for the other issues, especially for the United Kingdom. The correlation is mostly better when including the per705 category, though only for Germany and the United Kingdom is it significantly improved and for France it is weaker.

To summarize, it seems that attention to immigration is captured by a number of different categories in the CMP dataset. Including the four categories related to national way of life and multiculturalism provide estimations relatively close to the CAP measure in terms of levels of attention, though typically lower. This makes the inclusion of further categories appealing, but Table 34.5 would indicate that including per705 implies capturing attention that is not immigration related. No matter which solution is applied, the correlation is clearly weaker than for the other issues. Thus, the immigration measures that can be developed from the CMP dataset seem the most different from the CAP ones. This is not surprising, given that they were also not designed with only immigration-related content in mind.

The third and final question raised above with regard to the CMP coding scheme was the implication of certain policy issues being completely absent from the scheme, in the sense that they have no specific category. Energy policy was mentioned above, and another example is healthcare. In the CMP coding scheme, attention to healthcare is handled by per504 and per505, which capture statements about welfare-state expansion and welfare-state

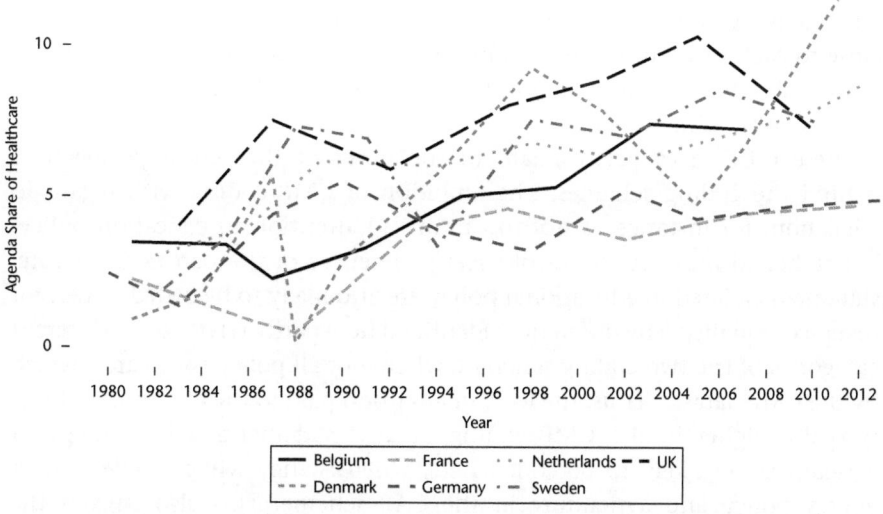

Figure 34.1. Attention to healthcare in seven countries, 1980–2013
Source: Comparative Agendas Project

limitation. The CAP coding scheme has a major topic for healthcare and a series of subtopics capturing different aspects of healthcare such as facilities construction, regulation, and payments (322) and disease prevention, treatment, and health promotion (331). Figure 34.1 shows the development of attention to healthcare in the seven countries based on the CAP data. In all countries, attention to healthcare has risen, and in several countries quite substantially. This significant development cannot be observed through the CMP dataset.

34.4 Conclusions

The comparison of the level of attention to different policy issues in the CMP and the CAP coding schemes show relatively similar levels of attention to many issues. Furthermore, the differences were typically in the same direction, indicating that they were due to one coding system systematically leading to higher or lower levels of attention in all countries. Relatively high levels of correlation between the CMP and the CAP measures were also generally found, but with significant exceptions. The biggest differences in terms of levels of attention were found with regard to the environment, whereas the weakest correlations were with regard to immigration, no matter which measure of immigration from the CMP dataset was used. Generally, crime and justice was the issue where the two measures were closest to each other, both in terms of levels of attention and correlation, and immigration was the issue where they were furthest from each other. This is not surprising when looking at the codebooks. The categories for crime and justice are quite close to each other in the two coding schemes, whereas they differ substantially with regard to immigration. Here, the issue is only measured indirectly in the CMP coding scheme.

These differences partly relate to the different theoretical perspectives behind the coding schemes. The ambition of CMP coding with regard to education, for instance, is not to capture all attention to education policy, but rather to measure the ideological preferences of the parties. Therefore, statements related to educational policy are also likely to be coded under, for instance, equality. The differences identified here partly relate to the different categories of the two coding schemes, where not all policy issues are covered by the CMP dataset. Thus, the level of attention paid to the environment was typically higher in the CMP coding because statements about energy or agriculture are likely to be coded here, whereas they will be coded under energy policy and agriculture in the CAP scheme. This also stresses the importance of evaluating the coding schemes in total. What is coded under one category depends on the alternative categories offered.

It is also worth noting that the differences in coding units do not seem to make a substantial difference. The CMP data use quasi-sentences as coding units, which is also the coding unit used in the CAP coding of party manifestos in the United Kingdom, Sweden, France, and Belgium. However, for Germany and Denmark, natural sentences were used as coding units for the CAP coding, and in the Dutch case, paragraphs were used. The tables shown above do not indicate that the relationships between the CAP and CMP were any weaker for the three countries with a different coding unit for the CAP data—not even for the Netherlands, where paragraphs were used. This follows the findings of Dâubler et al. (2012), who also conclude that the use of natural sentences instead of quasi-sentences provides very similar results in substantial terms.

To conclude, in terms of the use of the CMP dataset to study policy issues, the findings here suggest that this should be done, but with caution. The CMP coding scheme is not based on a policy logic, and in some (but not all) cases, this makes a substantial difference.

Acknowledgements

Thanks to Christian Breunig and Nicolas Merz for very constructive criticism of an earlier version of this chapter.

Notes

1. The codebook can be found here: https://manifestoproject.wzb.eu/down/data/2016b/codebooks/codebook_MPDataset_MPDS2016b.pdf. A newer version of the codebook exists with more subcategories, but these codes have only been used for the most recent documents.
2. The detailed coding instruction of the CMP dataset can be found at https://manifestoproject.wzb.eu/down/papers/handbook_2014_version_5.pdf
3. The CMP project uses quasi-sentences as the coding unit.
4. This worry is supported by the fact that the recent Version 5.0 of the codebook has divided the four categories into two each, one general and one immigration related.
5. Potentially, one could also develop positional measures from the CAP scheme by subtracting the saliency of from the different policy issues.
6. Both coding schemes only allow one code for each coding unit.
7. The CAP coding scheme has a Master Codebook that can be found at http://sbevan.com/cap-master-codebook.html together with the crosswalk, which ties national versions of the codebook to the Master Codebook. The description of the CAP manifesto dataset (Green-Pedersen 2018) contains an overview of how the different subtopics from the CAP coding scheme have been combined into the policy issues.

8. What has not been feasible is a systematic sentence-by-sentence comparison of two different codings of the same manifesto. Even for the countries where quasi-sentences were also used as the coding unit for the CAP coding, the coding into quasi-sentences was done separately for the two datasets, implying differences in the exact quasi-sentences identified. Therefore, a direct comparison of the coding at the sentence level would first require an inspection of the data to ensure that only the coding of identical quasi-sentences is compared.

9. In the CMP dataset, downloaded from https://manifesto-project.wzb.eu/May 2016, un-codeable sentences are reported as a category alongside the substantial categories. In the following, the percentages in the CMP dataset have been recoded as percentages of total coded sentences, i.e., excluding the un-codeable sentences. This is the typical approach of the CAP scheme, where a total agenda summing to 100 is calculated based only on coded units.

10. For individual manifestos, 69 percent of the cases have higher values based on the CAP scheme.

11. For individual manifestos, 62 percent of the cases have higher values based on the CAP scheme.

12. In the CAP Master Codebook, 1910 refers to Western Europe and European integration, but for most countries, this sub-code has been split into 1910 for European integration and 1913 for Western Europe.

13. For individual manifestos, 71 percent of the cases have higher values based on the CMP scheme.

14. The CAP categories added to the environment are 1902, 2100, 2101, 2013, and 2199 and, for some countries, 407 (regulation of agriculture).

15. In the CAP coding scheme, regulation of agriculture, including for environmental purposes, will be coded under agriculture. However, some of the countries have generated a specific subtopic, 407, for environmental regulation of agriculture, and attention in this subtopic has been included in environmental attention in this chapter.

16. For individual manifestos, 65 percent of the cases have higher values based on the CMP scheme.

17. For individual manifestos, 59 percent of the cases have higher values based on the CAP scheme.

18. For individual manifestos, 69 percent of the cases have higher values based on the CMP scheme.

References

Abou-Chadi, T. (2016). Niche Party Success and Mainstream Party Policy Shifts. *British Journal of Political Science*, 46(2): 417–36.

Albright, J. (2010). The Multidimensional Nature of Party Competition. *Party Politics*, 16(6): 699–719.

Alonso, S., and da Fonseca, S. C. (2012). Immigration Left and Right. *Party Politics*, 18(6): 865–86.

Baumgartner, F. R., Jones, B. D., and Wilkerson, J. D. (2002). Studying Policy Dynamics. In *Policy Dynamics*, ed. F. R. Baumgartner and B. D. Jones. Chicago: University of Chicago Press, 29–46.

Breunig, C., and Luedtke, A. (2008). What Motivates the Gatekeepers? Explaining Governing Party Preferences on Immigration. *Governance*, 21(1): 123–46.

Brouard, S., Grossman, E., and Guinaudeau, I. (2012). "La compétition partisane française au prisme des priorités électorales." *Revue française de science politique*, 62(2): 255–76.

Budge, I., Klingeman, Hans-D., Volkens, A. et al. (2001). *Mapping Policy Preferences: Estimates for Parties, Electors, and Governments 1945–1998*. Oxford: Oxford University Press.

Budge, I., and Meyer, T. (2013). Understanding and Validating the Left–Right Scale (RILE). In *Mapping Policy Preferences from Texts III*, ed. A. Volkens, J. Bara, I. Budge et al. Oxford: Oxford University Press, 85–106.

Busemeyer, M. R., Simon, T. F., and Garritzmann, J. L. (2013). Who Owns Education? Cleavage Structures in the Partisan Competition over Educational Expansion. *West European Politics*, 36(3): 521–46.

Carter, N., Ladrech, R., Little, C., and Tsagkroni, V. (2017). Political Parties and Climate Policy: A New Approach to Measuring Parties' Climate Policy Preferences. *Party Politics*. https://doi.org/10.1177/1354068817697630

Curini, L., and Martelli, P. (2015). A Case of Valence Competition in Elections: Parties' Emphasis on Corruption in Electoral Manifestos. *Party Politics*, 21(5): 686–98.

Däubler, T., Benoit, K., Mikhaylov, S., and Laver, M. (2012). Natural Sentences as Valid Units for Coded Political Texts. *British Journal of Political Science*, 42(4): 937–51.

Dinas, E., and Gemenis, K. (2010). Measuring Parties Ideological Positions with Manifesto Data. *Party Politics*, 16(4): 427–50.

Froio, C., Bevan, S., and Jennings, W. (2017). Party Mandates and the Politics of Attention: Party Platforms, Public Priorities and the Policy Agenda in Britain. *Party Politics*, 23(6): 692–703.

Gemenis, K. (2013). What to Do and Not to Do with the Comparative Manifesto Dataset. *Political Studies*, 61(1): 3–23.

Green-Pedersen, C. (2007). The Growing Importance of Issue Competition: The Changing Nature of Party Competition in Western Europe. *Political Studies*, 55(4): 608–28.

Green-Pedersen, C. (2018). The CAP Party Manifesto Datatset. Department of Political Science, Aarhus University available at agendasetting.dk.

Green-Pedersen, C., and Krogstrup, J. (2008). Immigration as a Political Issue in Denmark and Sweden: How Party Competition Shapes Political Agendas. *European Journal of Political Research*, 47 (5): 610–34.

Helbling, M., and Tresch, A. (2011). Measuring Party Positions and Issue Salience from Media Coverage: Discussing and Cross-validating New Indicators. *Electoral Studies*, 30(1): 174–83.

Horn, A., Kevins, A., Jensen, C., and van Kersbergen, K. (2017). Peeping at the Corpus: What Is Really Going on behind the Equality and Welfare Items of the Manifesto Project? *Journal of European Social Policy*, 27(5): 1–15.

Jakobi, A. P. (2011). Political Parties and the Institutionalization of Education. *Comparative Education Review*, 55(2): 189–209.

Jensen, C., and Seeberg, H. (2015). The Power of Talk and the Welfare State. *Socio-Economic Review*, 13 (2): 215–33.

Lowe, W., Benoit, K., Mikhaylov, S., and Laver, M. (2011). Scaling Policy Preferences from Coded Political Texts. *Legislative Studies Quarterly*, 36(1): 123–54.

Meguid, B. (2008). *Party Competition between Unequals: Strategies and Electoral Fortunes in Western Europe*. Cambridge: Cambridge University Press.

Mikhaylov, S., Laver, M., and Benoit, K. R. (2012). Coder Reliability and Misclassification in the Human Coding of Party Manifestos. *Political Analysis*, 20(1): 78–91.

Müller, W. C., and Thurner, P. W. (eds.). (2017). *The Politics of Nuclear Energy in Western Europe*. Oxford: Oxford University Press.

Robertson, David. 1976. *A Theory of Party Competition*. London: Wiley.

Senninger, R. (2017). Issue Expansion and Selective Scrutiny—How Opposition Parties Used Parliamentary Questions about the European Union in the National Arena from 1973 to 2013. *European Union Politics*, 18(2): 283–306.

Spoon, J. J., Hobolt, S. B., and de Vries, C. (2014). Going Green: Explaining Issue Competition on the Environment. *European Journal of Political Research*, 53(2): 363–80.

Tavits, M., and Potter, J. D. (2015). The Effect of Inequality and Identity on Party Strategies. *American Journal of Political Science*, 59(3): 744–58.

Toubeau, S., and Wagner, M. (2016). Party Competition over Decentralisation: The Influence of Ideology and Electoral Incentives on Issue Emphasis. *European Journal of Political Research*, 55(2): 340–57.

Volkens, A. (2001). Quantifying the Election Programmes: Coding Procedures and Controls. In *Mapping Policy Preferences: Estimates for Parties, Electors, and Governments 1945–1998*, ed. I. Budge, Hans-D. Klingeman, A. Volkens et al. Oxford: Oxford University Press, 93–109.

Volkens, A., Bara, J., Budge, I. et al. (eds) (2013). *Mapping Policy Preferences from Texts III*. Oxford: Oxford University Press.

Ward, D., Kim, J. H., Tavits, M., and Graham, M. (2015). How Economic Integration Affects Party Competition. *Comparative Political Studies*, 48(10): 1227–59.

Zulianello, M. (2014). Analyzing Party Competition through the Comparative Manifesto Data: Some Theoretical and Methodological Considerations. *Quality & Quantity*, 48(3): 1723–37.

35

Advancing the Study of Comparative Public Policy

Frank R. Baumgartner, Christian Breunig, and Emiliano Grossman

Throughout the preceding chapters, the contributors to this book have explained the shared methodology that characterizes the Comparative Agendas Project (CAP) and have explored some of the policy-related, institutional, and comparative questions that can be addressed using our approach and infrastructure. This volume merely scratches the surface, however, in addressing the range of practical and theoretical questions that can be examined through the shared resources of the CAP. In this concluding chapter we assess the contributions and possibilities of the CAP.

35.1 A Vast Infrastructure for the Study of Comparative Public Policy

To date, the comparative study of public policy can be considered still to be in its infancy. Unlike the comparative study of voting, partisanship, attitudes, or elections, most comparative studies of public policy typically have been relatively small in scope: either just a few countries compared, or a single policy domain (often the "old standards" of the welfare state: pensions, health, or different forms of poverty assistance). As with any research approach where the underlying issues are highly complex and the available data are limited, attention often focuses on peculiarities and idiosyncrasies of particular country- or institution-specific situations that generate a given outcome or cross-national difference. But perhaps we see these trees because we lack the perspective to see the forest. Of course, detailed observations of an individual policy are worthwhile, just as a botanist would benefit from studies of an individual species of tree. But it is also useful to understand the structure of the forest. Understanding one enhances the understanding of the other.

Deeply detailed analyses of individual cases will remain a staple of the comparative approach to the study of public policy, as well they should. But so far the vast majority of research on public policy has concentrated on individual policy fields. The real challenge is to embed these detailed comparisons into the larger patterns and broad categories into which they might fit. For example, French and Italian voters may relate to their respective political parties in different and sometimes idiosyncratic ways, but they can still be understood with some common characteristics similar across multiparty systems. By the same token, each advanced democracy has faced growing pressures on their healthcare systems as costs have risen and technologies have advanced, on pensions as the population has aged, and on immigration systems as the numbers demanding entry have increased. Those of us involved in the CAP seek to allow scholars of comparative public policy to do what scholars in other fields of comparative politics have long been able to do: observe both the broadest patterns according to policy domain, institutional design, and political system, as well as explore the detailed and historically contingent development of public policy within individual systems. Doing both can only be done if we have the resources and perspective to see the broad patterns.

As each of the chapters in this volume has made clear, the CAP provides the opportunity to ask the same question in multiple contexts. With close attention to the differences across national systems, we nonetheless can get equivalent indicators about such basic elements as the legislative process, executive actions, spending, and media coverage. And with our consistent coding of policy topics, we know that what is called "endangered species protection" in one country can be easily identified in another. Our primary goal is to reduce the barriers to systematic comparison. This consistency enables several types of comparison: over time (as our databases typically cover many decades of political history); across policy domains (as all our projects are comprehensive, covering all actions of public policy from agriculture to defense, economics, foreign affairs, and everything in between); and across countries and political systems (the CAP network has over twenty national teams and continues to grow).

Over twenty years ago Frank Baumgartner and Beth Leech (1998) reviewed the US literature on interest groups and lobbying and noted that the literature was essentially based on case studies. While each individual study may have been well done, they noted, the accumulated literature was arguably less than the sum of its parts. This drawback prevailed because each study was *designed specifically* to be different from all previous studies: authors purposefully emphasized different aspects of lobbying strategies that led to success, for example, so that they could claim a theoretical innovation as well as an observational one. After all, a single new case confirming old theoretical perspectives while adding nothing to the theory would not be published, nor would the authors be recognized as leading scholars in the field. Professional norms, in effect, demanded incomparability, ensuring that the literature could not accumulate as one might hope. Baumgartner and Leech argued that interest-group scholars needed to find a way to build shared infrastructure, and with the CAP we are making the same argument here. By sharing resources, we reduce the costs of comparisons and we make possible what had previously not been feasible at all.

Of course, scholars cannot merely replicate studies in new domains; there will always be theoretical innovations, disputes, and advances. But to the extent that a broad community of scholars can be built who share some common resources, we promote shared knowledge and theory is likely to grow more quickly than if we each build our own case study. Such, in a nutshell, is the motivation of the CAP.

Comparative studies of public policy are usually limited to clearly circumscribed policy areas: healthcare, energy, immigration, employment, pensions, foreign trade, and so on. This domain restriction is intended to control for policy-specific constraints and dynamics, as well as for the way in which policies interact with country-specific variables and institutional setups. In some cases, such as for welfare policies, entire academic communities have emerged to address the difficulties of comparison. It is a way of holding constant at least some variables in exceedingly complex contexts. Similar attempts exist in other areas, but tend to federate a smaller research community. Our hope is to allow these scholarly communities to communicate and to allow individual scholars or teams to increase the number of observations in their work.

Just as scholars of the welfare state, pensions, or energy policy typically work in only one or a few policy domains, those interested in the policy process often engage in only the most limited comparisons: perhaps two countries, rarely more than a dozen of the advanced democracies. Some scholars of the developing world have used larger research designs to explore such things as the degree of institutionalization in the policy process in a relatively large sample of countries (Scartascini and Tommasi, 2012; Shugart and Haggard, 2001), or the conditions under which political leaders deliver private or public goods and policies (Bueno de Mesquita et al., 2005). However, we are aware of no studies of advanced industrial democracies with a similar focus on such important elements of the policy process as opinion-policy responsiveness (but for smaller comparisons see Soroka and Wlezien, 2010 or, on the topic of negativity, Soroka, 2014). Similarly, studies of the dynamics of how various institutions of government interact with each other have mostly been limited to a single country at a time (see, e.g., Baumgartner and Jones, 2015;

Chaqués-Bonafont et al., 2015; John et al., 2013), but some scholars, drawing from our datasets, have taken a different approach: a similar set of policy issues compared across a larger number of countries and political systems (e.g., Engeli et al., 2012).

We have been able to address some generalizable issues by using the databases of the CAP. In one paper (Jones et al., 2009) we postulated a "general law of public budgeting"—that the annual distributions of changes in spending follows, inevitably and in every country, a "fat tailed" distribution because of the overwhelming complexity of decision-making and the vast array of public policy concerns that affect every modern government. Using data from the CAP, we looked at patterns of budgeting in twelve different budgetary systems in seven nations. In that same year we published another comparison of many different policymaking processes in three countries (the United States, Belgium, Denmark), showing similar and predictable increases in the institutional friction associated with monitoring functions of government, law-making and policymaking, and budgeting (see Baumgartner et al., 2009). More recently, a team took the budgeting idea more broadly and compared the distribution of budget changes in democratic systems and in autocracies (see Baumgartner et al., 2017). These studies were very much "inside" the CAP, in that the authors were assessing questions derived from the punctuated equilibrium perspective and were using data from the national projects described here. The autocracy article added some further breadth and pushed beyond the "usual suspects" of the advanced industrial world.

CAP has progressively also included media data and has studied the influence of the media on policy agenda-setting. While much of the early work was essentially limited to single-country case studies, this has recently changed. A paper by Vliegenthart and colleagues (2016a) has illustrated how media attention may influence the focus of attention of parliamentary debates. A related piece (Vliegenthart et al., 2016b) shows how the media may filter the influence of protest on parliamentary debates, by relaying certain protests more than others. While debates do not equate political action or public policy, of course, the media thus have a very sizeable and concrete effect on the debates that may lead to the adoption of policy.

Our hope and expectation is that the CAP will continue to grow and our own members will of course continue to be active in the analysis of the data we have been collecting. However, more important than that is the multiplication of studies using the data as a starting point by scholars fully disconnected with any of our work, both intellectually and in terms of scholarly networks. By making the data freely available, we hope to reduce the cost of comparative analysis of public policy across the board. Logically, the subsidy to research inherent in the CAP should lead to more, bigger, and better studies. Of course, bigger by itself is not necessarily better. But certainly we can hope that more scholars will take the data we provide as a starting point for a variety of questions that can now be addressed in a larger scale and fully comparative manner.

35.2 Setting Standards for Collecting and Assembling Comparative Policy Data

The main strengths of the CAP have been outlined throughout this volume. The chapters highlight how CAP would contribute to the emergence of a more powerful research agenda in comparative public policy. The first reason has to do with the transparency of the data collection process. Building on the experience of early projects, CAP has been able to avoid many of the dangers and errors that have bedeviled may other comparative projects. From the very beginning, CAP has been a largely decentralized project, building on the research goals of national research teams. While this loose structure could have been a disadvantage, making coordination more difficult, it ensured that national teams had an independent and autonomous interest in the continued success of the project.

Despite this apparently dispersed data collection process, we have developed a single standard for categorizing all public policies in a hierarchical taxonomy that has proved workable in every country. The US project was the first in chronological order, and when the Danish team sought to apply the US codes in their country, a number of anomalies became immediately apparent. With time and the development of many projects, we have established a standard applicable to all. In the interest of maximum use to all audiences, most national projects also provide a country-specific codebook with some differences from the international classification and thereby many projects offer distinctions that seem indispensable for national experts but not generalizable to other systems. This coordination on the basis of subject matter for each political activity is the most important defining feature of the CAP. As explained in the introductory section, coordination meetings have taken place on a regular basis since 2007, leading common standards, similar data-collection procedures, and intercoder reliability tests (see Bevan in this volume).

For a long time, many similar efforts have restricted data access or provided data in raw format only. While this has changed in recent years, CAP stands out in its will to make all data easily available. Access has taken several forms. During the first years, national projects have maintained dedicated websites with spreadsheets giving access to some of the data. Increasingly, though, there was a will to conform to a common Master Codebook, beyond existing national specificities. More importantly, this led to the creation of dedicated website that allows for easy data retrieval, of course, but which allows also for much more complex operations. The new website allows for selective retrieval, limiting data to certain types of agendas, certain topic codes, certain countries, and so on. Its online visualization tool, moreover, allows researchers to explore possible relations or dynamics in the data and thus to draw preliminary conclusions concerning the interest of a given research project.

35.3 The Future of Comparative Public Policy Studies

The CAP allows scholars to look across countries, across time, across institutional venues of politics, across media systems, and across policy domains in ways that have not previously been possible. The data are all made available at the micro-level, meaning that scholars can easily re-tool them to fit many needs, even if those have nothing to do with the original intent of the compilers of the databases. While most of the uses of the CAP thus far have been oriented toward quantitative usages, the databases themselves should be used for qualitative studies as well; they can provide the "first cut" before a deeper dive into the intricacies of policy development in a particular area, and they can provide the context to situate a detailed case study into its larger environment (as illustrated by Shpaizman in this volume).

More important than what the CAP currently allows might be what it could allow in the future. By moving from a single county to a growing international infrastructure, questions that were once addressed within a single national system now become amenable to systematic comparisons, rendering national structures variables rather than givens. We provide a few examples here.

How do different bureaucratic structures, media systems, partisan systems, federalism, active/reactive judiciaries, electoral systems affect the policy process? We have the opportunity to assess systematic variation in how various institutional structures affect the policy process. And of course, there is no single "policy process" but rather many elements of interest in considering the roles of interest groups, legislatures, executives, journalists, campaigners, and other actors in the policy process.

What do all political systems appear to have in common? No modern state fails to be involved in healthcare, and yet it would be hypothetically possible for a state to leave that to the private market. What are the common features of all governments? We literally have not addressed this issue at all. But we could begin. What issues are addressed in some countries but not in others? What contrasts can we draw between those issues that are commonly addressed in every country and that smaller set of issues that concern political leaders in some countries but not others?

What has been the range of responses to common public policy challenges? Is that range wider in some policy domains and more constrained in others?

What issue-characteristics explain the degree of cross-national variance in response? What system-level characteristics explain the variation in responses to a single policy challenge? Every Western democracy faces a powerful challenge to its pension system as an aging population moves increasingly toward retirement, and fewer are working. Every country faces increased demographic diversity in its schools, greater concern with environmental sustainability, and an employment threat from robots. What has been the timing of these common issues on the agendas of different states, and what has been the range of response?

How do elections and party leaders translate concrete policy challenges into the ideological structure of debate? Any review of the myriad challenges facing a modern government can quickly be summarized as overwhelming, complex, and bewildering. And yet partisan political leaders compete for control of government based on policy programs that are supposed to suggest a way forward in all those areas. How is the diversity of policy attention translated into the partisan structure of politics?

How do different type of media or media systems publicize the policy process and how does this affect it? Are there certain media systems that have a greater influence over policymaking or does it depend on specific issues? Does it vary over time?

How do citizens respond to policy failures and successes of their governments? Do they even realize that there are successes and failures? What models should we propose for evaluating the role of the citizen in public policy debates?

How have policy dynamics affected/been affected by partisan turnover? How do the policy agendas in those countries with historically stable party systems differ from those with greater "churning" in the party system? If we leave democratic polities, which issues do autocrats address? Who is reporting on the unaddressed problems given the likelihood of repercussions? Are autocratic leaders addressing fewer problems concerning the public and focusing more on issues that enable regime stability?

We purposefully conclude our review of the CAP with a series of questions. We have provided a tool. We hope that others will use it to address these and a wide variety of other puzzles.

References

Baumgartner, F. R., Breunig, C., Green-Pedersen, C. et al. (2009). Punctuated Equilibrium in Comparative Perspective. *American Journal of Political Science*, 53(3): 602–19.

Baumgartner, F. R., Carammia, M., Epp, D. A. et al. (2017). Budgetary Change in Authoritarian and Democratic Regimes. *Journal of European Public Policy*, 24(6): 792–808.

Baumgartner, F. R., and Jones, B. D. (2015). *The Politics of Information*. Chicago: University of Chicago Press.

Baumgartner, F. R., and Leech, B. L. (1998). *Basic Interests: The Importance of Groups in Politics and in Political Science*. Princeton: Princeton University Press.

Chaqués-Bonafont, L., Roqué, A. M. P., and Baumgartner, F. R. (2015). *Agenda Dynamics in Spain*. London: Palgrave Macmillan.

De Mesquita, B. B. (2005). *The Logic of Political Survival*. Cambridge, MA: MIT press.

Engeli, I., Green-Pedersen, C., and Larsen, L. T. (eds) (2012). *Morality Politics in Western Europe: Parties, Agendas and Policy Choices*. London: Palgrave Macmillan.

John, P., Bertelli, A., Jennings, W., and Bevan, S. (2013). *Policy Agendas in British Politics*. London: Palgrave Macmillan.

Jones, B. D., Baumgartner, F. R., Breunig, C. et al. (2009). A General Empirical Law for Public Budgets: A Comparative Analysis. *American Journal of Political Science*, 53(4): 855–73.

Scartascini, C., and Tommasi, M. (2012). The Making of Policy: Institutionalized or Not? *American Journal of Political Science, 56*(4): 787–801.

Shugart, M. S., and Haggard, S. (2001). Institutions and Public Policy in Presidential Systems. In *Presidents, Parliaments, and Policy*, ed. M. S. Shugart and S. Haggard. Cambridge: Cambridge University Press, 64–102.

Soroka, S. N. (2014). *Negativity in Democratic Politics: Causes and Consequences*. New York: Cambridge University Press.

Soroka, S. N., and Wlezien, C. (2010). *Degrees of Democracy: Politics, Public Opinion, and Policy*. New York: Cambridge University Press.

Vliegenthart, R., Walgrave, S., Chaqués-Bonafont, L. et al. (2016a). Do the Media Set the Parliamentary Agenda? A Comparative Study in Seven Countries. *European Journal of Political Research*, 55(2): 283–301.

Vliegenthart, R., Walgrave, S., Wouters, R. et al. (2016b). The Media as a Dual Mediator of the Political Agenda–Setting Effect of Protest: A Longitudinal Study in Six Western European Countries. *Social Forces*, 95(2): 837–59.

Index